The Chef's Library

Jenny Linford

A Quintessence book

Copyright © 2016 Quintessence Editions Ltd.
Jacket illustrations © Incomible / Shutterstock.com / gradedesign.com

This book was produced by
Quintessence Editions Ltd.
The Old Brewery
6 Blundell Street
London N7 9BH

For Quintessence

Project Editor	Sophie Blackman	**Picture Researchers**	Hannah Phillips
Editor	Fiona Plowman		Ouassila Mebarek
Design and layout	gradedesign.com	**Production Manager**	Anna Pauletti
Photography	Phil Wilkins	**Editorial Director**	Ruth Patrick
Proofreader	Sarah Kaikini	**Publisher**	Philip Cooper

For Abrams

Managing Editor	Leily Kleinbard
Editor	Michael Sand

In all cases, we have attempted to feature the first edition of each title in the language
in which it was originally published, but this has not always been possible.

Spelling and grammar within quoted material remains unedited.

Library of Congress Control Number: 2015955594

ISBN: 978-1-4197-2080-2

10 9 8 7 6 5 4 3 2 1

Abrams books are available at special discounts when purchased in quantity for
premiums and promotions as well as fundraising or educational use. Special editions
can also be created to specification. For details, contact specialsales@abramsbooks.com
or the address below.

Color reproduction by Bright Arts, Hong Kong.
Printed in China by C&C Offset Printing Co., LTD.

ABRAMS The Art of Books
115 West 18th Street, New York, NY 10011
abramsbooks.com

The Chef's Library

Favorite Cookbooks from the World's Great Kitchens

Jenny Linford

Abrams / New York

The Chef's Library *Contents*

Introduction 6

Chapter 1:
The Chefs' Favorites

Andoni Luis Aduriz 10
Livre de Michel Bras by Michel Bras, Alain Boudier, and Christian Millau

Darina Allen 12
The Ballymaloe Cookbook by Myrtle Allen

Michael Anthony 14
Cooking by Hand by Paul Bertolli

Juan Mari Arzak and Elena Arzak 16
Cocinar para viver by Fernando Fombellida and Andoni Luis Aduriz

Jason Atherton 18
The French Laundry Cookbook by Thomas Keller with Susie Heller and Michael Ruhlman

Sat Bains 20
White Heat by Marco Pierre White

Dan Barber 22
Much Depends on Dinner by Margaret

Nieves Barragán Mohacho 24
Nose to Tail Eating by Fergus Henderson

Rainer Becker 26
Les Recettes de L'Auberge de L'Ill by Paul and Jean-Pierre Haeberlin

Emma Bengtsson 28
The Nordic Cookbook by Magnus Nilsson

Claude Bosi 30
Too Many Chiefs Only One Indian by Sat Bains

Massimo Bottura 32
La scienza in cucina e l'arte di mangiar bene by Pellegrino Artusi

Jackson Boxer 34
Arabella Boxer's Book of English Food by Arabella Boxer

Michel Bras 36
La Cuisine c'est beaucoup plus que des recettes by Alain Chapel

Sébastien Bras 38
Les Secrets de la casserole by Hervé This

Stuart Brioza 40
The River Cottage Meat Book by Hugh Fearnley-Whittingstall

Sean Brock 42
The Unrivalled Cook-Book and Housekeeper's Guide by Mrs. Washington

André Chiang 44
Chef, La Grenouillère by Alexandre Gauthier

Sally Clarke 46
The Chez Panisse Menu Cookbook by Alice Waters

Mauro Colagraco 48
Clorofilia by Andoni Luis Aduriz

Tom Colicchio 50
Unplugged Kitchen by Viana la Place

Richard Corrigan 52
Sex & Drugs & Sausage Rolls by Graham Garrett and Cat Black

Wylie Dufresne 54
Essential Cuisine by Michel Bras

André Garrett 56
Roast Chicken and Other Stories by Simon Hopkinson

Suzanne Goin 58
Paula Wolfert's World of Food by Paula Wolfert

Peter Gordon 60
Fire by Christine Manfield

Bill Granger 62
Charmaine Solomon's Enclopedia of Asian Food, Charmaine Solomon

Michel Guérard 64
Éloge de la cuisine Française by Édouard Nignon

Skye Gyngell 66
The Zuni Cafe Cookbook by Judy Rodgers

Anna Hansen 68
Thai Food by David Thompson

Stephen Harris 70
Cuisine Actuelle Patricia Wells presents the food of Joel Robuchon

Angela Hartnett 72
The Classic Italian Cookbook by Marcella

Shaun Hill 74
The Best of Jane Grigson by Jane Grigson, compiled by Roy Fullick

Mark Hix 76
Gastronomy of Italy by Anna del Conte

Ken Hom 78
The Key to Chinese Cooking by Irene Kuo

Simon Hopkinson 80
The French Menu Cookbook by Richard Olney

Daniel Humm 82
4 Saisons á la Table No. 5 by Yannick Alléno and Kazuko Masui

Margot Janse 84
French Provincial Cooking by Elizabeth David

Thomas Keller 86
Ma Gastronomie by Fernand Point

Tom Kerridge 88
Grande Livre de Cuisine by Alain Ducasse with Jean-François Piège

Tom Kitchin 90
Memories of Gascony by Pierre Koffmann

Florence Knight 92
Honey From a Weed by Patience Gray

Pierre Koffmann 94
Le Répertoire de la cuisine by Louis Saulnier

Nicole Krasinski 96
Flatbreads and Flavors by Jeffrey Alford and Naomi Duguid

Cory Lee 98
Great Chefs of France by Anthony Blake and Quentin Crewe

Jeremy Lee 100
Charcuterie and French Pork Cookery by Jane Grigson

David Everitt-Matthias 102
Charcuterie and French Pork Cookery by Jane Grigson

Andrew McConnell 104
Nose to Tail Eating by Fergus Henderson

Jennifer McLagan 106
Jane Grigson's Fruit Book by Jane Grigson

David McMillan and Frédéric Morin 108
La Cuisine du marché by Paul Bocuse

Joyce Molyneux 110
French Provincial Cooking by Elizabeth David

Anton Mosimann 112
Opera dell'arte del Cucinare by Bartolomeo Scappi

Jamie Oliver 114
Good Food by Ambrose Heath

Shane Osborn 116
White Heat by Marco Pierre White

Sarit Packer 118
Delia's Cakes by Delia Smith

Stevie Parle 120
Honey From a Weed by Patience Gray

Neil Perry 122
Great Chefs of France by Anthony Blake and Quentin Crewe

Gary Rhodes 124
Great Chefs of France by Anthony Blake and Quentin Crewe

Joan Roca 126
La Cuisine spontanée by Frédy Girardet

Jordi Roca 128
Perfume by Patrick Süskind

Josep Roca 130
Com Usar Bé de Beure e Menjar by
Francesc Eiximenis

Simon Rogan 132
Herbs, Spices and Flavourings by
Tom Stobart

Ruth Rogers 134
The Classic Italian Cookbook by
Marcella Hazan

Søren Selin 136
Noma by René Redzepi

Chris Shepherd 138
The French Laundry Cookbook by
Thomas Keller with Susie Heller and
Michael Ruhlman

Bryce Shuman 140
Eleven Madison Park by Daniel Humm
and Will Guidara

Vivek Singh 142
Prashād by J. Inder Singh Kalra

Clare Smyth 144
Grand Livre de Cuisine by Alain Ducasse

Itamar Srulovich 146
My Favourite Ingredients by Skye Gyngell

Cathy Whims 148
Essentials of Classic Italian Cooking by
Marcella Hazan

Michael Wignall 150
Origin by Ben Shewry

Chapter 2:
Influential Cookbooks

Grant Achatz, *Alinea* 154
Ferran Adrià, Juli Soler and Albert Adrià,
A day at elBulli 156
Andoni Luis Aduriz, *Mugaritz* 158
Darina Allen, *Thirty Years at Ballymaloe* 160
Michael Anthony, *The Gramercy Tavern
Cookbook* 162
Juan Mari Arzak, *Arzak Secrets* 164
Alex Atala, *D.O.M. Rediscovering
Brazilian Ingredients* 166
Jason Atherton, *Social Suppers* 168
Sat Bains, *Two Many Chiefs Only
One Indian* 170
Pascal Barbot, Christophe Rohat and
Chihiro Masui, *Astrance* 172
Paul Bertolli, *Cooking by Hand* 174
Mark Best and Pasi Patanen, *Marque* 176
Raymond Blanc, *Recipes from Le Manoir
aux Quat' Saisons* 178

Heston Blumenthal, *The Big Fat Duck
Cookbook* 180
Paul Bocuse, *La Cuisine du marché* 182
Massimo Bottura, *Never Trust a Italian
Skinny Chef* 184
Daniel Boulud and Sylvie Bigar,
Daniel 186
Michel Bras, *Bras* 188
Sean Brock, *Heritage* 190
David Chang and Peter Meehan,
Momofuku 192
Sam and Sam Clark, *Moro* 194
Tom Colicchio, *Think Like a Chef* 196
Dominique Crenn, *Atelier Crenn* 198
The Culinary Institute of America,
The Professional Chef 200
Ollie Dabbous, *Dabbous* 202
Alain Ducasse and Jean-François Revel,
L'Atelier of Alain Ducasse 204
Auguste Escoffier, *La Guide culinaire* 206
The French Culinary Institute with
Judith Choate, *The Fundamental
Techniques of Classic Cuisine* 208
Graham Garrett, *Sex & Drugs &
Sausage Rolls* 210
Peter Gilmore, *Quay: Food Inspired
by Nature* 212
Gunnar Karl Gíslason and Jody Eddy,
North 214
Suzanne Goin with Teri Gelber, *Sunday
Suppers at Lucque* 216
Bill Granger, *bills Sydney Food* 218
Rose Gray and Ruth Rogers, *The River
Cafe Cookbook* 220
Michel Guérard, *Cuisine Minceur* 222
Simon Hopkinson and Lindsey Bareham,
Roast Chicken and Other Stories 224
Daniel Humm and Will Guidara, *Eleven
Madison Park* 226
Mollie Katzen, *The Moosewood
Cookbook* 228
Thomas Keller, *The French Laundry
Cookbook* 230
Tom Kerridge, *Tom Kerridge's Best
Ever Dishes* 232
David Kinch, *Manresa* 234
Pierre Koffmann and Timothy Shaw,
La Tante Claire 236
Nico Ladenis, *My Gastronomy* 238
Maguy Le Coze and Eric Ripert,
Le Bernardin Cookbook 240
Corey Lee, *Benu* 242
Alastair Little with Richard Whittingdon,
Keep It Simple 244

Deborah Madison with Edward Espe
Brown, *The Greens Cookbook* 246
Christine Manfield, *Spice* 248
Nobuyuki Matsuhisa, *Nobu* 250
Jennifer McLagan, *Fat* 252
Masaharu Morimoto, *Morimoto* 254
Magnus Nilsson, *Fäviken* 256
Russell Norman, *Polpo* 258
Yotam Ottolenghi and Sami Tamimi,
Ottolenghi 260
Nathan Outlaw, *Nathan Outlaw's
British Seafood* 262
Alain Passard, *Collages & Recettes* 264
Daniel Patterson, *Coi* 266
Jacques Pépin, *La Technique* 268
Neil Perry, *Balance and
Harmony* 270
Elisabeth M. Prueitt and Chad
Robertson, *Tartine* 272
Christian F. Puglisi, *Relæ* 274
Gordon Ramsay with Roz Denny,
A Chef For All Seasons 276
René Redzepi, *Noma* 278
Joël Robuchon, *Les Dimanches de
Joël Robuchon* 280
Judy Rodgers, *The Zuni Cafe
Cookbook* 282
Albert Roux and Michel Roux,
La Pâtisserie des frères Roux 284
Gabriel Rucker and Meredith Erickson
with Lauren and Andrew Fortgang,
Le Pigeon 286
Ben Shewry, *Origin* 288
Jean-Georges Vongerichten and
Mark Bittman, *Simple Good Food* 290
Tetsuya Wakuda, *Tetsuya* 292
Alice Waters, *The Chez Panisse Menu
Cookbook* 294
Marco Pierre White, *White Heat* 296

Chapter 3:
Cookbook Directory

COOKBOOKS OF THE WORLD 300
GENERAL COOKBOOKS 328
SPECIALTY COOKBOOKS 336
HISTORICAL COOKBOOKS 344

Index 348
Picture and Publisher Credits 351
Acknowledgments 352

Introduction
Jenny Linford

This book celebrates cookbooks as a source of knowledge and inspiration. It also salutes chefs—their hard work, commitment, creativity, and culinary skills—with specially chosen cookbooks by chefs offering a window into their world.

What was striking about writing this book was the willingness with which great chefs from around the world—among them Michel Bras (see p.36), Corey Lee (see p.98), the Roca brothers (see pp.126–131), and Clare Smyth (see p.144)—shared their favorite books. Cookbooks, it is clear, are meaningful for chefs and are held by them in affection and respect. Many chefs, it turns out, have their own personal "libraries" of cookbooks, collections of hundreds of volumes. It became apparent that asking them to choose one favorite caused a fair amount of mental anguish and much deliberation.

The reasons given by the chefs for their favorite cookbook choices varied. A number of chefs chose books that they had encountered while young, books that set them on the path to becoming a chef, or, if already working as apprentices, confirmed that this was a dream they should pursue. You can see this strand in the choices of Margot Janse (see p.84) of The Tasting Room at Le Quartier Français, Franschhoek, South Africa, and Sat Bains (see p.20) of Restaurant Sat Bains, Nottingham, UK. Others chose books by chefs who they respect enormously and who have influenced them, sometimes mentor figures with whom they have worked during their careers. There were also—in a spirit of affectionate camaraderie—choices for books written by friends, other chefs they knew well. The capacity of great food writers to nourish, stimulate, and inspire chefs is clear, too, with classic works by Elizabeth David, Jane Grigson, and Marcella Hazan chosen by several chefs. Charting the cookbook choices as they came through was a fascinating process; it became apparent that certain cookbooks have struck a resonant chord among chefs around the world.

Not only were the reasons for selecting cookbooks varied, the chosen titles themselves form a diverse collection. In terms of history alone, the range is impressive. They span hundreds of years, from the fascinating Catalan manuscript *Com Usar Bé de*

Beure e Menjar ("How to Eat and Drink Well") written in 1384 by Francesc Eiximenis (see p.130) to recently published cookbooks, such as Magnus Nilsson's *The Nordic Cookbook* (see p.30). The choices include tomes focused on one specific chef and also more general works on national cuisines, including Chinese, French, Indian, or Italian. Subjects range from a historical insight into Southern cooking in the United States to a Modernist work, focused on the science of cooking. It is notable that many of the choices have a huge sense of personality: a characterful voice speaking from the pages, whether Fergus Henderson (see p.24, 104), writing with quirky humor on the pleasures of offal, or Judy Rodgers's (see p.66, 282) generous, hospitable tones in *The Zuni Café Cookbook*. Not all the books chosen were cookbooks: one food book choice being Margaret Visser's masterpiece of culinary anthropology *Much Depends on Dinner* (see p.22), which dissects North American eating habits in witty style. One famous Spanish chef, in maverick mode, even chose a novel instead of a cookery or food book (see p.128).

In addition to these favorite books chosen by chefs, this book also offers entries on classic cookbooks, old and new, written both by chefs and by food writers. Chapter two, "Influential Cookbooks," focuses on classic restaurant and chef cookbooks. Reading the books in this genre one gains a sense of the demanding journeys that chefs embark upon in order to pursue their vision. Books such as Andoni Luis Aduriz's *Mugaritz* (see p.158), Pierre Koffmann's *La Tante Claire* (see p.236), Magnus Nilsson's *Fäviken* (see p.256), or Ben Shewry's *Origin* (see p.288) are far more than a collection of recipes; the authors share their personal philosophy and provide insights into what has shaped them and their approach to food. Cookbooks offer an important opportunity to chefs to record their cuisine for the future. Acclaimed chef Corey Lee, of restaurant Benu, San Francisco, recognized this, writing in his own *Benu* cookbook (see p.242) that his book "is meant to archive and share with you something that our team works so tirelessly to execute every day. Food is an ephemeral form of expression, and I want to document some of our hard work." Although the legendary French restaurant La Pyramide at Vienne has long gone, through *Ma Gastronomie*—with his maxims and recipes for luxurious dishes—the hospitable, generous spirit of French chef Fernand Point lives on. The titles in the "Cookbook Directory" remind one of the wonderful variety of voices the cookbook form offers, from Hannah Glasse's forthright *The Art of Cookery Made Plain and Easy* (1747; see p.346) to Claudia Roden's authoritative *A Book of Middle Eastern Food* (1968; see p.319), which was written from a powerful urge to chronicle a vanishing world.

Food is an expression of society and culture and cookbooks offer an invaluable record. In the seminal work *Great Chefs of France*, Quentin Crewe writes a history of haute cuisine, using cookbooks from la Varenne's *Le Cuisinier François* (1651; see p.344) to Curnonsky's *Recettes Des Provinces De France* (1933; see p.313) as building blocks with which to construct it. One of the interesting aspects of this book is that it allows the reader to form a picture of the overlapping influence of cookbooks and chefs. The famous *Ma Gastronomie*, for example, by

Fernand Point of La Pyramide, Vienne, France, is championed by American chef Thomas Keller (see p.18, 86, 138, 230), for whom it is a very special book. In turn, Keller's own elegant work, *The French Laundry Cookbook*, is chosen by Jason Atherton (see p.18), a leading figure in Britain's food scene. Among the many famous French chefs who worked with Fernand Point, and were much influenced by him, is the huge figure of Paul Bocuse (see p.108, 182). *La Cuisine du marché* by Paul Bocuse, is the book chosen by Canadian chefs David McMillan and Frédéric Morin of Joe Beef, Montreal (see p.108).

The special joy of cookbooks to anybody interested in food and cooking is that they are useful—and used. Cookbooks are read for pleasure, looked through for ideas of what to make for a dinner party, and recipes from them are cooked, resulting in tell-tale stains on pages; they become a companionable presence in our lives. It is this special power of cookbooks to touch lives that the chefs who took part in this book recognize and acknowledge. Reading and researching the many different volumes has been a fascinating labor for me and an inspiring reminder of the richness of great food writing from around the world. I hope readers of this book will find many cookbooks they want to buy and keep for themselves—while researching it, I certainly did!

Chapter One
The Chefs' Favorites

In this section of *The Chef's Library*, an international array of acclaimed chefs share their favorite cookbook choices. The result is an illuminating read for anyone interested in chefs, restaurants, cookbooks, and food. The chefs contributing to this book come from countries around the world—America, Australia, Denmark, France, Britain, Italy, Korea, Spain, Sweden, Taiwan—so offer a cosmopolitan selection. The roll call of names includes leading figures in the world of gastronomy: chefs who have shaped restaurant cuisine through their imagination, skill, and dedication. Included, too, is a younger generation of chefs, talents to watch with interest. It is fascinating to see which books the chefs have chosen and also to read of their reasons for choosing them: some deeply personal, others distinctly professional. It is also interesting to see which titles have been chosen by more than one chef, testifying to the influence of certain books. Cookbooks are meaningful for chefs. At the most fundamental level, they offer chefs, especially when starting out, a chance to learn about and understand food and cooking. The best cookbooks, however, offer much more than simply well-written recipes. One can see this in the variety of reasons given for choosing titles. It might be the story of a great chef—or great chefs—which resonates; a book that offers a meaningful insight into a cuisine, such as French or Italian; the distinctive voice of a wonderful food writer. Cookbooks are a vital repository of knowledge and inspiration to chefs—in effect, food for the mind.

Andoni Luis Aduriz

RESTAURANT

Mugaritz, San Sebastián, Spain, opened 1998

Le Livre de Michel Bras
Michel Bras, Alain Boudier, and Christian Millau

BOOK DETAILS

Published 1991, Éditions du Rouergue, 316 pages, photography by Willy Abplanalp and Alain Willaume

The thoughtful and intellectual Basque chef Andoni Luis Aduriz offers something special at his restaurant, Mugaritz (see p.158)—food that is emotionally charged as well as innovative and imaginative. His culinary creations include Edible Stones, which are designed to trick the eye and delight the palate. The restaurant is remotely located—hidden away in the hills above San Sebastián—and it is these rural surroundings that have inspired Aduriz in his cuisine. The open-minded Aduriz is active across many fields; characteristically, he set up Los Diálogos de Cocina (Kitchen Dialogues) in 2007 to promote the exchange of ideas. Not content with having already stretched the boundaries of haute cuisine dining, Aduriz's creativity and curiosity continue to motivate his culinary exploration.

Andoni Luis Aduriz's choice is for *Le Livre de Michel Bras* by French chef Michel Bras. "It was a book that was ahead of its time and laid the foundations and concepts that led the entire movement of wild and local cooking linked to creativity," says Aduriz, with characteristic eloquence. Stunning photographs of the magnificent Aubrac scenery set the scene for Bras's cooking, which, famously, draws inspiration from the landscape around him. "His best language is cooking. It is the vehicle for his tenderness, his complete love for nature, his integrity, and his joy at sharing," writes Christian Millau of Bras. This poetically conceived book uses both images and carefully chosen words to express Bras's philosophy. Pictures of the landscape—fast-flowing streams, verdant meadows—are interposed with images of Bras at work, meticulously creating his famous Gargouillou de Jeunes Légumes, offering an insight into his creative process. "From my point of view, it is the perfect book of what is called a signature cuisine because all the work of this kitchen genius is contextualised in it," declares Aduriz emphatically.

> *"It is a book that—even though it is twenty-five years old—is timeless and exudes inspiration."*
>
> ANDONI LUIS ADURIZ

Basque chef Andoni Luis Aduriz, whose imaginative, innovative cooking is showcased at his famous restaurant, Mugaritz.

"The much-loved Ballymaloe Cookbook *remains an important cultural and culinary milestone in the history of Irish food."*

DARINA ALLEN

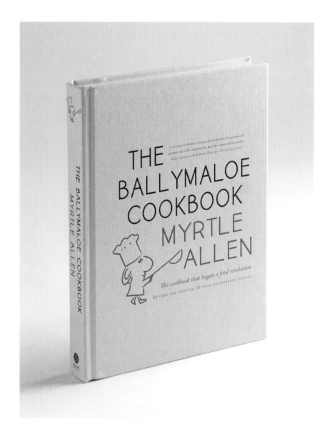

Irish chef, broadcaster, and writer Darina Allen, founder of the world-famous Ballymaloe Cookery School.

Darina Allen

COOKERY SCHOOL

Ballymaloe Cookery School, Shanagarry, County Cork, Ireland, opened 1983

The Ballymaloe Cookbook Myrtle Allen

BOOK DETAILS

Published 1977, Gill & Macmillan, 344 pages, photography by Joanne Murphy, Tim Allen, and Joleen Cronin, illustrations by Mel Calman

The power of a good teacher to influence lives and inspire students is exemplified by Irish chef and food writer Darina Allen (see p.160). As a young sous chef, her first job was at Ballymaloe House in County Cork, Ireland, working for Myrtle Allen. After marrying Myrtle's son Tim, Darina and her brother Rory O'Connell cofounded the Ballymaloe Cookery School in 1983. Such is the school's reputation that it attracts teachers and students from all around the world. Charismatic and passionate, Darina, like her mother-in-law Myrtle, has been a driving force in Ireland's food scene, campaigning passionately and eloquently for causes she believes in: local food producers, organic farming, farmers' markets, and the Slow Food movement. An experienced television broadcaster and bestselling author, she has a huge and loyal following, among them the many alumni of Ballymaloe Cookery School.

Darina Allen's choice of favorite, most inspiring cookbook was immediate and unhesitating: *The Ballymaloe Cookbook,* written by her mother-in-law, the remarkable Myrtle Allen. "The cookbook that began a food revolution" reads the subtitle on the 2014 edition. In this bestselling cookbook, which has never been out of print since it was first published in 1977, Myrtle Allen presented her philosophy of food with simplicity, candor, and engaging humor. The cooking she showcased at Ballymaloe and her recipe writing—which placed locally produced, seasonal food firmly centerstage—is now de rigueur, but was distinctly radical in the 1970s. Myrtle Allen's food is rooted in a sense of place; she writes of heading out to pick mussels from the strand when a "gourmet" arrives unexpectedly for supper and portrays food producers, such as Tommy Sliney, the Ballycotton fisherman. Recipes include classics such as Irish Stew, Soufflé Omelette, and Ballymaloe Brown Bread. Shrewd and down-to-earth—as when writing on how long fresh fish is stored for—one also senses that she is a formidable campaigner. "She had a deep appreciation and understanding of the quality of Irish produce at a time when many still had an inferiority complex," writes Darina on Myrtle's championing of Irish food. At once charming and redoubtable, Myrtle Allen's influence continues to ripple on.

Michael Anthony

RESTAURANT
Gramercy Tavern, New York City, New York, USA, opened 1994 (Anthony joined in 2006)

Cooking by Hand Paul Bertolli

BOOK DETAILS
Published 2003, Random House Inc., 270 pages, photography by Gail Skoff and Judy Dater

"I fell in love with the practical nature of the delicious instructions in the book and the poetic love for food and its impact on our loved ones."
MICHAEL ANTHONY

There is a warm-heartedness to acclaimed American chef Michael Anthony and his vision of dining. He regards his New York restaurant, Gramercy Tavern (see p.162), as a "place where people can come together." This togetherness not only involves offering warm hospitality to guests, but also creating meaningful, respectful relationships with everyone from his staff to his suppliers. Committed to using locally produced, seasonal ingredients, Anthony's cooking is at once sophisticated and gloriously delicious. In signature creations such as Slow-Roasted Pork with Bacon Broth and Corn Bread, he demonstrates his ability to create contemporary American food with flair.

A fascination with the craft of food is the hallmark of Michael Anthony's favorite cookbook. In *Cooking by Hand,* its author, chef Paul Bertolli, writing with charisma and intelligence, offers a fascinating, in-depth exploration of how to cook well. Fittingly, given Anthony's own commitment to supporting local food producers, the book highlights the importance of using fresh, truly seasonal ingredients. Bertolli offers genuinely useful advice, weighted with years of experience, on sourcing and choosing and using ingredients such as pears, tomatoes, and pork. The book offers an interesting mix of essays and recipes. Bertolli's commitment to sharing his knowledge is marked; he patiently outlines, for example, the five steps to creating a Ragu alla Bolognese, then gives a Southern-Style Ragu. While the information contained is extensive, Bertolli writes with grace and sensibility, conveying the emotional power that the growing, cooking, and eating of food has. He conveys the power of ingredients to stimulate his creativity—something that Anthony, too, appreciates.

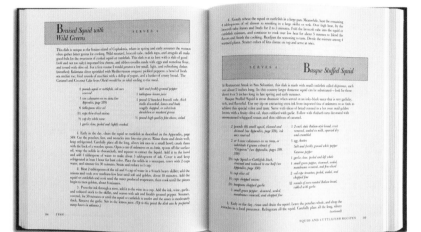

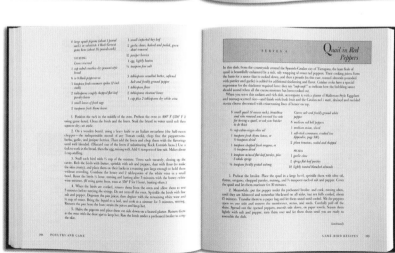

American chef Michael Anthony, champion of seasonally led fine dining at New York's Gramercy Tavern.

"It is a book, as the title says, that helps you live better and eat healthier."
JUAN MARI AND ELENA ARZAK

Working together in creative collaboration, formidably talented Spanish chefs—and father and daughter—Juan Mari and Elena Arzak.

Juan Mari Arzak and Elena Arzak

RESTAURANT

Arzak, San Sebastián, Spain, opened 1890s (Juan Mari Arzak took over the family restaurant in 1966)

Cocinar para vivir
Fernando Fombellida and Andoni Luis Aduriz

BOOK DETAILS

Published 2015, Ediciones Destino, 488 pages

Intellectually curious, imaginative, and supremely talented, Catalan chef Juan Mari Arzak (see p.164) is a major figure in contemporary gastronomy, inspiring figures such as Ferran Adrià (see p.156) to push the creative boundaries of the restaurant experience. His innovative, experimental cooking played a seminal part in putting Spanish haute cuisine on the gastronomic map. His daughter, the acclaimed chef Elena Arzak, cooks with her father at their family establishment, bringing her own innovative talents to their partnership. An emphasis on collaboration and teamwork is a hallmark of their approach to cooking and to life. Noted for their avant-garde, ever-evolving Basque cuisine, which uses impeccable local ingredients in intriguing ways, their hospitable San Sebastián restaurant attracts diners from around the world.

The cookbook choice of Juan Mari and Elena Arzak is a volume that is modest in appearance and accessible, but written on a very important subject. *Cocinar para vivir* is the result of a collaboration between Dr. Fernando Fombellida and renowned chef Andoni Luis Aduriz of Mugaritz (see p.158), the latter being known for his intellectual curiosity. As the authors make clear in their first chapter, the aim of this book about healthy eating is to empower its readers: "You will be able to redefine what you mean by good food and come up with your own food plan." The book explains the cancer-preventing properties of

particular ingredients and how to cook with them, while providing generous amounts of background information. The recipes themselves are designed by Aduriz to be dishes that are "tasty but which preserve the nutritious properties of the food." They are intended to offer a starting point, from which "you will be in a position to let your imagination run free and create your own dishes." As Juan Mari and Elena Arzak observe, it is a book "that teaches you how to shop for food in a practical way. It is very up-to-date and will serve as a daily manual. We are proud of it as we consider the authors part of our family."

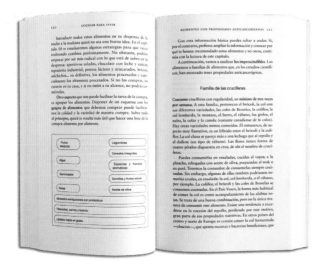

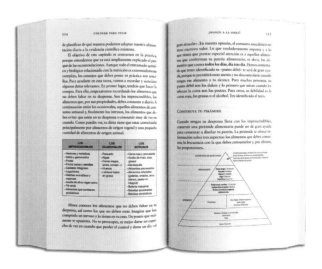

Jason Atherton

RESTAURANT
Pollen Street Social, London, UK, opened 2011

The French Laundry Cookbook
Thomas Keller with Susie Heller and Michael Ruhlman

BOOK DETAILS
Published 1999, Artisan Books, 326 pages, photography by Deborah Jones

Courteous, soft-spoken, and modest in person, British chef Jason Atherton (see p.168) is an impressively talented chef and a highly successful restaurateur. Always hungry for knowledge, he has worked with some great chefs, including Pierre Koffmann (see p.94, 236), Nico Ladenis (see p.238), and Marco Pierre White (see p.20, 116, 296). Notably, he was the first British chef to complete a stage at Ferran Adrià's elBulli restaurant in Spain (see p.156), which proved to be a career-defining experience. After a period working for Gordon Ramsay (see p.276), for whom he launched Maze, Atherton set up his own restaurant company in 2010. He now has a globe-trotting array of establishments, including Pollen Street Social and City Social in London. In his own cooking, Atherton offers an intensity of flavor combined with a deft lightness and sophistication of execution.

Noted for his refined cuisine, British chef Jason Atherton has opened successful restaurants around the world.

There is a calm elegance to Jason Atherton's favorite cookbook, *The French Laundry Cookbook* by renowned American chef Thomas Keller. It is a well-designed, harmonious tome, written with thoughtful intelligence and offering an in-depth insight into the creation of The French Laundry, the restaurant that helped redefine American fine dining. The story of Keller's quest to become a chef is an inspiring one: "In these great French kitchens—Taillevent, Guy Savoy, and Pré Catelan among them—what I learned once again was respect for food, but here it had a new depth and dimension." The recipes for luxurious dishes such as White Truffle Oil-Infused Custards with Black Truffle Ragout; Poached Moulard Duck Foie Gras au Torchon with Pickled Cherries; or Strawberry Sorbet Shortcakes with Sweetened Crème Fraîche Sauce are long and detailed, reflecting Keller's meticulous approach to the craft of cooking. His writing about dishes such as soup or hollandaise is illuminating, expressing his personal culinary philosophy. "The way to keep the experience fresh," writes Keller, "is not by adding more flavors, but rather by focusing more on specific flavors, either by making them more intense than the foods from which they come, or by varying the preparation technique." In his own restaurants, Atherton offers a refined experience that is also hospitable. One can see why this sophisticated cookbook, which depicts the graciousness of fine dining so alluringly, appeals to him.

"It's such a beautifully produced book and each time I open it, I find something in there to inspire me."

JASON ATHERTON

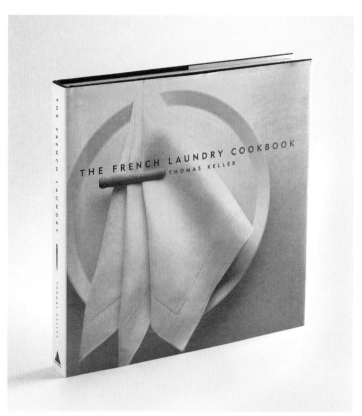

Preceding spread, left: Dungeness Crab Salad, page 92. Above: Salad of Petite Summer Tomatoes, page 56; right: Vine-Ripe Tomato Sorbet with Tomato Tartare, page 57.

First Course 55

"I obsessively read books by top chefs in the UK and France, in particular Marco Pierre White's White Heat.*"*

SAT BAINS

The dynamic and creative British chef Sat Bains is noted for his innovative cooking.

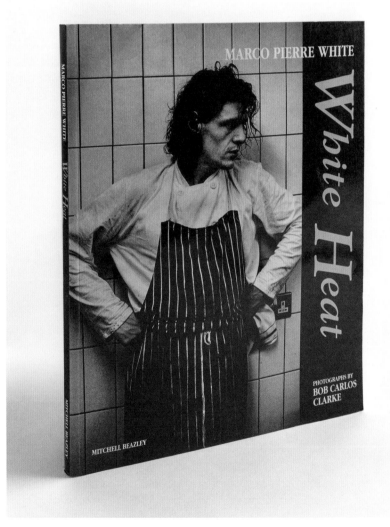

Sat Bains

RESTAURANT
Restaurant Sat Bains, Nottingham, UK, opened 2002

White Heat Marco Pierre White

BOOK DETAILS
Published 1990, Mitchell Beazley, 128 pages, photography by Michael Boys and Bob Carlos Clarke, illustrations by Edward Bawden

Food as an expression of a chef's personality is on offer at Sat Bains's acclaimed Midlands restaurant (see p.170), which he and his wife, Amanda, set up in 2002 and run together. Such is the appeal of Bains's characterful, highly skilful cooking that, despite its industrial location in the city outskirts of Nottingham, their restaurant is a popular dining destination. The drive and energy that Bains has in person is reflected in his culinary creations—which surprise and intrigue in their combinations of flavors and textures, and the flair with which they are put together. Underlying his cuisine is an impressive technical ability; while Bains talks about food and cooking with humor and practicality, his creative commitment to the business of being a great chef is undeniable.

Bains's choice is Marco Pierre White's *White Heat* (see p.116, 296), which he came across as a young chef, starting out in the restaurant world. "When I bought it, it completely blew me away! He was probably the most influential chef in the UK, and at the time every chef of my generation had his book." A charismatic cookbook by a charismatic chef, one can see why it would appeal to the young Bains. The black-and-white photography of Marco and his brigade has a rock 'n' roll quality to it: the sense of a life being lived dangerously, excitingly, fully. Such was the book's legendary status that

twenty-five years later, a revised edition was published, with yet more candid photographs plus testimony from chefs as to how this book transformed their lives and made them want to be like Marco. The contrast between the images of carefully composed, immaculate dishes—Ravioli of Lobster with a Beurre Soy Sauce; Tranche of Calves' Liver with Sauce of Lime—and the kitchen scenes is deliberate. The impeccably presented food is serene and perfect, while behind the scenes one glimpses the drama and adrenaline of a busy, professional kitchen, with a dynamic figure at its heart.

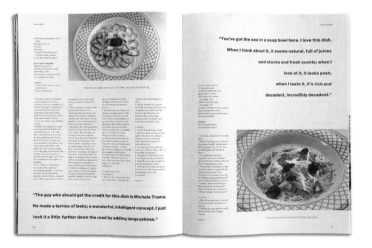

Dan Barber

RESTAURANT

Blue Hill at Stone Barns, Pocantico Hills, New York, USA, opened 2004

Much Depends on Dinner Margaret Visser

BOOK DETAILS

First published 1986, McClelland and Stewart Limited, 352 pages, illustrations by Mary Firth; this edition published by Penguin Books, 1989

"Subjected to Visser's anthropological eye, each ingredient emerges with its own enthralling history."

DAN BARBER

There is an intellectual quality to Dan Barber—he is a thinker as well as a great chef. The results of that approach manifest themselves in his food, his restaurants, and his writing. He is famed as an eloquent champion of the "farm-to-fork" movement in dining. At his acclaimed restaurants Blue Hill at Stone Barns in the Pocantico Hills and Blue Hill, in New York City's Greenwich Village, Barber offers diners meals created using food from farms including Blue Hills Farm and the Stone Barns Center for Food and Agriculture. Barber's vision, however, reaches far beyond tracking food miles or celebrating seasonal produce; he promotes responsible agriculture—and aquaculture—and addresses environmental issues. He is a campaigner who uses his influence as a famous chef to raise awareness.

"Margaret Visser's *Much Depends on Dinner* is not a cookbook per se, but its anatomy of the American dinner plate introduced a new kind of 'recipe,' as much cultural as culinary," explains Dan Barber of his choice. Taking as its starting point an "ordinary meal" in North America, Visser digs deep beneath the surface of everyday foods such as salt, butter, and lettuce, weaving together history, science, and social observation to fascinating effect. Despite its scholarly aspect, Visser's writing has a verve and power to it, making for gripping reading: "Each of the foodstuffs I have chosen," she writes, "has a weird, passionate, often savage history of its own; each has dragged the human race in its wake, constrained us, enticed us, harried and goaded us in its own particular fashion." As Barber says, "Subjected to Visser's anthropological eye, each ingredient emerges with its own enthralling history, and commonplace dishes like roast chicken, corn on the cob, and ice cream become complex lenses through which we understand our own identity." It is a book that shows, with intelligence and a fierce, shrewd wit, how much lies behind the food we eat.

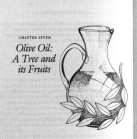

American chef Dan Barber of Blue Hill, a committed and articulate champion of the importance of sustainable food.

"Fergus is a genius."
NIEVES BARRAGÁN MOHACHO

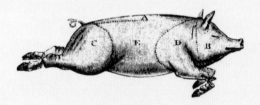

NOSE
TO
TAIL
EATING

A KIND
OF BRITISH
COOKING

FERGUS HENDERSON
With an introduction by Anthony Bourdain

Basque chef Nieves Barragán
Mohacho has a devoted following
for her Spanish cooking at
London's Barrafina restaurants.

Nieves Barragán Mohacho

RESTAURANT

Barrafina, London, UK, opened 2007

Nose to Tail Eating Fergus Henderson

BOOK DETAILS

Published 1999, Bloomsbury Publishing, 221 pages, photography by Jason Lowe

Basque-born chef Nieves Barragán Mohacho has made her name in London, working in fruitful partnership for the restaurateurs Sam and Eddie Hart. She began working for the Hart brothers in 2003, as sous chef at Fino in London. Appreciating her talents, the Harts opened their tapas bar Barrafina in London's Soho in 2008 with head chef Barragán Mohacho garnering great acclaim and perennial queues for seats at the bar. Her creative cooking draws on her Basque heritage, with dishes ranging from renditions of classics—Bocadillo de Calamar Encebollado, Arroz de Marisco, Milk-Fed Lamb's Brain—to innovative riffs—Crab Croquetas, Morcilla and Piquillo Pepper Tortilla—with the quality of her cooking attracting a committed following.

"Fergus doesn't mess around—he's a risk taker—which is why he's one of my favourites and why I love this book so much," declares Barragán Mohacho firmly of her cookbook choice, *Nose to Tail Eating: A Kind of British Cooking* by Fergus Henderson (see p.104). "He doesn't waste anything; this book is a lesson in getting the most out of your ingredients." In this appealing, quirky, characterful cookbook, British chef Fergus Henderson sets out his own distinctive approach to food and cooking, showcased to great effect at his iconic St. John restaurant, a short stroll away from Smithfield, London's historic meat market. Despite being written by a chef who has been hugely influential—much admired and much followed—it is a cookbook that is resolutely "un-cheffy" in tone or approach. Henderson demystifies processes such as making stock, clarification, and rendering, as well as sharing recipes including Ham in Hay; Blood Cake and Fried Eggs; and Duck's Neck Terrine. "Fergus just gets on with it; he really cooks and that greatly inspires me," says Barragán Mohaco simply.

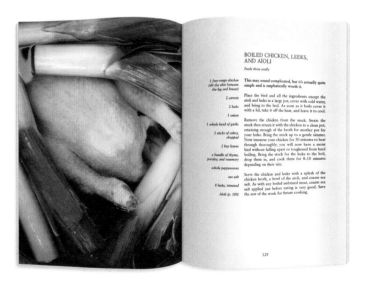

Rainer Becker

RESTAURANT

Zuma London, London, UK, opened 2002

Les Recettes de L'Auberge de L'Ill
Paul and Jean-Pierre Haeberlin

BOOK DETAILS

Published 1982, Flammarion, 238 pages, photography by Johan Willsberger

Ever since he was a young apprentice, training in some of Germany's most prestigious kitchens, German chef Rainer Becker has brought a distinct discipline and perfectionism to his work. Having worked in Australia, he was appointed executive chef at the Park Hyatt Tokyo, where he worked for five years in 1994. Japanese food culture, with its exquisite aesthetics and focus on discipline and excellence, struck a chord with Becker, who immersed himself in it while in Japan. Zuma, his glamorous, sophisticated, Japanese-inspired restaurant brand, has proved a hit globally. Becker's latest restaurant venture, Oblix, located on the thirty-second floor of London's Shard, sees him moving away from Japanese cuisine. Charismatic, driven, and influential, Becker is a figure the restaurant world watches with interest.

A cookbook acquired when one is young and dreaming of a career as a chef can be a powerful thing. "I proudly bought this book when I was sixteen years old, and my dream at that time was to cook like the Haeberlin Brothers in Alsace," explains Rainer Becker. The cookbook he purchased as a teenager, and that he has selected now that he is a world-renowned chef, is *Les Recettes de L'Auberge de L'Ill* by Paul and Jean-Pierre Haeberlin. It is a cookbook that celebrates and records the legendary three Michelin–starred restaurant created by the brothers at

their Alsace family auberge. The tersely written recipes are for opulent, haute cuisine creations such as Terrine de Foie Gras Truffe; Veau Curnonsky; Fraises Romanoff. A picture of the Auberge de L'Ill guestbook is revealing of the caliber of visitors to his French institution: Marlene Dietrich, Elizabeth R (Queen Elizabeth), Jean-Paul Sartre, Orson Welles . . . "I remember I was fascinated by the photos and the look of the dishes," says Becker fondly. "It gave me a lasting memory and was my favourite cookbook for many years, and, because of the fond memories, it still is."

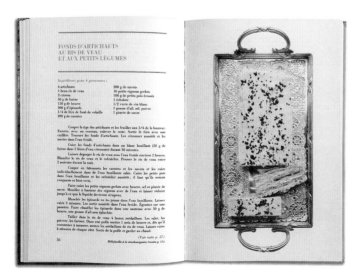

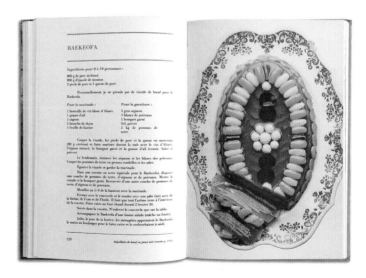

"My first ever cookbook was the Auberge de L'Ill."
RAINER BECKER

German chef Rainer Becker,
famed for his uber-stylish
restaurants, including Zuma
and Roka.

"I read it like a page-turner and think it's that rare cookbook that will appeal equally to both professional chefs and home cooks."

EMMA BENGTSSON

Swedish chef Emma Bengtsson demonstrates her considerable culinary skills at New York's Aquavit restaurant.

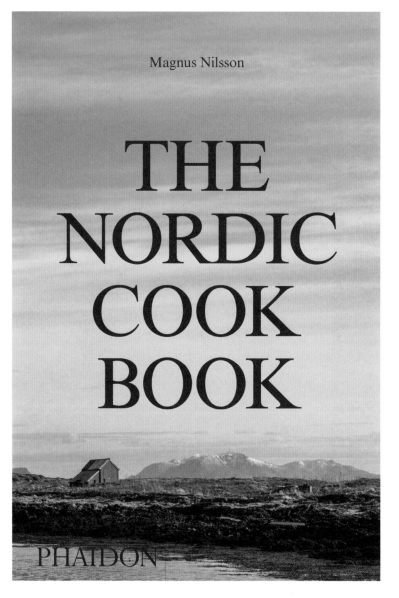

Magnus Nilsson

THE NORDIC COOK BOOK

PHAIDON

Emma Bengtsson

RESTAURANT

Aquavit, New York City, New York, USA, opened 1987

The Nordic Cookbook Magnus Nilsson

BOOK DETAILS

Published 2015, Phaidon, 768 pages, photography by Magnus Nilsson

Since arriving in the United States, Swedish chef Emma Bengtsson has established a name for herself. From a young age, she knew that she wanted to cook professionally. Her career in Sweden saw her working for national culinary institutions including Edsbacka Krog, where she became fascinated by working with pastry; busy Stockholm bistro Restaurant Prinsen; and Operakällaren in Stockholm's Opera House. She joined Aquavit—New York's long-established, upmarket, modern Nordic restaurant—as pastry chef in 2010, where she draws on the rich tradition of Scandinavian baking to excellent effect. Her considerable talents were recognized with a promotion to executive chef in spring 2014 and she was rewarded in the fall of the same year with Aquavit's second Michelin star, making her America's second female chef to hold those coveted two Michelin stars.

Emma Bengtsson's choice is for Magnus Nilsson's remarkable tome *The Nordic Cookbook*. "Professional chefs will appreciate its encyclopaedic scope—it's a great research tool," while "home cooks will admire the accessibility of the recipes," she says. For Bengtsson, the book is an important work in offering an insight into the complexities of Nordic cuisine. "The book raises awareness about how countries whose cuisines are often grouped together—Sweden, Denmark, Norway—by those living outside the region each actually has a distinctly unique cuisine; the same with the Faroe Islands, Greenland, and Iceland, which the book also covers."

Nilsson undertook his mission to chart the complexities of Nordic food culture with characteristic commitment, collecting a vast amount of information and recipes, the latter ranging from the everyday and humble to the rare and distinctive. Although documentary in feel, his own voice—perceptive, down-to-earth, opinionated, and often humorous—also comes across clearly. "Chef Nilsson visited all these places, spoke to the locals, elicited their recipes, and took beautiful photos, too," enthuses Bengtsson. "Best of all, he's also not afraid to suggest modifications regardless of how revered the preparation is."

Claude Bosi

RESTAURANT

Hibiscus, Ludlow, Shropshire, UK, opened 2000 (the restaurant moved to London in 2007)

Too Many Chiefs Only One Indian Sat Bains

BOOK DETAILS

Published 2012, Face Publications, 448 pages, photography by John Arandhara-Blackwell

Restaurants are in Claude Bosi's genes; born in Lyon in France, his parents had a restaurant, so the world of the professional kitchen was one familiar to him from a young age. His training as a chef saw a formative period at Alain Passard's L'Arpège in Paris (see p.88, 144, 264), followed by a spell working for Alain Ducasse (see p.204). Bosi made his name in Ludlow, a picturesque, food-loving town in the United Kingdom, where, as chef-owner, he opened Hibiscus in 2000, gaining two Michelin stars by 2003. In 2007, Bosi relocated Hibiscus to London, where he continued offering the distinctive, creative cuisine, founded on classic technique, for which he is known. Committed to seasonality and local sourcing, Bosi uses quality British ingredients, from seafood and game, in elegant, contemporary style.

Claude Bosi's choice of cookbook is by his friend Sat Bains (see p.20, 170), an acclaimed British chef who is renowned for his culinary panache. With its distinctive appearance, the intriguingly titled *Too Many Chiefs Only One Indian* is a generously illustrated autobiographical cookbook, which chronicles Bains's interesting life and career as well as his recipes. Writing with a straightforward vigor and humor, Bains offers a glimpse into the hardworking, driven world of the professional chef. On tasting menus, he explains, "It's not about using the customers as guinea pigs—that's our job.

So we'll try and test, try and test, try and test, taste, and only then does it go on the menu." His Nottingham restaurant, Restaurant Sat Bains, is known for its contemporary, innovative food, which draws on cutting-edge cooking methods to exciting effect. The intricately composed, strikingly portrayed recipes, complete with information on seasonality and taste profile, testify to his imaginative powers. In this book, for example, are recipes for both his famous Ham/Eggs/Peas dish, and the Evolved version, offering a fascinating insight into Bains's creative process.

TOO
MANY
CHIEFS
ONLY
ONE
INDIAN/
SAT
BAINS/

French chef Claude Bosi, known for his classic yet creative cooking at Hibiscus restaurant, London.

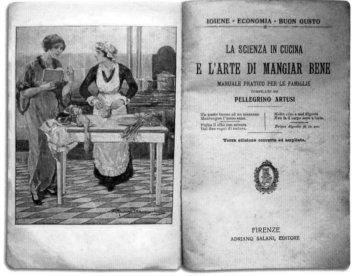

Charismatic Italian chef
Massimo Bottura, noted for his
creative riffs on Italian cuisine
at his restaurant Osteria
Francescana in Modena, Italy.

Massimo Bottura

RESTAURANT

Osteria Francescana, Modena, Italy, opened 1995

La scienza in cucina e l'arte di mangiar bene
Pellegrino Artusi

BOOK DETAILS

Published 1891, L'Arte della Stampa; published in English as *Science in the Kitchen and the Art of Eating Well*, 1997, Marsilio Publishers

"To do contemporary cooking, you have to know everything and forget about everything."

MASSIMO BOTTURA

A charismatic, vivacious personality, Italian chef Massimo Bottura (see p.184) delights in pushing the boundaries of Italian cuisine, challenging its traditional conservatism and bringing a freshness of vision. Famous regional delicacies, such as Parmigiano-Reggiano, prosciutto di Parma, or aceto balsamico tradizionale di Modena, are given new life and form in Bottura's inventive menu; classic dishes are creatively reinterpreted in innovative style. His culinary creations, such as An Eel Swimming Up the Po River, are playful and sophisticated. This irreverent, imaginative approach has seen his Osteria Francescana garner numerous accolades, including three Michelin stars, and an international reputation as one of the most exciting places to eat in Italy.

Massimo Bottura's favorite cookbook is a magnificent classic of Italian cuisine, Pellegrino Artusi's *La scienza in cucina e l'arte di mangiar bene*. Published three decades after the Unification of Italy in 1891, Artusi's work was seminal in that it included recipes from across the newly unified nation and so played a part in forging a sense of Italian identity. As well as being an important cookbook, it is a characterful and engaging one, written in a conversational, digressive style and filled with anecdotes. His writing conveys a vivid sense of the times he lived in: Minestrone, for him, is associated with an outbreak of cholera in Livorno. Artusi's jovial sense of humor pervades the pages, as with his warning regarding cookbooks: "Beware of books that deal with this art: most of them are incomprehensible, especially the Italian ones . . ." His recipes, however, are shrewdly written and rooted in a genuine knowledge of cookery. There is a democratic inclusiveness to his approach: "Dear Mr. Meat Loaf, please come forward, do not be shy, I want to introduce you to my readers. I know that you are modest and humble, because given your background you feel inferior to many others . . .".

Jackson Boxer

RESTAURANT

Brunswick House, London, UK, opened 2010

Arabella Boxer's Book of English Food Arabella Boxer

BOOK DETAILS

Published 1991, Hodder & Stoughton Ltd, 270 pages, illustrations by Jessica Gwynne

There is an energy to Britain's dining scene—a real appetite for genuinely good food—and chef Jackson Boxer fits well into the current zeitgeist. Food was very much part of his family heritage and interested him from an early age. Fergus Henderson's pared-down approach to food (see p.24, 104), as displayed at St. John's in London's Clerkenwell, is an inspiration for Boxer's own style, which focuses on sourcing excellent ingredients and cooking them simply but very, very well. His restaurant, Brunswick House, is located in a Georgian mansion, built for the Duke of Brunswick in 1758. The historical setting, given fresh life through the relaxed restaurant, is an appropriate backdrop for Boxer's thoughtful cooking, which appreciates the culinary past, while also being distinctly contemporary.

Jackson Boxer's choice is for a book with which he has a direct connection: Arabella Boxer's *Book of English Food*. "It has always held a profound fascination for me," says Jackson of the book, written by his "hugely inspirational grandmother." Arabella's book explores English food between the wars, "a time in which English food asserted itself confidently as a proto-modern expression of simplicity, clarity, seasonality, and locality," explains her grandson. "It is fascinating how this anticipates a contemporary approach to eating, to which we popularly give reverent credit to Italian cookery, when in fact it sees its precursor already comfortably ensconced in the great English kitchen half a century before. In a sense English food, under the imaginative guidance of Fergus Henderson first and foremost, is picking up where the Second World War so abruptly cut it off. In this way, it is a somewhat speculative cuisine, not based on continuous tradition, but on radical breaks and re-imaginings, underpinned by a firm nativist attachment to the simple presentation of the products of our soil. It is from this I derive most of my inspiration."

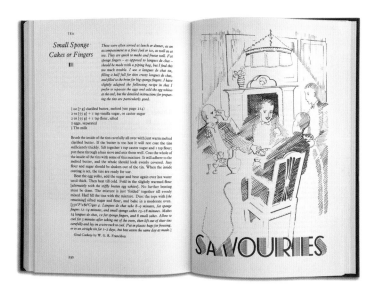

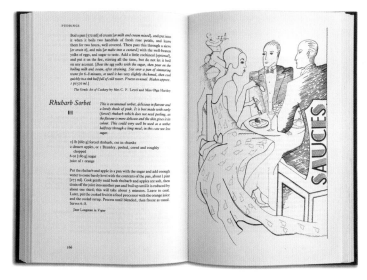

"It's certainly the book that's had the greatest influence on me, and one of my favourites to read."

JACKSON BOXER

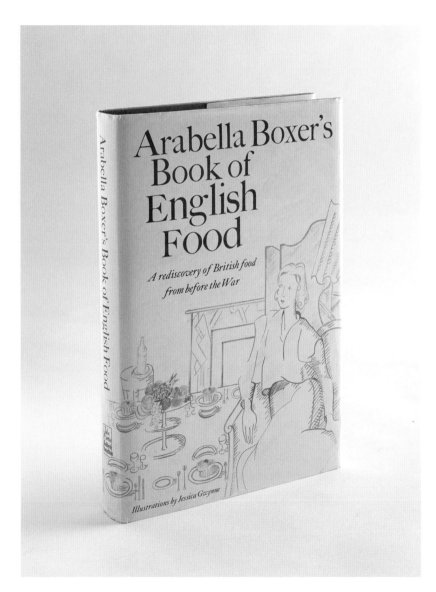

British seasonal cooking is on the menu at Jackson Boxer's atmospheric London restaurant, Brunswick House.

*"As a cook, I am a merchant of happiness. I respect the producer,
I respect my guest, but in between, I respect my collaborators."*
MICHEL BRAS

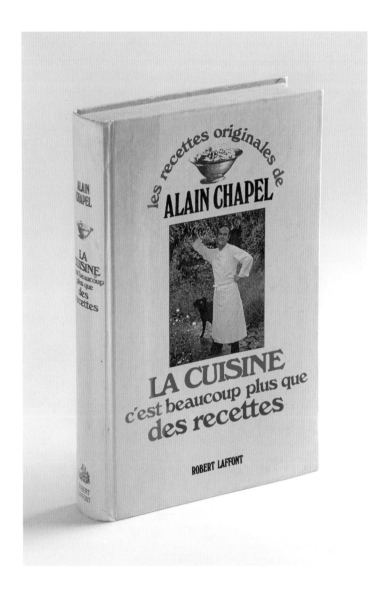

Michel Bras

RESTAURANT
Restaurant Bras, Laguiole, France, opened 1992

La Cuisine c'est beaucoup plus que des recettes
Alain Chapel

BOOK DETAILS
Published 1980, Éditions Robert Laffont, 443 pages, photography by Marc Tulane-Rapho

The great French chef Michel Bras (see p.10, 54, 188) draws inspiration for his food from the landscape around him in L'Aubrac. Here, perched high on the summit of Le Suquet, is his striking Restaurant Bras, where he works now in partnership with his son, chef Sébastien Bras (see p.38). Michel Bras's celebrated dish La Gargouillou—a joyous, seasonally changing composition of vegetables, herbs, and seeds—was inspired by seeing a meadow covered with flowers when he went for a stroll one day. In many aspects of his cuisine—from an early championing of veg-centric menus to his redefining of what "luxury" in fine dining should mean—he has been a pioneering figure. These as well as Bras's connectivity to the land—his ability to express this relationship through the plate, the integrity of his vision—have been profoundly influential for many of today's leading chefs.

The cookbook chosen by Michel Bras is *La Cuisine c'est beaucoup plus que des recettes* by the renowned French chef Alain Chapel, who died suddenly at the age of fifty-three in 1990. As a young man, he trained under the legendary Fernand Point at La Pyramide, Vienne. Having taken over the family bistro, renaming it Alain Chapel in 1970, he elevated its cooking, moving from one to three Michelin stars in six years. His cookbook, as its subtitle suggests, has a thoughtful, philosophical aspect to it, expressed with Gallic eloquence. In his heartfelt introduction, he champions creativity in the kitchen, rather than following recipes by rote, making the case for "freedom of creation, including culinary creation, that comes about through the various pleasures of change, innovation, and surprise." Despite his reservations, in this volume Chapel does share his recipes for legendary dishes such as Gâteau de foies blonds de poulardes de Bresse baigné d'une sauce aux queues d'écrevisses à la Lucien Tendret. Chapel's distinctive cuisine, impeccable in style and technique, drawing on classic tradition, yet also daring, profoundly creative, and innovative, influenced many other great chefs, including Heston Blumenthal, Michel Roux, Jr., and David Kinch. With his great restaurant closed, this cookbook offers an important record of Chapel's culinary genius.

Legendary French chef Michel Bras of Restaurant Bras, Laguiole, France, whose creative cooking has inspired chefs around the world.

Sébastien Bras

RESTAURANT

Restaurant Bras, Laguiole, France, opened 1992

Les Secrets de la casserole Hervé This

BOOK DETAILS

Published 1993, Éditions Belin, 232 pages, illustrations by Alain Kugel

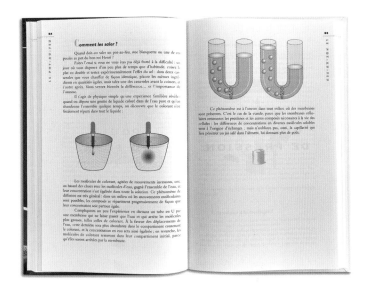

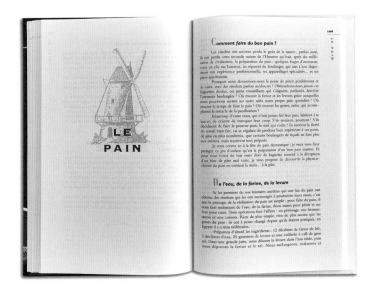

Ever since he was a small boy, Sébastien Bras knew that food and cooking were for him and that he would follow in the footsteps of his father, renowned chef Michel Bras (see p.10, 54, 188), and work as a professional chef: "At the age when you're making your own Laguiole knives out of hazelnut twigs, I was already dreaming of cooking. I inherited that particular trait from my father." His affinity with his father—and their mutual respect and camaraderie—has seen the two men working together harmoniously for several years at Restaurant Bras, the acclaimed restaurant established by Michel Bras in 1992. Sébastien is inspired by a love of nature and a sense of terroir: "I want my cuisine to pay tribute to L'Aubrac, a part of the country I could not dream of living without."

Sébastien Bras's book choice is *Les Secrets de la casserole* ("The Secrets of the Pan") by Hervé This, the renowned French chemical scientist from the Institut National de la Recherche Agronomique at AgroParisTech, Paris, France. In his book, This sets out to explain and clarify the science behind everyday acts of food preparation and cooking, enabling the reader to understand what is happening when, for example, they make a soufflé. It is a book, in effect, written to address the gaps left by conventional cookbooks, which give instructions without explaining the processes involved. While the work is, by its nature, scholarly—and comes complete with diagrams—This generally presents his information with admirable clarity and conciseness. In one section, he explores how much mayonnaise can be made from one egg yolk. American scientist Harold McGee (see p.337) prepared 50 pints (24 litres) from one yolk; "naturally he was helped by science," observes This. Thought-provoking and intriguing, it is a book for the curious-minded food lover, keen to learn more about the alchemy of cooking.

"I am self-taught and I acquired my culinary techniques through a scientific approach."

SÉBASTIEN BRAS

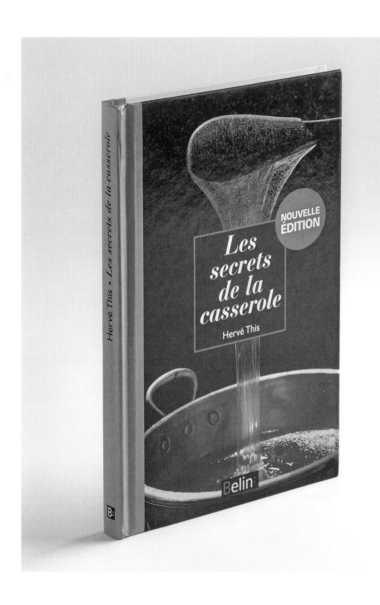

French chef Sébastien Bras, son of Michel Bras, offers cuisine inspired by the natural world at the acclaimed Restaurant Bras, France.

Stuart Brioza

RESTAURANT

State Bird Provisions, San Francisco, California, USA, opened 2011

The River Cottage Meat Book
Hugh Fearnley-Whittingstall

BOOK DETAILS

Published 2004, Hodder & Stoughton Ltd, 544 pages, photography by Simon Wheeler

There is an open-mindedness and an energy to American chef Stuart Brioza's approach to food. Ever since he and his pastry-chef wife, Nicole Krasinski (see p.96), opened State Bird Provisions in San Francisco in 2011, it has enjoyed critical and popular acclaim, quickly achieving cult status in the Bay area. Brioza's freshness of approach is apparent in the trademark, frequently changing menu of imaginative, small dishes, allowing him to explore and invent, which he does with relish. His cooking reveals a flair for putting together a cosmopolitan range of ingredients in unexpected ways to excellent and satisfying effect: Sourdough, Sauerkraut, Pecorino, and Ricotta Pancakes; Garlic Bread with Burrata; Lap Cheong with Long Pepper Yogurt. Brioza brings a sense of humor and fun to the business of food, and his enjoyment is infectious.

Stuart Brioza's choice is Hugh Fearnley-Whittingstall's hefty tome, *The River Cottage Meat Book*. Just as there is a lack of fuss and pretension to Brioza and Krasinski's State Bird Provisions, so is this cookbook straightforward and down-to-earth in its approach and style. Fearnley-Whittingstall, a noted British food promoter, is a great believer in sharing knowledge and informing people so that they can understand their food choices. In characteristically thorough fashion, he first explores issues to do with meat: the morality of eating it; how livestock is reared and killed (including witnessing how two of his own North Devon cattle are slaughtered); how to choose meat. Regarding the latter, the author is clear: Animals that have led good lives—free-range, organically reared—make for better meat than intensively reared, factory farmed creatures. Supermarket chill cabinets, writes Fearnley-Whittingstall, are "strip-lit morgues for millions of miserable pigs." The second part of the book explores how to cook meat, with Fearnley-Whittingstall explaining cooking processes, from grilling to making sausages. Fearnley-Whittingstall's writing is clear and accessible, whether on curing meat or cooking techniques. The recipes themselves are for uncomplicated, often hearty dishes—A Provençal Daube; Calf's Liver with Little Onions, Sage and Aged Vinegar; Roast Belly of Pork with Apple Sauce—with the focus firmly on achieving tasty results.

American chef Stuart Brioza, whose food can be enjoyed at State Bird Provisions restaurant, cofounded with his wife Nicole Krasinski, in San Francisco.

"Kitchens have a way of just absorbing you and taking you in, and it's hard not to get hooked. I think that one of the first things that really captured me is just the use of all my senses as I cook."

STUART BRIOZA

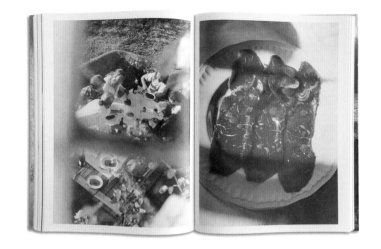

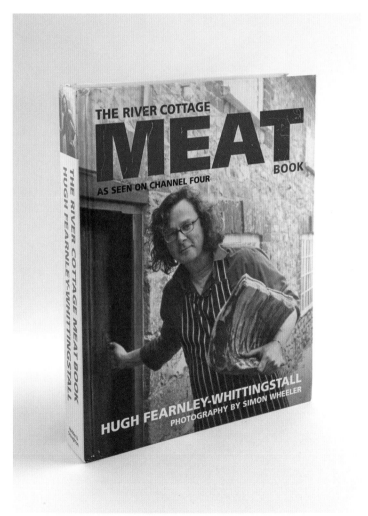

"The books of this time period inspire my cooking every day."
SEAN BROCK

THE

UNRIVALLED COOK-BOOK

AND

HOUSEKEEPER'S GUIDE

By MRS. WASHINGTON

NEW YORK
HARPER & BROTHERS, FRANKLIN SQUARE
1886

American chef Sean Brock is a champion of the rich heritage of Southern cooking.

Sean Brock

RESTAURANT

Husk, Charleston, South Carolina, USA, opened 2010

The Unrivalled Cook-Book and Housekeeper's Guide
Mrs. Washington

BOOK DETAILS

Published 1886, Harper & Brothers, 640 pages

Eloquent and passionate, Sean Brock (see p.190) is noted for his heartfelt championship of his beloved Southern cuisine, with the roots of his interest lying deep in his own rural Virginia childhood, in a society where people grew the food they cooked. While pursuing a successful career as a chef, Brock, a man with an appetite for knowledge, also followed his interest in Southern cuisine: researching its history, charting it, and, increasingly, preserving its traditions. There is an impressively obsessive quality to this aspect of his work, with Brock committed to seed preservation, growing endangered heirloom crops, and sourcing heritage breeds. Diners can taste the fruits of his labors for themselves at his acclaimed restaurants in Charleston and Nashville, which serve the Southern cuisine he loves.

Sean Brock's fascination with the history of America's Southern cuisine is manifest in his cookbook choice, *The Unrivalled Cook-Book* by Mrs. Washington. Told of the book's existence by Dr. David Shields of the University of South Carolina, Brock "searched and searched for an original copy." He remembers the thrill of discovery: "When I finally found and started flipping through it, my hands started trembling with excitement. It's so inspiring to read through a book that was one of the first definitive Southern cookbooks. It's a unique look into the way people used to approach food, a peek into the heyday of Southern cuisine." Using Mrs. Washington as a nom de plume, the book's author writes with patriotic pride: "A long residency in

foreign countries has convinced the editor that the American cuisine, where it is good, is, as is the American market, the best in the world." The book prides itself on its comprehensive nature, including recipes for griddle-cakes and catsups as well as game and fish. "It is filled full of amazing recipes like the Deer's-Head Soup à la Malmesbury, flavored with marigold and laurel, and the first recorded recipe for boiled peanuts," enthuses Brock. Having first made copious notes, Brock generously gave his precious copy of *The Unrivalled Cook-Book* to Dr. Shields. "I felt it only fitting to gift him that book. So I'm in the market for another if anyone ever runs across one," he explains.

André Chiang

RESTAURANT

Restaurant André, Singapore, opened 2010

Chef, La Grenouillère Alexandre Gauthier

BOOK DETAILS

Published 2014, Éditions de La Martinière, 333 pages, photography by Marie Pierre Morel

There is a willingness to take risks, a daring quality, to Taiwanese chef André Chiang's approach to food, which is much admired. Chiang's commitment to learning from the best saw him working at Pierre Gagnaire, L'Atelier de Joël Robuchon (see p.280), Astrance (see p.172), and Le Jardin des Sens. He made his name with Jaan Par André, Swissotel, in Singapore in 2008, which rapidly gained international acclaim. Following his own path, he set up Restaurant André in 2010. In his intimate Singaporean restaurant, Chiang serves his own emotionally charged cuisine, created according to his own Octaphilosophy, which focuses on eight elements that form his signature approach to food: Unique, Pure, Texture, Memory, Salt, South, Artisan, Terroir. Creative and intellectual, chef André Chiang is a talent to watch.

Intensely aesthetic, daringly conceived, a desirable object—one can understand why André Chiang was drawn to Alexandre Gauthier's distinctive book *Chef, La Grenouillère.* "The photographer is one of the best photographers in France and the whole book has very little text, but conveys so much. And the book is very well designed. You feel like you are really walking into the restaurant, by the visuals," enthuses Chiang. To look at the book is indeed to be transported to Gauthier's famous restaurant, La Grenouillère, housed in a sixteenth-century farmhouse. The serene, beautifully composed images depict the restaurant itself, its natural surroundings and Gauthier's dishes. The pictures allow the reader's eyes to see and understand how the chef is inspired by the landscape around him, sensing relationships between textures, colors, and forms. The recipes themselves are concisely written, simply outlining the method and allowing the images of the exquisite food to do the talking. "To me there is no other cookbook like this on the market at the moment," says Andre admiringly. "A very bold idea, certainly risky, but I admire his courage and creativity."

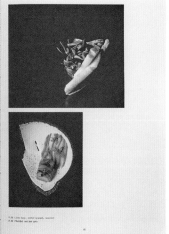

"It was a complete idea of Alexandre: He basically designed the book first and then went to the publisher. Everything was his."

ANDRÉ CHIANG

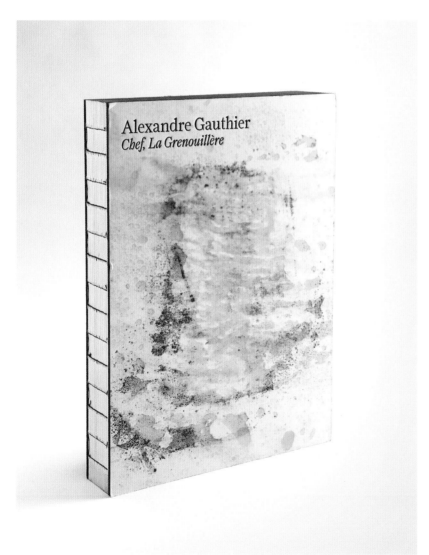

Noted for his Octaphilosopy, Taiwanese chef André Chiang of Restaurant André, Singapore, is a creative force in the world of haute cuisine.

British chef Sally Clarke is a long-time champion of carefully sourced, seasonal, British produce at her acclaimed restaurant, Clarke's, in London.

Sally Clarke

RESTAURANT
Clarke's, London, UK, opened 1984

The Chez Panisse Menu Cookbook Alice Waters

BOOK DETAILS
Published 1982, Random House Inc., 318 pages, illustrations by David Lance Goines

"I had a copy inscribed by Alice—'You will always be part of the famille Panisse'—which was stolen from me. If anyone finds it, please return it!"
SALLY CLARKE

There is an impressive integrity to British chef Sally Clarke's approach to food and dining. When she opened Clarke's in Kensington, London, she was unusual in being a female chef-owner in a male-dominated world. Furthermore, what she offered was then far from the norm: seasonally inspired menus that changed daily, and a single-option dinner menu. Clarke's inspiration was Alice Waters's California restaurant, Chez Panisse (see p.294): "When she opened Clarke's, she became the only admirer of Chez Panisse to actually adopt this format, our most idiosyncratic feature," observed Waters. Clarke put considerable work and energy into sourcing ingredients in order to ensure the quality she sought. Her cooking is discreetly elegant, rather than overtly showy, and she has never been afraid to embrace simplicity.

Sally Clarke's choice—*The Chez Panisse Menu Cookbook* by Alice Waters—is a deeply personal one, a book by her mentor that is freighted with significance. "It was Alice's first book and the first book I owned of hers," explains Clarke. "It has a slightly young, fragile feel about it, yet her voice throughout comes across as authoritative." This famous cookbook is, in a sense, a manifesto, in which Waters sets out to define and convey her own deeply held philosophy of food. The book contains a distinctly appetizing selection of Chez Panisse menus—A Garlic Dinner, A Menu for the Zinfandel Festival—and the ingredients-focused recipes for them. She presents her ideas about food with conviction, unafraid of championing the simple things in life, such as rounding off a meal with ripe fruit or a glass of Sauternes. Waters writes thoughtfully and intelligently on how to compose a menu. "Marrying the elements of a meal correctly so as to achieve that elusive equilibrium requires an understanding of each separate course and its importance within the overall structure of the menu. To succeed, first consider what foods are at their peak that particular day," she counsels. Far away from Berkeley, California, in the busy metropolis of London, chef Sally Clarke read, understood, and acted on Waters's book.

Mauro Colagreco

RESTAURANT

Mirazur, Menton, France, opened 2006

Clorofilia Andoni Luis Aduriz

BOOK DETAILS

Published 2004, Mugaritz, 224 pages, photography by José Luis López de Zubiria

Charismatic and creative, Italo-Argentine chef Mauro Colagreco has made his name with his restaurant Mirazur, which is located in the hills of Menton on the French Riviera. Colagreco's career has been marked by a drive and determination that saw him leave Argentina as a young man to work in France as a chef. There he worked first for Bernard Loiseau until his death in 2003, then for chefs including Alain Ducasse (see p.88, 144, 204) and Alain Passard at L'Arpège (see p.264), with the latter opening Colagreco's eyes to the potential of cooking creatively with vegetables. In 2006, Colagreco opened his own restaurant Mirazur and it swiftly garnered enormous acclaim. The beautiful natural surroundings, the location close to Italy and the restaurant's large organic garden offer inspiration for his elegant cooking, which is rooted in terroir and noted for its use of fresh seafood, produce, and herbs.

Mauro Colagreco's fascination with the natural world is reflected in his book choice, *Clorofilia* by the acclaimed Spanish chef Andoni Luis Aduriz (see p.158). "It is a book that offers important research on herbs and their use in the kitchen," explains Colagreco. At Mugaritz, his internationally renowned restaurant, Aduriz is noted for his imaginative interpretation of nature, and in this distinctive, elegant cookbook he celebrates the use of plants, offering recipes for fifty different herbs, from *Achillea millefolium* (common yarrow) to *Viola riviniana* (common dog violet). The recipes for exquisitely presented dishes—for example, Gelatinous Veil of Bonito, Rosemary Flowers, and Whipped Honey on Quinoa Seasoned with Idiazabal Cheese—reveal Aduriz's impressive creativity and technical mastery. Characteristically, Aduriz worked in collaboration with scientists, botanists, and writers, with each herb given an individual entry that explores its folklore and history. In his lucid introduction to the book, Aduriz sets out his personal manifesto as a chef, writing with eloquence of the importance of eschewing conventional definitions of luxury: "Overwhelmed by all that is unctuous and overloaded, we should be reaching out to the opposite," he declares.

"For me, this is a book that has had a great impact on modern cuisine and in chefs' minds."
MAURO COLAGRECO

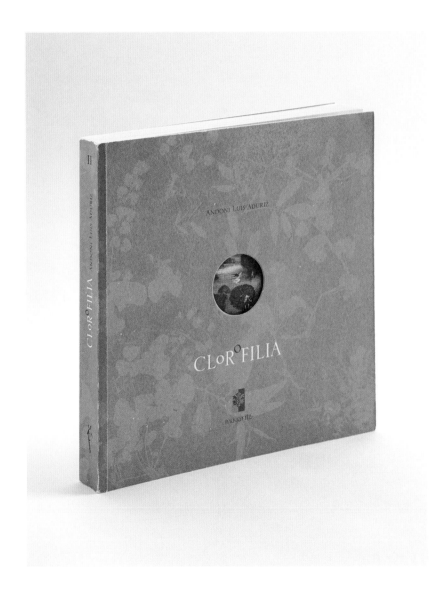

Argentinian chef Mauro Colagreco's exquiste food reflects his restaurant's idyllic Côte d'Azur setting.

"Every home cook should have a copy."
TOM COLICCHIO

American chef, restaurateur, and television personality Tom Colicchio, whose food emphasizes the craftsmanship of cookery.

Tom Colicchio

RESTAURANT

Craft, New York City, New York, USA, opened 2001

Unplugged Kitchen Viana La Place

BOOK DETAILS

Published 1996, William Morrow and Company, 354 pages, photography by Maria Robledo, illustrations by Ann Field

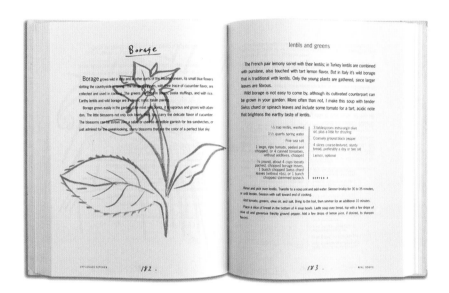

Having been acclaimed for his cooking at such illustrious New York restaurants as Mondrian and Gramercy Tavern (see p.162), American chef Tom Colicchio (see p.196) has forged his own career as chef and restaurateur. His restaurant Craft, which he opened in New York in 2001, gave him a chance to express his own approach to food and dining—seasonal ingredients, chosen when they are at their very best, cooked simply in order to let them shine, served in a relaxed, hospitable atmosphere. Since then, Colicchio has gone on to open numerous other restaurants, with the emphasis—naturally—always on the craft of creating good food. Colicchio's interest in food also extends beyond the kitchen and he frequently raises awareness of various food issues, including the abuse of antibiotics in the food chain.

"I love Viana's approach to cooking in this book," says Tom Colicchio enthusiastically of his choice, *Unplugged Kitchen* by Viana La Place. Inspired by her Italian-American heritage, La Place offers a straightforward, rooted approach to making and eating food. She begins by championing home cooking over restaurant cooking, pointing out that "In many countries around the world, home cooking is considered to be the paradigm of good cooking." La Place expresses her approach to food and cooking with a lively conviction and humor, advocating hopping outside the "twilight zone" of supermarkets and drawing inspiration instead from food markets and small shops run by real people. Her recipes are as vivacious as her writing: Tabbouleh (dressed with lime juice rather than lemon), Innocent Fettuccine, Unplugged Pesto (made without pine nuts). Every single delicious dish is explained with friendly enthusiasm. As someone who eats very little meat, vegetables and fruit are the stars of the show, used by La Place with creative relish in dishes from fresh salads and heartening soups to simple but tasty panini. As Colicchio remarks, "She takes simple everyday recipes that make cooking accessible for anyone."

Richard Corrigan

RESTAURANT

Bentley's Oyster Bar & Grill, London, UK, opened 1916 (bought and refurbished by Corrigan in 2005)

Sex & Drugs & Sausage Rolls
Graham Garrett and Cat Black

BOOK DETAILS

Published 2015, Face Publications, 288 pages, photography by Adrian Franklin

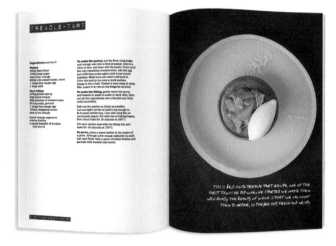

A childhood on a small farm in County Meath, Ireland, saw Irish chef Richard Corrigan learn for himself, from a young age, the hard work and effort that goes into producing food. One of the hallmarks of his cooking, broadcasting, and food writing has been a commitment to first-class ingredients and a championing of excellent food producers. Corrigan made his name in England, first winning a Michelin star while head chef for Stephen Bull's Fulham Road restaurant in London, then at his own restaurant, Lindsay House, Soho, London, which he opened in 1997. His successful revival of a British culinary institution—Bentley's Oyster Bar & Grill in London—has garnered him many plaudits; he is renowned for his refined yet flavorful classic cooking.

Richard Corrigan—a jovial bon viveur and raconteur—has chosen, appropriately, a cookbook with spirit and a sense of humor. *Sex & Drugs & Sausage Rolls* by British chef Graham Garrett (see p.65, 210) is, as the title suggests, not a dull tome; it is distinctive and vigorous both in appearance and content. Garrett—a rock musician turned chef—tells the story of his colorful life through the cookbook format. Following his career as a drummer in bands including the Dumb Blondes and the Ya Yas, Garrett decided at the age of thirty-one to pursue his passion for food and become a chef, establishing his Michelin-starred restaurant, The West House, in Kent, England. In down-to-earth, engaging, eminently readable prose, Garrett conveys the mad worlds of musicians and chefs with cheerful candor, mixing in recipes en route that demonstrate his excellent eye and commitment to the craft of food. As the writer of the foreword, Corrigan has, himself, a connection to this cookbook, writing affectionately of his friend and colleague: "Graham is one of those people who grab life by the 'proverbials' and attack any project with the gusto and enthusiasm of a master."

"One of the best cookery books in a long, long time; a reflection of Graham's colourful rock 'n' roll life, a collection of wonderful stories and, of course, fine recipes."
RICHARD CORRIGAN

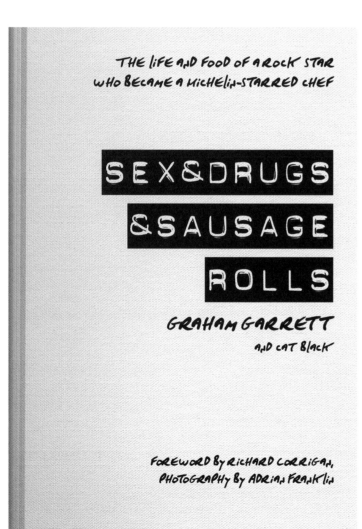

Irish chef Richard Corrigan, whose restaurants showcase prime ingredients from fish to game.

"We've taken a page out of the Bras book—the schmear, the spoon drag, putting food on a plate like it fell off a tree."
WYLIE DUFRESNE

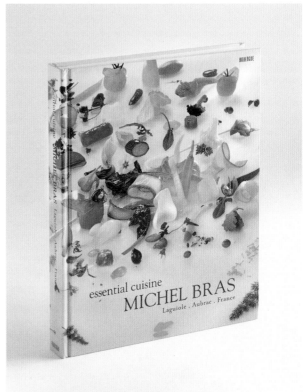

American chef Wylie Dufresne is famous for his innovative, modernist cooking.

Wylie Dufresne

RESTAURANT

wd~50, New York City, New York, USA, 2003–2014

Essential Cuisine Michel Bras

BOOK DETAILS

Published in English as *Essential Cuisine*, 2008, Éditions du Rouergue, 272 pages, photography by Christian Palis and Jean-Pierre Trébosc; first published in French as *Bras: Laguiole, Aubrac, France*, 2002

There is an open-minded curiosity to chef Wylie Dufresne, which is reflected in his innovative cooking. Having trained with Jean-Georges Vongerichten (see p.290) in the 1990s, he opened his own restaurant wd~50 in New York City's Lower East Side, its name referencing his own initials and the location. Here, Dufresne expressed himself in his own style, inspired by the science-based approach of modernist cuisine and becoming noted for his cutting-edge creativity. Hallmark creations included his deconstructed Eggs Benedict—looking strikingly different from the conventional version, yet containing all the classic elements of the dish, reimagined for maximum effect. He closed both wd~50 and his bistro Alder in 2014 and 2015, with new projects—and more imaginative cooking—promised.

Wylie Dufresne's choice is a cookbook by a legendary French chef, *Bras: Laguiole, Aubrac, France* by Michel Bras (see p.10, 36, 188). The book celebrates the cuisine that Michel, together with his son Sébastien (see p.38), serves at Bras, his world-renowned restaurant at Laguiole in France. "Celebrates" is the right word to use as there is a delightful exuberance to the book, with its full-page, colorful photographs of culinary creations such as Fromage Blanc Tartine with Butternut Confit and Chives; Crusted Prawns with Foamy Potatoes and Meadow Mushroom Soup; or Gentian Leaves Filled With Apple Compote, Frosted Black and Red Berries, and Spicy Jus. Bras presents his dishes with inventive wit and flair and it is notable that his plates of food frequently evoke natural landscapes—mountains, streams, rocks, and earth—a reminder that a love of nature is fundamental to Bras's creativity as a chef. The book opens with a quote by the great French writer Jean Giono that seems to perfectly encapsulate Bras's philosophy and approach to his cuisine: "When you love your land / You want to make it known to as many people as possible / And to make it rich. / Gastronomy is a magnificent way to do all that."

grilled john dory fillets, with a hearty stock, buckwheat cake and parsley

"gargouillou" of leaves, roots, mushrooms and fruits in autumn

"This book has been with me for years and every time I pick it up and read it, I smile."

ANDRÉ GARRETT

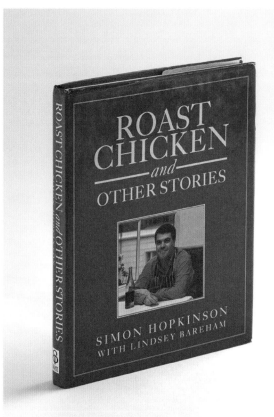

Acclaimed for his elegant, classic cooking, André Garrett's cuisine can be enjoyed in the lovely surroundings of Cliveden, UK.

André Garrett

RESTAURANT

André Garrett at Cliveden, Taplow, Berkshire, UK, opened 2013

Roast Chicken and Other Stories Simon Hopkinson

BOOK DETAILS

Published 1994, Ebury Press, 230 pages, illustrations by Flo Bayley

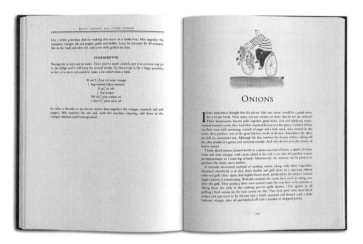

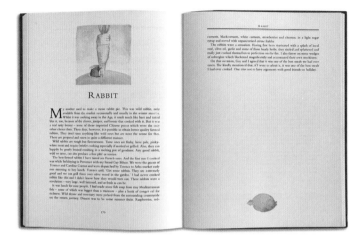

British chef André Garrett has worked for notable chefs during his career, among them Nico Ladenis (see p.238) and Bruno Loubet. In 2002, Garrett began working for Chris Galvin at the Michelin-starred Orrery, London, the beginning of a rewarding relationship that saw him swiftly promoted from senior sous chef to head chef within a year. In 2002, Garrett also won that year's Roux Scholarship, using the opportunity to work at three Michelin-starred restaurant Guy Savoy in Paris. In 2006, Galvin at Windows at the London Hilton, Park Lane, opened, with Garrett as head chef, making a name and gaining a Michelin star for his accomplished French cuisine. These days, diners can enjoy Garrett's harmonious, elegant cooking at his own restaurant in the beautiful surroundings of Cliveden House.

André Garrett's affection for *Roast Chicken and Other Stories* by Simon Hopkinson (see p.80, 224) is palpable: "I really love this book and it is timeless," he enthuses. "The style is simple: Simon picks key ingredients and has a number of great recipes around these. What is really great is the stories around the ingredients and recipes." Garrett has accurately pinpointed the special quality of Hopkinson's famous cookbook—the straightforward format allows Hopkinson to champion his favorite foods, which he does with charm and character, often writing so evocatively that he makes the reader hungry. Memories of encounters with ingredients and kitchen stories give a personal dimension to the writing, as with his humorous account of having to make a huge amount of garlic butter by hand while apprenticing at Yves Champeau's La Normandie in Birtle, U.K. Often cheerfully maverick, there is a beautiful audacity to noted chef Hopkinson's affirmation of the pleasures of a simple roast chicken: "Roasting a chicken is a joy for me; and if I am pressed to name my favourite food, then roast chicken it must be."

Suzanne Goin

RESTAURANT

Lucques, Los Angeles, California, USA, opened 1998

Paula Wolfert's World of Food Paula Wolfert

BOOK DETAILS

Published 1988, Harper & Row Publishers, 361 pages

Californian chef and restaurateur Suzanne Goin (see p.216) has that special ability to transmit her love of food through her cooking, her restaurants, and her food writing. The early years of her career saw her working in restaurants including Alice Waters's Chez Panisse in Berkeley (see p.294) and Alain Passard's L'Arpège in Paris (see p.264). In 1998, she opened her own restaurant, Lucques in Los Angeles, to acclaim from critics and diners alike. She is a thoughtful chef with strong convictions about the role of food in bringing people together, typified by the Sunday Suppers at Lucques, which were inspired by her own memories of family dinners. Her Mediterranean-influenced cooking is at once rustic and elegant, simple and sophisticated, grounded in classic technique, but also rooted in the personal connections she has to the food she cooks.

"I love all of Paula Wolfert's books [see p.313] but *World of Food* is my favorite," says chef Suzanne Goin warmly of her cookbook choice. "It's so personal and diverse—you can tell these are Paula's real favorite recipes to cook." As the inclusive title suggests, it is a book of recipes drawn from around the world: Sicily, Morocco, France, Greece . . . Wolfert sets out her criteria for inclusion, with the simple but important question: "Do I want to eat this dish again?" being for her "the ultimate test." Wolfert's considerable culinary intelligence underlies the carefully chosen contents. The book's recipes, she explains, include

dishes with "big taste," but also dishes which are "refined" with "real polish"— for example, French chef Michel Bras's elegant Cèpe Tart with Walnut Cream. Cooking techniques, similarly, range from long, slow cooking to the more sophisticated. Another theme throughout the book is "the attainment of richness without heaviness." It is a vibrant and beguiling mixture, written with equal measures of practicality and charm. It is a book that still continues to inspire Goin: "I cooked my way through this book at an early age and still use so many of the techniques and flavor profiles."

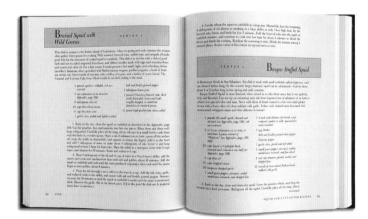

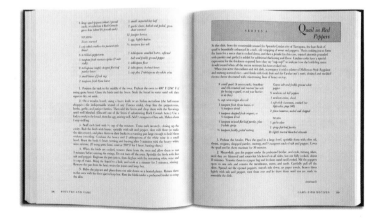

"My copy is tattered and torn!"
SUZANNE GOIN

Californian chef Suzanne Goin, whose cooking at her restaurant Lucques, Los Angeles is influenced by the simplicity of classic Mediterranean cuisine.

"I've been a huge admirer of Christine's food for several decades and of all her books, this is the one I find most inspirational, and all encompassing."
PETER GORDON

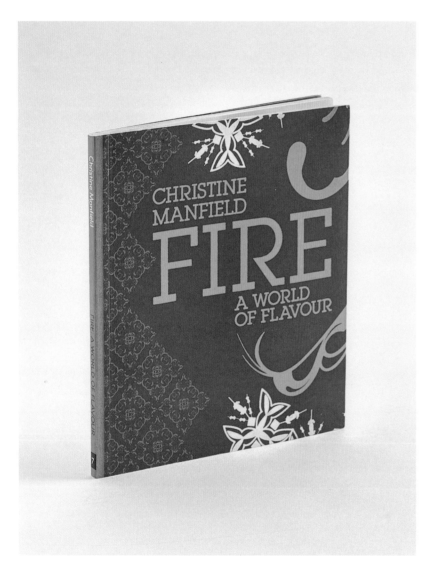

New Zealand chef Peter Gordon draws inspiration from around the world for his imaginative dishes.

Peter Gordon

RESTAURANT

The Providores and Tapa Room, London, UK, opened 2001

Fire: A World of Flavour   Christine Manfield

BOOK DETAILS

Published 2008, Penguin Books Australia, 574 pages

New Zealand chef Peter Gordon is a champion of "fusion cuisine" and his cooking reflects both his intelligent interest in food from around the world and his considerable creative culinary talents. Having made his name as chef at The Sugar Club, first in Wellington, then with its London incarnation in 1995, Gordon set up his own restaurant, The Providores and Tapa Room, in Marylebone, London, in 2001, showcasing his distinctively cosmopolitan cuisine. The menus in both the informal downstairs area and the restaurant upstairs change often, reflecting Gordon's fascination with ingredients from spelt to the citrus fruit yuzu. Gordon's capacity to bring foods from different cuisines together with flair is impressive.

Peter Gordon's choice is *Fire* by Australian chef, restaurateur, and writer Christine Manfield (see p.248). "It's a travel journal and a culinary encyclopaedia in one; it covers dishes she's experienced in her travels, but always with that 'Chris' touch. It has savoury dishes and desserts, small plates, large plates, a bit of everything. Her understanding of 'foreign' cuisines is second to none, and she has a great love of flavour. What's not to like?" he says admiringly. One can see why Manfield's open-minded exploration of world cuisines would appeal to Gordon, whose own cooking is similarly omnivorous. There is a stimulating energy to *Fire*, in which Manfield takes the reader on a globe-trotting spin around the world, from Asia to Europe. Each section begins with a piece of travel writing to set the scene, then moves on to recipes. Her own cooking reveals a flair for combining flavors and textures to exciting effect. Dishes such as Black Pepper Snow Crab Salad or Lobster Lollipops reflect her capacity to refine and play with classic dishes from cuisines she loves.

Bill Granger

RESTAURANT
bills, Sydney, Australia, opened 1993

Charmaine Solomon's Encyclopedia of Asian Food
Charmaine Solomon with Nina Solomon

BOOK DETAILS
Published 1996, William Heinemann Australia, 480 pages, photography by Richard l'Anson, Tom Cockrem, Greg Elms, and Brian Gilkes, illustrations by Peter Schouten

Self-taught Australian chef, restaurateur, broadcaster, and food writer Bill Granger (see p.218) established his name with his iconic Sydney café bills, which he opened in 1993 at the age of twenty-four. Now with a number of restaurants around the world, his name has come to characterize a laid-back, informal approach to food and dining. From the early days of bills, Granger's own cooking has always reflected a cosmopolitan attitude to food, with his menus at the café drawing inspiration from the multicultural communities living in Sydney. The vibrant flavors of Asian food—with ingredients such as fragrant lemongrass, aromatic ginger, or hot, pungent chiles—are something he has embraced and championed with relish in his own cooking, encapsulated in his own attractive, characteristically accessible and appetising cookbook *Bill's Everyday Asian*.

Bill Granger's cookbook choice—*Charmaine Solomon's Encyclopedia of Asian Food*—reflects his long-held interest in Asian food. Born in Sri Lanka, but moving to Australia as a young woman, Charmaine Solomon has done an enormous amount to introduce and popularize Asian food within her adopted country, notably through her bestselling *Complete Asian Cookbook*. Her *Encyclopedia* is another ambitious achievement, lovingly charting ingredients from across Asia in order to demystify these "exotic foods." She provides clear guidance on how to prepare and use ingredients from kaffir lime leaves to Maldive fish, describes

cooking techniques, and includes a diverse selection of mouthwatering recipes. Her writing is clear, accessible, and often humorous, demonstrated in a lively entry on the notoriously pungent durian. The range of content is impressive, with information given on both the macro level—with national cuisines of countries outlined—and the micro, with entries, for example, on both dried shrimp paste and shrimp sauce. On Australian food, Solomon writes with, one feels, justifiable pleasure: "Instead of being a culinary outpost of Britain as it was for so long, Australian cuisine is developing its own personality, one with a distinctly Asian bias."

"Packed full of the classics as well as the more unusual, Charmaine translates the mysteries of the Asian kitchen concisely for the home cook."

BILL GRANGER

Australian chef Bill Granger, whose relaxed, friendly restaurants have an international following.

"Édouard Nignon was visionary."
MICHEL GUÉRARD

French chef Michel Guérard,
famous for his *cuisine minceur*,
which offers a lighter take on
haute cuisine dining.

Michel Guérard

RESTAURANT
Les Prés d'Eugénie, Eugénie-les-Bains, France, opened 1974

Éloges de la cuisine Française Édouard Nignon

BOOK DETAILS
Published 1933, L'Édition d'art H. Piazza et Cie, 559 pages

An elegant, witty figure, Michel Guérard's vitality makes him an excellent advertisement for *cuisine minceur*—the healthy cooking he has championed for so many years (see p.222). That energy is appropriate as, throughout his career, he has been a revitalizing force in French cuisine, offering his own creative reimagining of French food. He made his name first in Paris, with his restaurant Pot-au-Feu, then, having married and moved to Eugénie-les-Bains, with his famous Prés d'Eugénie. It was here, in the surroundings of a luxurious spa, that Guérard came up with his famed *cuisine minceur*, with which his name is synonymous. It is a style of cooking that moved away from the dependence on cream and butter traditionally used in luxurious French cooking, while offering a satisfying intensity and purity of flavor.

Michel Guérard's cookbook choice is for a book published in 1933—"the year I was born," he points out. It is *Éloges de la Cuisine Française*, by Édouard Nignon, a chef, whom explains Guérard, "had a huge influence on French chefs like me or Joël Robuchon [see p.280]." In the illustrious canon of great French chefs, Nignon has a particularly special place; born in 1865, his considerable talents saw him cooking for the crowned heads of Europe at the tender age of twenty-seven. In 1908, he took over Restaurant Larue in Paris, swiftly making it one of *the* places to dine. Nignon opens his

book in eloquent style: "I have chosen today, the 9th of November 1932, and my birthday, to deliver through these pages the account of what was the loveliest, noblest, and most captivating work of my life." Setting out to capture and communicate "the very best" of his work, Nignon initially lays out his thoughts on eating well, before moving on to offer recipes for classic French dishes including Suprême de Turbot Excellence or Escalopes de Homard Colbert. It is a glimpse into the world of French haute cuisine, written with poetic panache by a master chef.

Skye Gyngell

RESTAURANT
Spring, London, UK, opened 2014

The Zuni Café Cookbook Judy Rodgers

BOOK DETAILS
Published 2002, W. W. Norton & Company, 546 pages, photography by Gentl & Hyers/Edge, Steven Rothfeld, and Mazin Nasser

"It is the book that has remained by my bedside for over a decade."
SKYE GYNGELL

Noted for her ingredients-led cuisine and ability to combine flavors to great effect, Skye Gyngell's food can be enjoyed at Spring in London.

Australian-born chef Skye Gyngell trained in Europe, notably under Anton Mosimann (see p.112) at The Dorchester in London. She made her name as head chef of the Petersham Nurseries Café, located in idyllic surroundings in a plant nursery by the banks of the River Thames at Richmond, London. Here, working with ingredients freshly picked from the kitchen gardens, she created her signature style—one that was elegantly rustic, focused on truly seasonal, high-quality ingredients, used with imagination and flair. In 2014, Gyngell opened her restaurant Spring, located in historic Somerset House in London. Here, too, the menu focuses on seasonal ingredients, changing daily in order to reflect what is best and using straightforward cooking methods to allow the carefully sourced produce to star on the plate.

"I've loved so many books over the years and I still get great pleasure and excitement when I find a new book that I simply must have," says Skye Gyngell with the relish of a true cookbook lover. "But the book that I have returned to and that has influenced me more than any other is *The Zuni Café Cookbook* by Judy Rodgers (see p.282). Its integrity, purity, and precision never fails to dazzle me." There is indeed something very special about Rodgers's cookbook, based on food she cooked and served at her own, much-loved restaurant the Zuni Café in San Francisco. Her ability to take simple ingredients and use them to great effect is apparent in dishes such as the trademark Zuni Salt-Cured Anchovies, served with "shards of Parmigiano-Reggiano and cold, crisp sliced celery." Rather than simply offering recipes, in her cookbook Rodgers also shares her thoughts on cooking, food, hospitality, and the convivial pleasures of dining, all of which contribute to make it a rich and beguiling read. Writing in a distinctive, characterful voice, she offers advice expressed with charm but also conviction: "Cookbooks will give you ideas, but the market will give you dinner—study your market at least as avidly as you study your library." Rodgers cooked from the heart—and that simple but powerful fact shines through her cookbook.

> *"I haven't found another book that conjures up such fresh and delicious Asian recipes; it's unrivalled."*
>
> ANNA HANSEN

Anna Hansen's aptly named restaurant Modern Pantry captures her adventurous, cosmopolitan approach to food.

Anna Hansen

RESTAURANT
The Modern Pantry, London, UK, opened 2008

Thai Food David Thompson

BOOK DETAILS
Published 2002, Ten Speed Press, 673 pages, photography by Earl Carter

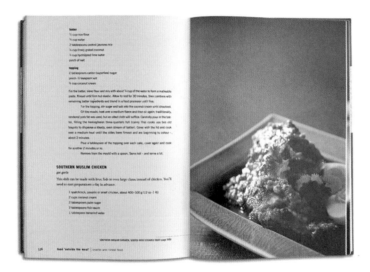

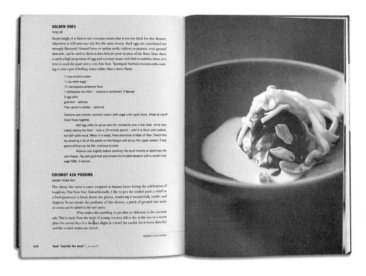

There is a cosmopolitan quality to Anna Hansen's life and cooking. Born in Australia but raised in New Zealand, she has made her name as a chef in the United Kingdom, where she trained under Fergus Henderson (see p.24, 104) at The French House Dining Room in London. In 2001, in partnership with Peter Gordon (see p.60), she opened The Providores in London, a restaurant noted for its imaginative use of globe-trotting ingredients. In 2008, Hansen went solo to open The Modern Pantry in London's fashionable Clerkenwell, which showcased her inventive approach to ingredients and fascination with cuisines from around the world in an informal atmosphere. Dishes such as a signature Sugar-Cured Prawn Omelette with Smoked Chilli Sambal reflect her ability to put together flavors and textures with flair and panache.

"I have been cooking from David Thompson's *Thai Food* for years," says Anna Hansen about her favorite cookbook. The short, simple title of this acclaimed cookbook belies its considerable scale. Australian chef David Thompson became enthralled by Thai cuisine and has spent years researching, cooking, and recording it; this book is an extraordinary chronicle of Thai food, impressive in both its breadth and depth. Thompson sets the cuisine he loves in the context of Thai geography, history, and politics, then explores it with relish and in great detail. Here are authentic recipes ranging from everyday street and market food to historic, courtly dishes, from the simple to the extraordinarily intricate. Thompson's depth of knowledge of Thai ingredients and cooking techniques is apparent throughout, with his excitement about Thai food both engaging and infectious. For anyone interested in the richness of Southeast Asian cuisine—as Hansen is—the book provides a fascinating insight into its enormous range and complexity. "It's a real go-to for me whenever I need a bit of inspiration," says Hansen, "as the scope of recipes and depth of knowledge is utterly amazing."

Stephen Harris

RESTAURANT
The Sportsman, Seasalter, UK, opened 1999

Cuisine Actuelle Patricia Wells presents the cuisine of Joël Robuchon

BOOK DETAILS
Published 1993, William Morrow and Company, 336 pages, photography by Steven Rothfeld and Robert Fréson

"I bought this book when I was a frustrated chef, trying to teach myself."
STEPHEN HARRIS

Stephen Harris is now acclaimed for his intelligent, flavorful cooking; however, it was only in his thirties that he came to his career as a chef. Working as a financial advisor, Harris had become increasingly fascinated by food and cooking, experimenting at home; a revelatory meal at Chez Nico at 90 Park Lane (see p.238) proved a turning point. In 1999, self-taught chef Harris took over a pub in a remote spot on the Kentish coast, The Sportsman. The aim was always to use local produce, and the Kent coast as well as its agricultural land offer rich pickings—with his menus featuring ingredients such as salt marsh lamb, foraged plants, shellfish, and seaweed, all cooked with care, attention, and excellent technique.

Stephen Harris's choice is for a book learnt from during his quest to become a chef: *Cuisine Actuelle, Patricia Wells Presents the Cuisine of Joël Robuchon.* Harris wanted an insight into how professional chefs cook and "this book was the closest I could get," he explains. The book is a collaboration between legendary French chef Robuchon (see p.280) and American food writer—and French food lover—Patricia Wells (see p.314). It is a fruitful partnership because Wells is able to describe Robuchon's cooking with intelligent appreciation, highlighting his emphasis on respecting ingredients and his ability to "work magic with the simplest of ingredients." In addition to clearly written versions of Robuchon's dishes, including his famous Potato Purée, there is an illuminating interview with Robuchon himself. Keen to eat Robuchon's food, Harris remembers how "when he opened his Atelier place in 2003, I was straight over there with Dan, my chef. We ordered everything on the menu and were given a guard of honour by the staff as we left the restaurant! The biggest thing I learnt from Robuchon was how small finishing touches can turn a good dish into a great one."

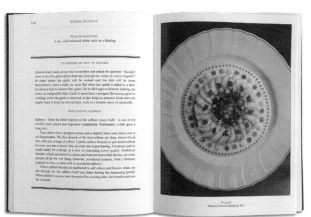

At his restaurant The Sportsman, British chef Stephen Harris expresses the terroir of the Kentish coast with wit and intelligence.

"One of the first cookery books I ever bought. My mum bought a copy for my brother before he went off to uni, and I have loved Hazan's books ever since."

ANGELA HARTNETT

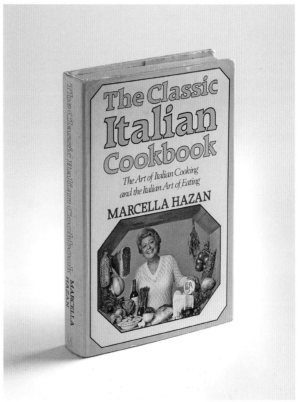

Her Italian heritage informs British chef Angela Hartnett's approach to food, expressed at her elegant London restaurant Murano.

Angela Hartnett

RESTAURANT

Murano, London, UK, opened 2008

The Classic Italian Cookbook Marcella Hazan

BOOK DETAILS

First published 1973, Alfred A. Knopf, 414 pages, illustrations by Karin Kretschmann; this edition published 1980, Macmillan

British chef Angela Hartnett's Italian heritage, via her mother and grandmother, has been an important, defining force in her approach to food. She worked for several years for Gordon Ramsay (see p.276), who recognized her culinary talents, working with her to launch numerous restaurants, including Amaryllis in Scotland, Verre in Dubai, and Angela Hartnett at The Grill Room at the Connaught, London. She is now a restaurateur in her own right, with her flagship establishment Murano in Mayfair, London, where she is chef-owner. Here, she showcases an Italian-inspired menu that is contemporary and accessible in style, yet focused on quality ingredients. Straightforward and warm in person, Hartnett's restaurants reflect her belief that dining is about hospitality and conviviality, rather than excessive formality or pomp and ceremony.

Angela Hartnett's choice—*The Classic Italian Cookbook* by Marcella Hazan (see p.134, 148)—reflects the English chef's deeply held affection for the Italian cuisine that is part of her heritage. "There are no pictures," says Hartnett, "just illustrations of pasta. Every recipe works, and she shows all the different regions of Italy." It is indeed the quality of the writing—both elegant and informative—which has made this bestselling book such an enduring success. Hazan was a notable cooking teacher, and her ability to explain and communicate is evident in her text, which gives a true insight into the nature of Italian food: "The cooking of Italy is really the cooking of its regions, regions that until 1861 were separate, independent, and usually hostile states." The well-written recipes are grouped together in a way that reflects the structure of an Italian meal. Hazan, with characteristic thoroughness, first outlines a technique, such as the making of fresh pasta, then gives a range of recipes using it: Trenette al Pesto, Cappelletti in Brodo, for example. It is a book that is intensely affirmative about the pleasures of good food: "Not everyone in Italy may know how to cook, but nearly everyone knows how to eat."

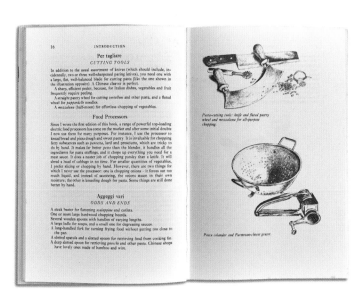

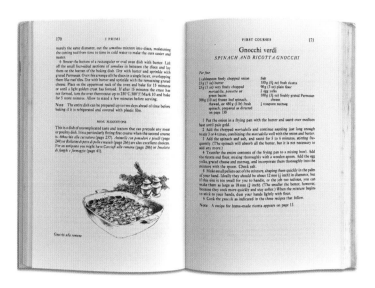

Shaun Hill

RESTAURANT
The Walnut Tree, Abergavenny, Wales, UK, reopened by Hill in 2007

The Best of Jane Grigson
Jane Grigson, compiled by Roy Fullick

BOOK DETAILS
Published 1992, Michael Joseph, 468 pages

"I was torn between Jane Grigson's Good Things *and* English Food, *then I remembered that* The Best of Jane Grigson *was compiled and published."*
SHAUN HILL

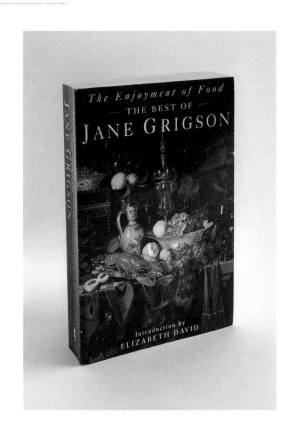

Noted for his intelligent, unpretentious approach to cooking and food, British chef Shaun Hill began cooking at Robert Carrier's restaurant in Islington, London, in the late 1960s. He made his name first as head chef of the renowned country house hotel Gidleigh Park, at Chagford in Devon, before moving to set up Merchant House, situated on the ground floor of his home in Ludlow. Here, famously, Hill did his own shopping, cooking, and dish washing, serving simple but excellent food on a small scale and acquiring a devoted and loyal following. In 2007, Hill took over The Walnut Tree at Abergavenny, a restaurant that had fallen on hard times and closed down, breathing new life into this cherished institution with his characterful, eclectic cooking.

"Such a joy to be treated as an intelligent and interested person by the author," observes Shaun Hill on *The Best of Jane Grigson*. This compilation celebrates the considerable talents of the much-loved food writer Jane Grigson (see p.100, 102, 106, 329). As no less than Elizabeth David (see p.84, 110, 332) wrote in the introduction, thinking back to reading Grigson's first book on charcuterie: "The clarity of the writing, and the confident knowledge of its subject and its history displayed by this young author were new treats for us all." The range of Grigson's food knowledge is amply displayed in this collection. Her writing is rich and varied, with fascinating nuggets of history and literary references, while also rooted in practicality. The book climaxes with "Treats and Celebrations," which offers fine pieces on meals with friends, advice on picnics, and recipes from Meat Loaf to Lobster with Grilled Oysters. "Grigson's books on *Fruit* and the like were, of course, magisterial, but will be less so with changing availabilities and possibilities," reflects Hill, "but the good advice will always have a place."

British chef Shaun Hill's characterful cooking—based firmly on what he likes to cook—has gained him a loyal following at The Walnut Tree in Wales.

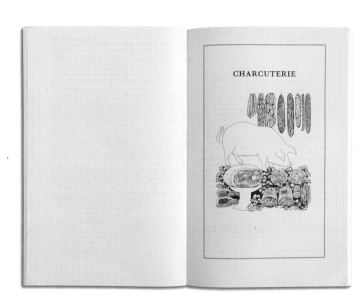

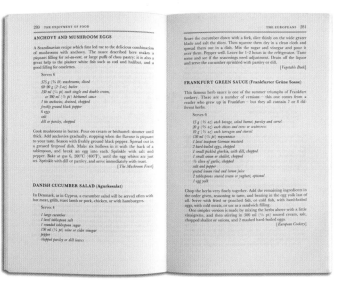

"I always go back to Anna del Conte."
MARK HIX

In both his cooking and
his food writing, chef and
restaurateur Mark Hix has
been a pioneering champion
of British food producers.

Mark Hix

RESTAURANT

HIX Oyster and Chop House, London, UK, opened 2008

Gastronomy of Italy Anna del Conte

BOOK DETAILS

Published 1987, Bantam Press, 384 pages, photography by Laura Edwards

British chef Mark Hix (see p.308) originally made his name in elegant, well-known London restaurants Le Caprice and The Ivy, offering what became a trademark line in upmarket comfort food, including his famous fish pie. Moving on to become a highly successful restaurateur in his own right, Hix has a number of his own restaurants, including the HIX Oyster and Fish House, which looks out over the Jurassic Coast at Lyme Regis in his native Dorset; the restaurant showcases very fresh, locally caught fish and seafood. Both in his cooking and in his recipe writing, Hix was an early pioneer in championing Britain's food culture, long before it was fashionable to do so. The menus at his restaurants highlight high-quality local ingredients, which are sourced from British food producers, from lovingly made farmhouse cheeses to Somerset apple brandy.

Anna del Conte's (see p.315) magisterial work, *Gastronomy of Italy*, the book selected by Mark Hix, celebrates Italian food culture through the format of a gastronomic dictionary. The entries are ordered alphabetically by their Italian name, beginning with Abbacchio (baby lamb) and ending with Zuppa Inglese (custard and cake dessert) in the revised 2013 edition. While the book is filled with plenty of comprehensive and detailed information, it is far from being simply a dull collection of dry facts. Del Conte's affection and respect for her native cuisine infuses the text, and she roots her descriptions of food in culture, history, and her own, personal

evocative memories. The entry on Cipolla (onion), for example, references the Roman gastronome Apicius and the Renaissance cook Bartolomeo Scappi; it outlines regional onion varieties and ways of cooking with them, describes the tradition of onions roasted in braziers on winter mornings, and includes a recipe for sweet and sour Cipolline in Agrodolce. Reading del Conte's admirable book, one appreciates the considerable role food can play in creating a sense of place, making it an appropriate choice for a chef who has done so much to generate a new sense of pride in his native British cuisine.

Ken Hom

RESTAURANT

Mee, Rio de Janeiro, Brazil, opened 2014

The Key to Chinese Cooking Irene Kuo

BOOK DETAILS

Published 1977, Alfred A. Knopf, 532 pages, illustrations by Carolyn Moy, calligraphic seals designed by C. C. Kuo

"A thoughtful book that will always remain a classic on Chinese food."
KEN HOM

Chef, broadcaster, cooking teacher, and author Ken Hom is renowned around the world for his championing of Asian food. Born in the United States and of Chinese heritage, Hom started working in his uncle's restaurant at the age of eleven and began working as a cookery instructor as a young man. He made his name with the BBC television program *Ken Hom's Chinese Cookery* in 1983, which was a huge hit. An engaging personality, with a capacity to make cooking accessible and inviting, Hom has gone on to make many other successful television series since. He is the author of thirty-six books, including the bestselling *Ken Hom's Chinese Cookery*. His career has been a busy and productive one and he continues to travel the world explaining the food the loves.

It is appropriate that Ken Hom, who has done so much to bring an understanding of Chinese food to a wider audience, has chosen a cookbook that is truly illuminating on Chinese cuisine. Irene Kuo's *The Key to Chinese Cooking* is a lucid, deeply intelligent book written to give a genuine insight into Chinese cookery for a non-Chinese audience. It is edited, Hom points out, by "Judith Jones, who edited Julia Child." In her introduction, Kuo explains how cooking techniques, each allowing for variation, are at the heart of Chinese cuisine. The first part of the book offers a foundation, with Kuo outlining utensils, the key role of cleavers, and four major techniques, such as cooking in oil, with recipes illustrating these ways of cooking. With the reader now "familiar with the basic techniques," Section Two sees Kuo reveal the richness of Chinese cuisine with a fascinating, wide-ranging collection of recipes. Her elegant writing sets Chinese food in its cultural context, so one comes away having learned much. "I love the way Irene Kuo took the mystery out of Chinese cooking and made one of the world's great cuisines accessible with her passion and clear explanation," says Hom.

For equipment, you will need a small, sharp paring knife and a cleaver to crack the leg bones.

Remove the bird from the water and pat it dry. Give it an overall massage to loosen the skin, taking great care not to puncture the skin.

Now, starting with the neck: 1) With your fingers and the tip of the paring knife slid between membrane and skin, cut and pull the skin free of connecting tissue and meat. Roll the skin downward as you go (almost inside out), until you reach the wings. 2) Using the paring knife, cut through the joint to detach the wing, and keep rolling and cutting away the skin from meat until you reach the second joint of the wing. 3) Cut through this and remove the wing plus bone of the upper part of the wing; you now have the wing tip still within skin but only a pocket of skin for the upper part. Do the same for the other wing.

Continue with the main body of the bird, always cutting just in front of the rolled-back skin, which you hold firmly with the other hand. The cutting is particularly delicate over the back, where the skin is tight over the bones. The action should be almost a vertical cutting—keep lifting the skin up and back and carefully scrape the edge of the paring knife against the bones (not the skin!).

4) When you reach the thighs, cut through the joint to detach the whole leg; then roll the skin down to the tip of the leg bones. Put the skinned fowl across your board with the attached skin off to your right; lift the cleaver carefully and chop through the lower leg bone decisively, keeping knobby end plus about 1½ inches of bone with the skin. If you find it easier, place the blade on the bone and bang the top of your cleaver with a mallet. Turn the bird around with the skin off to the left and do the same with the other leg.

Roll the skin down to the cavity and reveal the tiny tail bone, which is attached to the spine. Cut through this bone (leaving the tail still on) and then around the edge of the cavity to free the skin completely. Turn the skin right side up and you have a whole chicken or duck skin with wing tips and partial leg bones, ready for luscious stuffing. There may be little holes until you have practiced a few times, especially if you've used a tender young chicken, but don't despair—patch them with dabs of beaten egg.

糯米鶏 **BONELESS WHOLE CHICKEN WITH RICE STUFFING**

This chicken is skinned, and the skin is filled with chicken meat, glutinous rice, and vegetables. The re-formed chicken is then steamed, coated with a batter, and deep-fried until crisp and brown. It is a rich dish and will serve

SKINNING A WHOLE FOWL

VEGETABLES

There is a far greater variety of vegetables in China than here. Aside from having a wider range of types and numerous forms of dried and processed vegetarian products, bean curd being particularly notable, the Chinese also relish parts of vegetables generally discarded in Western cooking, such as radish greens, cucumber skins, or the red roots of spinach. For lack of proper refrigeration and transportation, however, many regional specialties never travel beyond their own provincial boundaries. Consequently, the unique flavor and texture of the blue turnips of Tientsin in the north might be totally unknown to a southerner, and by the same token, a northerner might never taste the bitter melons of the south.

The Chinese cook vegetables primarily by the stir-frying method, and the results are spectacular. The brief searing in hot oil followed by vigorous steam-cooking with a small amount of liquid gives vegetables a plump crispness and vivid coloring that are really extraordinary. After trying green beans and broccoli this way, you may never want to boil them again. Seldom ever turning soggy or becoming discolored, stir-fried vegetables are delicious hot and cold.

I have kept most of the vegetable dishes here simple, and unless you wish to make special trips to the Chinese grocer, you will be able to enjoy vegetables the Chinese way from produce found right in the supermarket—Chilled Sweet and Sour Onions and Spicy Minced Watercress being good examples of the transformations wrought by Chinese cooking methods and seasonings.

炒菠菜 **STIR-FRIED SPINACH**

Spinach, containing a good deal of salt and iron, sometimes leaves one with a puckery aftertaste unless a little sugar is added. It needs a good amount of oil to give it luster and a smooth texture, garlic and sesame oil

to enrich the flavor, and a very brief parboiling to prevent it from turning watery. This soft, shiny spinach is delicious hot or cold. *Serves 2 to 4*

2 pounds spinach	¾ teaspoon salt
4 tablespoons oil	1 teaspoon sugar
2 large cloves garlic, lightly crushed and peeled	2 teaspoons sesame oil

Wash the spinach well. If it has roots, separate them and cut into 2 or 4 pieces—they are extremely sweet and succulent. Chop stems if long.

Bring a large pot of water to a rolling boil, add the spinach, and stir to submerge it. When the water begins to boil again, in about a minute, pour the spinach into a colander and spray with cold water to stop the cooking. Press down lightly to extract excess water.

Heat a wok or large, heavy skillet over high heat until hot; add the oil, swirl, and heat about 30 seconds till hot. Toss in the garlic cloves and press them against the pan a few times. Add the spinach and poke and shake to separate the mass; then stir in fast turning motions to coat it with oil. Sprinkle in the salt and sugar and stir briskly for about 1 minute. Add the sesame oil, give a few fast turns, and pour into a hot serving dish, discarding the garlic.

炒青豆 **STIR-FRIED GREEN PEAS**

While there is nothing to compare with eating fresh peas at their peak season, for year-round enjoyment there is nothing quite as convenient as frozen peas. Rapidly stir-fried and briefly steam-cooked, these peas are firm and tender, each one a burst of sweetness. Unlike fresh, you must not use the tiny frozen peas—they are too fragile; they tend to be creamy rather than slightly crisp. *Serves 2 to 4.*

1 ten-ounce package frozen green peas, thoroughly defrosted	½ teaspoon salt
3 tablespoons oil	¼ teaspoon sugar
	¼ cup chicken stock

Heat a wok or large, heavy skillet over high heat until hot; add the oil, swirl, and heat for 30 seconds. Pour in the peas and stir rapidly for 5 seconds. Add the salt, sugar, and stock, lower the heat, cover, and steam-cook for about 2 minutes. Uncover and stir lightly and rapidly until there is no more liquid, then pour into a hot serving dish.

TV chef and restaurateur Ken Hom has shared his knowledge of Chinese food and cooking with people around the globe.

"Immaculate instruction. Glorious prose. Recipes for serious kitchen folk. My most treasured cookery book."

SIMON HOPKINSON

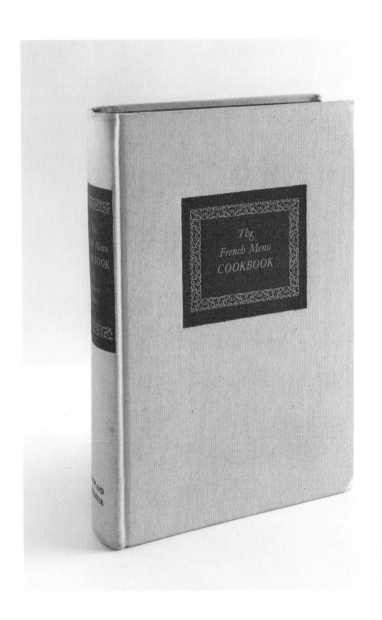

British chef, food writer, and broadcaster Simon Hopkinson has been an influential figure in shaping Britain's food culture.

Simon Hopkinson

RESTAURANT

Bibendum, London, UK, opened 1987 (Hopkinson was chef from 1987 to 1995)

The French Menu Cookbook Richard Olney

BOOK DETAILS

Published 1970, Simon and Schuster, 446 pages, illustrations by Gösta Viertel

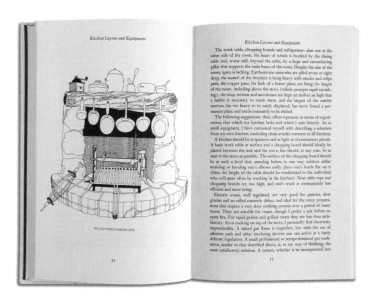

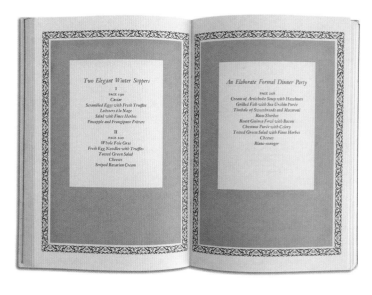

A love of good food is, of course, something that many chefs share. British chef Simon Hopkinson (see p.56, 224) has the ability to communicate his affection through his characterful writing about ingredients and dishes. Meticulous, masterful recipes have gained him a strong following among cooks, with his cookbook *Roast Chicken and Other Stories* (1994) remaining an enduring classic. Hopkinson worked as a chef for several years, opening Bibendum in London with restaurateur Terence Conran in 1987 to great acclaim. Since leaving the world of the professional kitchen, Hopkinson has focused on writing and broadcasting, bringing his distinctive, immediately recognizable voice and an admirable eye for what makes a recipe great, rather than simply satisfactory, to his work.

Simon Hopkinson's choice is, tellingly, for a cookbook whose enduring appeal rests in the prose style and superb recipe writing, rather than beautiful photography or striking visuals. Richard Olney's *The French Menu Cookbook* is an iconic work by the eminent American food writer and editor who lived in France for many years, writing about its cuisine with great knowledge, careful attention, and flair. Olney's charismatic personality infuses the book, as he shares his opinions with conviction: "Good and honest cooking and good and honest French cooking are the same thing." Whether writing on how to compose a menu, explaining the three different types of skimming (*écumer*, *dégraisser*, *dépouiller*), or conveying the sensual pleasures of truffles, he is always interesting. The recipes themselves are written with an impressive thoroughness and precision, informed by Olney's emphasis on what he called "'tactile' sense . . . the awareness through touching, and also through smelling, hearing, seeing, and tasting that something is 'just right.'" This is food writing of great intelligence and style, to be savored and relished.

Daniel Humm

RESTAURANT

Eleven Madison Park, New York City, New York, USA, opened in 1998 (Humm joined in 2006)

4 Saisons à la Table No. 5 Yannick Alléno, Kazuko Masui

BOOK DETAILS

Published 2006, Éditions Glénat, 274 pages, photography by Philippe Barret, Ryusuke Hayashi, and Kazuko Masui; published in English as *4 Seasons at Table No. 5*, 2007, Glénat

Swiss chef Daniel Humm (see p.140, 226) credits his mother with nurturing his love of food, and his ability in the kitchen, even as a young chef, meant that he was a talent to watch. In 2003 he moved from Switzerland to the United States, taking over Campton Place Restaurant in San Francisco, and quickly receiving rapturous reviews for his fresh, sophisticated cooking. Humm's culinary talents brought him to the attention of restaurateur Danny Meyer (see p.335), who lured him to work in partnership with Will Guidara and reimagine Eleven Madison Park, which the pair did in triumphant style. Today this iconic New York restaurant is known for Humm's refined, witty cuisine and the charm and elegance of the dining experience it offers.

Daniel Humm's choice—*4 Saisons à la Table No. 5* by Yannick Alléno and Kazuko Masui—is a book as stately as Le Meurice, the famous Parisian restaurant that the book celebrates. The enigmatic title refers to the way in which Japanese journalist Masui became enthralled by French chef Yannick Alléno's cooking, dining regularly at Le Meurice, always at table no. 5. The book offers an appreciative collaboration between Masui, a noted connoisseur of French food, and chef Alléno, in which the chef's dishes are discussed and explored by Masui. The book presents the recipes according to season, beginning with fall—with ingredients such as partridge, eggplant, and the shellfish abalone to the fore—and ending with summer creations such as Filet de Rouget Barbet Sous le Gril or Fraises des Bois Juste Sucrées. The full-page photographs of the intricately constructed dishes—Noix de Coquilles Saint-Jacques et Foie Gras Iodé aux Langues d'Oursin and Foie de Veau à la Fleur d'Oranger—demonstrate the skilful intricacy of Alléno's cuisine, a fact reinforced by the technically complex recipes.

"I like to be very open as far as seeing what's out there, what other people do, and take in as much influence as I can. But at the end of the day, I'm more of a traditionalist."

DANIEL HUMM

Swiss-born chef Daniel Humm expresses his culinary talents at New York's Eleven Madison Park.

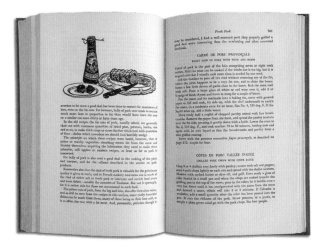

Dutch chef Margot Janse is noted for her
creative, expressive cuisine at The Tasting
Room, Franschhoek, South Africa.

Margot Janse

RESTAURANT

The Tasting Room at Le Quartier Français, Franschhoek, South Africa, opened 2004
(Janse has been Executive Chef at Le Quartier Français since 1996)

French Provincial Cooking
Elizabeth David

BOOK DETAILS

Published 1960, Michael Joseph, 524 pages, illustrations by Juliet Renny

"This book inspired me immensely and made me change my direction."
MARGOT JANSE

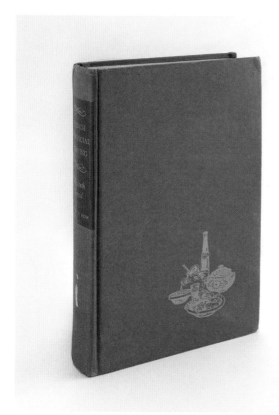

The emotional power of food and its capacity to tell stories are at the heart of Dutch chef Margot Janse's vision of food. At her restaurant The Tasting Room at Le Quartier Français in Franschhoek, South Africa, Janse is noted for her creative cooking. Janse's choice is for a cookbook that was hugely influential on her. She had arrived in Johannesburg in 1990 "with little money to spare," she remembers. "I loved cooking, but, due to budget restraints, cookbooks were a major treat. It would still be another three years before I made it into my first kitchen and realised my dream to make cooking my career. I used to browse the shops and found *French Provincial Cooking* in a second hand book shop. I had no idea then who Elizabeth David was."

Janse had come across a Cookery Book Club edition. "Nothing really said 'pick me up'," she says, "Yet I did, somehow I realised it was special. I do not have all those fortunate memories of a granny at the stove. But somehow Elizabeth David (see p.110, 317) managed to remind me of the memories that have shaped my culinary character—the small delicious details that are clearly embedded in my brain. I love the way it is written from a very personal perspective. The ingredients are not actually listed in any order; the recipes are more like beautiful descriptions and read like short stories that make your mouth water. It is honest, regional cooking, written by a woman who was quite a revolutionary—she was way ahead of her time. David taught herself to cook after studying French history and literature in Paris, where she became obsessed with food. Once back in England she wanted to be able to reproduce the dishes she so loved. She was opinionated, unconventional, and led an exciting life; traveling, eating, and writing cookbooks. She really changed the way people thought about food."

Thomas Keller

RESTAURANT

The French Laundry, Yountville, California, USA, opened 1978 (Keller became chef-owner in 1994)

Ma Gastronomie Fernand Point

BOOK DETAILS

Published 1969, Flammarion, 240 pages; published in English as *Ma Gastronomie*, 1974, Rookery

There is a thoughtful, gracious quality both to chef Thomas Keller (see p.18, 138, 230) as a man, and to his food. A perfectionist by nature, his quest to become a chef saw him travel to France to work in restaurants such as Le Taillevent to learn about haute cuisine. He then became chef-owner of The French Laundry in Napa Valley, California, in 1994. Under Keller, The French Laundry helped redefine American fine dining. Keller writes eloquently about being a chef: "When you acknowledge, as you must, that there is no such thing as perfect food, only the idea of it, then the real purpose of striving towards perfection becomes clear: to make people happy. That is what cooking is all about."

Thomas Keller has chosen a cookbook that influenced him profoundly, *Ma Gastronomie*, by the French chef Fernand Point. In his introduction to a 2008 edition of the book, Keller tells how he first came across Point's book as a young man, when he was lent a copy by his mentor Roland Henin. "Through Chef Point's words," explains Keller, "I finally understood and discovered a higher sense of purpose for my chosen profession: cooking was not just about technique and providing sustenance; it was about nurturing." This generous message was at the heart of Point's approach to food at his famous restaurant La Pyramide, Vienne. The book provides a vivid picture of Point: his charm, his knowledge of food, and the principles by which he cooked. Here are his recipes for luxurious dishes, such as Parfait de Foie Gras Fernand, as well as extracts from his notebooks. His aphorisms, such as "Success is the sum of a lot of small things correctly done," have been cherished by generations of chefs.

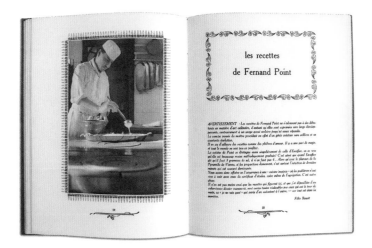

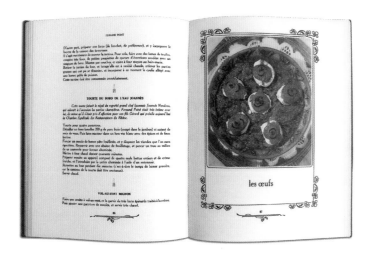

"Through Chef Point's words, I finally understood and discovered a higher sense of purpose for my chosen profession: cooking was not just about technique and providing sustenance; it was about nurturing."
THOMAS KELLER

American chef Thomas Keller of The French Laundry, Napa Valley, a hugely influential, respected figure in America's restaurant scene.

"It's a book of kings!"

TOM KERRIDGE

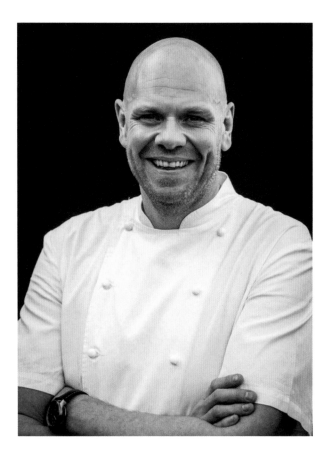

British chef and broadcaster
Tom Kerridge, whose The
Hand & Flowers pub at Marlow
is a dining destination.

Tom Kerridge

RESTAURANT

The Hand & Flowers, Marlow, UK, opened 2005

Grand Livre de Cuisine
Alain Ducasse with Jean-François Piège

BOOK DETAILS

Published 2004, Ducasse Books, 1078 pages, photography by Didier Loire

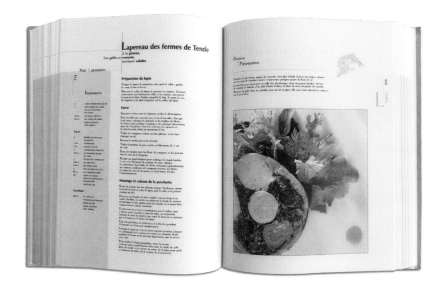

The fact that British chef Tom Kerridge has made his name with a pub that has two Michelin stars says much about Kerridge's approach to food (see p.232). When he set up The Hand & Flowers with his wife, Beth, their vision was to create a democratic, accessible establishment that also served wonderful food. The menu at The Hand & Flowers reflects Kerridge's ability to create elegant versions of British comfort food, coaxing the maximum flavor out of ingredients—as shown by signature dishes such as Slow-Cooked Aylesbury Duck with Duck Fat Chips and Gravy. Kerridge's hunch that the food he was creating would be appreciated has paid off, with a successful TV career making him a household name in the UK.

Tom Kerridge is exuberantly enthusiastic about his cookbook choice: *Grand Livre de Cuisine* by Alain Ducasse (see p.144, 204). "It's a phenomenal encyclopaedic cookbook that is both informative and educational as well as being a beautiful and stunning piece of work from unquestionably one of the greatest chefs of all time, where the produce is allowed to shine and luxury ingredients are used to extravagance." This impressive tome is, in effect, an encyclopaedia of recipes, arranged alphabetically by ingredient, beginning with acacia—with a recipe for

Acacia Blossom Fritters—and ending with zucchini, an entry with numerous recipes. As the recipes are from the French chef Alain Ducasse and his protégés, this is haute cuisine territory, both in terms of culinary technique and ingredients. Truffles are abundantly present, as is foie gras. The recipes outline ingredients, instruction, finish, and presentation. The instructions are detailed, with the images of the immaculately presented dishes showing the precision with which Ducasse expects his dishes to be arranged.

Tom Kitchin

RESTAURANT

The Kitchin, Edinburgh, UK, opened 2006

Memories of Gascony
Pierre Koffmann with Timothy Shaw

BOOK DETAILS

Published 1990, Mitchell Beazley, 256 pages, photography by Anthony Blake

"From nature to plate" is how Scottish chef Tom Kitchin describes his own cuisine. At his award-winning restaurant The Kitchin in Edinburgh, he showcases the best of Scottish ingredients—seafood, fish, venison, game birds, lamb—using them to elegant yet flavorful effect in skillfully constructed dishes such as A Rockpool of Local Shellfish and Sea Vegetables Served with a Shellfish Consommé, or Boned and Rolled Pig's Head, Served with Roasted Tail of Langoustine from Tobermory and a Crispy Ear Salad. Kitchin's career saw him work in renowned three Michelin–starred restaurants, including Guy Savoy in Paris, Alain Ducasse's Le Louis XV in Monte Carlo (see p.88, 144, 204), and, influentially at La Tante Claire, Pierre Koffmann's London restaurant (see p.94, 236). Kitchin's impressive cooking draws on his classic training and celebrates seasonality as well as his beloved Scotland.

Tom Kitchin's favorite cookbook is by a chef he respects hugely and values as a mentor—Pierre Koffmann's *Memories of Gascony*. Born in Tarbes in southwestern France, Koffmann is a Gascon by birth and in this deeply personal cookbook he pays loving tribute to his grandparents, Camille and Marcel Cadeillan, focusing on the village of Saint-Puy in central Gascony, where they lived on their farm. Koffmann established his name as a chef in London with his legendary restaurant La Tante Claire and his cooking—even at exalted levels—has famously drawn on his Gascon heritage, as witnessed by his signature classic dish of Stuffed Pig's

Trotters with Sweetbreads and Morels. "Like many other Frenchmen, I have retained all my life the taste of the food I ate as a child," he writes. In this book, he celebrates the rustic country cooking of his grandparents, interspersing classic recipes with long evocative passages describing his childhood visits to their farm. Writing with eloquence and an intense nostalgia, Koffmann takes the reader on a journey through the seasons and the enduring patterns of rural life: the start of the fishing season, haymaking, harvesting, hunting for furred and feathered game, picking cèpes, the *vendage* (harvesting of grapes), the killing of pigs in January.

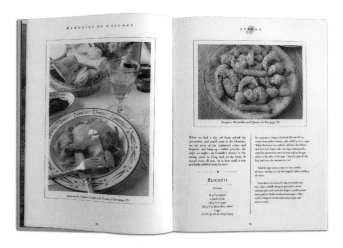

"Memories of Gascony tells the story of his culinary journey and truly reflects his passion for cooking—it's definitely the most used cookbook in my home kitchen."

TOM KITCHIN

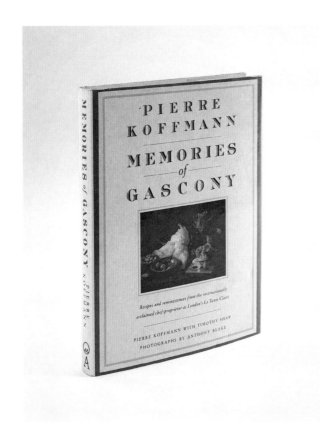

A commitment to showcasing Scottish produce at its best lies at the heart of Tom Kitchin's cuisine.

"A book everyone should find a space for on their shelves."
FLORENCE KNIGHT

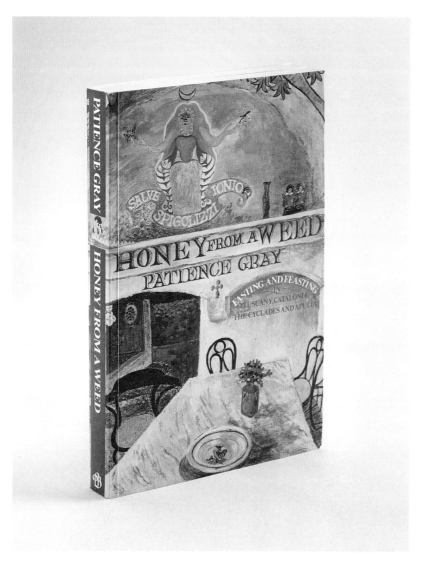

Young British chef Florence Knight, who made her name at Polpetto, is a talent to watch.

Florence Knight

RESTAURANT

Polpetto, London, UK, opened 2010 (Knight was head chef from 2010 to 2015)

Honey From a Weed: Fasting and Feasting in Tuscany, Catalonia, the Cyclades and Apulia Patience Gray

BOOK DETAILS

Published 1986, Harper & Row, 374 pages, illustrations by Corinna Sargood

Talented young British chef Florence Knight came to public attention through her work as head chef at Polpetto in London, the small restaurant inspired by Venetian bars and owned by restaurateur Russell Norman (see p.258). Here, her ability to cook simple but refined dishes—such as an exemplary Baccalá Mantecato (beaten salt cod) and a delicate-textured Maple Custard Tart—was noticed. "'Less is more' typifies Florence's style," observes Norman, also noting her "attention to detail." Her first cookbook, *One: A Cook and Her Cupboard,* was published in 2013. In 2015, she left Polpetto to open a new restaurant. Admirers of her cooking will be waiting with interest.

"This book brought the warmth and simplicity of the Mediterranean to England, for which I'm very grateful," says Florence Knight of her cookbook choice, Patience Gray's *Honey From a Weed* (see p.120). Gray's book is remarkable—based on the author's nomadic life in the Mediterranean, it offers a fascinating chronicle of an ancient, rooted, simple way of life. Gray's writing weaves together evocative anecdotes, ancient history, and perceptively written recipes for

dishes such as Partridge in the Manner of Vicenza; Spinach with Raisins and Pine Kernels; and Purée of Dried Broad Beans with Wild Chicory. One only has to open it to find an intriguing piece of information or expressive phrase. Knight is eloquent on the book's special qualities: "My imagination is always revived by the vivid descriptions of dishes, which make the most of the season's humble and wild ingredients, and the love and time taken in each creation reminds me to appreciate life's quiet moments."

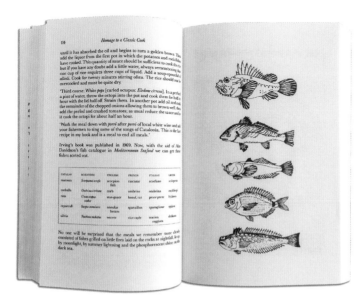

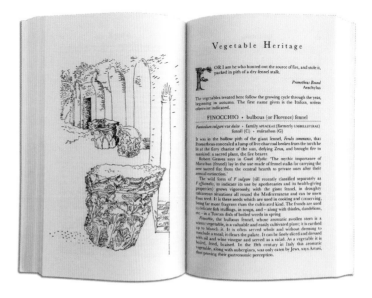

Pierre Koffmann

RESTAURANT
Koffmann's, Berkeley Hotel, London, UK, opened 2010

Le Répertoire de la cuisine Louis Saulnier

BOOK DETAILS
Published 1914, Flammarion, 264 pages; published in English as *Le Répertoire de la Cuisine*, 1924, Leon Jaeggi & Sons Ltd

French chef Pierre Koffmann (see p.90, 236) is a proud Gascon by birth and his approach to food and cooking has been shaped by the childhood he spent there, in particular visits to the farm of his beloved grandparents, which offered an insight into the seasonal pattern of agricultural life. Koffmann's career, however, blossomed in Britain, where he is a major and influential figure in the world of fine dining. He worked for notable chefs and restaurateurs the Roux Brothers (see p.284), who gave him the role of head chef at The Waterside Inn, Bray, Berkshire, when they established it in 1972. Following that, Koffmann and his wife, Annie, set up his famous restaurant La Tante Claire in London in 1977, where he gained three Michelin stars. Today, diners can enjoy his classic French cuisine at Koffmann's at The Berkeley Hotel in London.

Pierre Koffmann's cookbook choice is for a key text in French cuisine, *Le Répertoire de la cuisine*, by Louis Saulnier. It is a book used by generations of French chefs ever since its publication in 1914. "If you are after traditional French cooking," explains Koffmann, "this book gives you all the recipes you could possibly want. The traditional technical skills involved means that it acts as the foundation for much modern cuisine." Saulnier's carefully compiled reference work offers a guide to his mentor, the great Auguste Escoffier, and his magisterial writings. Rather than giving Escoffier's recipes in full, Saulnier presents brief accounts of how dishes such as Eggs Perigueux or Consommé Blanc are made. It is, in effect, a culinary aide-mémoire: "All chefs will find *Le Répertoire* an invaluable help, for even the best informed could not carry so many recipes of the past and present in his memory." It is a masterpiece of condensation, admirably comprehensive, containing around 7,000 methods for dishes and much tersely expressed useful information. Reading the book, with its roll call of traditional French dishes and the overlapping elements used to create them, one gains an understanding of the intricate and orderly nature of classic French cuisine.

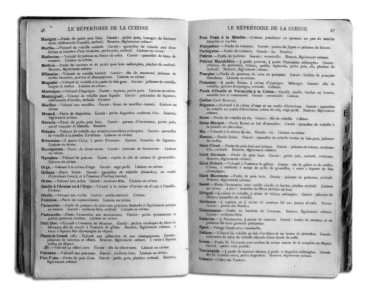

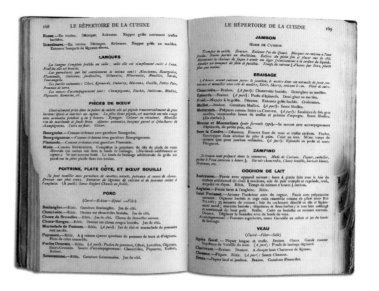

"This book is the bible of French cooks."

PIERRE KOFFMANN

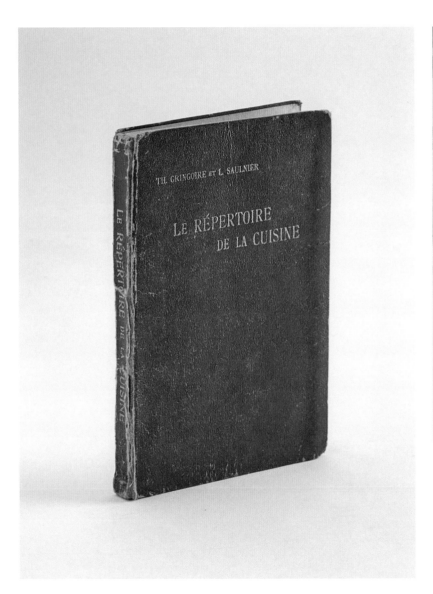

French chef Pierre Koffmann, whose Gascon heritage has been a great influence on his cooking.

Nicole Krasinski

RESTAURANT

State Bird Provisions, San Francisco, California, USA, opened 2011

Flatbreads & Flavors: A Baker's Atlas
Jeffrey Alford and Naomi Duguid

BOOK DETAILS

Published 1995, William Morrow and Company, 441 pages, photography by Gentl & Hyers, Jeffrey Alford and Naomi Duguid

"Flatbreads & Flavors *was one of the first cookbooks I bought as a young cook in a pre-internet era. Jeffrey Alford and Naomi Duguid provided a unique perspective and holistic view of the food and the stories behind the recipes in the book.*"

NICOLE KRASINSKI

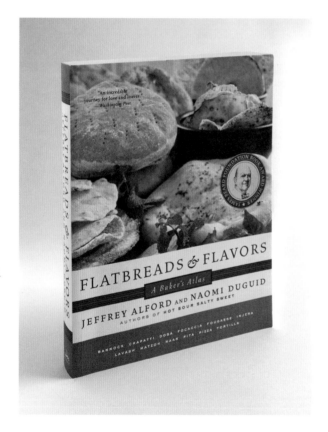

Nicole Krasinski's love of baking stems back to her days as a photography student. She came to realize that this, rather than photography, was what she wanted to pursue, moving from Chicago's Art Institute to work at the city's Red Hen Bakery under chef Nancy Carey, an influential figure in Krasinki's life. Her career as a pastry chef saw her working in partnership with her husband, Stuart Brioza (see p.40), at Tapawingo in Michigan, before taking over Rubicon in San Francisco. The couple's vision of dining is expressed in their award-winning restaurant State Bird Provisions, which they opened in 2011. As pastry chef there, Krasinski's influence is clear in the dessert section, with its cosmopolitan, witty array of sweet treats.

Nicole Krasinski's choice, *Flatbreads and Flavors: A Baker's Atlas* by Jeffrey Alford and Naomi Duguid, reflects her own interest in baking. A fascination with flatbreads saw travelers and food writers Jeffrey Alford and Naomi Duguid embark on several journeys to learn more about the world's oldest breads. The result is a cookbook that is evocative, and appetizing: "This cookbook is in part a journal, a travel diary, a record of events, and memories expressed in recipes," they write. The book is grouped geographically, allowing the authors to give a cultural context. Bringing life to the recipes are tales of places visited and people met on their travels: a poignant encounter with Afghan refugees in Pakistan; the story of Varusai, a chapatti street vendor in Penang; New Year's Eve in Vietnam. Naturally, given the book's range, the recipes are international: Pakistani Hunza Sprouted Wheat Breads; Vietnamese Fresh Rice Papers; Indian Dosa; Norwegian Crispbread. "We began this book with a passion for flatbreads," wrote the authors—and their passion is infectious.

Celebrated American pastry chef Nicole Krasinski delights diners at her San Francisco restaurant, State Bird Provisions, with her cleverly conceived desserts.

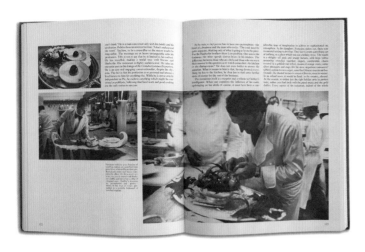

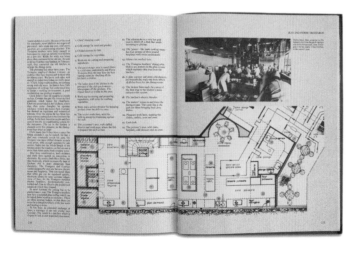

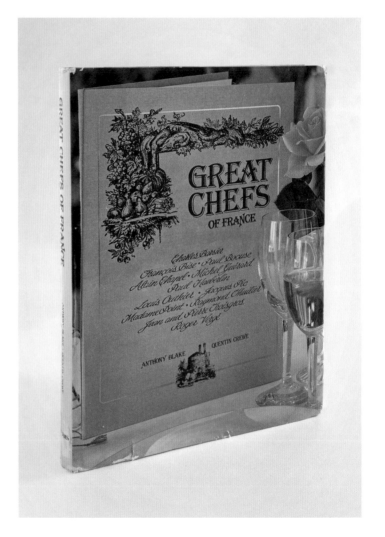

Corey Lee

RESTAURANT
Benu, San Francisco, California, USA, opened in 2010

Great Chefs of France Anthony Blake and Quentin Crewe

BOOK DETAILS
Published 1978, Harry N. Abrams Inc., 239 pages, photography by Anthony Blake

At Benu, his internationally acclaimed San Francisco restaurant, chef Corey Lee offers his exquisite, aesthetic cuisine.

"I discovered this book when I was a teenager, first starting out in the kitchen."
COREY LEE

Corey Lee's career exemplifies the commitment, drive, and sheer hard work that is required of chefs. Reflecting on Lee's drive to become a chef, Thomas Keller (see p.18, 86, 138, 230) wrote: "Corey embarked on that pursuit at a young age, and his dedication to it has never wavered." Fascinated by French haute cuisine, Lee spent years working in some of the finest restaurants, including a tenure as head chef at Keller's The French Laundry. Lee's cooking at his own three-starred San Francisco restaurant, Benu (see p.242), expresses both his creativity and an in-depth knowledge of Asian and French cooking techniques, which he draws on to create his unique and intelligent cuisine. Lee is a chef driven by the pursuit of perfection—who brings a holistic appreciation of food and aesthetics to the dining experience.

Corey Lee's book choice, Anthony Blake and Quentin Crewe's *Great Chefs of France* (see p.122, 124), celebrates both the world of the chef and French cuisine with eloquence and erudition. The book opens with an adrenaline-raising account of "The Day of the Chefs," offering verbal snapshots across the kitchens of the twelve three-starred French chefs profiled in the volume, from 6 A.M., with François Bise making croissants, through the drama of lunchtime service to midnight. "The chefs who live through such a day as this are not slaves, nor are they driven by financial greed. They are artists dedicated to the pursuit of excellence," writes Crewe stirringly. In a long and fascinating essay, he then charts the "story of haute cuisine," describing the remarkable way in which cooking in France rose to be an art: from medieval times to the contemporary period. While the knowledge is scholarly, Crewe's writing is entertaining and characterful; his portraits of historical figures such as Brillat-Savarin or Carême are as vivid as his profiles of the contemporary chefs. Anthony Blake's remarkable, intimate portraits of the legendary chefs at work complement the text. While it features many recipes, this unique and fascinating book, in Lee's words, "reads more like a biography of twelve French chefs that gives an insight into the dedication, passion, and respect for tradition that goes into running a great restaurant."

Jeremy Lee

RESTAURANT

Quo Vadis, London, UK, opened 1926 (Lee has been head chef and partner since 2012)

Charcuterie and French Pork Cookery Jane Grigson

BOOK DETAILS

Published 1967, Michael Joseph, 348 pages

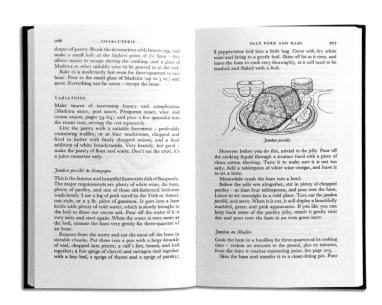

Born and raised in Dundee, Scotland, Jeremy Lee learned the craft of cooking while working for British chefs Simon Hopkinson (see p.80, 224) and Alastair Little (see p.244). As head chef of Terence Conran's The Blueprint Café, with its wonderful Thameside location, Lee became famed for his distinctive British cooking. Lee has long been a champion of seasonal, local produce and is noted for the discernment with which he sources ingredients. His menu at Soho's historic Quo Vadis restaurant is a daily-changing affair, reflecting his engaging personality through tasty dishes that charm and surprise: Smoked Eel Sandwich; Roast Duck, Potato Cakes and Pickled Prunes; Pistachio and Rhubarb Trifle. Lee's knowledge of British food is considerable and his ability to use his favorite produce to create riffs on classic dishes impressive.

Jane Grigson (see p.74, 102, 106, 329) is a writer whom Jeremy Lee holds in huge affection and who continues to be an important source of inspiration to him. *Charcuterie and French Pork Cookery*, her first book, "began a brilliant career in food writing," he explains, "and inspired, among many others including my mother, a young interested cook from Dundee who still bows down to her knowledge to this day." Lee is right to highlight the considerable extent of Grigson's culinary knowledge—she brought a genuine curiosity, both intellectual and practical, to her research. Such is the charm of her writing style—

she has a particular companionable quality to her voice—that she wears her authority lightly. The wide range of content in this book, however, is quite remarkable and impressive, with Grigson offering practical recipes on the intricacies of making everything from Galantines to Boudin Noir aux Pommes. Grigson's enormous enthusiasm for charcuterie makes her an engaging guide to the subject: "Pig's ears are one of the most appealing delicacies in the charcuterie, lying swathed in jelly on their white tray. Expensive, too, you will find. Here in England your butcher will very likely give them to you free."

"I love this extraordinary woman, who was such a pioneer both as a cook and as a woman, who had such a witty, gentle, and learned approach to a traditionally very male-dominated subject."

JEREMY LEE

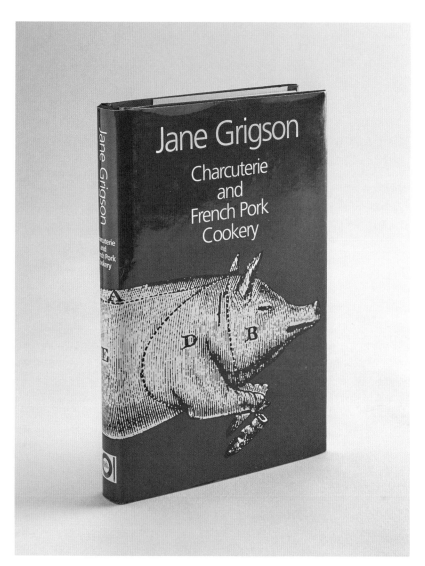

Scottish chef Jeremy Lee's cooking at Quo Vadis champions seasonal British produce.

David Everitt-Matthias

RESTAURANT

Le Champignon Sauvage, Cheltenham, Gloucestershire, UK, opened 1987

Charcuterie and French Pork Cookery Jane Grigson

BOOK DETAILS

Published 1967, Michael Joseph, 348 pages

"It is a magical book with the insight into all forms of charcuterie."

DAVID EVERITT-MATTHIAS

British chef David Everitt-Matthias is noted for his rich and subtle cuisine at acclaimed restaurant Le Champignon Sauvage, Cheltenham, UK.

A deeply held commitment to excellence underlies the food at David Everitt-Matthias's restaurant, Le Champignon Sauvage, which he opened with his wife Helen in 1987 and which has kept two Michelin stars since 2000. This is a truly personal venture: While Helen oversees front of house, David is head chef; admirably neither has ever missed a service. The result is an intimate, genuinely hospitable restaurant, much loved by diners. Hugely respected by his peers, David's cooking style reflects both his culinary craftsmanship and his willingness to experiment. While eschewing novelty for novelty's sake, his thoughtful interest in cookery sees him constantly developing his style, creating food which, in the words of Australian chef Brett Graham, "demands to be eaten."

"I love Jane's style of writing, as she exudes enjoyment of food in her words," explains David Everitt-Matthias, who has chosen Grigson's (see p.74, 100, 106, 329) first-ever book as his favorite. The book opens in characteristically thoughtful style: "It could be said that European civilization—and Chinese civilization too—has been founded on the pig." Her book, inspired by the abundant variety of French charcuterie, offers extensive guidance to the domestic cook on how to make products from pâtés to black pudding (blood sausage). Eminently sensible, Grigson advocates

using all parts of the animal, as the chapters entitled "Extremities" and "The Insides" demonstrate. The "commercial debasement" of food such as black pudding and brawn (head cheese) "have misled people into feeling that only the expensive parts of a pig are worth eating," she notes sadly. Grigson, a truly cultured food writer, has the gift of conveying her interest in a subject in an infectious way. Chef Everitt-Matthias is noted as an early champion of previously overlooked, humble ingredients, so this cookbook—celebrating a thrifty tradition in which nothing is wasted—is an apt choice.

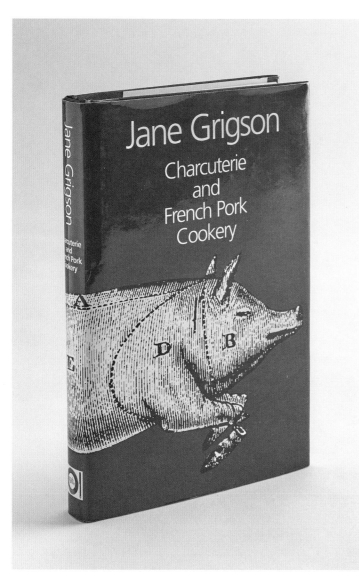

Andrew McConnell

RESTAURANT
Cumulus Inc., Melbourne, Australia, opened 2008

Nose to Tail Eating Fergus Henderson

BOOK DETAILS
Published 1999, Bloomsbury Publishing, 221 pages, photography by Jason Lowe

"Keeping things fresh, and looking for the best way to bring the most flavour out of produce, is key."
ANDREW McCONNELL

Melbourne-born and bred, chef and restaurateur Andrew McConnell is having a huge influence on his native city's dining scene, as executive chef and co-owner of five Melbourne restaurants. He began his career working in Melbourne, then cooked in London, Hong Kong, and Shanghai before returning to open his first venture, Diningroom, in 2012. With his restaurant Cumulus Inc., McConnell demonstrated his ability to offer high-end, yet relaxed dining, with both the mellow atmosphere and cosmopolitan recipes striking a chord with Melbourne's discerning diners. Each of his restaurants have their own individual style and character, with McConnell interested in exploring the possibilities of dining, and showing an ability to be in tune with the city's culinary zeitgeist.

Andrew McConnell's favorite cookbook is *Nose to Tail Eating*, by British chef Fergus Henderson (see p.24), who with his characterful approach to cooking, typified at his St. John restaurant in London, has influenced many other chefs around the world. The book, much like the menu at St. John, has a pared-back quality to it, and yet is also delightfully idiosyncratic. Henderson, with characteristic succinctness, lays out what is, in effect, his own culinary manifesto: He explains clearly and simply that nose to tail eating "means that it would be disingenuous to the animal not to make the most of the whole beast; there is a set of delights, textural and flavoursome, which is beyond the fillet." He then sets out recipes demonstrating these pleasures. The book, as McConnell appreciates, is wonderfully grounded in genuine knowledge of ingredients and cooking. The no-frills recipes include such simple pleasures as How to Eat Radishes at Their Peak, as well as more notably carnivorous dishes such as Cold Lamb's Brains on Toast. Henderson writes with wit and wisdom, conveying his love of food in his own distinctive style; his Fish Pie recipe ends, "Even just writing this recipe down, its soothing qualities have quite restored me from the fragile state in which I was."

Australian chef and restaurateur Andrew McConnell, an energizing and trend-setting force in Australia's dining scene.

NOSE
TO
TAIL
EATING

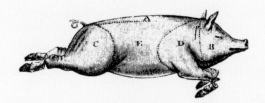

A KIND
OF BRITISH
COOKING

FERGUS HENDERSON

With an introduction by Anthony Bourdain

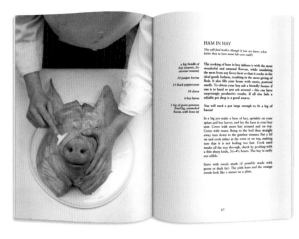

"When I began writing cookbooks, I knew I didn't want to write simply recipes with head notes—that would be too boring. I turned to Jane Grigson who I had read when I first began cooking."

JENNIFER McLAGAN

Australian chef Jennifer McLagan, whose award-winning food writing has gained her a loyal readership.

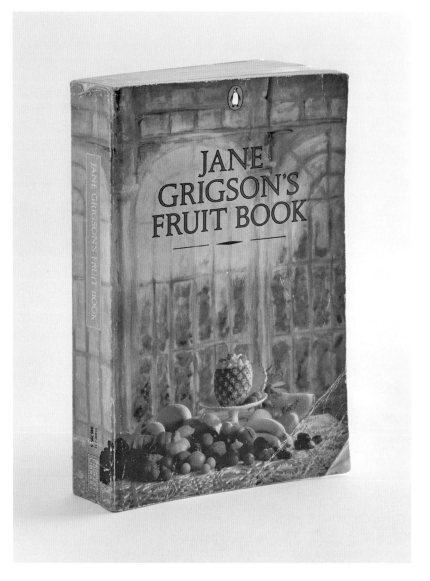

Jennifer McLagan

BOOKS
Bones (2005), *Fat* (2008), *Odd Bits* (2011), and *Bitter* (2014)

Jane Grigson's Fruit Book Jane Grigson

BOOK DETAILS
Published 1982, Michael Joseph, 528 pages, illustrations by Yvonne Skargon

Just as a good chef will transform unloved, unfashionable cuts of meat into flavorful meals, so Australian-born chef and acclaimed food writer Jennifer McLagan (see p.252) has taken neglected aspects of food—bones, fat, and bitterness—and transformed them into award-winning cookbooks. Having worked as a chef in Australia, the United Kingdom, and France, she brings a cosmopolitan sensibility to her well-written recipes. What makes McLagan such a fascinating food writer, however, is the range of reference she brings to her subjects, setting them in a cultural and historical context. Her writing, while knowledgeable, is deft and witty, making her cookbooks a pleasure to read.

British food writer Jane Grigson (see p.74, 100, 102, 329) is a much-loved and hugely influential figure, a woman who has inspired generations of cooks, chefs, and food writers through her distinctive, intelligent, cultured food writing. When McLagan began writing cookbooks herself, it was to Jane Grigson that she looked. "Her book, *Fruit*, is one of my favourites," she explains. "In it Grigson introduces you to each fruit, recalls her experiences with it, and adds historical nuggets, literary references, and lines of poetry, all of which are just as interesting as the recipes." Grigson's *Fruit Book*, like her seminal *Vegetable Book*, is an appealing mixture: at once down-to-earth and eminently practical, yet also a fascinating and evocative read. Grigson's ability to convey her delight in an ingredient is a hallmark of her writing. Hers is a cookbook model that McLagan has embraced with relish. "Food, just like art, literature, music, and poetry, is a building block of our culture," she says. "All the arts can find a place in a cookery book; the only problem is getting an editor to let you include them."

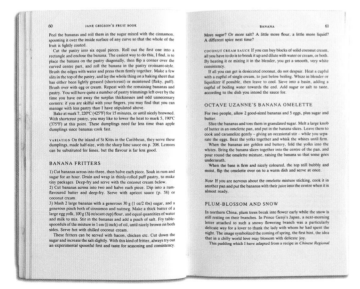

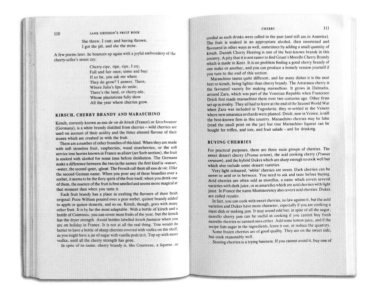

"We see the restaurant as an extension of our houses—we don't see it as a public space. It's our restaurant and we welcome visitors as we would guests in our home."

DAVID McMILLAN

Canadian chefs David McMillan and Frédéric Morin, whose Joe Beef restaurant in Montreal has a devoted following.

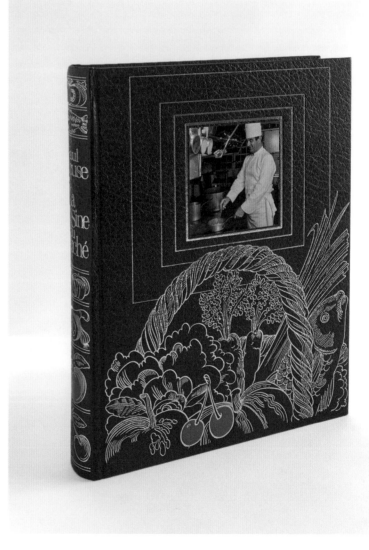

David McMillan and Frédéric Morin

RESTAURANT
Joe Beef, Montreal, Canada, opened 2005

La Cuisine du marché Paul Bocuse

BOOK DETAILS
Published 1976, Flammarion, 712 pages, photography by J.-P. Chatelin and P. Ginet; published in English as *The New Cuisine*, 1978, Granada Publishing

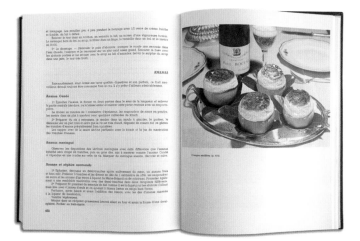

The culinary partnership between Canadian chefs David McMillan and Frédéric Morin has been a fruitful one. Wanting to set up their own place, the two found a small rundown café in a working-class quarter of Montreal and, together with Allison Cunningham, founded Joe Beef. The food they served—and continue to serve—draws on classic French cuisine, but often with an irreverent humorous twist. They swiftly acquired cult status, gaining first a national, then an international, following for their addictively flavorful and creative French-inspired cuisine. In person, the pair are charismatic, outspoken, and down-to-earth, with clear ideas about what good food and dining should be.

David McMillan and Frédéric Morin's choice of *La Cuisine du marché*, written by the eminent chef Paul Bocuse (see p.182), makes sense given that they have described their own food as Bocusian-Lyonnais. Written with calm authority, this book offers a great insight into Bocuse's philosophy of cooking. Bocuse shares his thoughts on matters such as the key importance of selecting the ingredients carefully and well, respecting seasonality, retaining the flavor of ingredients when one cooks them, and the importance of the dishes one enjoys preparing: "I never forget another of Fernand Point's maxims: you can only cook well, he used to say, if you cook with love, creating friendship and fraternity 'round your table. I believe that is essential." Bocuse stresses the importance of understanding the principles of cooking and following them accordingly. Recipes for classic dishes such as Quenelles de Brochet à la Lyonnaise are written with elegance and precision. His knowledge is impressive, as his instructions on matters from skinning hares to poaching eggs make clear.

Joyce Molyneux

RESTAURANT
The Carved Angel, Dartmouth, UK, opened 1974 (Molyneux retired in 1999)

French Provincial Cooking Elizabeth David

BOOK DETAILS
Published 1960, Michael Joseph, 523 pages, illustrations by Juliet Renny

British chef and restaurateur Joyce Molyneux, whose pioneering approach to food at her much-loved restaurant, The Carved Angel, was highly influential.

"It's a book that you can always read for pleasure."
JOYCE MOLYNEUX

In 1974, chef Joyce Molyneux, together with Tom Jaine, George Perry-Smith, and Heather Crosbie, set up The Carved Angel restaurant in the English seaside town of Dartmouth. It was a quietly revolutionary restaurant and its influence rippled out to touch and inspire numerous figures in Britain's food world. Innately modest, yet with strongly held convictions on the quality of food and service, Molyneux championed local produce, seasonality, and creating an informal, welcoming restaurant environment—complete with open kitchen—at a time when these were far from the norm. Reading her delightful *The Carved Angel Cookbook*, published in 1990, it is striking how her fuss-free approach to food and cooking—centered on local food producers and a deep understanding of ingredients—resonates with Britain's food scene today.

Joyce Molyneux's memories of her favorite cookbook, Elizabeth David's *French Provincial Cooking*, (see p.84, 332) date back to her days working for George Perry-Smith at his iconic Hole in the Wall restaurant in Bath: "George was making things that you never had in those days: moussaka, taramasalata, pepperonata, and ratatouille," she remembers. "When Elizabeth David brought *French Provincial Cooking* out, George gave all us cooks in the kitchen a copy of her book in hardback. We cooked from it next thing—oxtail with grapes, chicken with tarragon, made a whole gamut of things, marvellous." Elizabeth David was to influence Molyneux's cooking both in her own home—"I always remember cooking a saddle of hare in cream from her *French Provincial Cooking*, it was absolutely terrific"—and at her much-loved restaurant, The Carved Angel. "The fish soup goes back to Elizabeth David. Being in Dartmouth, there was lovely fish debris that you could use. We'd have a turbot and you could use the head and the trimmings and make a nice bisque with all the debris from the lobsters and crabs. It's the aioli that's lovely—it enriches it."

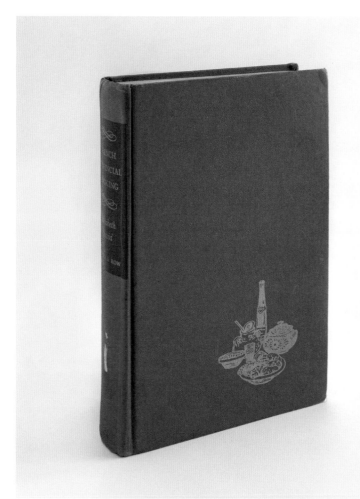

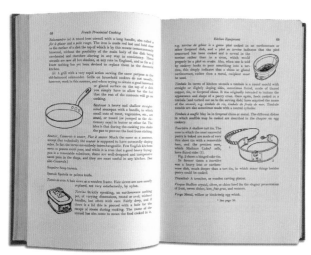

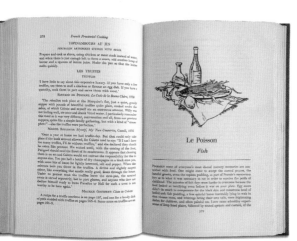

BARTOLOMEO SCAPPI

Cuoco segreto di Papa Pio V

OPERA

DELL'ARTE DEL CUCINARE

Saggio introduttivo di Giancarlo Roversi

VOL. I

ARNALDO FORNI EDITORE

Anton Mosimann

RESTAURANT
Private Dining Club: Mosimann's, London, UK, opened 1988

Opera dell'arte del Cucinare Bartolomeo Scappi

BOOK DETAILS
First published 1570, Michele Tramezzino, 800 pages, illustrations by Bartolomeo Scappi; this edition published 2007, Arnaldo Forni Editore

"It is probably the history cookbooks that have inspired me the most."
ANTON MOSIMANN

Impeccable in style and manner, Swiss-born chef Anton Mosimann is known for the elegance and deftness of his cooking. Concerned about the issue of healthy eating, he has long advocated *cuisine naturelle*, offering lighter food that is cooked without the use of butter, cream, or alcohol, yet which is flavorful and beautifully presented. At the age of twenty-eight, Mosimann became maître chef de cuisines at London's Dorchester Hotel, where he worked for thirteen years. Following his own vision, however, he left the hotel—and the two Michelin stars he had gained there—to set up Mosimann's, his luxurious, exclusive private dining club in London's Belgravia, offering his signature cooking to the great and the good of British society, in elegant surroundings.

"I have been collecting cookery books ever since I earned my income from cooking—more than forty years ago," explains Anton Mosimann. "Now I have more than 6,000 cookery books in my library, and all of them are there because they have given me something special. My favourite was written by Bartolomeo Scappi, a chef to the Pope in the sixteenth century." Mosimann's choice is a fascinating and important book in the history of Western cookery; as the first illustrated cookbook, it offers a remarkable glimpse into the past.

Scappi himself worked for the great and the good in his society. His book sets out to share his knowledge and pass on his considerable experience to other, younger cooks. The "ideal personal qualities" for the job of a cook are "punctuality, modesty, sobriety" he writes. The illustrations of the kitchen—with its "*tavola da pasta*" complete with rolling pin—convey the hard manual work of kitchen life. "It is amazing how little has changed," observes Mosimann, "ladles, pots, fish kettle, and other kitchen equipment, just as you see it today."

Swiss chef Anton Mosimann, whose elegant, light cuisine has gained him a strong following.

Jamie Oliver

RESTAURANT

Fifteen, London, UK, opened 2002

Good Food Ambrose Heath

BOOK DETAILS

Published 1932, Faber & Faber Limited, 280 pages, illustrations by Edward Bawden

There is an admirable energy about British chef Jamie Oliver (see p.331). Relaxed, likable, and with an infectious enthusiasm for good food, he made his name as a young man with the hugely successful *Naked Chef* TV series, in which he made cooking look fun and accessible. Rather than simply relishing his new celebrity status, however, Oliver has used his fame as an effective platform from which to campaign on issues such as raising the standards of school dinners and combating childhood obesity and the perils of excess sugar. Laudably, his restaurant Fifteen was created to offer disadvantaged youngsters a chance to learn life-changing skills. An expert communicator, Oliver's capacity to reach audiences through social media, TV series, and vlogs, as well as books, makes him a force to be reckoned with.

Lively and characterful, Ambrose Heath's voice reaches out across the decades. "In this little book I have attempted two things. First, to show how easy good cooking can be; and second, to demonstrate that it need not be expensive, as so many seem to think it must be," he writes in the introduction to his 1932 cookbook. These sentiments are a good fit with Jamie Oliver, who chose this as his favorite cookbook. It is presented in the form of a calendar, with Heath highlighting ingredients and recipes appropriate to each month: "Food which is in season is the best food of all. This should never be forgotten. Good things

out of season are but a ghost of their true selves . . ." Heath, like Oliver, is at once informative and entertaining. From his evocative monthly prefaces to the conversational asides and humorous observations, one senses Heath's enjoyment of food. The recipes are cheerfully eclectic and cosmopolitan—Iced Polish Soup, Mussel Pilaf, Beef Stroganoff, Partridges en Cocotte—written with common sense and an eye for thrift. Edmund Bawden's delightful illustrations complement this charming cookbook perfectly, with Oliver looking to *Good Food* as a source of inspiration for the cover of his own book *Jamie at Home*.

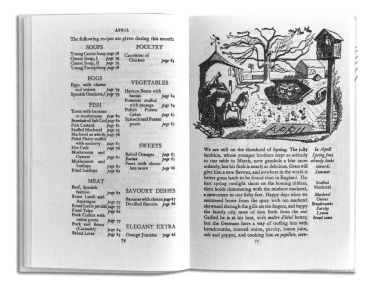

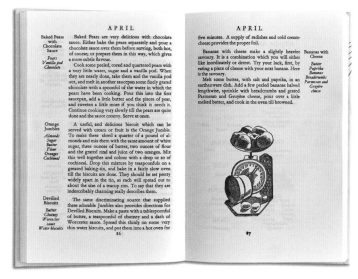

"I think food and cooking are among the most important things out there for us to learn about."
JAMIE OLIVER

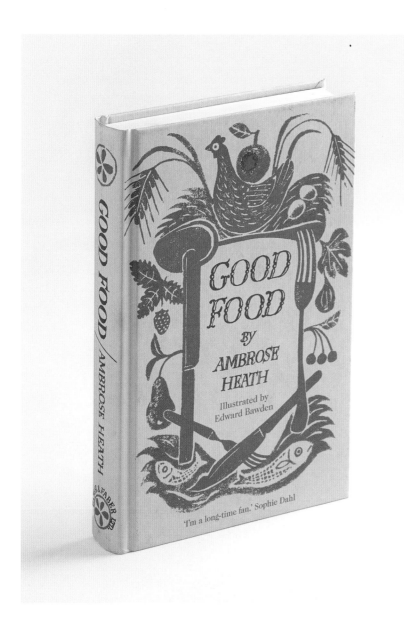

Celebrity British chef, restaurateur, and broadcaster Jamie Oliver campaigns on issues close to his heart.

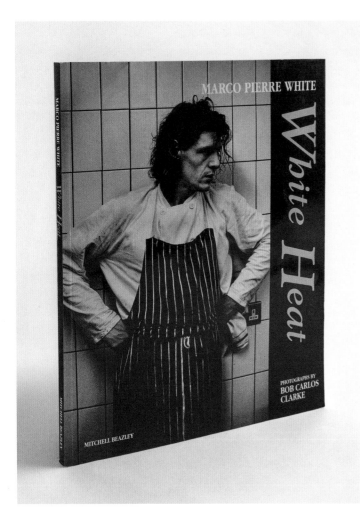

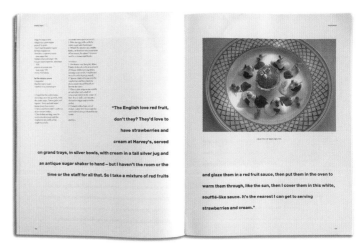

"If I went to the Gavroche, I'd order lemon tart. It's one of my great favourites — a wonderful way of finishing a meal, and a real chef's pudding. Any chef worthy of the name has a lemon tart on his menu. We cook one twice a day: in the morning just before lunch service, and at 7 p.m. just before the dinner service, so it's always fresh and fragrant."

"Passion fruit has a persistent flavour: eat it, and you've still got the flavour in your mouth five minutes later. That's exactly what you need for a soufflé: something sharpish and long to match the sweet, eggy blandness."

"A soufflé needs heart. A lot of people go crazy trying to make them as light as possible, but you end up losing texture and substance. A good soufflé has an inside and an outside — and a middle, a heart."

"The English love red fruit, don't they? They'd love to have strawberries and cream at Harvey's, served on grand trays, in silver bowls, with cream in a tall silver jug and an antique sugar shaker to hand – but I haven't the room or the time or the staff for all that. So I take a mixture of red fruits

and glaze them in a red fruit sauce, then put them in the oven to warm them through, like the sun, then I cover them in this white, soufflé-like sauce. It's the nearest I can get to serving strawberries and cream."

Shane Osborn

RESTAURANT
Arcane, Hong Kong, opened 2014

White Heat Marco Pierre White

BOOK DETAILS
Published 1990, Mitchell Beazley, 128 pages, photography by Michael Boys and Bob Carlos Clarke, illustrations by Edward Bawden

Australian chef Shane Osborn is noted for his skillful, stylish cooking, showcased at his Hong Kong restaurant Arcane.

"This cookbook had the most profound effect on my career."
SHANE OSBORN

Shane Osborn was born in Perth, Australia, and his career as a chef has seen him travel the world. The lure of Europe saw him arrive there as a young man, where he worked in England and Sweden. While working at London's Pied à Terre, Osborn was recognized for his considerable culinary talents and he became head chef and joint owner in 2001, gaining the restaurant a second Michelin star during his time there. Now chef-owner of Arcane in Hong Kong, Osborn offers his refined harmonious food—Carpaccio of Turnip with Smoked Eel, Braised Wagyu Shortribs, Caramelized Pear with Hokkaido Cream. Osborn's skillful cooking is grounded in great technique, drawing on the knowledge he's gained through several years of hard work and travel.

Osborn has vivid memories of his choice, *White Heat* by Marco Pierre White (see p.20, 296): "It had just been published when I arrived in the UK and the hype around Marco was incredible." Like its author, the book is a dashing affair, illustrated with Bob Carlos Clarke's grainy black-and-white photos of White at work. Proving that White could write as well as cook, the text, in his unmistakable voice, is vivid, candid, and challenging: "I wish I wasn't a cook. I wish cooking was just a passionate hobby, but it's an obsession." White tells the story of his journey to chef superstardom, writing perceptively of mentors such as Michael Lawson, Albert Roux (see p.284), Nico Ladenis (see p.238), Pierre Koffmann (see p.90, 94,

236). The recipes for refined, beautifully presented creations such as Feuillantine of Sweetbreads or Navarin of Fish are brought to life by White's comments, expressing his thoughts on ingredients, flavor combining, and cooking methods in pithy form. He has a candid eloquence about food that brings a sense of his personality to the page: "There's only one dish on my menu which is perfect, and that's the tagliatelle of oysters with caviar. It's pure theatre to make and it's pure theatre to eat." Osborn remembers the time he was lucky enough to eat at Harvey's: "I studied the book night and day leading up to the day of my visit. The meal exceeded my expectations; the food was beautiful and absolutely delicious."

Sarit Packer

RESTAURANT

Honey & Co., London, UK, opened 2012

Delia's Cakes Delia Smith

BOOK DETAILS

Published 1977, Hodder & Stoughton Ltd, 223 pages, photography by Dan Jones

Israeli chef Sarit Packer has come to public attention with Honey & Co. (see p.318), the beguiling, relaxed, and intimate restaurant she and her husband, Itamar Srulovich (see p.146), founded in London in 2012, which quickly established a devoted following. Packer's experience as a chef includes working as pastry chef under Chris Galvin at The Orrery, as head of pastry at Ottolenghi (see p.260, 318), and as executive chef at Nopi. The cooking at Honey & Co., which serves breakfast, lunch, and dinner, allows Packer to display her range of skills. The changing menu offers everything from luscious cakes and desserts—such as a signature Feta and Honey Cheesecake on a Kadaif Pastry Base—to Middle Eastern–inspired savory dishes.

Given that the tempting display of cakes in the window of Honey & Co. acts as an attention-grabbing lure for passersby, Sarit Packer's choice of *Delia's Cakes* is very apt. The fact that Packer selected this cookbook—domestic in tone, written for the home cook rather the professional chef—says much about Delia Smith's (see p.310) qualities as a cookery writer. Her ability to write easy-to-follow recipes that work—despite the inexperience of the cook—is a hallmark of Smith's work and has given her a special place in British affections.

Notably democratic rather than elitist in her approach to food, she is keen to empower her readers. On cake-making, she declares encouragingly: "what homemade cakes have got going for them is that they provide you with something really luxurious at very little cost." Smith offers reliable recipes for an array of British treats: Old-Fashioned Cherry Cake, Iced Lemon Curd Layer Cake and a classic Madeira Cake. Straightforward and practical, this cookbook reminds readers of the richness of Britain's baking heritage.

"Because no one beats Delia on great recipes that work time and again to produce great cakes that don't try too hard, but win hearts and mouths every time."

SARIT PACKER

Talented Israeli chef Sarit Packer, whose cooking delights diners at London's Honey & Co.

"My favourite book is, and has been for many years, Patience Gray's Honey From a Weed."

STEVIE PARLE

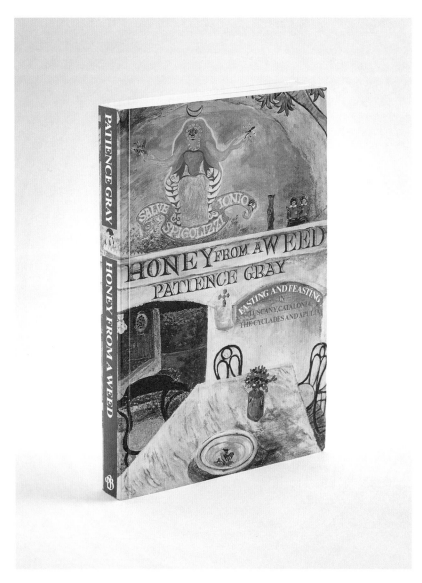

British chef Stevie Parle brings creative energy and imagination to his cooking at Craft London.

Stevie Parle

RESTAURANT

Craft London, London, UK, opened 2015

Honey From a Weed: Fasting and Feasting in Tuscany, Catalonia, The Cyclades and Apulia Patience Gray

BOOK DETAILS

Published 1986, Harper & Row Publishers, 374 pages, illustrations by Corinna Sargood

Stevie Parle studied at Ballymaloe Cookery School in Ireland (see p.12, 160) at the age of sixteen, and his career saw him working in some notable British restaurant kitchens: The River Cafe (see p.220), Moro (see p.194), and the Petersham Nurseries. In 2009, he set up Dock Kitchen, housed in a converted wharf building and offering an eclectic, frequently changing menu. His recent venture, Craft London in Greenwich, is a project with Tom Dixon, who designed the striking décor. The concept sees Parle focusing on the craft of food, from curing meat or smoking fish to growing vegetables and keeping bees. Known for culinary creativity and flair, dishes such as his signature Clay Roasted Duck have ensured Parle a committed following.

"It's a wonderfully eccentric mixture of recipes and storytelling from a life lived in wonderful places with wonderful people," observes Stevie Parle affectionately of his favorite book, Patience Gray's *Honey From a Weed* (see p.92). "It's a real insight into a lifestyle that we are losing more every year, culinary traditions and knowledge from remote areas of Europe that can't be found elsewhere." As evocative as its title suggests, Gray's remarkable book charts her journeys through the landscape and seascape of the Mediterranean,

sharing the nomadic life of her sculptor companion: "A vein of marble runs through this book. Marble determined where, how, and among whom we lived; always in primitive conditions." With her distinctive prose, Gray conveys the frugal peasant life she observed and took part in—the gathering of land snails to cook with spaghetti, the picking of figs, mulberries, and edible weeds, the laborious harvesting of olives. Offering a remarkable breadth of knowledge— intensely cultured and deeply rooted— it is an enthralling, memorable book.

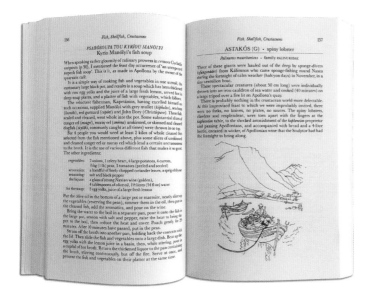

Neil Perry

RESTAURANT
Rockpool, Sydney, Australia, opened 1989

Great Chefs of France Anthony Blake and Quentin Crewe

BOOK DETAILS
Published 1978, Harry N. Abrams Inc, 239 pages, photography by Anthony Blake

With his iconic Sydney restaurant Rockpool, Australian chef, restaurateur, and broadcaster Neil Perry helped redefine Australian fine dining. Perry's cuisine is sophisticated and cosmopolitan, drawing on classic French cooking techniques, yet also looking for inspiration to Asia. Ingredients—pandan, shiso, and konbu sit alongside Australian lamb, kingfish, and blue swimmer crab—are combined with an appreciation for texture and flavor that has garnered Perry numerous plaudits. Ever since he took over the Blue Water Grill on Bondi Beach, transforming it into a success, Perry has been an important and dynamic figure on Australia's gastronomic scene, adding to its range and vibrancy. An energetic man—he has seven restaurants and is the author of nine cookbooks—he has helped shape modern Australian cuisine.

Neil Perry's choice is for a cookbook that has profoundly inspired him: Anthony Blake and Quentin Crewe's seminal work *Great Chefs of France* (see p.98, 124). Based on an idea of renowned photographer Anthony Blake, the book set out to pay homage to twelve master French chefs, each possessing three Michelin stars. Both in its approach and its subject, this fascinating book is eminently civilized. First, the scene is set: the long, hardworking day in the professional kitchen is depicted in verbal snapshots. Next, comes "The Story of Haute Cuisine," told at length and with panache by Crewe. The book

then lovingly portrays each of the chefs in turn, both in words and in Blake's intimate photographs, beginning with Madame Point, with whose husband—the legendary chef Fernand Point (see p.86)—so many of the chefs in the book had trained. Each chef portrait—Paul Bocuse (see p.108, 182), the Haeberlin brothers, Jean and Pierre Troisgros among them—is wonderfully vivid; one glimpses the characters of the people, as well as that of their restaurants and food. The extraordinary commitment to their profession displayed by all the chefs is amply conveyed with respect and affection in this remarkable book.

"After reading it, I fell in love with the idea of the work and ethic behind creating a great restaurant."
NEIL PERRY

A leading figure in the world of Australian dining, Neil Perry's restaurant, Rockpool, is internationally acclaimed.

"This book has become an obsession—today I own five copies and would add more to the pack!"
GARY RHODES

British chef and broadcaster Gary Rhodes, a long-time champion of British cuisine.

Gary Rhodes

RESTAURANT
Rhodes Twenty10, Dubai, UAE, opened 2010

Great Chefs of France
Anthony Blake and Quentin Crewe

BOOK DETAILS
Published 1978, Harry N. Abrams Inc, 239 pages, photography by Anthony Blake

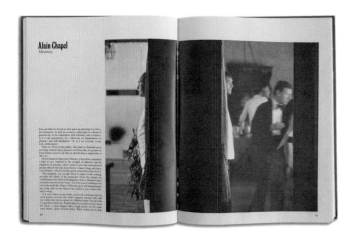

In Britain's food scene, Gary Rhodes was among the first of a new generation of celebrity chefs, becoming a household name in the United Kindom through television series such as *Rhodes Around Britain*. His training included a time in Amsterdam, but he made his name at the Castle Hotel, Taunton, Somerset, retaining a Michelin star as head chef there at the age of twenty-six years. A pioneering champion of British food, Rhodes's culinary skills garnered him plaudits as executive chef at The Greenhouse, London, where he offered refined versions of classic dishes such as fishcakes and bread-and-butter pudding. Following this, in 1997 he opened his first restaurant, the upmarket City Rhodes in London's financial district. In 2006, this experienced chef and restaurateur was awarded an OBE for his services to the hospitality industry.

Gary Rhodes's cookbook choice is a title that he was first given as a Christmas present in 1979: Anthony Blake and Quentin Crewe's *Great Chefs of France* (see p.98, 122). "I was working at the Amsterdam Hilton," recalls Rhodes, "and on reading and studying the pages, the book became a culinary dream, offering and presenting to me a new inspiration, one that still continues as I glance through the pages today." Photographer Anthony Blake had conceived of the idea to celebrate twelve great living French chefs, working in partnership with Quentin Crewe to create this unique book, which weaves together Blake's revealing photographs and Crewe's

knowledgeable text—offering in-depth profiles of the chefs—to wonderful effect. As Rhodes explains, "The book holds a combination of culinary legends, chefs you dream of working for and with: Jacques Pic, Alain Chapel (see p.36), Troisgros Brothers, Paul Bocuse (see p.108, 182), Michel Guérard (see p.222), and more." The book celebrates French cuisine as a great achievement of human culture, with the chef as hero. It is also rooted in a realistic understanding of the demands of the chef's work, as "The Day of Chefs" section shows. The hard labor, the rigorous discipline required by a professional kitchen, the drive and energy needed are respected and made clear.

Joan Roca

RESTAURANT
El Celler de Can Roca, Girona, Spain, opened 1986

La Cuisine spontanée: les recettes originales de Girardet Frédy Girardet

BOOK DETAILS
Published 1982, Éditions Robert Laffont, 266 pages, illustrations by Julien van der Wal; published in English as *Cuisine Spontanée*, 1985, Macmillan

Restaurants are a way of life for Spanish chef Joan Roca, who learned about cooking in his parents' Catalan restaurant. Today, the Roca family name is known worldwide, with El Celler de Can Roca—the restaurant that Joan founded with his two brothers Josep (see p.130) and Jordi (see p.128)—feted and lauded by food critics and diners alike. Although they work together, the brothers each have separate roles within the restaurant, with Joan, the eldest, its head chef (Jordi is pastry chef and Josep the sommelier). His elegant cooking—while rooted in the rich, traditional cuisine of Catalonia—is also experimental and innovative. The thoughtful and philosophical Joan Roca brings a depth to his cuisine, often drawing on the emotional charge that food can bring, its power to evoke memories and feelings, but also a light playfulness and wit.

Joan Roca's choice is *La Cuisine Spontanée* by legendary Swiss chef Frédy Girardet, from whom Roca learned while training as a chef. Girardet's eponymous restaurant at Crissier, near Lausanne in Switzerland, had an international acclaim, attracting gourmands from around the world. Such was Girardet's reputation that, in 1975, he was awarded the Gault-Millau Guide Cle d'Or, a signal honor in the restaurant trade. Despite Girardet's grand reputation, there is a distinctly accessible air to this modestly presented cookbook, with its content centered primarily on the recipes. Girardet's cooking focused on the ingredients local to his part of Switzerland, with the emphasis on sourcing the best. There is an admirable precision to the recipe-writing: when it is required, exact measurements are given for prepping ingredients and timings are in seconds. Despite the book's straightforward appearance, however, the recipes within it are luxurious, representing the impeccable haute cuisine for which Girardet was famed: Salad of Little Artichokes with Hot Foie Gras; Fillets of Sea Bass with Oysters; Saddle of Hare in Strips with Pears. It is a glimpse into a world of classic French cooking, which rests on superb technique.

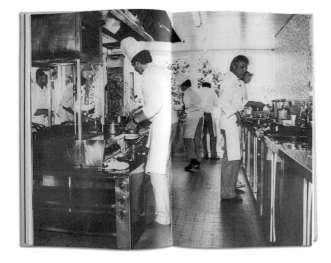

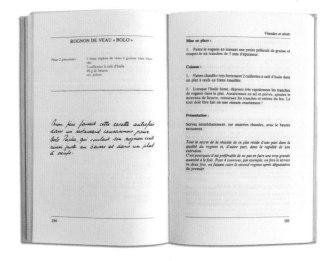

"I think dining is often about the memories of food, the sensory experience and how you will remember it. I develop my own food to heighten the senses for customers."
JOAN ROCA

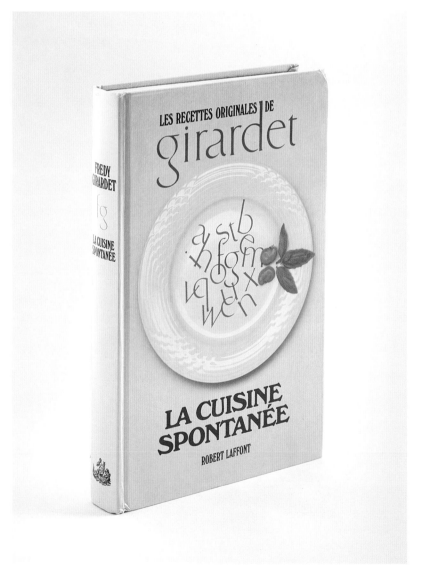

Spanish chef Joan Roca, whose restaurant El Celler de Can Roca in Girona, cofounded with his brothers, is famous worldwide.

"A walk, a landscape, a smell, a story, a noise, a transgression, an emotion—any road can lead to creativity."

JORDI ROCA

Spanish pastry chef Jordi Roca's creative desserts delight diners at El Celler de Can Roca, the celebrated family restaurant he joined in 1999.

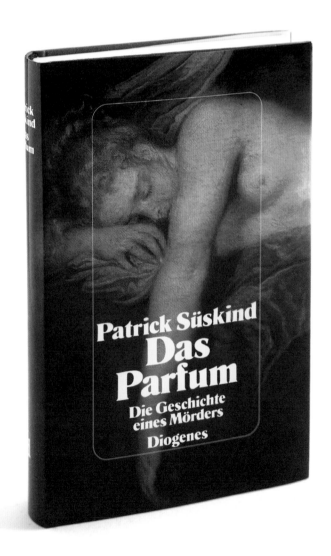

Jordi Roca

RESTAURANT

El Celler de Can Roca, Girona, Spain, opened 1986

Das Parfum Patrick Süskind

BOOK DETAILS

Published 1985, Diogenes Verlag, 263 pages; this edition published 2006, 319 pages; published in English as *Perfume*, 1986, Alfred A. Knopf

Jordi Roca, head pastry chef of the legendary El Celler de Can Roca, the Spanish restaurant that his brothers Joan (see p.126) and Josep (see p.130) cofounded and which he joined in 1999, is a chef who delights in creativity. While food and kitchens were part of his life from an early age, he became fascinated by desserts in particular "under the guidance of Damian Allsop," a British pastry chef who had arrived to work at El Celler de Can Roca in the late 1990s. Having studied his craft in-depth, Roca draws on his considerable skills and understanding of the underlying science to let his inventiveness soar. Taking pleasure in surprising his diners, Roca's original, playful, and delectable desserts are a wonderful note on which to end a meal at El Celler de Can Roca.

Jordi Roca's book choice is a striking one—not a cookbook or even a food book. Instead he has selected a novel: *Das Parfum* by Patrick Süskind. Although not overtly about food, the novel is centered on the sense of smell, which is crucial to our ability to detect flavors. Süskind's macabre book relates the tale of Grenouille, born a grotesque, unloved child, in eighteenth-century Paris, whose one gift in life is his extraordinary sense of smell. Süskind writes with sensuous intensity of the smells that Grenouille's hypersensitive nose encounters: the odor of pressed silk, the scent of the sea, the freshness of a frosty wind, the complex web of odors that make up the smell of the city of Paris. Just as a young man interested in food might become an apprentice chef, so Grenouille hunts out master perfumers to learn the business of creating perfumes, acquiring the skills of distillation and enfleurage. *Das Parfum* is a fascinating, thought-provoking tour de force chosen by a pâtissier who revels in the power of imagination. Significantly, Jordi Roca is known for his desserts based on deconstructed perfumes.

Josep Roca

RESTAURANT

El Celler de Can Roca, Girona, Spain, opened 1986

Com Usar Bé de Beure e Menjar Francesc Eiximenis

BOOK DETAILS

Manuscript written 1384, published 1977, Curial Edicions Catalanes, 150 pages

The role of the reflective and eloquent Josep Roca at El Celler de Can Roca—the internationally acclaimed restaurant that he founded together with his brothers, Joan and Jordi, in 1986—is the keeper of the wines. El Celler de Can Roca is renowned for the extent and range of its large wine cellar and, naturally, for the quality of the wines themselves, which are carefully and knowledgeably selected by Josep. His fascination with wine is evident in the way in which he talks about the subject. In this gracious, hospitable restaurant, he regards the communication side of his role as an important one—the ability to engage with customers and listen to what they want—and much prefers to describe himself as a wine waiter, rather than a sommelier.

Josep Roca's choice is for an important historical document, *Com Usar Bé de Beure e Menjar* ("How To Eat and Drink Well") written in 1384 by Francesc Eiximenis, a noted Catalan writer. The work forms part of a major literary project Eiximenis undertook called *Lo Crestià* ("The Christian"). In it, Eiximenis explores the relationship between man and food. It is a fitting and witty choice by Roca, as a considerable portion of the work is concerned with wine and drunkenness, with Eiximenis warning of the arguments and fights that ensue when wine has been consumed

to excess. The importance of good manners when eating and drinking is a major theme. Eiximenis also writes with pride of Catalan dining habits. In his chapter "Com Catalans menjen pus graciosament e ab millor manera que altres nacions" ("How Catalans eat much more graciously and in a better way than other nations"), he praises the way in which Catalans eat seasonally, choose their dishes well, and drink moderately. Eiximenis's work is a fascinating glimpse into the world of Catalan fine dining many centuries ago, and which still resonates today.

"I like wine. I'm drawn by our fascinating dialogue with it, a dialogue of man and nature."

JOSEP ROCA

Sommelier Josep Roca is keeper of the wines at the acclaimed El Celler de Can Roca.

Simon Rogan

RESTAURANT

L'Enclume, Cartmel, Cumbria, UK, opened 2002

Herbs, Spices and Flavourings Tom Stobart

BOOK DETAILS

Published 1970, The International Wine and Food Publishing Company, 262 pages, illustrations by Ian Garrard

A commitment to expressing a sense of place through his cuisine is at the heart of British chef Simon Rogan's internationally renowned L'Enclume restaurant. Its beautiful, natural setting in the Cumbrian hills inspired Rogan to begin using locally foraged ingredients, which grew wild in the countryside around him. He also set up his own farm, growing vegetables, fruits, and herbs for his restaurants, including Fera, at London's Claridge's Hotel. While the inspiration is rustic, Rogan's cuisine —presented with a fine aesthetic sensibility—is notably sophisticated and playful, drawing on modern cooking techniques in order to create a series of dainty, complex dishes. Imaginatively conceived creations such as Shorthorn, Charcoal Oil, Mustard, Apple, and Celeriac show his ability to intrigue and delight diners.

At first glance, Simon Rogan's favorite cookbook, *Herbs, Spices and Flavourings* by Tom Stobart, a text-based reference book, might appear rather scholarly. The content, however, is lively and engaging. Stobart, a great traveler, opens the book with a vivid account of a cave exploration in Sardinia, where he discovered jars containing food "some four thousand years old." Afterward, eating lamb roasted over an "aromatic" fire of rosemary, he thought of the way in which humans have used herbs to flavor foods for centuries. The alphabetically arranged entries—on subjects as diverse as anchovy, bulrush, meadowsweet, and galangal—have a magpie quality to them, offering a mix of history, botany, and cooking advice. His traveler's tales, too, provide zest: "Anyone who visits the Corbett National Park in Kumaon will notice the strong appetizing smell of curry as their elephant bursts through the thickets and bruises the leaves of this plant," he writes airily of curry leaves. "I actually stumbled across my copy in an antiques store many years ago and it turns out it previously belonged to the one and only Elizabeth David," explains Rogan. "It's a book that I hold very dear for both sentimental as well as practical reasons."

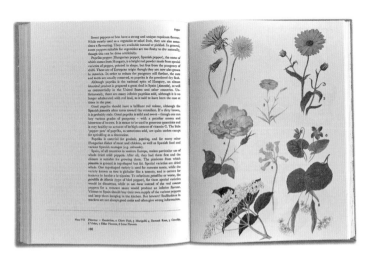

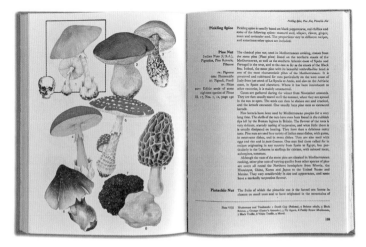

"Tom Stobart's Herbs, Spices and Flavourings *is one of my oldest herbs and spices books."*

SIMON ROGAN

A fascination with expressing a sense of place through food is a hallmark of British chef Simon Rogan's cooking at L'Enclume.

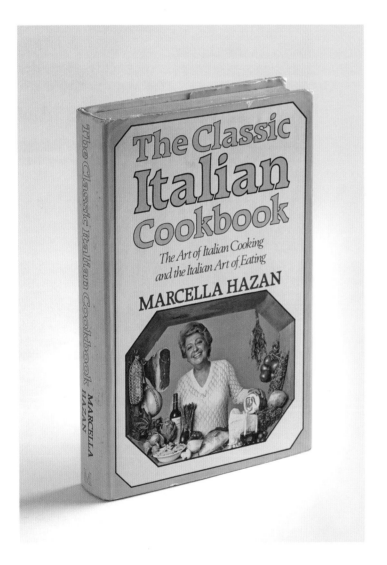

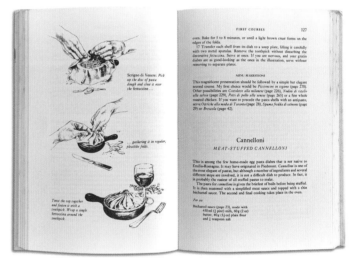

Scrigno di Venere: Pick up the disc of pasta and cover with the fettuccine ...

... gathering it in regular, pleatlike folds.

Twist the top together and fasten it with a toothpick. Wrap a single fettuccina around the toothpick.

oven. Bake for 5 to 8 minutes, or until a light brown crust forms on the edges of the folds.

17 Transfer each shell from its dish to a soup plate, lifting it carefully with two metal spatulas. Remove the toothpick without disturbing the decorative *fettuccine*. Serve at once. If you are nervous, and your gratin dishes are as good-looking as the ones in the illustration, serve without removing to separate plates.

MENU SUGGESTIONS

This magnificent presentation should be followed by a simple but elegant second course. My first choice would be *Piccione in tegame* (page 270). Other possibilities are *Costolette alla milanese* (page 226), *Nodini di vitello alla salvia* (page 229), *Petti di pollo alla senese* (page 265) or a fine whole roasted chicken. If you want to precede the pasta shells with an antipasto, serve *Ostriche alla moda di Taranto* (page 28), *Spuma fredda di salmone* (page 29) or *Bresaola* (page 42).

Cannelloni
MEAT-STUFFED CANNELLONI

This is among the few home-made egg pasta dishes that is not native to Emilia-Romagna. It may have originated in Piedmont. *Cannelloni* is one of the most elegant of pastas, but although a number of ingredients and several different steps are involved, it is not a difficult dish to produce. In fact, it is probably the easiest of all stuffed pastas to make.

The pasta for *cannelloni* is given the briefest of boils before being stuffed. It is then seasoned with a simplified meat sauce and topped with a thin béchamel sauce. The second and final cooking takes place in the oven.

For six

Béchamel sauce (page 23), made with
  450 ml (¾ pint) milk, 60 g (2 oz)
  butter, 40 g (1½ oz) plain flour
  and ¼ teaspoon salt

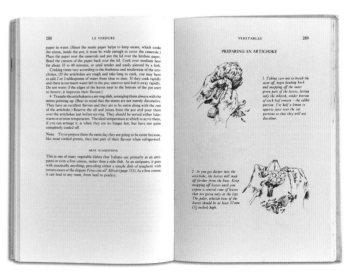

paper in water. (Since the moist paper helps to keep steam, which cooks the stems, inside the pot, it must be wide enough to cover the casserole.) Place the paper over the casserole and put the lid over the kitchen paper. Bend the corners of the paper back over the lid. Cook over medium heat for about 35 to 40 minutes, or until tender and easily pierced by a fork.

Cooking times vary according to the freshness and tenderness of the artichokes. (If the artichokes are tough and take long to cook, you may have to add 2 or 3 tablespoons of water from time to time. If they cook rapidly and there is too much water left in the pot, uncover and boil it away rapidly. Do not worry if the edges of the leaves next to the bottom of the pot start to brown; it improves their flavour.)

4 Transfer the artichokes to a serving dish, arranging them always with the stems pointing up. (Bear in mind that the stems are not merely decorative. They have an excellent flavour and they are to be eaten along with the rest of the artichoke.) Reserve the oil and juices from the pot and pour them over the artichokes just before serving. They should be served either lukewarm or at room temperature. The ideal temperature at which to serve them, if you can arrange it, is when they are no longer hot, but have not quite completely cooled off.

Note   Try to prepare them the same day they are going to be eaten because, like most cooked greens, they lose part of their flavour when refrigerated.

MENU SUGGESTIONS

This is one of many vegetable dishes that Italians use primarily as an antipasto or even a first course, rather than a side dish. As an antipasto, it goes with practically anything, preceding either a simple dish of spaghetti with tomato sauce or the elegant *Fettuccine all'Alfredo* (page 111). As a first course it can lead to any roast, from beef to poultry.

PREPARING AN ARTICHOKE

1 Taking care not to break the stem off, begin bending back and snapping off the outer green part of the leaves, letting only the whitish, tender bottom of each leaf remain – the edible portion. Use half a lemon to squeeze over the cut portions so that they will not discolour.

2 As you get deeper into the artichoke, the leaves will snap off further from the base. Keep snapping off leaves until you expose a central cone of leaves that are green only at the tips. The paler, whitish base of the leaves should be at least 37 mm (1½ inches) high.

Ruth Rogers

RESTAURANT
The River Cafe, London, UK, opened 1987

The Classic Italian Cookbook
Marcella Hazan

BOOK DETAILS
Published 1973, Alfred A. Knopf, 414 pages, illustrations by Karin Kretschmann

"Marcella Hazan's Classic Italian Cookbook *was the defining book for Rose and me when we first started The River Cafe."*
RUTH ROGERS

A great friendship—that between Ruth Rogers and British chef Rose Gray—was at the heart of their decision to set up The River Cafe in London in 1987 (see p.220). Their restaurant, founded in a shared vision and with mutual support, was groundbreaking in many ways: from the collaborative way that the open-plan kitchen was run to the daily-changing, seasonal, Italian-inspired menu, focused on what ingredients were at their best that day. A side street in west London was an unlikely location for a restaurant championing the essence of Italian cuisine, and yet The River Cafe has proved to be an influential restaurant. Sadly, Rose Gray died in 2010, but the restaurant created with such imagination and conviction carries on under Rogers.

Ruth Rogers's choice is for a cookbook that was very important to both her and Rose Gray when they founded The River Cafe, namely *The Classic Italian Cookbook* by Marcella Hazan (see p.72, 148). Written with an elegance of style, Hazan set out to elucidate the qualities of Italian cuisine. She begins by setting the context for Italian cuisine, focusing on its regional nature, and highlighting the importance of geography—citing "the two dominant elements of the Italian landscape—the mountain and the sea" as forces shaping Italian gastronomy.

Hazan's rooted approach to explaining what Italian cuisine is about makes this a wise and perceptive book. Her clear recipes, for classics such as Venice's Risi e Bisi or Trieste's Lo "Schinco," set the dishes in context of place and culture. "In the beginning we did not waiver from her recipes," explains Rogers, "but with more experience and travels to Italy, we expanded our interpretations. I look at it less often now but when I do, I am reminded of what inspired us to open River Cafe, why we love Italian food, and most of all memories of Rose."

British chef Ruth Rogers, whose partnership with chef Rose Gray at The River Café changed the face of British dining.

"A local cuisine that's rooted in Danish ingredients and seasons, and a natural cuisine where the raw materials are the stars."

SØREN SELIN

Danish chef Søren Selin of AOC, Copenhagen, Denmark, is noted for his meticulous cuisine.

Søren Selin

RESTAURANT

AOC, Copenhagen, Denmark, opened 2009 (Selin joined in 2013)

Noma: Time and Place in Nordic Cuisine René Redzepi

BOOK DETAILS

Published 2010, Phaidon, 320 pages, photography by Ditte Isager

A desire to express the beauty of Nordic nature is at the heart of acclaimed Danish chef Søren Selin's cooking. Having worked at restaurants including Le Relais Louis XIII in Paris, it is at Restaurant AOC that Selin has come to international attention, joining as head chef in 2013 and gaining the establishment a second Michelin star in 2015. Noted for his creativity and also his perfectionism, Selin's cuisine sees him use local ingredients with imagination and flair. Dishes such as Squid, Lard, and Fermented Parsnip Broth or Green Juniper Berries, Pears, and Buttermilk reflect his ability to create skillful, intriguing dishes, presented with an aesthetic sensibility.

"A game changer" says Søren Selin simply of his chosen cookbook—René Redzepi's *Noma: Time and Place in Nordic Cuisine* (see p.278). Beautifully and carefully produced, this large volume explores Redzepi's culinary journey in creating his iconic restaurant, Noma. It is an intelligent charting, including essays by artist Olafur Eliasson and journalist Rune Skyum-Nielsen in addition to Redzepi's own diaries of his North Atlantic research trip and affectionately written descriptions of his food producers.

Redzepi is candid about his culinary baggage acquired while working as a young chef at great restaurants. Of his time at Spain's elBulli he says: "I wasn't listening enough to myself." The book also uses pictures to excellent effect. Images of Redzepi's exquisite, pure-looking dishes—Dessert of Flowers; Fresh Cheese and Spruce Shoots; Asparagus, Bulrush, and Duck Eggs—are interspersed with photographs of nature. Nature shapes the menu at Noma and one understands Redzepi's intense appreciation for it.

Chris Shepherd

RESTAURANT
Underbelly, Houston, Texas, USA, opened 2012

The French Laundry Cookbook
Thomas Keller with Susie Heller and Michael Ruhlman

BOOK DETAILS
Published 1999, Artisan Books, 326 pages, photography by Deborah Jones

Chris Shepherd is a chef with a vision—and it is a democratic and inclusive one. With his acclaimed restaurant Underbelly, of which he is chef-owner, he celebrates the city of Houston, in all its ethnic diversity: "We have a few rules at Underbelly. We buy directly from farmers. We only use the whole animal. Our food is inspired by the cultures of Houston." Shepherd is a man committed to community, using food as a way of bringing people together. Offering "new American Creole cuisine," the menu changes daily and is a diverse affair. Dishes such as Singaporean Sweet Chili Blue Crab sit alongside UB Hickory King Grits, Braised Country Ham, Leeks, evidence of Shepherd's open-minded fascination with food.

Chris Shepherd's choice is *The French Laundry Cookbook* by Thomas Keller (see p.18, 86, 230): "It came out in 1999, an influential time for me as a cook. I was just starting to understand dining and not just cooking." As elegantly presented as the food it portrays, Thomas Keller's classic cookbook celebrates his famous California restaurant. Evocative photos depict a gracious dining experience and the devoted work by Keller and his team to create it. Studding the book are short, thoughtful essays by Keller, in which he shares his thoughts on food and restaurants. Underlying the beauty of The French Laundry, one understands, is Keller's determination and vision. He gives glimpses of key moments in his career—learning the "real fundamentals" of cooking as a young chef from Roland Henin—including his arrival at The French Laundry in 1992: "It seemed as if I'd been heading there my whole working life." Keller's book is one that inspired Shepherd to follow his own dreams: "It showed me what it takes to succeed—as a cook, the only thing that stops you is yourself."

"It came out in 1999, an influential time for me as a cook."

CHRIS SHEPHERD

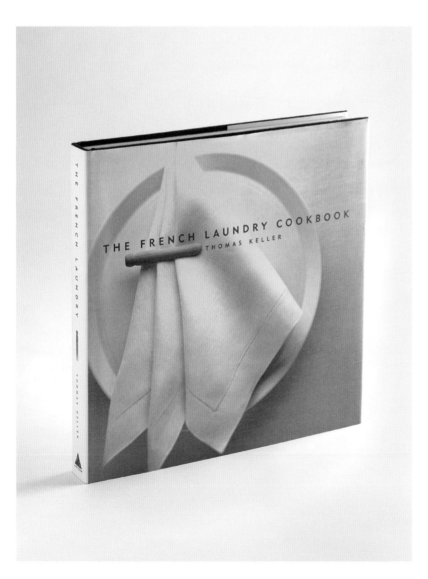

American chef Chris Shepherd
pursues his vision of "new
American Creole cuisine" at
Underbelly, Houston, Texas.

"I learned a lot about the cookbook production process and it deepened my appreciation for how much work is involved."

BRYCE SHUMAN

American chef Bryce Shuman, whose sophisticated Modern American cuisine is on offer at Betony, New York City.

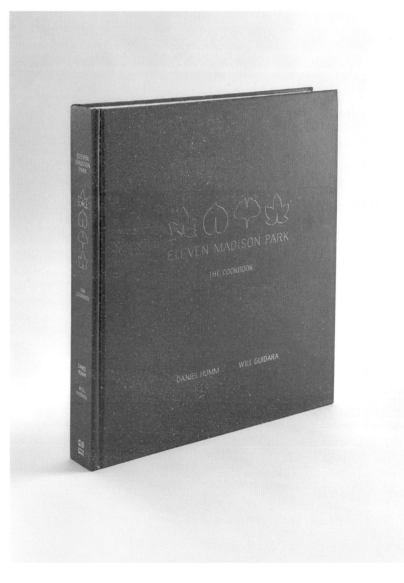

Bryce Shuman

RESTAURANT

Betony, New York City, New York, USA, opened 2013

Eleven Madison Park: The Cookbook
Daniel Humm and Will Guidara

BOOK DETAILS

Published 2011, Little, Brown, 384 pages, photography by Francesco Tonelli

These are exciting times for chef Bryce Shuman. In 2013, he opened Betony in New York City with former Eleven Madison Park colleague Eamon Rockey as general manager. Sophisticated and refined, Betony has been greeted with critical plaudits and awards. Shuman's career has seen him work in the United States and Europe, including with Stuart Brioza (see p.40) and Nicole Krasinski (see p.96) at Rubicon in San Francisco. Shuman worked for six years at New York's Eleven Madison Park under chef Daniel Humm (see p.82, 226). Having learned from the best, Betony sees Shuman expressing his own culinary talents in style.

Bryce Shuman's choice is for a cookbook that means a lot to him, as he was involved in its making. "*Eleven Madison Park: The Cookbook* is my favourite cookbook as it represents a few years of my life helping chef Daniel Humm to test and edit every recipe in it and working closely with him and master food photographer Francesco Tonelli to prepare the food for the photoshoot," explains Shuman. The result of all this hard, meticulous work was a cookbook

as handsome as the famous New York restaurant it celebrates. The book tells the story of how Eleven Madison Park was created in great detail, charting the history and explaining Humm and Guidara's vision of what it could be. The food, of course, plays a key part, with Humm revealing the ideas behind his witty, exquisite dishes. The striking photographs testify to Humm's culinary skill and creativity; no wonder Shuman is proud to have been part of this.

Vivek Singh

RESTAURANT
The Cinnamon Club, London, UK, opened 2001

Prashād: Cooking with Indian Masters
J. Inder Singh Kalra

BOOK DETAILS
Published 1986, Allied Publishers Private Limited, 214 pages, photography by Pradeep Das Gupta

Indian chef Vivek Singh, known for his stylish Indian cooking at The Cinnamon Club, London.

"This is possibly the **Larousse Gastronomique** *of Indian cuisine."*
VIVEK SINGH

Rather than follow in his father's footsteps and become an engineer, Vivek Singh surprised his family by choosing to become a chef. After catering college, he began working for the Oberoi Hotel Group. He joined as a specialist in Indian cuisine, rising through the ranks to become the chef at the group's luxurious, flagship Rajvilas hotel in Jaipur. While his training in Indian food was classical, Singh's own cuisine fuses French culinary techniques with Indian cooking. When restaurateur Iqbal Wahhab and chef Vivek Singh teamed up to open The Cinnamon Club in London in 2001, they redefined the Indian restaurant in Britain, offering a dining experience that was luxurious, sophisticated, and contemporary.

Vivek Singh's choice is a classic cookbook that has played an important role in Indian food culture, a book that champions Indian chefs, recognizing them as culinary artists. In *Prashād: Cooking with Indian Masters*, its author, J. Inder Singh Kalra, set out to record the masters of that cuisine. "It is a great documentary of sterling dishes being cooked in hotels by professional chefs, masterfully curated by J. Inder Singh Kalra," explains Singh. *Prashād* brought together "for the first time, recipes from various hotels and chefs cooking in different parts of the country, a feat that hadn't been achieved before." The book, written in campaigning spirit and a lively style, gives an insight through the chefs and their recipes of the intricacies of Indian cuisine. The rich, multifarious, regional nature of Indian cuisine is apparent in the range of recipes contained in this book: game dishes, such as Maas Ke Sule, from Rajasthan, Goa's Prawn Balchao, and Punjabi Punj Rattani Dal. While charting the history of techniques such as Dum Pukht, it is also forward looking and appreciative of culinary creativity. "It is no secret that Indian cuisine is 'in' and the time ripe to introduce the 'Grand Ol' Men' and the 'Whiz Kids' of the Indian kitchen," writes Kalra with characteristic verve.

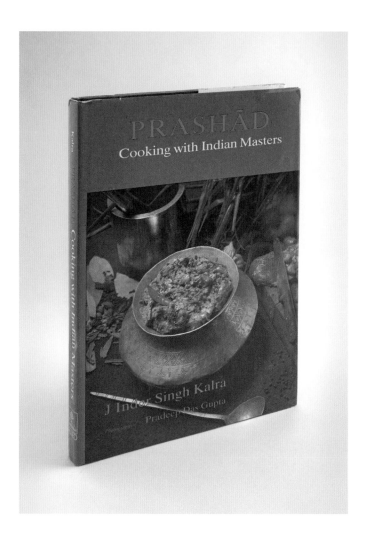

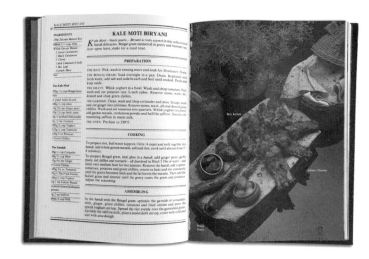

"When I was a young chef, this was the book to have."
CLARE SMYTH

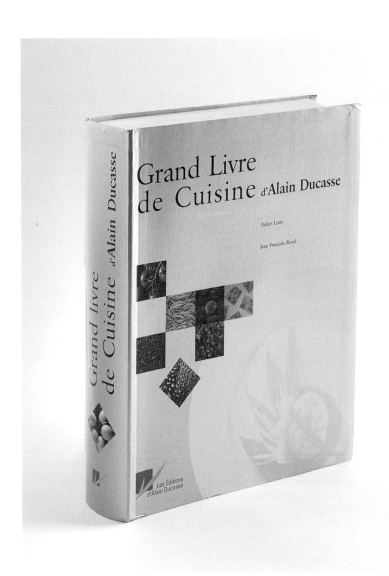

Acclaimed British chef Clare Smyth, formerly of Restaurant Gordon Ramsay, London, is known for her skillful, beautifully presented food.

Clare Smyth

RESTAURANT

Restaurant Gordon Ramsay, London, UK, opened 1998 (Smyth was head chef in 2007)

Grand Livre de Cuisine Alain Ducasse

BOOK DETAILS

Published 2004, Ducasse Books, 1078 pages, photography by Didier Loire

The first and only female chef to run a three Michelin–starred restaurant in the United Kingdom, Clare Smyth is a formidable culinary talent. Born in Northern Ireland, her focus and dedication were obvious from an early age. She joined Restaurant Gordon Ramsay (see p.276) in London in 2002, working her way up to become senior sous chef. In 2005, driven by her quest for knowledge, she left to work at Alain Ducasse's legendary Le Louis XV in Monte Carlo (see p.204). Returning to London in 2007, she joined Restaurant Gordon Ramsay as head chef, becoming chef-owner in 2012. Her ability to offer immaculate, beautifully presented Michelin-star food is clear. Now having left Restaurant Gordon Ramsay to set up her own restaurant, her next move is eagerly anticipated.

"It was this huge encyclopaedia, so expensive at the time, other chefs were truly envious if you had one," remembers British chef Clare Smyth of her cookbook choice, *Grand Livre de Cuisine* by Alain Ducasse (see p.84). "It's a beautifully done book, that still inspires me today." Truly an imposing tome, this work, by acclaimed French chef Ducasse and his chef protégés, offers a fascinating look into the work and skill required by the world of haute cuisine restaurants. Written for professional chefs, it contains an array of recipes for savory dishes, arranged alphabetically by main ingredient. The recipe instructions are meticulous, with a considerable emphasis on presentation; the food photography offers a visual representation of how the dishes should look. This is a world in which foie gras is trimmed, cooked mussels have their frills painstakingly removed, parsley leaves are pressed between folded layers of fresh pasta, and frog's legs are boned: a world of perfectionist, obsessive attention to detail. There is, it turns out, also a personal reason for Smyth's choice: "Having worked with the man himself, it has that extra special place on my shelf."

Itamar Srulovich

RESTAURANT

Honey & Co., London, UK, opened 2012

My Favourite Ingredients Skye Gyngell

BOOK DETAILS

Published 2008, Quadrille Publishing Ltd, 255 pages, photography by Jason Lowe

Extroverted, exuberant, and humorous, Israeli chef Itamar Srulovich brings a jovial, hospitable showmanship to Honey & Co. (see p.318), the small restaurant he and his wife, Sarit Packer (see p.118), established in a peaceful Fitzrovia sidestreet in London in 2012. He trained as a chef in Tel Aviv and met Packer in an Italian restaurant in the city where they were both working. Honey & Co., their first solo project—with its menu influenced by the vibrant flavors of the Middle East—has proved a great success, quickly acquiring cult status among the capital's food lovers. The intimate space is perennially filled with diners enjoying food from morning to night—for example, a shakshuka (dish of eggs poached in tomato sauce), fragrant with spices, for breakfast; a selection of trademark mezze at lunch; an enticing cake for tea; followed by slow-cooked lamb at suppertime.

Itamar Srulovich's favorite cookbook is *My Favourite Ingredients* by Australian chef Skye Gyngell. In this beautifully presented book, written while she was still working at Petersham Nurseries in Richmond, London, Gyngell, as she explains, "highlights some of the rich and beautiful ingredients that I am privileged to work with through the culinary year. Most of the recipes are simple in their execution." As with the recipes, the format is clear and straightforward. Each section is focused on a favorite ingredient such as "Cherries" or "Vinegar," starting with an evocative piece of writing about what that particular foodstuff means to her and how she likes to use it in the kitchen,

followed by a few recipes. Gyngell writes sensuously and well of these foods she loves: from the "grassy, slightly peppery, pungent, and completely summery" smell of a tomato plant to honey which, in contrast to "one-dimensional" sugar, "is complex and lends subtle flavour notes to dishes." She explores key ingredients, such as extra-virgin olive oil. Her recipes—Lobster Salad with Fennel and Blood Orange; Borlotti, Clams, and Fino; Pickled Pumpkin with Burrata— are often creative variants of classics, with Gyngell adept at combining flavors to surprising and interesting effect. Of Gyngell's recipes, Srulovich says simply: "I wish I could cook like that."

"Her simple and clever combinations work to create really beautiful and tasty dishes."
ITAMAR SRULOVICH

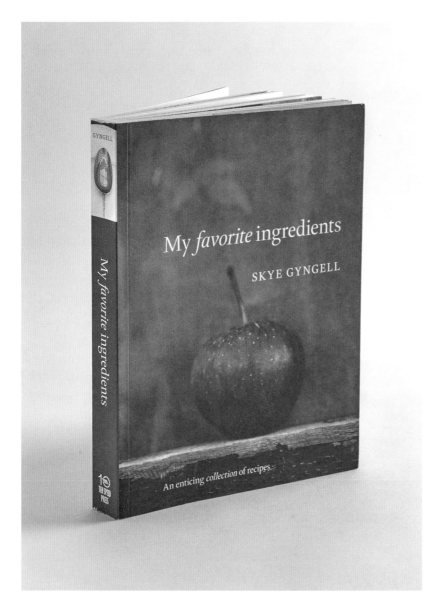

Israeli chef Itamar Srulovich brings a zest for life to his popular restaurant, Honey & Co., London.

Cathy Whims

RESTAURANT

Nostrana, Portland, Oregon, USA, opened 2005

Essentials of Classic Italian Cooking Marcella Hazan

BOOK DETAILS

Published 1992, Alfred A. Knopf, 722 pages, illustrations by Karin Kretschmann

"Marcella Hazan's cookbooks have been, and continue to be, perhaps my greatest learning tools. I constantly re-read them and consult them."
CATHY WHIMS

American chef Cathy Whims of Nostrana, Portland, whose love of Italian food is manifest in her own cooking.

A love of Italy and Italian food is a recurring theme of Cathy Whims's life, who, having studied Latin in college, also studied Italian cookery with Marcella and Victor Hazan (see p.72, 134) in Venice. She cooked in Italian restaurants in Barbaresco and Alba and returns to Italy frequently. A six-time James Beard finalist, Whims was co-owner of Genoa in Portland, before moving on to found Nostrana there with her partner, David West. Here, in relaxed surroundings, diners are offered a taste of Whims's much-praised Italian cooking—pizzas, freshly cooked in a wood-fired oven; handmade pasta; and classic *secondi*, such as *tagliata* or *porchetta*—deceptively simple dishes which, in true Italian fashion, allow the quality of the ingredients to shine through.

Cathy Whims's favorite cookbook is *Essentials of Classic Italian Cooking* by the esteemed Italian food writer Marcella Hazan. In it Hazan rewrote and reshaped the contents of her earlier cookbooks, adding an entire new chapter called "Fundamentals" and distilling the wisdom of many years into characteristically beautifully written prose and recipes. Whims describes how she once had the honor of cooking for Marcella and Victor Hazan at Nostrana. "We attempted a very difficult pasta called Venus' Jewel Purses from [Marcella's] first book. We practiced it for a month before the dinner. When Victor heard that we were doing that particular dish, from a previously famous restaurant in Bologna, Diana, he said 'Good luck!' We were so concerned what they would think! After the dinner, Marcella paid me the highest compliment I have ever received in my career. She said that there were only two professional chefs in her career that understood and executed her recipes correctly. One was a chef in a famous Michelin-star restaurant in Hong Kong, and the other was me! I guess all of that study paid off!"

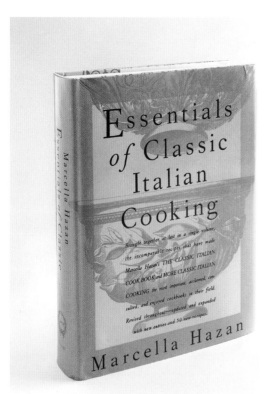

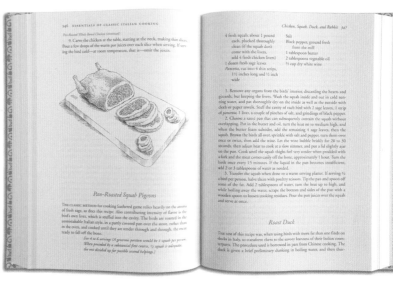

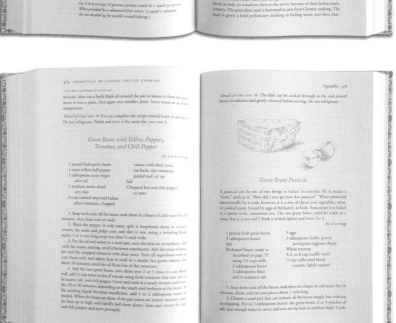

"For me, a cookbook needs to tell a story and not just be about the chef's ego or how amazing the food and restaurant is."

MICHAEL WIGNALL

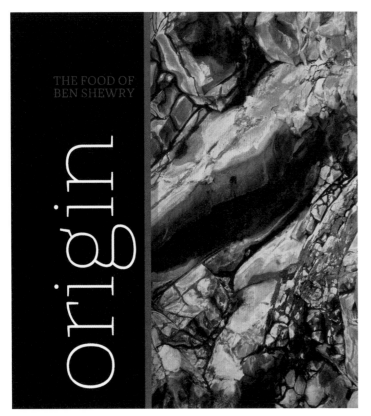

Acclaimed British chef Michael Wignall, who showcases his formidable culinary technique at Gidleigh Park.

Michael Wignall

RESTAURANT

Gidleigh Park, Dartmoor, Devon, UK, opened 2016

Origin: The Food of Ben Shewry Ben Shewry

BOOK DETAILS

Published 2012, Murdoch Books, 304 pages, photography by Colin Page

There is an energy about British chef Michael Wignall, both to the man himself and to his career. As a teenager, he was keen to pursue a career as a professional BMX biker, however, his parents sent him to catering college, where his love of food triumphed. Wignall's career saw him working in restaurants around Britain, both retaining and acquiring Michelin stars. He made his name with Michael Wignall at the Latymer, Surrey, which opened in 2007 and gained its second Michelin star in 2012. Driven and perfectionistic in all he does, his cooking is complex, drawing on his formidable culinary technique to great effect. In 2016, Wignall began a new chapter in his career, as executive chef of the famed Gidleigh Park in Devon.

Michael Wignall is very clear about what he looks for in a cookbook: "The recipes should evoke the imagination and, for a chef, intrigue and inspire the creative process." His favorite cookbook, *Origin* by New Zealand chef Ben Shewry (see p.288), is indeed an inspiring one, written with compelling eloquence and offering a fascinating insight into Shewry's own life and work as a chef. Wignall, noted for the way in which he presents his food, is very aware of the visual aspect of a cookbook: "For me, the overall feel and design of the book is just as important as the content, as is the style of the photographer and the photography." *Origin* is a notably handsome book: impressively large, with exquisite photographs of dishes such as Wild Weeds and Salted Fish as well as striking pictures of the natural environment that inspires Shewry. The matching of form and content is important to Wignall: "All should work in harmony with the food. Like a chef creating a new dish, everything on the plate should be there to complement each element, not over-shadow."

Chapter Two
Influential Cookbooks

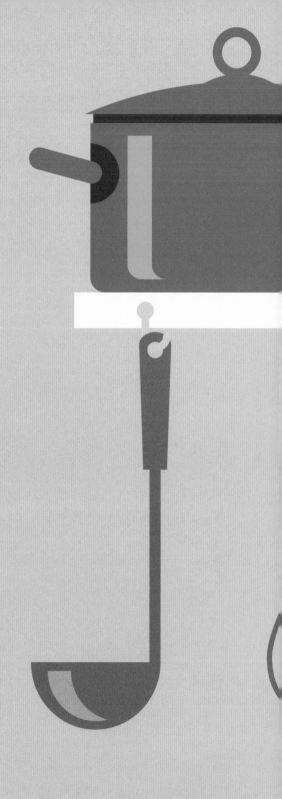

The focus here is on a particular genre within cookbooks: the chef and restaurant cookbook. Works within this section range from classic texts, such as *Le Guide Culinaire* by the great French chef Auguste Escoffier, whose legacy lives on in the brigade system used by restaurants to this day, to contemporary cookbooks, such as Sat Bains's *Too Many Chiefs Only One Indian*, which is presented with imaginative flair. This category of cookbook offers chefs a vital opportunity to create a record for posterity of their otherwise ephemeral work. The importance of chronicling their food, their vision, and their creative process is recognized by chefs themselves, with much thoughtful work going into the creation of heartfelt books such as *Mugaritz* by Andoni Luis Aduriz or Ben Shewry's *Origin*. The generosity with which knowledge is shared is noteworthy—and the value offered by these cookbooks to those interested in chefs and restaurants is immense. The sheer charisma of British chef Marco Pierre White, chronicled while in his prime at London restaurant Harvey's, leaps off the pages of *White Heat*, a book that inspired so many people to become chefs. Danish chef René Redzepi charts the creative process behind his restaurant Noma with candor and generosity in his inspiring cookbook. The last two decades have been exciting times for the world of dining, with the influence of Modernist cuisine, a fascination among chefs in exploring a sense of place deeply and imaginatively, and a move toward a new informality resonating around the globe. It is important that these changes are documented. Reading these books, too, shines a light on the sheer hard graft and dedication that chefs bring to the business of making food and running restaurants.

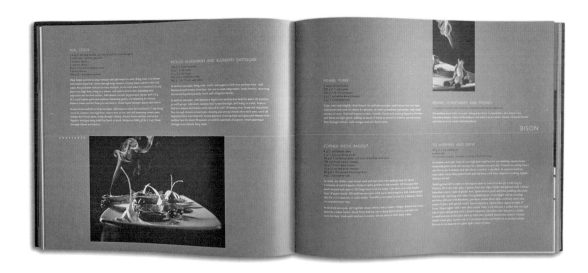

Alinea
Grant Achatz

RESTAURANT
Alinea, Chicago, Illinois, USA, opened 2005

BOOK DETAILS
Published 2008, Ten Speed Press, 396 pages, photography by Lara Kastner

"Following ideas from conception to realization is incredibly satisfying, but devising my own ideas and then watching people interact with them, both in the kitchen and in the dining room, is even more rewarding."
GRANT ACHATZ

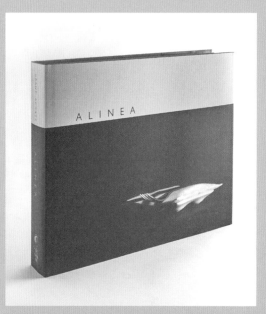

Charismatic and talented, American chef Grant Achatz's unique approach to food is expressed at his Chicago restaurant, Alinea, which he cofounded with businessman Nick Kokonas. In this intimate space, diners are offered a truly innovative and adventurous tasting menu, which challenges any preconceptions and cheerfully defies convention. "Most restaurants seek to help their guests momentarily escape from engagement. We insist on the opposite," explains Kokonas. Achatz's cooking is often categorized as molecular gastronomy, a phrase that conveys his fascination with scientific techniques and his willingness to plunder the "postmodern pantry." The intensity and focus that Achatz brings to creating his menu also characterizes the dishes themselves— each is memorable and vividly experienced.

Those interested in learning more about how Grant Achatz approaches food and cooking will be rewarded by reading *Alinea* the book. This is a substantial and serious-minded work, intended to illuminate the creative processes that have made the restaurant Alinea a phenomenon. A series of well-written essays by luminaries, including food critic Jeffrey Steingarten, help the reader gain a sense of context for both Achatz and his remarkable restaurant. Achatz himself writes coherently, and at length, on how he and his team conceptualize dishes, outlining approaches such as Reversal, Profile Replication, Form Mimicking, Texture Manipulation, Ingredient Expression, Bouncing Flavors, and Global Awareness.

He brings an intellectual rigor to the craft of creating food, as well as a relish for being playful and surprising. Scientific methods are used to transform the culinary experience of a familiar ingredient, which constantly amazes and intrigues diners. The tersely named recipes themselves—Oyster, Ginger, Steelhead Roe, Beer; or Yolk Drops, Asparagus, Meyer Lemon, Black Pepper—belie the amount of complex work that goes into creating the food. As Nick Kokonas writes, "Grant is fond of saying that manipulation is not a bad word at Alinea."

Grant Achatz ignites the oak leaves that feature in his pheasant breast dish.

A Day at elBulli: An Insight into the Ideas, Methods and Creativity of Ferran Adrià
Ferran Adrià, Juli Soler, and Albert Adrià

RESTAURANT
elBulli, Roses, Spain, 1984–2011

BOOK DETAILS
Published 2008, Phaidon, 538 pages, photography by Maribel Ruiz de Erenchum

> *"To eat here is to engage in an experience that is both intensely communal and solitary and subjective. . . . Tonight's dinner involves all the senses, it engages the mind, and is also, at times, a strangely emotional experience."*
>
> ADRIAN SEARLE, THE *GUARDIAN*

The story of how a small, Spanish restaurant in a remote location by the sea became "the most famous restaurant in the world" is remarkable. Under the creative genius of Ferran Adrià, elBulli—where Adrià began working as a chef in 1984—was transformed into a remarkable restaurant that galvanized and stimulated the world of haute cuisine. Inspired by Jacques Maximin's statement at a conference in 1987, "creativity is not copying," Adrià set out on a journey of culinary exploration focused on originality.

As his vision of elBulli developed, the restaurant closed for six months each year while Adrià and his team created one hundred new dishes in his Barcelona "workshop" using innovative, imaginative techniques that pushed boundaries. Such was elBulli's fame at its peak that it received two million reservation requests every year for just 8,000 places. Charismatic, intellectual, and always looking for new challenges, Adrià closed the restaurant in 2011, announcing that he would set up the elBulli Foundation.

Through the simple device of following a day's service at elBulli, this cookbook offers an intimate insight into Adrià's work. Illustrated with more than 1,000 photographs, the book opens with a serene 6:05 A.M. image of the sea at Cap de Creus, the restaurant's idyllic location and a source of inspiration to the team. A thoughtful Ferran Adrià arrives at his workshop at 10 A.M. The extraordinary amount of meticulous, detailed, skillful work that went into producing the tasting menus at elBulli is depicted: the reader is shown how the team created hibiscus paper, painstakingly measured pineapple batons, created salt hemispheres, and made salt spaghettini. The down-to-earth side of life at this legendary restaurant is also shown—the trip to the local shop to buy kombu (seaweed); deliveries from local producers; staff sitting down for "the family meal." This book offers the closest "taste" of that remarkable establishment one can now have. It is an absorbing, inspiring, and stimulating portrait of a truly fascinating and creative chef.

A talk by chef Jacques Maximin in 1987 inspired Ferran Adrià to create the unique elBulli experience.

The elBulli garden

Nature's textures

Ferran arrives at the secret workshop

Árbol de fruta de la pasión
(Passion fruit tree)

The search for new ideas: preparations, styles and characteristics

Map of elBulli's cuisine

AMONG
THE FERNS,
WEEDS
AND BABY
CARROTS...

AN ODE TO
UNCERTAINTY

SHARING

THIS IS A RECIPE BOOK

Mugaritz: A Natural Science of Cooking
Andoni Luis Aduriz

RESTAURANT

Mugaritz, San Sebastián, Spain, opened 1998

BOOK DETAILS

Published 2012, Phaidon, 254 pages, photography by Jose Luis Lopez de Zubiria and Per-Anders Jorgensen

"Few professional chefs have changed the course of culinary history. Andoni is one of them."

FERRAN ADRIÀ

Notoriously hard to find, hidden away in a remote location in the hills outside San Sebastián, Mugaritz restaurant's fame is such that it attracts gastronomic pilgrims from around the world. While the scenery is beautiful, the magnetic pull is the chance to experience the creative wizardry of Basque chef Andoni Luis Aduriz. As a young chef, Aduriz spent two years working for Ferran Adrià (see p.156) at elBulli, witnessing Adrià's obsession with finding perfection, an experience that left "an indelible mark" on him. Having decided to set up his own establishment, Aduriz converted a derelict dairy in the countryside. The name Mugaritz refers to a tree, the border oak, which is part of the landscape there with deep roots, and it is a name that captures Aduriz's approach to his cuisine.

Written with a thoughtful, philosophical intelligence, *Mugaritz: A Natural Science of Cooking* is a large, handsome volume, which offers a genuine insight into Aduriz's journey from a young chef, hungry for knowledge, to his present position at the cutting edge of restaurant cuisine. Aduriz writes with humor of how he, a city dweller, slowly began to engage with his rural surroundings and realize that by venturing out into the landscape that the "grass backdrop" was, in fact, "a field of herbs." He decided to use the "overlooked" seasonal produce in his restaurant, creating dishes that included ingredients such as pumpkin, sheep's milk curd, fern, and hay, with the hay acting as "a powerful, evocative spice." He shares the process of how his own philosophy of food emerged, how he developed his dishes, and how his menu evolved. Here, too, are the intricate, complex recipes for his poetically named creations, including his famous Edible Stones, Shhhhhh … Cat got your Tongue, and Evoking a Spring Morning, together with photographs of these beautiful, intriguing dishes. Aduriz writes of the emotional power of food and of the way he uses the element of "unpredictability" to engage his guests. Reading this cookbook, one appreciates that eating a tasting menu at Mugaritz promises to be a joyful, enchanting, and thrilling experience, and one that is well worth the long journey.

Spanish chef Andoni Luis Aduriz is noted for his striking cuisine, at once intellectual and gloriously playful.

Thirty Years at Ballymaloe: A Celebration of the World-Renowned Cookery School with Over 100 New Recipes
Darina Allen

RESTAURANT

Ballymaloe Cookery School, Cork, Ireland, opened 1983

BOOK DETAILS

Published 2013, Kyle Books, 304 pages, photography by Laura Edwards

"Ballymaloe's great and powerful message is not just about bringing back an appreciation of food and taste, but an understanding of the culture of food, and of Ireland: a culture of stewardship of the land, tradition, hospitality, and, above all, beauty."

ALICE WATERS

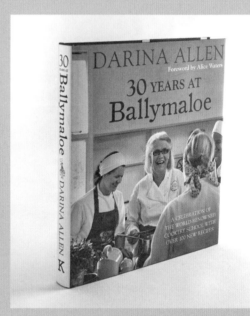

As a young sous chef, Darina Allen fell first in love with Myrtle Allen's Ballymaloe House, and then with Myrtle's son, Tim, whom she married in 1970. Encouraged by her mother-in-law, Darina set up the Ballymaloe Cookery School in 1983 with her brother, Rory O'Connell. Despite its remote location in County Cork, Ireland, the school, situated on a 100-acre (40-ha) organic farm, garnered an international reputation and many of its pupils went on to work in the food world. Darina Allen herself has been a notable exponent of farm-to-fork eating and a champion of Irish artisan food producers. She set up Ireland's farmers' market movement, promoted the Slow Food movement, and is an experienced TV broadcaster.

The cookbook is a celebratory record of Ballymaloe's first three decades, tracing the origins of the school and its evolution. A fascinating array of prominent figures have taught at the school, including Jane Grigson (see p.74, 102, 106, 308, 329), Marcella Hazan (see p.72, 134, 148), Rose Gray, and Ruth Rogers (see p.134, 220). Reading *Thirty Years at Ballymaloe* offers an insight into the way the food culture in Ireland and the United Kingdom has changed. Concerns over issues such as BSE, foot-and-mouth disease, and the horsemeat scandal prompted Allen to seek out artisan producers and take up organic farming. The simple, appetizing recipes here reflect both Allen's interest in local ingredients and her fascination with foods from around the world, with trips abroad treated as research opportunities. The recipes are studded with practical nuggets of information; one can see that these are written by a cookery teacher. Her recipe for Ballycotton Prawns reads: "Bring the water to the boil and add the salt (it may sound a lot, but this is the secret of real flavor when cooking prawns or shrimps)." Her tone of voice is always supportive and encouraging. The strength of her personality—lively, hospitable, intelligent, fired by convictions—leaps off the pages.

Darina Allen of Ballymaloe, a renowned cookery teacher and food campaigner.

Heirloom Tomato Salad with Wasabi Mascarpone

Cooking with Spices

MODESTO GOES TO MARKET
MODESTO BATISTA
CHIEF STEWARD • SINCE 1994

MARINATED ARCTIC CHAR AND CUCUMBER BROTH

SERVES 4

MARINADE

½ cup extra-virgin olive oil, plus more for seasoning

2 tablespoons store dashi

2 tablespoons fresh lemon juice, plus more for seasoning

1 tablespoon white balsamic vinegar

½ garlic clove, thinly sliced

Salt and pepper

4 baby turnips, peeled and quartered

5 radishes, 4 quartered, 1 sliced paper-thin

1 cup diced cucumbers, plus 2 tablespoons minced cucumber and a 1-inch piece of cucumber, sliced paper-thin

1 large shallot, minced

One ½-pound skinless Arctic char fillet, cut into dice slightly larger than the cucumbers

A few dill fronds

ARCTIC CHAR WITH GREEN CABBAGE, CAULIFLOWER, AND AMERICAN CAVIAR

SERVES 4

½ head cauliflower

6 tablespoons olive oil

½ cup minced onion

¼ cup thinly sliced leek (white and pale green parts, halved lengthwise)

1 shallot, minced

1 garlic clove, minced

1 cup Vegetable Broth or water

1 cup whole milk, or more

Salt and pepper

4 cups very thinly sliced savoy cabbage

1 tablespoon unsalted butter

2 teaspoons white balsamic vinegar, or more if needed

Fresh lemon juice

Four 6-ounce skinless Arctic char fillets

1 heaping tablespoon American paddlefish caviar

1 tablespoon finely chopped chives

The Gramercy Tavern Cookbook
Michael Anthony

RESTAURANT
Gramercy Tavern, New York City, New York, USA, opened 1994

BOOK DETAILS
Published 2013, Clarkson Potter, 352 pages, photography by Maura McEvoy

"To me, there was a visceral link between the taverns in Greece or Italy and taverns dating back to colonial America, they were always the best places to gather and eat in any town. And that's what Gramercy Tavern was meant to be."

DANNY MEYER

Now an iconic New York gastronomic institution, Gramercy Tavern is a much-loved restaurant created by visionary restaurateur Danny Meyer that has showcased the talents of American chef Michael Anthony since 2006. During his career as a chef, Anthony has worked in both Japan and France, including time at both L'Arpège and Astrance in Paris, experiences that helped form his respect for natural ingredients. Having returned to the United States, he was the opening executive chef at Blue Hill, Stone Barns in New York, with its farm-to-fork approach to dining, before moving to Gramercy Tavern. His cooking draws on French techniques but is distinctly American, using impeccable, carefully sourced local ingredients to create accomplished and inviting food that has ensured him a loyal following among diners.

This handsomely presented book includes a history of Gramercy Tavern by Danny Meyers, which offers an interesting insight into the roller coaster challenges of creating a restaurant. Gramercy Tavern, he explains, was conceived as "the love child" of Taillevent in Paris and Union Square Cafe in New York, with the word "tavern" carefully chosen. The cookbook, Michael Anthony explains, sets out to convey the spirit of Gramercy Tavern and "the warm welcome" it offers.

Anthony's cooking is noted for its use of natural produce and the book is structured seasonally. Here are signature recipes for popular dishes, such as Baked Clams, and Striped Bass with Summer Squash and Pepper Sauce. The tone of the book is encouraging and helpful to the home cook: "Yes, the book will look great on your coffee table, but I want you to take it into the kitchen and use it well," writes Anthony.

In addition to the carefully written methods, generously abundant notes on how the dishes were originated—and essays on subjects such as pickles, the influence of Japanese cuisine, and how dishes are named—reveal Anthony's creative process in an in-depth and informative way.

Michael Anthony, whose refined cooking at Gramercy Tavern is noted for its use of seasonal, locally produced ingredients.

Arzak Secrets
Juan Mari Arzak

RESTAURANT
Arzak, San Sebastián, Spain, opened 1890s

BOOK DETAILS
Published 2015, Grub Street Publishing Ltd, 278 pages

"What we eat, how we eat, is in our culture. Our signature cuisine is Basque. Our taste is from here. We were born here. We cook unconsciously with this identity."

ELENA ARZAK

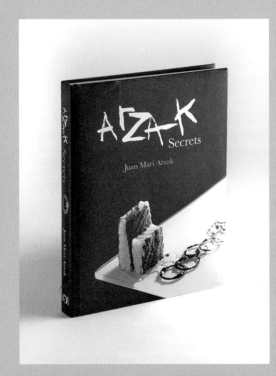

A major, trailblazing figure in the creation of the New Basque Cuisine movement, Spanish chef Juan Mari Arzak began working in 1966 at his family restaurant in San Sebastián, a much-loved local institution. Inspired by Paul Bocuse (see p.108, 182), the 1970s saw him begin exploring new ways of expressing Basque cuisine. Arzak's willingness to push boundaries saw him pioneering a hugely influential scientific approach to cooking, and he was among the first chefs to set up a "laboratory" exploring textures and flavors. Today the restaurant Arzak, where he works in partnership with his daughter, the chef Elena Arzak, is known around the world for its innovative avant-garde cuisine, which retains its deeply rooted sense of Basque identity and is presented with hospitable warmth.

In his lucid, elegantly written prologue to this cookbook, Juan Mari Arzak outlines his approach to his cuisine, emphasizing the "team" and "teamwork" that lie behind the creative and practical development of the recipes, which have made the restaurant Arzak internationally famous. Research, he writes, is "an important factor in the development of all enterprises and, of course, the most creative." Arzak's own culinary curiosity—his fascination with learning about food, with exploring and discovering—is manifest in this cookbook, with its thoughtful, intelligent words on subjects from "The Flavour of Porcelain" and "The Subversion of Colour" to "The Gelatine Revival" and "Consensual Deception." With these, Arzak generously shares his thoughts on food, science, art, and culture, which make this cookbook a rich and fascinating read.

The strikingly presented, technically sophisticated recipes here illustrate the wit and imagination that Arzak and his team are known for. The titles of the recipes themselves intrigue and fascinate: The Disappearance; Pumice Stone; Mimetic Sole; Necklace For a Mandarin. The book's title itself is a tease—"the secrets" mentioned in this book are nothing but "the wide open doors of our kitchen" he writes—with the book offering an insight into the world of Arzak.

Juan Mari Arzak, a pioneering figure of the groundbreaking New Basque Cuisine.

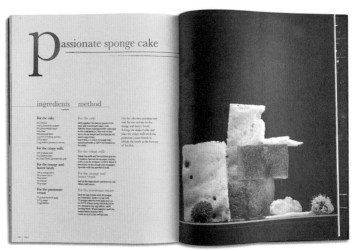

Beef tongue with parsley purée

Lamb thymus with artichoke

River fish

Tapioca

D.O.M. Rediscovering Brazilian Ingredients
Alex Atala

RESTAURANT

D.O.M., São Paulo, Brazil, opened 1999

BOOK DETAILS

Published 2013, Phaidon, 292 pages, photography by Sergio Coimbra and Edu Simões

"To walk in the rain forest, to explore unknown, undervalued flavors, are things that I have done forever."

ALEX ATALA

A tall man, with his body decorated with tattoos, chef Alex Atala is a striking figure. His impact, however, goes far beyond his appearance. This charismatic chef has brought Brazilian gastronomy to world attention through his much-lauded restaurant, D.O.M., in São Paulo. Here, the menu offers truly rare ingredients—Amazonian foodstuffs barely known in Brazil, let alone in other parts of the world—that have been hunted out and sourced by Atala, and then transformed with humor and panache into elegant dishes, such as Heart of Palm Fettuccine Carbonara or Ants and Pineapples. Atala's mission to breathe new life into Brazilian cuisine by combining traditionally humble ingredients with classic cooking techniques has seen him attract much interest and acclaim.

This handsome cookbook tells the story of Atala's personal journey, from his early days on the streets of Brazil, involved in a world of drugs and violence, to becoming a passionate young chef. At the age of nineteen, he began working in Belgium, followed by France and Italy. In 1994, he returned to Brazil to open a restaurant, and realized that he wanted to offer truly Brazilian cuisine. Brazil is his inspiration: "its wild flavors have been part of my life since childhood," he says.

Atala embarked on expeditions into the Amazon rain forest, meeting indigenous people, learning from them about the ingredients they used, and researching the history of ancient South American culinary techniques. The recipes in *D.O.M. Rediscovering Brazilian Ingredients* are full of unfamiliar foodstuffs: *saúva* ants, which are used by the Tucano people as a seasoning; Amazonian river fish, such as *pirarucu*; Brazilian sea snails; fruit such as *bacuri* and *pequi*; and the herb *jambu*.

Writing at once passionately and intelligently, Atala also makes clear his environmental concerns—the important need to respect the lives of the indigenous people, the forests, the rivers, and to sustain the natural world from where these riches come. He hopes that by spreading knowledge of these wild foods, their value will increase, and the rain forest will be perceived as a more useful resource while it is living than when felled for timber.

With his exciting, accomplished cooking showcasing Amazonian ingredients, chef Alex Atala has revitalized Brazilian cuisine.

Social Suppers
Jason Atherton

RESTAURANT

Pollen Street Social, London, UK, opened 2011

BOOK DETAILS

Published 2014, Absolute Press, 240 pages, photography by John Carey

"Jason is one of the greats. He's the best of both worlds. He has the prowess of a Michelin-starred chef with accolades from every corner of the globe, but he is also the person you want to be preparing your Sunday supper."

THOMAS KELLER

Jason Atherton came to public attention as executive head chef of Gordon Ramsay's Maze restaurant in London, delighting diners with witty dishes like his famous deconstructed BLT—pork belly, brioche, lettuce, and tomato. With Pollen Street Social, his first UK solo venture as chef-owner, he breathed new life into fine dining, showing that a Mayfair restaurant could offer a more informal approach, as well as wonderful food and wine and excellent service. Noted for his perfectionism, his cooking has acquired a loyal clientele. Following Pollen Street Social's success, he now has a string of successful restaurants around the world, in cities including New York, Shanghai, and Singapore—a tribute to his organizational and management skills as well as his culinary prowess.

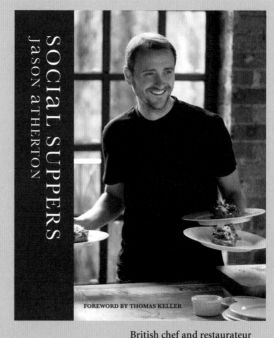

British chef and restaurateur Jason Atherton has drawn an international following for his elegant, flavorsome cooking.

Despite his achievements, the introduction to Atherton's cookbook is modest and unaffected. Rather than sharing his life story, he focuses on his approach to food: "It might sound obvious, but the recipes in this book are all about flavours," he says. He then goes on to advocate "adding your own flair," using these recipes as a starting point.

A characteristic of Atherton's cuisine is that not only is it technically accomplished and sophisticated, it is food that you want to eat. The recipes in *Social Suppers* are often inspired by classic dishes and well-known flavors: Mrs. Tee's Wild Mushrooms on Toast with Bacon Jam; Potato and Parsley Soup with Black Pudding and Cheddar Toasties; or Spiced Melon Soup with Ginger Sorbet and Basil. His characteristically elegant, visually appealing dishes are put together with a fine eye for detail; for example, in the dish Cornish Cod with Braised Lentils and Lardo di Colonnata, the lardo is sliced thinly and placed on the just-fried fish so that it melts over it.

A formidably talented chef, Atherton has written a notably accessible book aimed at the home cook. He says, "I would love this book to inspire you to cook and I hope that you can use the joy of food and wine to bring your nearest and dearest back around the table to experience love, joy and laughter together."

MAIN COURSES

SQUID AND PRAWN BURGER WITH SMOKED TOMATO CHUTNEY

SERVES 2

For the smoked tomato chutney

PORK SHANKS WITH HARICOT BEANS

SERVES 4

For the haricot beans

Too Many Chiefs Only One Indian
Sat Bains

RESTAURANT

Restaurant Sat Bains, Nottingham, UK, opened 2002

BOOK DETAILS

Published 2012, Face Publications, 448 pages, photography by John Arandhara-Blackwell

"One of the most memorable meals I've ever had was at his restaurant, and I reckon he's one of the best chefs this country has produced."

HESTON BLUMENTHAL

Charismatic chef Satwant Singh Bains, known simply as Sat Bains, is an inspiring figure in Britain's dining scene. His road to success involved much effort, hard work, and self-belief, and his wife Amanda, who oversees the staff at his restaurant, has been a supportive presence in his life and work. Winning the Roux Scholarship as a young chef was a formative experience and enabled him to work in France. In 2002, he opened Restaurant Sat Bains, famously situated in unlikely urban surroundings on the outskirts of Nottingham. Here he made his name with his tasting menus, offering intriguing and original culinary creations put together with masterful skill, reflecting an adventurous mind, and engendering a rapt response from critics and diners alike.

British chef Sat Bains, who is noted for his imaginative and characterful cuisine.

Sat Bains's food is unexpected and engaging. So, too, is his autobiographical cookbook, *Too Many Chiefs Only One Indian*. A strikingly handsome, huge, impressive tome, it is also funny and irreverent. An engaging narrative, woven through with numerous photographs, this book traces Sat's life, from his early days as a young boy who started cooking when he was sixteen years old to his happiness at receiving two Michelin stars for his eponymous restaurant in the city of Nottingham.

Among the gems hidden in these pages are a collection of humorous emails from prolific chefs, such as Alex Atala of D.O.M. in Brazil (see p.166), René Redzepi of Noma in Denmark (see p.278), and Jason Atherton of Pollen Street Social in England (see p.18, 168), in response to Sat's request for "lines/quotes/stories" about what gets them up in the morning.

Sat's own culinary philosophy is clearly expressed: "The way I work to create new ideas or new dishes is never about reinventing, or inventing anything new: it's always about reintroducing." The recipes for tersely named dishes, such as his signature Ham/Egg/Peas or Scallop/Smoked/Charred, reveal the level of technical skill with which Bains combines ingredients, while short but eloquent notes explain the thinking behind the dishes. Richly inventive, both in its presentation and content, this is a deeply personal cookbook from a remarkable chef.

Astrance: Livre de Cuisine
Pascal Barbot, Christophe Rohat, Chihiro Masui

RESTAURANT
Astrance, Paris, France, opened 2000

BOOK DETAILS
Published 2012, Éditions du Chêne, 352 pages, photography by Richard Haughton; published in English as *Astrance: A Cook's Book*, 2013

"We are not a typical Three Star [. . .] we don't have fancy cutlery or décor or even a menu. We are more like a small bistro than a grand restaurant."
PASCAL BARBOT

A partnership between the imaginative culinary talents of French chef Pascal Barbot and the hospitable charm of maître d'hôtel Christophe Rohat, who met while working at L'Arpège, lies at the heart of Astrance, their Paris restaurant. This intimate establishment has garnered much acclaim since it opened in 2000, and is known for its groundbreaking role in redefining French fine dining. Famously, rather than being offered a conventional menu, diners at Astrance are asked simply how many plates they would like and the kitchen then sends out a series of "surprise" dishes. These are innovative, elegantly presented creations in which Barbot demonstrates his fresh approach to cuisine and his ability to produce food that intrigues and enthralls.

Just as Astrance the restaurant delights and surprises, *Astrance: A Cook's Book* does the same. Written with culinary author Chihiro Masui, it opens with a description of her first visit to Astrance and her surprise and fascination with the food she was served. Masui's elegantly expressed appreciation of Barbot's cooking and Rohat's skill at managing the restaurant informs the book. Detailed descriptions of her encounters with the dishes offer an insight into Barbot's inventive way with food and the effect of his creations on the appreciative diner. Masui's "understanding of taste" grows with each visit to Astrance.

Rather than being presented as a catalog of recipes, the dishes in this book are accompanied by a list of their elements and a fascinating essay by Barbot on how he created them. For example, we learn that for his signature dish, Foie Gras with Button Mushroom and Roasted Lemon, Barbot asked himself, "What can I do with foie gras?" before exploring flavors, textures, and temperatures on his quest to find out.

Throughout the text, the reader glimpses the way that Barbot's mind works: his use of different cooking techniques, from heating to marinating to crystallizing; and his profound understanding of ingredients, from his beloved citrus fruits to the seaweed kombu. In contrast to the in-depth essays about the efforts behind each dish, the photographs are beguiling, playful, colorful, and inviting.

At his intimate Paris restaurant, Pascal Barbot surprises and delights with his creative approach to cooking and dining.

FOIE GRAS
CHAMPIGNON DE PARIS
CITRON RÔTI

LIÈVRE
COING
ÉCHALOTE GRISE

SAINT-JACQUES
KOMBU
HUÎTRE

ROGNON
RIS DE VEAU
MORILLE

BŒUF
CAPUCINE
HUÎTRE

Artichokes Braised in Olive Oil

Eggs Cooked in a Bain-Marie

Boning and Trimming the Leg

Removing the Tailbone, Pelvic Bone, and Aitchbone

Bitter Orange Cake with Compote of Blood Oranges

Compote of Blood Oranges

Weight

Cooking Backward
The Place of Dessert in a Menu

Introduction
Dessert First
A Menu of Roasted Courses
Associating Flavors
Weight
Texture
Color
Singular Flavors
Rich and Lean
Salty, Bitter, Sour, Sweet
Spring Is Here
Intensity
Autumn
The Shape of a Menu
Summer Peaches
Refreshment

Cooking by Hand
Paul Bertolli

RESTAURANT

Oliveto, Oakland, California, USA, 1995–2005 (Bertolli was chef-owner)

BOOK DETAILS

Published 2003, Random House Inc., 270 pages, photography by Gail Skoff and Judy Dater

"A rich memory for tastes and scents, whether gathered casually or cultivated consciously, lends emotional resonance to cooking."

PAUL BERTOLLI

A deep-rooted obsession with how food is made characterizes the career of Paul Bertolli. Born in California and of Italian heritage, he made his name with a tenure as chef at Alice Waters's restaurant Chez Panisse in California (see p.46, 294, 335). Following that, he set up Oliveto, offering the Italian food he loves. Increasingly fascinated by the process of making charcuteries, he moved on from working in restaurants and founded Fra' Mani Handcrafted Foods in 2006. Here, in his role as curemaster, he creates a range of award-winning cured meats using traditional methods. His fascination with preserving Italy's rich charcuterie heritage and keeping culinary traditions alive has seen him conduct extensive research into the subject and become hugely knowledgeable in the process.

That obsessive quest for knowledge is apparent in Bertolli's thoughtful book, *Cooking by Hand*, which was written a few years before he left Olive to follow his passion for charcuteries. The book opens with him asking, "What must be done in order to cook seriously well?" It then proceeds to explore the time and trouble that goes into truly understanding ingredients and using them to best effect. While the book contains an array of carefully worded, detailed recipes for dishes—such as Southern-Style Ragu, Spinach or Nettle Pasta, Fig and Balsamico Ice Cream with Saba, and Spiced Tomato Pudding—it is the long, informative essays that make it distinctive. Bertolli writes on a variety of culinary subjects: the venerable tradition of creating balsamic vinegar, how to make fresh pasta, and the place of dessert in a menu, offering in-depth insights into each topic. As one might expect, given his later career trajectory, one senses his fascination with charcuteries in the section "The Whole Hog," which focuses on sausages and cured meats.

Bertolli's writing is intelligent and reflective as he casts light on methods and techniques. In the chapter, "Cleaning the Fresco," he recounts an analogy that was described to him by a Florentine chef who tried to breathe new life into the tired, old, clichéd stalwarts of Tuscan cuisine, akin to clearing layers of dust off of a traditional artwork.

A fascination with the crafting of food is at the heart of Paul Bertolli's approach to cooking.

Marque: A Culinary Adventure
Mark Best and Pasi Petanen

RESTAURANT

Marque, Sydney, Australia, opened 1999

BOOK DETAILS

Published 2011, Hardie Grant Books, 304 pages, photography by Stuart Scott

"Everything in his restaurant—the décor, ambience, plateware, and even the food itself—is almost a complete reflection of him, which is even rarer than finding a chef with his self-perception intact."

RENÉ REDZEPI

Australian chef Mark Best is known for his imaginative cuisine, with diners at his acclaimed Sydney restaurant, Marque, offered intriguing, technically accomplished, cutting-edge dishes, such as Foie Gras Ice Cream, Beetroot Snow, and Maple Syrup; or Sea Urchin, Mandarin, and Green Tea. Brought up in the small town of Murray Bridge in South Australia, he came to professional cooking late in life, having first worked as an electrician in a gold mine. His journey to culinary acclaim has been a long and hard one. A seminal experience in his career was a meal at Alain Passard's famous L'Arpège restaurant (see p.264) in 1996; a meal so inspiring that he and his wife moved to France so that he could work at L'Arpège.

A sense of that determination comes through in this cookbook, which candidly charts the roller coaster of Best's career. There is also a dry, humorous quality to his writing and he conveys his sense of excitement about great food, restaurants, and chefs.

Despite his down-to-earth tone, the recipes themselves are complex, intricate, beautifully presented affairs, as the photographs illustrate. It is notable that several of the recipes start with the phrase: "Begin this recipe one day in advance"—a sign of the complexity of the processes involved. His knowledge of ingredients is evident, as are his decided views on certain foodstuffs, such as intensively bred wagyu beef, with its "boring" taste "almost of popcorn."

Australia's rich seafood bounty is used to striking effect in dishes such as Jellied Oyster with Honeydew, Avocado, Jellied Samphire and Watercress, and Cucumber Soda; or Prawn Cracker with Freshly Salted Mullet Roe. He pays an affectionate homage to the chefs who have inspired him, with Chaud-Froid Free-Range Egg and Grissini served at Marque as a tribute to Alain Passard, who invented it.

Best's sense of fun also appears in his dishes, for example, the surprising Potato and Parmesan Marshmallows have an intense tomato flavor, despite being white. "As an Australian," writes Best, tongue-in-cheek, "I also appreciated its resemblance to our national cake: the Lamington."

Australian chef Mark Best brings a commitment to quality to the table.

MARK BEST – A POTTED HISTORY

CHAUD-FROID FREE-RANGE EGG AND GRISSINI

SOUTHERN ROCK LOBSTER WITH SALTED BUTTER, WAKAME, CARAMELISED YOGHURT, CURRY LEAVES AND KOMBU

ROQUEFORT WITH BEETROOT, GUAVA AND RASPBERRIES

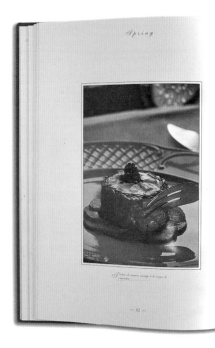

MOUSSETTE DE SAUMON FUME

Smoked salmon mousse

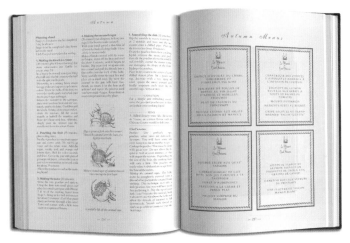

Recipes From Le Manoir aux Quat'Saisons
Raymond Blanc

RESTAURANT

Le Manoir aux Quat'Saisons, Great Milton, UK, opened 1984

BOOK DETAILS

Published 1988, Macdonald Orbis, 280 pages, photography and illustrations by Macdonald Orbis

"Raymond Blanc is an instinctive chef, perhaps the best such chef in England today."

HUGH JOHNSON

A rural childhood in Besançon, France, with mornings spent searching for wild mushrooms, afternoons fishing for trout, and nights hunting for frogs, gave the young Raymond Blanc a profound awareness of the seasons that was to influence his approach to cooking. Having decided as a young man that he wanted to cook professionally, he struggled to progress in the strict, hierarchical world of French restaurants. Coming to England in the 1970s gave Blanc the opportunity to work as a chef and to express his considerable culinary talents. He first opened a restaurant in Oxford, and 1983 saw him fall "in love" with Great Milton Manor in Oxfordshire, which Blanc transformed into his famous restaurant and hotel: Le Manoir aux Quat'Saisons.

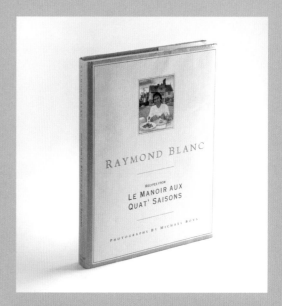

Written with eloquence and wit, this tastefully presented cookbook offers a considerable insight into Blanc's love of food. His voice comes through clearly, from his shock at the low quality of English ingredients—"the poor, tasteless, pellet-fed, hormone-ridden, battery farmed chickens"—to the humorous account of battling his head gardener at Le Manoir, who was determined to grow the largest vegetables possible, rather than the tender, baby ones that Blanc wanted.

Despite being a self-taught chef, Blanc's reverence for and knowledge of the classic techniques of French cuisine are apparent. The book opens with a section of fundamental recipes and methods for essentials, such as stock, beurre blanc, sabayon, and soufflé.

Reflecting Blanc's passion for seasonality, it then moves through a calendar year, featuring intricate recipes appropriate to each season. In spring, "A chef's imagination is fired by the sight of delicate, fresh leaves struggling to burst out," and ingredients such as wild salmon, lamb, and asparagus feature. Summer, when "flavors are triumphant," sees dishes such as Quenelles of Pike from the Windrush, simmered in a freshwater crayfish sauce. Game comes to the fore in fall, when cooking takes on "more powerful and rustic tastes, sauces with a hint of richness and deeper colours and flavours," while winter is a festive season, celebrated with dishes such as Praliné and Armagnac Mousses served with caramel sauce.

An appreciation of seasonality lies at the heart of Raymond Blanc's food.

The Big Fat Duck Cookbook
Heston Blumenthal

The Fat Duck, Bray, UK, opened in 1995

BOOK DETAILS
Published 2009, Bloomsbury Publishing, 532 pages, photography by Dominic Davies, Jose Luis Lopez de Zubiria, Nick Knight, and Ashley Palmer-Watts

"What fun it is to follow in this gastro-wizard's footsteps."
OBSERVER FOOD MONTHLY

The career of British chef Heston Blumenthal (see p.310) reflects his drive and commitment as well as his culinary talent. Following a short stint at Raymaond Blanc's Le Manoir aux Quat'Saisons (see p.178), he did a series of non food-related jobs for eleven years, saving money and teaching himself to cook. In 1995, at the age of twenty-nine, he bought The Bell, an old pub in the village of Bray, refurbished it and reopened it as The Fat Duck. Free at last to express himself without boundaries, he created a gastronomic sensation with his creative, science-driven cuisine. It was awarded its first Michelin star in 1999 and, by 2004, had achieved three. TV series have seen Blumenthal become a household name in the United Kingdom as well as an internationally acclaimed chef.

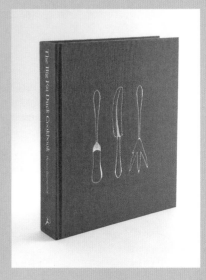

The heavy tome that is *The Big Fat Duck Cookbook* is, in the words of eminent food scientist Harold McGee, "a cookbook like no cookbook I've ever seen"—exuberant, verbose, and obsessive, just to read it requires energy. It is filled with humorous, colorful pictures, in which Blumenthal is depicted as a mad scientist, his massive brain teeming with ideas. The first part of the book intimately charts Blumenthal's personal journey, starting with the sixteen-year-old boy who fell in love with the theater of Michelin-starred dining during a visit with his family to L'Oustau de Baumanière in Provence, France. The second part contains the technically complex recipes for iconic dishes such as Snail Porridge, Sound of the Sea, and Sardine on Toast Sorbet, with Blumenthal charting his creative process for each one with an infectious enthusiasm. The third and final section details the science underlying the recipes, offering insight into Blumenthal's approach. We learn that combinations that may seem bizarre are, in fact, based on chemical similarities. The collaborative aspect of his work sees him including essays by scientists on subjects such as odor or multisensory perception. Blumenthal's appetite for knowledge, insatiable curiosity, and openness to ideas is manifest and impressive. Gloriously geeky and generous with its knowledge, *The Big Fat Duck Cookbook* conveys the extraordinary depth of Heston's genius—readers are given all the information needed to recreate his dishes—all they need is his energy.

Innovative chef Heston Blumenthal, whose restaurant The Fat Duck in Bray, UK, is internationally renowned.

180 INFLUENTIAL COOKBOOKS

APPLE PIE CARAMEL

'Edible Wrapper'

—— 2006 ——

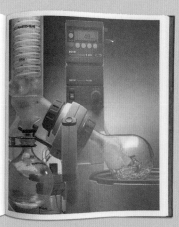

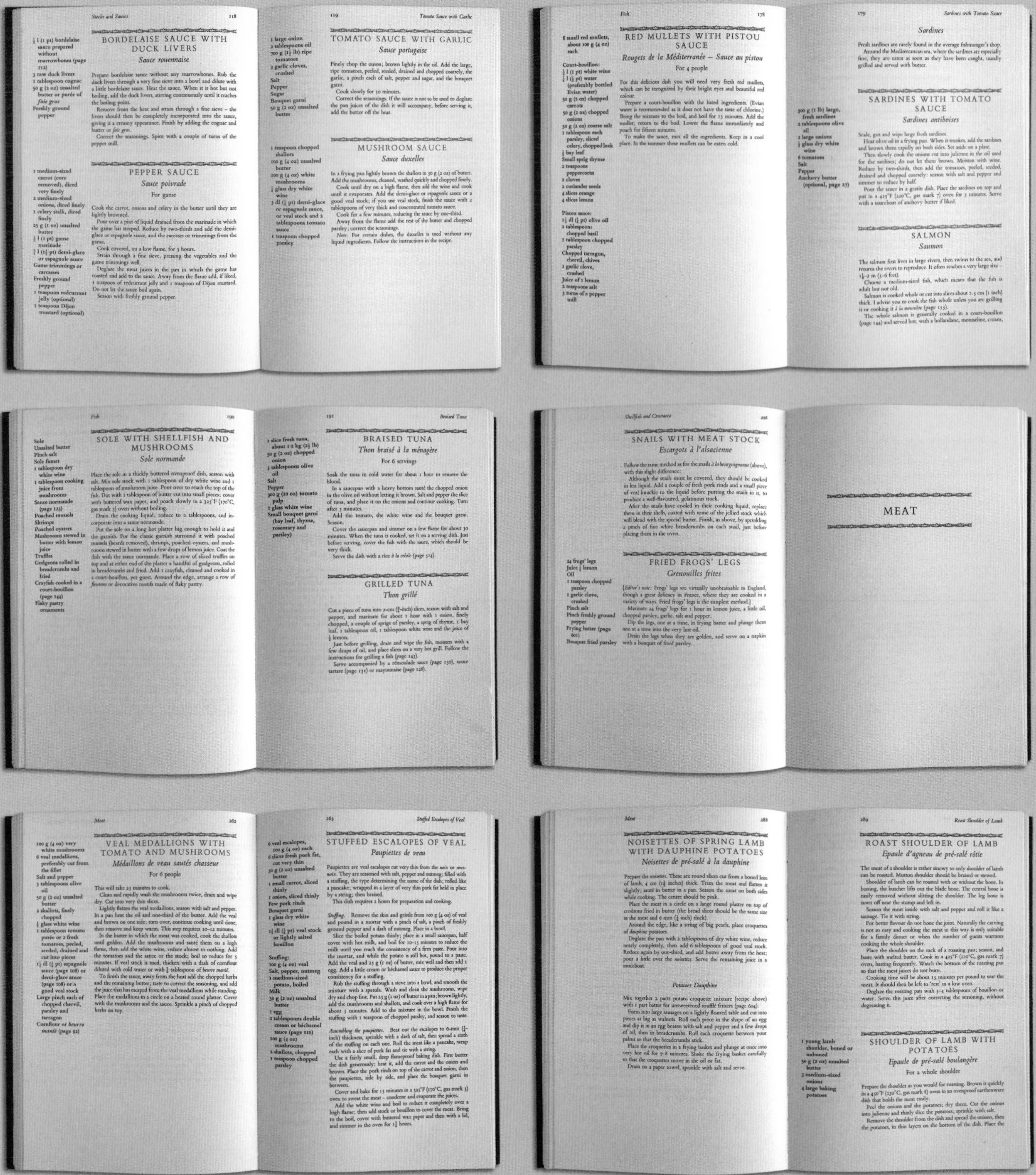

BORDELAISE SAUCE WITH DUCK LIVERS

Sauce rouennaise

- $\frac{1}{2}$ l (1 pt) bordelaise sauce prepared without marrowbones (page 112)
- 3 raw duck livers
- 1 tablespoon cognac
- 50 g (2 oz) unsalted butter or purée of *foie gras*
- Freshly ground pepper

Prepare bordelaise sauce without any marrowbones. Rub the duck livers through a very fine sieve into a bowl and dilute with a little bordelaise sauce. Heat the sauce. When it is hot but not boiling, add the duck livers, stirring continuously until it reaches the boiling point.

Remove from the heat and strain through a fine sieve – the livers should then be completely incorporated into the sauce, giving it a creamy appearance. Finish by adding the cognac and butter or *foie gras*.

Correct the seasonings. Spice with a couple of turns of the pepper mill.

PEPPER SAUCE

Sauce poivrade

For game

- 1 medium-sized carrot (core removed), diced very finely
- 2 medium-sized onions, diced finely
- 1 celery stalk, diced finely
- 25 g (1 oz) unsalted butter
- $\frac{1}{2}$ l (1 pt) game marinade
- $\frac{3}{4}$ l ($1\frac{1}{2}$ pt) demi-glace or espagnole sauce
- Game trimmings or carcasses
- Freshly ground pepper
- 1 teaspoon redcurrant jelly (optional)
- 1 teaspoon Dijon mustard (optional)

Cook the carrot, onions and celery in the butter until they are lightly browned.

Pour over a pint of liquid drained from the marinade in which the game has steeped. Reduce by two-thirds and add the demi-glace or espagnole sauce, and the carcases or trimmings from the game.

Cook covered, on a low flame, for 3 hours.

Strain through a fine sieve, pressing the vegetables and the game trimmings well.

Deglaze the meat juices in the pan in which the game has roasted and add to the sauce. Away from the flame add, if liked, 1 teaspoon of redcurrant jelly and 1 teaspoon of Dijon mustard. Do not let the sauce boil again.

Season with freshly ground pepper.

TOMATO SAUCE WITH GARLIC

Sauce portugaise

- 1 large onion
- 2 tablespoons oil
- 700 g ($1\frac{1}{2}$ lb) ripe tomatoes
- 3 garlic cloves, crushed
- Salt
- Pepper
- Sugar
- Bouquet garni
- 50 g (2 oz) unsalted butter

Finely chop the onion; brown lightly in the oil. Add the large, ripe tomatoes, peeled, seeded, drained and chopped coarsely, the garlic, a pinch each of salt, pepper and sugar, and the bouquet garni.

Cook slowly for 30 minutes.

Correct the seasonings. If the sauce is not to be used to deglaze the pan juices of the dish it will accompany, before serving it, add the butter off the heat.

MUSHROOM SAUCE

Sauce duxelles

- 1 teaspoon chopped shallots
- 100 g (4 oz) unsalted butter
- 100 g (4 oz) white mushrooms
- $\frac{1}{2}$ glass dry white wine
- 3 dl ($\frac{1}{2}$ pt) demi-glace or espagnole sauce, or veal stock and 2 tablespoons tomato sauce
- 1 teaspoon chopped parsley

In a frying pan lightly brown the shallots in 50 g (2 oz) of butter. Add the mushrooms, cleaned, washed quickly and chopped finely.

Cook until dry on a high flame, then add the wine and cook until it evaporates. Add the demi-glace or espagnole sauce or a good veal stock; if you use veal stock, finish the sauce with 2 tablespoons of very thick and concentrated tomato sauce.

Cook for a few minutes, reducing the sauce by one-third.

Away from the flame add the rest of the butter and chopped parsley; correct the seasonings.

Note: For certain dishes, the duxelles is used without any liquid ingredients. Follow the instructions in the recipe.

RED MULLETS WITH PISTOU SAUCE

Rougets de la Méditerranée – Sauce au pistou

For 4 people

- 8 small red mullets, about 100 g (4 oz) each

Court-bouillon:

- $\frac{1}{2}$ l (1 pt) white wine
- $\frac{1}{4}$ l ($\frac{1}{2}$ pt) water (preferably bottled Evian water)
- 50 g (2 oz) chopped carrots
- 50 g (2 oz) chopped onions
- 50 g (2 oz) coarse salt
- 1 tablespoon each parsley, sliced celery, chopped leek
- $\frac{1}{2}$ bay leaf
- Small sprig thyme
- 2 teaspoons peppercorns
- 2 cloves
- 2 coriander seeds
- 4 slices orange
- 4 slices lemon

Pistou sauce:

- $1\frac{1}{2}$ dl ($\frac{1}{4}$ pt) olive oil
- 2 tablespoons chopped basil
- 1 tablespoon chopped parsley
- Chopped tarragon, chervil, chives
- 1 garlic clove, crushed
- Juice of 1 lemon
- 2 teaspoons salt
- 3 turns of a pepper mill

For this delicious dish you will need very fresh red mullets, which can be recognized by their bright eyes and beautiful red colour.

Prepare a court-bouillon with the listed ingredients. (Evian water is recommended as it does not have the taste of chlorine.) Bring the mixture to the boil, and boil for 15 minutes. Add the mullet; return to the boil. Lower the flame immediately and poach for fifteen minutes.

To make the sauce, mix all the ingredients. Keep in a cool place. In the summer these mullets can be eaten cold.

Sardines

Fresh sardines are rarely found in the average fishmonger's shop.

Around the Mediterranean sea, where the sardines are especially fine, they are eaten as soon as they have been caught, usually grilled and served with butter.

SARDINES WITH TOMATO SAUCE

Sardines antiboises

- 500 g (1 lb) large, fresh sardines
- 2 tablespoons olive oil
- 2 large onions
- $\frac{1}{2}$ glass dry white wine
- 6 tomatoes
- Salt
- Pepper
- Anchovy butter (optional, page 27)

Scale, gut and wipe large fresh sardines.

Heat olive oil in a frying pan. When it smokes, add the sardines and brown them rapidly on both sides. Set aside on a plate.

Then slowly cook the onions cut into julienne in the oil used for the sardines; do not let them brown. Moisten with wine. Reduce by two-thirds, then add the tomatoes, peeled, seeded, drained and chopped coarsely: season with salt and pepper and simmer to reduce by half.

Pour the sauce in a gratin dish. Place the sardines on top and put in a 425°F (220°C, gas mark 7) oven for 5 minutes. Serve with a sauceboat of anchovy butter if liked.

SALMON

Saumon

The salmon first lives in large rivers, then swims to the sea, and returns the rivers to reproduce. It often reaches a very large size – $1\frac{1}{2}$–2 m (5–6 feet).

Choose a medium-sized fish, which means that the fish is adult but not old.

Salmon is cooked whole or cut into slices about 2.5 cm (1 inch) thick. I advise you to cook the fish whole unless you are grilling it or cooking it *à la meunière* (page 155).

The whole salmon is generally cooked in a court-bouillon (page 144) and served hot, with a hollandaise, mousseline, cream,

SOLE WITH SHELLFISH AND MUSHROOMS

Sole normande

- Sole
- Unsalted butter
- Pinch salt
- Sole fumet
- 1 tablespoon dry white wine
- 1 tablespoon cooking juice from mushrooms
- Sauce normande (page 123)
- Poached mussels
- Shrimps
- Poached oysters
- Mushrooms stewed in butter with lemon juice
- Truffles
- Gudgeons rolled in breadcrumbs and fried
- Crayfish cooked in a court-bouillon (page 144)
- Flaky pastry ornaments

Place the sole in a thickly buttered ovenproof dish, season with salt. Mix sole stock with 1 tablespoon of dry white wine and 1 tablespoon of mushroom juice. Pour over to reach the top of the fish. Dot with 1 tablespoon of butter cut into small pieces; cover with buttered wax paper, and poach slowly in a 325°F (170°C, gas mark 3) oven without boiling.

Drain the cooking liquid; reduce to 2 tablespoons, and incorporate into a sauce normande.

Put the sole on a long hot platter big enough to hold it and the garnish. For the classic garnish surround it with poached mussels (beards removed), shrimps, poached oysters, and mushrooms stewed in butter with a few drops of lemon juice. Coat the dish with the sauce normande. Place a row of sliced truffles on top and at either end of the platter a handful of gudgeons, rolled in breadcrumbs and fried. Add 1 crayfish, cleaned and cooked in a court-bouillon, per guest. Around the edge, arrange a row of *fleurons* or decorative motifs made of flaky pastry.

BRAISED TUNA

Thon braisé à la ménagère

For 6 servings

- 1 slice fresh tuna, about 1·2 kg ($2\frac{1}{2}$ lb)
- 50 g (2 oz) chopped onion
- 3 tablespoons olive oil
- Salt
- Pepper
- 300 g (10 oz) tomato pulp
- 1 glass white wine
- Small bouquet garni (bay leaf, thyme, rosemary and parsley)

Soak the tuna in cold water for about 1 hour to remove the blood.

In a saucepan with a heavy bottom sauté the chopped onion in the olive oil without letting it brown. Salt and pepper the slice of tuna, and place it on the onions and continue cooking. Turn after 5 minutes.

Add the tomato, the white wine and the bouquet garni. Season.

Cover the saucepan and simmer on a low flame for about 30 minutes. When the tuna is cooked, set it on a serving dish. Just before serving, cover the fish with the sauce, which should be very thick.

Serve the dish with a rice *à la créole* (page 514).

GRILLED TUNA

Thon grillé

Cut a piece of tuna into 2-cm ($\frac{3}{4}$-inch) slices, season with salt and pepper, and marinate for about 1 hour with 1 onion, finely chopped, a couple of sprigs of parsley, a sprig of thyme, 1 bay leaf, 1 tablespoon oil, 1 tablespoon white wine and the juice of $\frac{1}{2}$ lemon.

Just before grilling, drain and wipe the fish, moisten with a few drops of oil, and place slices on a very hot grill. Follow the instructions for grilling a fish (page 143).

Serve accompanied by a rémoulade sauce (page 130), sauce tartare (page 131) or mayonnaise (page 128).

SNAILS WITH MEAT STOCK

Escargots à l'alsacienne

Follow the same method as for the snails *à la bourguignonne* (above), with this slight difference:

Although the snails must be covered, they should be cooked in less liquid. Add a couple of fresh pork rinds and a small piece of veal knuckle to the liquid before putting the snails in it, to produce a well-flavoured, gelatinous stock.

After the snails have cooled in their cooking liquid, replace them in their shells, coated with some of the jellied stock which will blend with the special butter. Finish, as above, by sprinkling a pinch of fine white breadcrumbs on each snail, just before placing them in the oven.

FRIED FROGS' LEGS

Grenouilles frites

- 24 frogs' legs
- Juice $\frac{1}{2}$ lemon
- Oil
- 1 teaspoon chopped parsley
- 1 garlic clove, crushed
- Pinch salt
- Pinch freshly ground pepper
- Frying batter (page 601)
- Bouquet fried parsley

[*Editor's note*: Frogs' legs are virtually unobtainable in England, though a great delicacy in France, where they are cooked in a variety of ways. Fried frogs' legs is the simplest method.]

Marinate 24 frogs' legs for 1 hour in lemon juice, a little oil, chopped parsley, garlic, salt and pepper.

Dip the legs, one at a time, in frying batter and plunge them one at a time into the very hot oil.

Drain the legs when they are golden, and serve on a napkin with a bouquet of fried parsley.

MEAT

VEAL MEDALLIONS WITH TOMATO AND MUSHROOMS

Médaillons de veau sautés chasseur

For 6 people

- 100 g (4 oz) very white mushrooms
- 6 veal medallions, preferably cut from the fillet
- Salt and pepper
- 3 tablespoons olive oil
- 50 g (2 oz) unsalted butter
- 2 shallots, finely chopped
- $\frac{1}{2}$ glass white wine
- 1 tablespoon tomato purée or 2 fresh tomatoes, peeled, seeded, drained and cut into pieces
- $1\frac{1}{2}$ dl ($\frac{1}{4}$ pt) espagnole sauce (page 108) or demi-glace sauce (page 108) or a good veal stock
- Large pinch each of chopped chervil, parsley and tarragon
- Cornflour or *beurre manié* (page 92)

This will take 25 minutes to cook.

Clean and rapidly wash the mushrooms twice, drain and wipe dry. Cut into very thin slices.

Lightly flatten the veal medallions, season with salt and pepper. In a pan heat the oil and one-third of the butter. Add the veal and brown on one side; turn over, continue cooking until done, then remove and keep warm. This step requires 10–12 minutes.

In the butter in which the meat was cooked, cook the shallots until golden. Add the mushrooms and sauté them on a high flame, then add the white wine, reduce almost to nothing. Add the tomatoes and the sauce or the stock; boil to reduce for 5 minutes. If veal stock is used, thicken with a dash of cornflour diluted with cold water or with $\frac{1}{2}$ tablespoon of *beurre manié*.

To finish the sauce, away from the heat add the chopped herbs and the remaining butter; taste to correct the seasoning, and add the juice that has escaped from the veal medallions while standing. Place the medallions in a circle on a heated round platter. Cover with the mushrooms and the sauce. Sprinkle a pinch of chopped herbs on top.

STUFFED ESCALOPES OF VEAL

Paupiettes de veau

- 6 veal escalopes, 100 g (4 oz) each
- 6 slices fresh pork fat, cut very thin
- 50 g (2 oz) unsalted butter
- 1 small carrot, sliced thinly
- 1 onion, sliced thinly
- Few pork rinds
- Bouquet garni
- 1 glass dry white wine
- $1\frac{1}{2}$ dl ($\frac{1}{4}$ pt) veal stock or lightly salted bouillon

Stuffing:

- 100 g (4 oz) veal
- Salt, pepper, nutmeg
- 1 medium-sized potato, boiled
- Milk
- 50 g (2 oz) unsalted butter
- 1 egg
- 2 tablespoons double cream or béchamel sauce (page 110)
- 100 g (4 oz) mushrooms
- 2 shallots, chopped
- 1 teaspoon chopped parsley

Paupiettes are veal escalopes cut very thin from the *noix* or *sous-noix*. They are seasoned with salt, pepper and nutmeg; filled with a stuffing, the type determining the name of the dish; rolled like a pancake; wrapped in a layer of very thin pork fat held in place by a string; then braised.

This dish requires 2 hours for preparation and cooking.

Stuffing. Remove the skin and gristle from 100 g (4 oz) of veal and pound in a mortar with a pinch of salt, a pinch of freshly ground pepper and a dash of nutmeg. Place in a bowl.

Slice the boiled potato thinly; place in a small saucepan, half cover with hot milk, and boil for 10–15 minutes to reduce the milk until you reach the consistency of a firm paste. Pour into the mortar, and while the potato is still hot, pound to a paste. Add the veal and 25 g (1 oz) of butter, mix well and then add 1 egg. Add a little cream or béchamel sauce to produce the proper consistency for a stuffing.

Rub the stuffing through a sieve into a bowl, and smooth the mixture with a spatula. Wash and clean the mushrooms, wipe dry and chop fine. Put 25 g (1 oz) of butter in a pan; brown lightly, add the mushrooms and shallots, and cook over a high flame for about 5 minutes. Add to the mixture in the bowl. Finish the stuffing with 1 teaspoon of chopped parsley, and season to taste.

Assembling the paupiettes. Beat out the escalopes to 6-mm ($\frac{1}{4}$-inch) thickness, sprinkle with a dash of salt, then spread a sixth of the stuffing on each one. Roll the meat like a pancake, wrap each with a slice of pork fat and tie with a string.

Use a fairly small, deep flameproof baking dish. First butter the dish generously; heat it, add the carrot and the onion and brown. Place the pork rinds on top of the carrot and onion, then the paupiettes, side by side, and place the bouquet garni in between.

Cover and bake for 15 minutes in a 325°F (170°C, gas mark 3) oven to sweat the meat – condense and evaporate the juices.

Add the white wine and boil to reduce it completely over a high flame; then add stock or bouillon to cover the meat. Bring to the boil, cover with buttered wax paper and then with a lid, and simmer in the oven for $1\frac{1}{2}$ hours.

NOISETTES OF SPRING LAMB WITH DAUPHINE POTATOES

Noisettes de pré-salé à la dauphine

Prepare the *noisettes*. These are round slices cut from a boned loin of lamb, 4 cm ($1\frac{1}{2}$ inches) thick. Trim the meat and flatten it slightly; sauté in butter in a pan. Season the meat on both sides while cooking. The centre should be pink.

Place the meat in a circle on a large round platter on top of croûtons fried in butter (the bread slices should be the same size as the meat and 6 mm ($\frac{1}{4}$ inch) thick).

Around the edge, like a string of big pearls, place croquettes of *dauphine* potatoes.

Deglaze the pan with 2 tablespoons of dry white wine, reduce nearly completely, then add 6 tablespoons of good veal stock. Reduce again by one-third, and add butter away from the heat; pour a little over the *noisettes*. Serve the remaining juice in a sauceboat.

Potatoes Dauphine

Mix together 2 parts potato croquette mixture (recipe above) with 1 part batter for unsweetened soufflé fritters (page 604).

Form into large sausages on a lightly floured table and cut into pieces as big as walnuts. Roll each piece in the shape of an egg and dip it in an egg beaten with salt and pepper and a few drops of oil, then in breadcrumbs. Roll each croquette between your palms so that the breadcrumbs stick.

Place the croquettes in a frying basket and plunge at once into very hot oil for 7–8 minutes. Shake the frying basket carefully so that the croquettes move in the oil or fat.

Drain on a paper towel, sprinkle with salt and serve.

ROAST SHOULDER OF LAMB

Epaule d'agneau de pré-salé rôtie

The meat of a shoulder is rather sinewy so only shoulder of lamb can be roasted. Mutton shoulder should be braised or stewed.

Shoulder of lamb can be roasted with or without the bone. In boning, the butcher lifts out the blade bone. The central bone is easily removed without slitting the shoulder. The leg bone is sawn off near the stump and left in.

Season the meat inside with salt and pepper and roll it like a sausage. Tie it with string.

For better flavour do not bone the joint. Naturally the carving is not so easy and cooking the meat in this way is only suitable for a family dinner or when the number of guests warrants cooking the whole shoulder.

Place the shoulder on the rack of a roasting pan; season, and baste with melted butter. Cook in a 425°F (220°C, gas mark 7) oven, basting frequently. Watch the bottom of the roasting pan so that the meat juices do not burn.

Cooking time will be about 15 minutes per pound to sear the meat. It should then be left to 'rest' in a low oven.

Deglaze the roasting pan with 3–4 tablespoons of bouillon or water. Serve this juice after correcting the seasoning, without degreasing it.

SHOULDER OF LAMB WITH POTATOES

Epaule de pré-salé boulangère

For a whole shoulder

- 1 young lamb shoulder, boned or unboned
- 50 g (2 oz) unsalted butter
- 3 medium-sized onions
- 4 large baking potatoes

Prepare the shoulder as you would for roasting. Brown it quickly in a 450°F (230°C, gas mark 8) oven in an ovenproof earthenware dish that holds the meat easily.

Peel the onions and the potatoes; dry them. Cut the onions into julienne and thinly slice the potatoes; sprinkle with salt.

Remove the shoulder from the dish and spread the onions, then the potatoes, in thin layers on the bottom of the dish. Place the

La Cuisine du marché
Paul Bocuse

RESTAURANT

L'Auberge du Pont de Collonges, Collonges-au-Mont-d'Or, France, opened 1959

BOOK DETAILS

Published 1976, Flammarion, 712 pages, photography by J.-P. Chatelin and P. Ginet; published in English as *The New Cuisine*, 1978, Granada Publishing

"Paul Bocuse is our most admired culinary icon, whether locally in Lyon, across France or internationally, and for everyone from farmers and food artisans, pâtissiers and charcutiers, to chefs and restaurateurs around the world."

DANIEL BOULUD

To many people, the renowned Paul Bocuse epitomizes the classic French chef, committed to maintaining the exacting standards of haute cuisine. His culinary pedigree is impeccable. From a family of chefs, he trained under no less a figure than Fernand Point at the legendary restaurant La Pyramide in France before returning to take over the reins of his family restaurant, gaining the establishment its third Michelin star a few years later. The menu here offers diners a chance to enjoy skillfully executed versions of iconic, luxurious French dishes, such as Truffled Bresse Chicken Cooked in a Bladder, or Bocuse's famous Black Truffle Soup VGE, which was created for President Valéry Giscard d'Estaing in 1975. Such is his fame within the world of gastronomy that a prestigious chef's competition has been named after him: the Bocuse d'Or.

In this book, Bocuse explores "la nouvelle cuisine," the movement in the 1970s that saw a number of influential chefs in France move away from the traditional, over-complex, fussy dishes that had been de rigueur in fine dining, toward a simpler, fresher style. "One of the tenets of la nouvelle cuisine," observes Bocuse, "is that the food must keep its own taste, making the most of the original flavor. Previously in French cooking, there was a concern with ostentatious effect which had little to do with cooking."

Despite his awe-inspiring reputation, there is a commonsense aspect to his introduction. "Every morning I go to the market and wander about the stalls. This is a Lyonnais introduction, which I find hard to abandon." Shopping in this way allows him to buy what is best that day and then plan his menu: "Quite often, I have not decided what dishes to prepare for lunch; the market makes up my mind for me." The recipes, although drawn from the classic French tradition, are aimed at the home cook, clearly written with salient points included. Bocuse's in-depth knowledge of cooking—as well as his commitment to sharing it—comes through clearly.

A legend within his own lifetime, French chef Paul Bocuse has shaped French gastronomy.

Never Trust a Skinny Italian Chef
Massimo Bottura

RESTAURANT
Osteria Francescana, Modena, Italy, opened 1995

BOOK DETAILS
Published 2014, Phaidon, 296 pages, photography by Carlo Benvenuto and Stefano Graziani

"I often describe my kitchen as 'tradition seen from ten kilometres away.'"
MASSIMO BOTTURA

An exuberant culinary showman, acclaimed Italian chef Massimo Bottura is known for his irreverent creativity and flair. His roots are in the northern Italian province of Emilia-Romagna and the region's historic, rich food heritage is a source of much inspiration for the menu at his internationally lauded restaurant, Osteria Francescana. His dishes celebrate quintessential Italian ingredients and use them in surprising and intriguing ways. He is known for dishes such as Memory of a Mortadella Sandwich—inspired by the *panino di mortadella*, the everyday snack of his childhood—featuring a mortadella foam. Unafraid to challenge convention, his version of bollito misto is famously not boiled, as is traditional, and the meat is instead cooked *sous vide* (under vacuum).

This generously illustrated volume, Bottura's first book, is a celebration and an exploration of his career, and was created to offer an insight into how Bottura's cooking at Osteria Francescana has changed and developed since the restaurant opened in 1995.

As the title suggests—with Bottura himself a slender man—there is a playful and humorous quality to the writing in *Never Trust a Skinny Italian Chef*. It is a characteristic that is reflected in the names of Bottura's own creations, such as his famous dessert, Oops I Dropped the Lemon Tart. This playfulness, however, is combined with Bottura's personal mission "to bring the best from the past into the future." As he writes, he inspects the traditions of the Emilian kitchen "from under the table, through the eyes of a mischievous child."

Bottura narrates the stories of the recipes, and the imaginative and conceptual journeys he has taken in order to create dishes such as Tortellini Walking on Broth, which is thickened with agar; his Cappuccino, which looks sweet but tastes savory; and Five Ages of Parmigiano-Reggiano, which presents the cheese in a variety of unusual textures and forms. The reader gets a strong sense of Bottura's curiosity and his willingness to push the boundaries in order to explore how dishes can evolve. Although recipes are included, this is primarily a book about ideas, concepts, and creativity in cooking. It gives an insight into one of the most influential individuals in modern Italian cooking.

Creative and irreverent, chef Massimo Bottura has breathed new life into Italian cuisine.

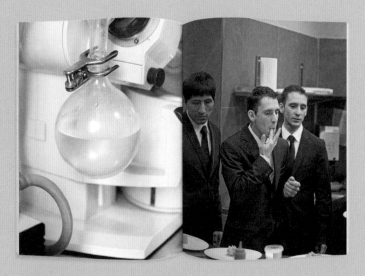

Five Ages of Parmigiano Reggiano

After selling my first restaurant, Trattoria del Campazzo, I left for Monte Carlo to study with Alain Ducasse for a year at the Hôtel de Paris. The year was 1994, and 'terroir' was the word. When I returned to Modena, I saw Emilian ingredients quite differently. One evening we were visited by a gentleman farmer named Umberto Panini, who owned a small dairy farm 15 minutes from Modena and was eager to taste the dish we were then calling Three Textures and Temperatures of Parmigiano Reggiano. I proposed to make something even better: not three, but four. We had been experimenting with a chilled foam to add another dimension to the original demi-soufflé, sauce and cracker. At the end of the meal, Umberto asked earnestly, 'Have you ever thought about what stagionatura means to a wheel of Parmigiano? It might help your recipe.'

I found out that Parmigiano Reggiano is not just any old cheese; it's a living and breathing portrait of Emilia-Romagna, created by Benedictine monks in the twelfth century. Roughly 500 litres (110 gallons) of milk are needed to make one 40-kilogram (88-pound) wheel of cheese. The coagulated curds are stirred in copper vats and heated to 55°C (131°F), where they form a mass which is shaped and place in a mould. The wheels float in salt water for 30 days and are then laid out on long wooden shelves, where they age in silence. After 12 months, an inspector taps each wheel with a small hammer and listens to the density; the sound is what determines whether it will be fire-branded with the seal of the Consortium of Parmigiano Reggiano. But the wheels must endure another year of damp winters and humid summers before they fulfil their destiny. I met cheese makers who were ageing wheels beyond the 24-month minimum requirement, for 28, 30 or 36 months and even longer, curious to see what could happen. Umberto was right. The subtle changes between a 24 and 40-month cheese changed our recipe dramatically in texture, flavour and

consistency. We began stashing away wheels of Parmigiano at dairies all over the region with handwritten labels that said: 'Osteria Francescana: Do not open until —'. Some of them are still sitting there. The characteristics of each wheel varied not only according to the ageing process, but also the landscape, the breed (Bianca Modenese, Rosso Reggiano or Jersey) and the cows' diet, whether mixed grains, free-range grass, or both.

As our wheels matured, the recipe evolved accordingly. A 24-month cheese became a demi-soufflé, a 30-month cheese became the warm, enveloping sauce, a 36-month cheese became a chilled foam mounted in a siphon, 40-month crusts became an intensely flavoured paper-thin water. Once we had shifted our focus from the transformations in the kitchen to those inside the cheese, the recipe was baptised Five Ages of Parmigiano Reggiano. It was no longer made with only one ingredient, but two: Parmigiano Reggiano and time.

Years later, we were invited to the Louvre for a demonstration. The Ducassian mantra of terroir was playing again in my head. I wanted to show the French audience something they did not know about Italy. For the event, we prepared my grandmother's recipe for Parmigiano broth using 50-month crusts. To that we added freshly grated 50-month cheese and left it for two days. Once filtered, it became pure and dense Parmigiano water. A whirl of a hand-held blender was all it took for the liquid to lift into the air and remain suspended like a cloud. From a crust of cheese we had created something ethereal, almost invisible, with intense flavour and a precise identity. Back at the restaurant, Four Ages of Parmigiano Reggiano soon became Five, and our tone poem was complete. The white-on-white monochrome, its temporal sculpture bathed in fog, silence and stagionatura, had become a portrait of the Emilian countryside seen from two kilometres away. And it only took 30 years to make.

32

Chicken, Chicken, Chicken, Where Are You?

My daughter, Alexa, used to play for hours with her plastic kitchen set. One afternoon she said, 'Papi, I'm going to make something for you.' She turned her back and banged away, then produced a beautiful mountain of plastic vegetables in a yellow saucepan. 'What are you serving me, Alexa?' I asked. She answered with a serious face, 'Chicken, chicken, chicken, where are you?' And we both fell to the floor laughing. Years later, a young waiter looking over the menu asked me, 'Isn't there any chicken on the menu?' I called out to the empty restaurant, 'Chicken, chicken, chicken, where are you?' Soon thereafter a chicken recipe found its way on to the menu. Thanks to Alexa's play on words, the objective of the dish was to create a chicken salad with incredibly intense chicken flavour, but no visible trace of the meat. Nine balls of julienned vegetables sit above a dense chicken vinaigrette. The plate looks like a game of noughts and crosses (tic-tac-toe). The table is bathed in a cloud of chicken vapour with a few sprays of an eau de cologne of roasted chicken. In this way the chicken is everywhere and nowhere all at once.

The idea of making chicken 'vapour' was inspired by a bronze self-portrait of Alighiero Boetti holding a rubber hose to his head. Water shoots out of the hose and a cloud of vapour escapes from the top of the artist's head. It looks like the thoughts coming magically to life, like ideas evaporating while the mind churns. The artist Bruce Nauman compared the practice of art to playing a game, with added responsibility: 'With a game you just follow the rules. But art is like cheating — it involves inverting the rules or taking the game apart and changing it.' Cooking is the same. By inverting the rules, we take responsibility for our actions and direct the diner's attention to what we think is important. We all agree that a well-made chicken salad is delicious. But like a game of noughts and crosses, it is also an easy win. My daughter is all grown up, but fortunately in the kitchen we can still act like children

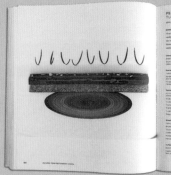

Daniel: My French Cuisine
Daniel Boulud and Sylvie Bigar

RESTAURANT
Daniel, New York City, New York, USA, opened in 1993

BOOK DETAILS
Published 2013, Grand Central Life & Style, 416 pages, photography
by Thomas Schauer

"I am a chef with soul: an American chef with a French soul or a French chef with an American soul. I have both influences in me and that's what keeps me grounded."

DANIEL BOULUD

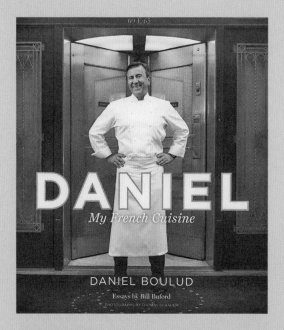

Born in Lyon, France, Daniel Boulud became interested in food at a young age, and by the time he was fourteen, he was peeling carrots in a restaurant kitchen. With the money he earned there, he bought Escoffier's *Le Guide Culinaire* (1975) and Gringoire and Saulnier's *Le Répertoire de la Cuisine* (1982). Intent on learning, he worked in some of France's best kitchens, and legendary chef Paul Bocuse (see p.108, 182), a notable influence, became his mentor. Working in America, however, Boulud's challenge was how to "translate traditional culinary experiences into modern recipes." This is something that Boulud pulled off with triumph with his New York City restaurant, Daniel, a huge success, both with diners and critics.

Daniel Boulud's cookbook, written with thoughtful intelligence, warmth, and charm, demonstrates the sheer range of his culinary knowledge. *Daniel: My French Cuisine* is divided into three sections: the first features the cuisine of restaurant Daniel, the second is made up of French classics, and the third is French regional cooking of the sort Boulud cooks at home. Here, in fully illustrated glory, are dishes that have attracted restaurant Daniel's devoted following among New York's gourmets: Citrus-Cured Fluke, Shiso Bavarois, Ponzu Gelée; Frog Leg Soupe en Croute VGE (a tribute to Bocuse); and Beaufort and Riesling Fondue Ravioli, Green Peppercorns, Sunchokes. The recipes for these exquisite dishes, works of art on a plate, are intricate and technically challenging, while the wit and creativity shines through. The second section, on iconic French dishes, written humorously by Bill Buford, reveal's Boulud's equal mastery of the grand tradition, exploring complex dishes such as Volaille à Noelle, or Poulet en Vessie. The final part of the book presents four menus from four regions of France, a demonstration of the diversity in terroir in French cuisine, with even Boulud's "home cooking" impeccably created and presented. Reading this, one understands that Boulud's playfulness when it comes to his menus rests on a formidable foundation of classic knowledge and skills.

Talented and committed, French chef Daniel Boulud has been a major influence in America's dining scene.

Bras: Laguiole, Aubrac, France
Michel Bras

RESTAURANT

Bras, Laguiole, France, opened 1992

BOOK DETAILS

Published 2008, Éditions du Rouergue, 272 pages, photography by Michel Bras, Christian Palis, and Jean-Pierre Trebosc, illustrations by Olivier Douzou; published in English as *Essential Cuisine*

"There is an expression I love from Jean-Paul Sartre:
'Nature talks, experience translates it.'
All the aesthetics of my plates, I picked up from nature."
MICHEL BRAS

Discreet, reserved, and thoughtful in person, French chef Michel Bras is a legendary figure in the world of gastronomy, widely revered by many contemporary chefs for his holistic and nature-centric approach to cooking. He made his name with his acclaimed restaurant Bras (previously Michel Bras) in Laguiole, France, situated in the lovely countryside of the Aubrac region. Bras's deep-rooted love of this area and the natural environment has shaped his food. One of the influential aspects of his cooking was his early pioneering of veg-centric haute cuisine—he offered a vegetable menu in 1978. Today, he and his son Sébastien both cook at restaurant Bras, with Michel also tending lovingly to the garden he has created, which supplies fresh produce for the restaurant.

A series of evocative essays add an extra personal dimension to this cookbook, illuminating Bras's particular sensibility and creativity. Bras writes poetically about his memories, such as eating eggs that were stolen from his neighbor's chickens on his way home from school, or the smell of Tuareg semolina bread baked in the sand and eaten under the Moroccan night sky. Reading these pieces offers a fascinating insight into Bras's creative processes and the way in which he uses memories and intense personal experiences as a starting point. The beautiful Aubrac landscape in which he lives is the inspiration for dishes such as his famous "Gargouillou" of Young Vegetables in Early Summer; and Light and Shadows, Mediterranean Monkfish Poached in Black Olive Oil with Mustard Greens. He writes thoughtfully about his and his son Sébastien's approach to food: "Sébastien and I like cheerful cooking that brings surprise and joy. It is why we enliven our plates with many different combinations that I call 'niac.' Niacs are structures of visual, scented and tactile elements that sharpen the senses and prepare for new discoveries." There is a joyful, vivacious quality to the food photographed for the book: colors leap from the pages, scattered petals add an appealing touch, and each dish is composed with a confident gracefulness.

The artistry of Michel Bras's cuisine has been a source of inspiration to numerous chefs.

Serves 4

HUILE RANCE
Huile rance (page 259)

CELTUCE OR ROMAINE
2 heads of celtuce or romaine

CARROTS, TURNIPS, CELERIAC, AND SWISS CHARD
4 carrots
4 turnips
4 small celeriac
Swiss chard, leaf and stalk separated

LEEKS
4 young leeks

SPINACH AND OTHER LEAVES
½ cup young spinach leaves
1 lb. (400 g) orache and amaranth leaves, washed and dried

PARSNIPS AND PARSLEY ROOTS
2 parsnips
2 parsley roots

PUMPKIN
1 potimarron squash or other small pumpkin
Butter
Cream
Salt
Demerara sugar

MUSHROOMS
8 oz. (200 g) cèpes
8 oz. (200 g) chanterelles
8 oz. (200 g) horn of plenty mushrooms

FRUIT REDUCTION
2 tbsp. (25 g) demerara sugar
4 tbsp. (50 g) red wine vinegar
2 tbsp. (25 g) sweet red wine
2 juniper berries
4 black figs

TO FINISH
4 slices of prosciutto
Huile rance
Hazelnut vinaigrette
14 hazelnuts
12 sprigs of burnet
Butter

HUILE RANCE
Prepare the huile rance several days in advance.
CELTUCE OR ROMAINE
Separate the leaves from the celtuce or romaine and set aside. Peel the fibers from the heart. Cut lengthwise with a knife or mandolin into slices ¼ in. (5 mm) thick. Boil in salted water.
CARROTS, TURNIPS, CELERIAC AND SWISS CHARD
Peel the carrots, turnips, and celeriac with a knife, leaving some of the shorter tops intact. Cut the carrots and turnips into pieces ¼ in. (5 mm) thick with a mandolin. Slice the celeriac into 8 pieces. Boil the vegetables separately in salted water.
LEEKS
Peel and slice the leeks, then boil them in salted water until tender.
SPINACH AND OTHER LEAVES
Carefully wash and dry the spinach, orache and amaranth leaves. Set aside.
PARSNIPS AND PARSLEY ROOTS
Peel and remove the tough bits on the parsnips and the parsley roots. Boil in salted water, then puree with butter and cream.

PUMPKIN
Peel the pumpkin and boil it in salted water until tender, then puree with butter, cream, and sugar 2 tbsp. (30 g) sugar per each ½ cup (100 g) puree.
MUSHROOMS
Wash and dry all the mushrooms carefully and set aside to be sautéed at the last minute.
FRUIT REDUCTION
To make the reduction, reduce the sugar, vinegar, and wine in a saucepan to a syrup. While the mixture is still hot, add the juniper berries and set aside. Reheat the reduction, immerse the figs, and poach them for 1 minute. Remove the figs and reduce the liquid again.
TO FINISH
Heat the lettuce hearts, the root vegetables, leeks, and swiss chard together in butter. Sauté the mushrooms in butter. Toss the assorted leaves in the hazelnut vinaigrette.
Spot each plate with the various purees and drizzle with the fruit reduction. Arrange the vegetables, mushrooms, and prosciutto, and add a few lettuce leaves here and there. Garnish with the hazelnuts and sprigs of burnet.

"gargouillou" of leaves, roots, mushrooms and fruits in autumn

---

Serves 4

JOHN DORY
2 john dory fish, about 2 lb. (800 g) each

HEARTY STOCK
3 tbsp. (50 g) butter
4 oz. (100 g) onions, chopped
4 tbsp. (55 g) chopped garlic
½-2 oz. (15 g) ham, chopped
2 oz. (60 g) john dory bones and trimmings
1 piece of lemon zest
1/3 cup (1/2 glass) white wine
1 cup (100 g) water

BUCKWHEAT CAKE
1/3 cup (100 g) milk
3 tbsp. (50 g) butter
1/4 tsp. (2 g) salt
1-1/4 oz. (30 g) buckwheat flakes
1 egg, separated

KASHA
2 tbsp. kasha
Salt

TO FINISH
Oil
Flat parsley, sliced

JOHN DORY
Rinse the fish under running water. Remove the guts and the scales and then fillet the fish, reserving the trimmings and the bones. Set aside in the refrigerator.
HEARTY STOCK
Brown the onions, garlic, and ham in the butter for 10 minutes. Add the bones and trimmings and continue to brown. Add the lemon zest, wine, and water and simmer for 10 minutes. Strain the fish trimmings and bones and reduce the stock.
BUCKWHEAT CAKE
Combine the milk, butter, and salt in a large saucepan and bring to a boil. Add the buckwheat flakes, cover, remove from the heat, and allow to swell for 15 minutes. Separate the egg into 2 bowls, beat the egg white until stiff. Whisk the yolk into the buckwheat mixture, fold in the white, and pour the butter onto a buttered baking dish. Bake for 30 minutes on the upper rack of the oven at 325°F (160°C). Remove and let cool.
KASHA
Pour the kasha into cold salted water. Bring to a boil and cook until tender. Rinse under cold water, drain well, and add salt to taste. Set aside.
TO FINISH
With a cookie cutter, cut cylinders out of the buckwheat cake and heat them in the oven. Oil the fish and broil or grill it. Quickly sauté the kasha in oil.
To serve, arrange the fish, buckwheat cakes and kasha on the plates. Drizzle the hearty sauce over the fish and garnish with some sliced parsley.

grilled john dory fillets, with a hearty stock, buckwheat cake   and parsley

GRILLED CHICKEN WINGS WITH BURNT-SCALLION BARBEQUE SAUCE

WILD-RAMP-AND-CRAB-STUFFED HUSHPUPPIES WITH GREEN GODDESS DRESSING

TENNESSEE FOIE GRAS WITH COUNTRY HAM, STRAWBERRY-MEYER LEMON JAM, AND HEIRLOOM JOHNNYCAKES

Heritage
Sean Brock

RESTAURANT

Husk, Charleston, South Carolina, USA, opened 2010

BOOK DETAILS

Published 2014, Artisan Books, 336 pages, photography by Peter
Frank Edwards

*"Sean Brock is one of the most important chefs in America.
In looking back at the roots of our cuisine, while always also looking
forward, he's changing the face of American food in wonderful ways."*
ANTHONY BOURDAIN

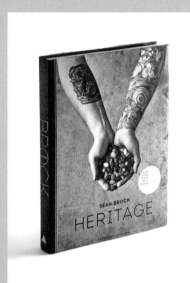

Virginia born and bred, chef Sean Brock is acclaimed for his championship
of Southern American food and culture. His highly praised restaurants—
Husk in Charleston and Nashville, and McGradys in Charleston—offer
a rich taste of Southern cuisine, expressive of the region's fascinating
and complex history and vanishing traditions. As part of this, he has
worked to create a network of local food producers, supporting, among
them, those trying to save endangered and rare traditional ingredients.
Southern cuisine, Brock understands, is the area's "living heritage," and
in his cooking he wants to honor it and share it with diners. Despite his
fascination with the past, however, Brock's cooking is also creative and
innovative; although deeply rooted in a sense of place and history, his
cuisine is also distinctly contemporary.

Written with verve and eloquence, Brock's first cookbook traces his food
obsession to his childhood in rural southwest Virginia, where living off the
land was the rule, not the exception. He writes affectionately of his grandmother,
a wonderful cook, as "the greatest influence" on his life. As the title
Heritage suggests, Brock is fascinated by the past, and he records the history
of Southern food in this book as well as offering recipes. Here, one learns about
traditional ingredients, such as Sea Island red peas, Carolina Gold rice, and seafood
such as wreckfish and amberjack. Food producers, such as "Clammer Dave" and
lamb and poultry farmer Craig Rogers, are profiled affectionately. The chapters
take the reader on a journey through the Southern landscape, beginning in "The
Garden," with recipes such as Creamed Corn, and Yellow Squash Marmalade,
and ending in "The Sweet Kitchen," where the Southern sweet tooth is
catered to, with recipes such as Chocolate Chess Pie and Black Walnut Pound
Cake with Chocolate Gravy. Local ways of preserving food, from smoking to
pickling, are explained en route. Brock's enthusiasm for the cuisine of his native
South is infectious, while his in-depth knowledge is truly impressive.

A glorious obsession with the
food of the American South is a
hallmark of Sean Brock's food.

Momofuku
David Chang and Peter Meehan

RESTAURANT
Momofuku, New York City, New York, USA, opened 2004

BOOK DETAILS
Published 2009, Clarkson Potter, 304 pages, photography by Gabriele Stabile

*"Ramen = broth + noodles + meat + toppings and garnishes.
It's that simple and that complex because the variations are endless."*
DAVID CHANG

The career of maverick restaurateur David Chang is a story of how one man's geeky fascination with a foodstuff—in Chang's case, noodles—became the starting point of a phenomenally successful restaurant group. Chang's restaurants, from his first small Momofuku Noodle Bar to Momofuku Ko (both in New York) have become cult dining destinations, attracting devoted customers and critical approval alike. Noodles were a part of his Korean roots, but a period living in Japan teaching English saw Chang become fascinated with ramen, eating in varied ramen shops, making notes about how these noodles worked, and what was in their dishes. Determination and persistence led him eventually to work as a chef in Japan. Returning to America, he opened Momofuku. Unorthodox and adventurous, he drew on his own Korean-American heritage and travels to offer his own versions of foods, such as noodle soups and savory buns.

"Koreans are notorious noodle eaters. I am no exception," begins Chang's forthright and entertaining account of the journey his ramen obsession took him on. The book offers an insight into how Chang works and traces the origins of his Noodle Bar, Ssäm Bar, and Ko, with recipes from each establishment.

Rather than being hidebound by tradition, he makes imaginative culinary leaps based on his well-informed palate. Back in America, we learn, he was struggling to source *katsuo-bushi* (dried fish flakes) of the quality he wanted in order to make dashi (the base for ramen broth). "So I got to thinking about how

else to get that smoky flavor, that meaty MSG that *katsuo-bushi* adds." Bacon provided an innovative solution, and the Bacon Dashi was key to Momofuku's polyglot culinary identity. The recipes give the readers a vivid taste of his gutsy, tasty, savory cooking, from Roasted Rice Cakes, tossed with a sweet-and-sour chile sauce, to the iconic Momofuku Steamed Buns filled with pork belly. The tone of voice is conversational and sprinkled with expletives. The practical issues of running restaurants are conveyed, and Chang's intelligence at solving problems is apparent. His book is food for the brain as well as the stomach.

Innovative, creative, and charismatic, David Chang is a vitalizing force in the restaurant world.

roasted mushroom salad braised pistachios, pickled jerusalem artichokes & radishes

soft-cooked hen egg caviar, onions & potato

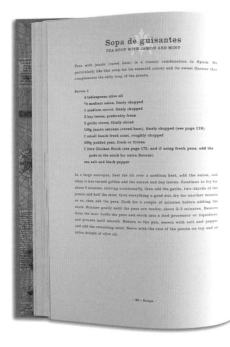

Sopa de guisantes
PEA SOUP WITH JAMON AND MINT

Peas with jamón (cured ham) is a classic combination in Spain. We particularly like this soup for its emerald colour and its sweet flavour that complements the salty tang of the jamón.

Serves 4

4 tablespoons olive oil
½ medium onion, finely chopped
1 medium carrot, finely chopped
2 bay leaves, preferably fresh
2 garlic cloves, thinly sliced
150g jamón serrano (cured ham), finely chopped (see page 116)
1 small bunch fresh mint, roughly chopped
500g podded peas, fresh or frozen
1 litre Chicken Stock (see page 175, and if using fresh peas, add the pods to the stock for extra flavour)
sea salt and black pepper

In a large saucepan, heat the oil over a medium heat, add the onion, and when it has turned golden add the carrot and bay leaves. Continue to fry for about 5 minutes, stirring occasionally, then add the garlic, two-thirds of the jamón and half the mint. Give everything a good stir, fry for another minute or so, then add the peas. Cook for a couple of minutes before adding the stock. Simmer gently until the peas are tender, about 2–3 minutes. Remove from the heat. Ladle the peas and stock into a food processor or liquidiser and process until smooth. Return to the pan, season with salt and pepper and add the remaining mint. Serve with the rest of the jamón on top and an extra drizzle of olive oil.

Esqueixada
SHREDDED SALT COD SALAD

'Esqueixada' is a refreshing and delicious Catalan salad made from raw salt cod. As the word 'esqueixar' (meaning 'to tear') suggests, the salt cod is literally shredded by hand. In Catalonia, market stalls specialising in salt cod sell esqueixada strips to make this dish. The simplicity of this salad does rely on good ingredients: sweet tomatoes and peppers in season, mild onion, fruity olive oil and good vinegar as well as a little time for all the flavours to infuse.

Serves 4

300g thick fillet of salt cod (dried weight), washed and soaked in the fridge for 48 hours, changing the water 4 times (see page 83)
1 green pepper, quartered, seeded and thinly sliced
1 red pepper, quartered, seeded and thinly sliced
10 cherry tomatoes (approx 225g), halved
1 large bunch fresh flat-leaf parsley, roughly chopped
½ small red onion, sliced water-thin
a handful of small black olives, like niçoises

DRESSING:
1 garlic clove, crushed to a paste with salt
1½ tablespoons good-quality red wine vinegar, or half red wine and half cherry vinegar
4 tablespoons extra virgin olive oil
sea salt and black pepper

Drain the salt cod and remove any skin or bones. Shred the cod between your fingers into soft, thread-like flakes. Transfer to a mixing bowl, and add the peppers, tomatoes, half the parsley and the onion.

For the dressing, whisk the garlic, vinegar and olive oil together, then season with salt and pepper. Pour over the salt cod, and gently toss together. Set aside for about an hour. Serve with the remaining parsley and the olives sprinkled on top.

½ x 400g tin whole plum tomatoes, drained of juice
1 fennel bulb, quartered, or 1 teaspoon fennel seeds
2 bay leaves, preferably fresh
1 teaspoon black peppercorns
a bunch of fresh flat-leaf parsley
sea salt and black pepper

Give the fish bones and head a good wash under cold water until the water runs at two runs clear, then transfer to a large saucepan and add all the other ingredients except for the salt and pepper. Generously cover with cold water (3 litres). Bring to the boil and then turn down the heat to a gentle simmer, skimming off any scum. Simmer for 15–30 minutes, but no longer, otherwise the stock will not taste fresh. Strain in a colander or fine-mesh sieve, then season with salt and pepper.

FISH MAIN COURSES

Moro: The Cookbook
Sam and Sam Clark

RESTAURANT
Moro, London, UK, opened 1997

BOOK DETAILS
Published 2001, Ebury Press, 288 pages, photography by Pia Tryde

> *"Calmly, steadily and surefootedly, Moro became part of its community. It became not only a destination restaurant but a local one too."*
> NIGEL SLATER

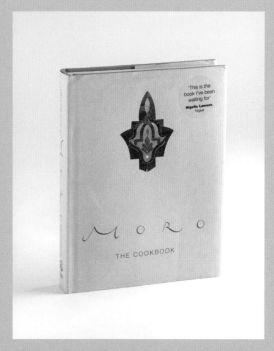

Husband-and-wife team Samuel and Samantha Clark breathed new life into London's dining world when they opened their restaurant Moro in 1997, setting a tone in both their approach to food and the restaurant's aesthetics that has been much imitated. Inspired by their three-month honeymoon driving around Spain and Morocco in a caravan, their cooking draws on both Arabic and Hispanic culinary traditions to create menus that are at once simple and yet imaginative, traditional, and also innovative. Friendly staff patiently explain unfamiliar ingredients such as pomegranate molasses, *mojama* (wind-dried tuna), and *freekeh* (roasted green wheat) to intrigued customers. There is a sense of adventure—of exploring cuisines with an open-minded interest—which "the Sams" (as they are affectionately called) bring from their own culinary odyssey to their restaurant.

The Moro cookbook, with its understated jacket, adorned with a small tiled pattern, was similarly refreshing in its approach. The matte pages are occasionally illustrated with a resolutely unfussy food photograph—a striking image of their famous, thick-crusted, freshly baked sourdough bread or a close-up shot of clams with manzanilla—pictures that make you want to eat that food now! The recipes are lucid and straightforward and knowledgeable, interspersed with information explaining the ingredients, their context, and how to use them.

"Moro was born of a desire to cook within the wonderful traditions of the Mediterranean, but with a need to explore new and exciting flavours," the Clarks write in their introduction, explaining how they explored the overlapping cuisines of Spain and the Muslim Mediterranean, connected by the 700-year occupation of Spain by the Moors. The quest to bring depth to their cooking means "we have ended up being surrounded by living things in the kitchen—we feed the culture for sourdough bread, we make live yoghurt daily, our wood oven and charcoal grills are fed continually." The recipes range from Moroccan-inspired Crab Brik to Catalan Fish Stew, with the Clarks's memories of how they encountered the dishes adding an evocative depth.

Sam and Sam Clark, the creative couple who founded the much-loved restaurant Moro.

Think Like a Chef
Tom Colicchio

RESTAURANT

Craft, New York City, New York, USA, opened 2002

BOOK DETAILS

Published 2000, Clarkson Potter, 272 pages, photography by Bill Bettencourt

"These days I'm excited by purity. I've started searching for the absolute essence of ingredients, veering away from showmanship and toward food that is clean and elemental."

TOM COLICCHIO

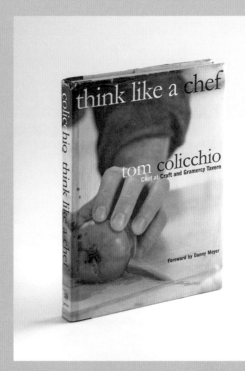

A love of food was part of American chef Tom Colicchio's life from a young age; he went fishing with his grandfather and sold vegetables for his uncle at a market in New Jersey. By the time he was fifteen years old, he was cooking in a professional kitchen. Buying Jacque Pépin's *La Technique* (see p.268), he worked his way through the book, treating it as an apprenticeship. He made his name at Le Mondrian, and also with Danny Meyer, at Gramercy Tavern (see p.162, 335), both in New York, before moving on to found his signature restaurant, Craft, to much acclaim. He is also noted for his campaigning spirit and founded Food Policy Action in 2012 to put pressure on legislators regarding food and farming policies.

In this clever, well-constructed cookbook Colicchio sets out, with an appealing generosity of spirit, to give his readers an understanding of how a chef works in ways that they can apply to their own cooking. Looking back to his own experience with Jacque Pépin's book, he lays out "Techniques," the "fundamental tools to creating great recipes."

Cooking methods such as roasting and making stocks and sauces are clearly explained. On sourcing ingredients, he advises, "When choosing vegetables, think like an Italian peasant. Even an Italian of the most modest means will spend a few extra lire on the best tomato, the freshest herbs, the fruitiest olive oil." He demonstrates how one core recipe can be the springboard for creativity, with Roasted Tomatoes, for example, leading to a vegetable lasagne, a risotto, and Clam Ragout with Pancetta and Seared Tuna with Roasted Tomato Vinaigrette. In his "Trilogies" section, he combines three major ingredients, all seasonally in context with one another, and cooks them in different ways—resulting in a Ragoût of Asparagus, Ramps, and Morels as well as Morel, Ramp, and Potato Gratin. His tone is conversational and helpful, with abundant advice on aspects of cooking. It is an accessible book, aimed at encouraging cooks. On readers making changes to his recipes, he writes: "Nothing is sacred or written in stone. I will forgive you. In fact, I'll be thrilled. Because when you do, you'll be thinking like a chef."

American chef Tom Colicchio brings a thoughtful, intelligent approach to his craft.

braised fresh "bacon"

SERVES 4

pan-roasted mushrooms

SERVES 4 AS A FIRST COURSE OR SIDE DISH

basic boiled lobster

YIELDS ABOUT 1½ POUNDS COOKED LOBSTER

lemon confit

Atelier Crenn: Metamorphosis of Taste
Dominique Crenn

RESTAURANT

Atelier Crenn, San Francisco, California, USA, opened 2011

BOOK DETAILS

Published 2015, Houghton Mifflin Harcourt, 359 pages, photography by Ed Anderson

"In French, the word atelier *can be used to refer to an artist's studio or an artisan's workshop, and I like the way it embodies the intersection between art and artisanship in the culinary world."*

DOMINIQUE CRENN

An appreciation of food and art was very much part of Dominique Crenn's French childhood, with her father, a food critic and a painter, hugely influential in this respect. From the age of eight, Crenn knew she wanted to be a chef, and she followed her dream with dedication. Her career as a chef saw her working in countries including Indonesia and the United States. Having fallen in love with the Bay Area, Crenn opened her first restaurant, Atelier Crenn, in San Francisco in 2011, garnering acclaim for her expressive, refined food, which draws on both modernist and classical culinary techniques. Inspired by her beloved father, she writes of opening Atelier Crenn: "I hung his pictures on the wall, wrote my menus as poems, and drew my inspiration from nature."

Fascinated by art and literature, Crenn subtitled her restaurant "Poetic Culinaria," expressing her philosophy that eating food at Atelier Crenn should reflect a poetic experience: "Each dish should contribute to the meaning of the meal in the way that a line of poetry conveys a layer of significance to a poem." Crenn's distinctive food philosophy, her sense that the food she cooks is emotionally charged and meaningful, permeates this eloquently written, visually striking cookbook.

The recipes are grouped together thematically: "Origin," "Plant," "Sea," "Land," "Dream," and "Craft." A recurrent motif is expressing an aspect of nature on a plate: A Walk in the Forest or The Sea. Beneath the aesthetic and graceful presentation, the intricate and time-consuming recipes themselves are composed of many carefully crafted elements. Crenn, writing thoughtfully and evocatively, explains her thought process behind dishes such as Le Jardin, Tomato (an homage to her mother's tomato salad), and Winter Squab. There is also a practical, grounded aspect to the cookbook—equipment explained ("We love our dehydrators at Atelier Crenn"), the restaurant routine made clear, fundamental recipes shared, an affectionate tribute to her pastry chef—which reflects the skilled craftsmanship, considerable labor, and teamwork that underlie Atelier Crenn's exquisite food.

French chef Dominique Crenn has made her name with her personal and poetic cuisine at Atelier Crenn.

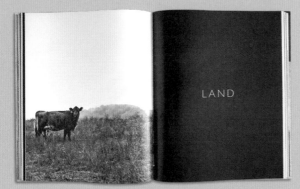

firm cheeses

Firm cheeses have a firm and drier texture than semisoft cheeses and a firm consistency. They slice and grate easily. Cheeses that fall into this category are made by varying processes. One of the most common is Cheddar. The cheddaring process originated in England, but a variety of cheeses that originated in the United States are made using the same method. Some examples are Colby, Monterey Jack, and dry Jack cheeses.

EMMENTALER
GRUYÈRE
MANCHEGO
AGED PROVOLONE
AGED GOUDA
RICOTTA SALATA
AGED PECORINO (ANTICO MUGELLO)
AGED CHEDDAR

Firm Cheeses

VARIETY	DESCRIPTION	COMMON CULINARY USES
CANTAL	Whole cow's milk. Light yellow cylinder. Mild, buttery flavor. Crumbly, firm	Table cheese. In salads, sandwiches. With fruit
CHEDDAR	Whole cow's milk. Light to medium yellow wheels or rectangles. Mild to sharp, depending on age. Sweet grassy aroma. Buttery, rich	Table cheese, with beer. In sandwiches. As cooking ingredient. Great melting cheese
EMMENTALER	Raw or pasteurized part-skim cow's milk. Light yellow wheel. Full flavored, nutty, fruity. Smooth, shiny, with large holes. Commonly called Swiss cheese	Table cheese. Great melting cheese. In fondues, sandwiches
GOUDA	Whole cow's milk. Wheel, usually coated with red wax; ranges from golden to amber, depending on age. Mild, creamy, slightly nutty flavor. Smooth, may have tiny holes. May be smoked	Table cheese. Great melting cheese. Aged Gouda can be grated
JARLSBERG	Part-skim cow's milk. Light yellow wheel. Sharp, nutty flavor. Large holes. Very popular in the United States	Table cheese. Great melting cheese
MANCHEGO	Whole sheep's milk. White to yellowish wheel; brownish-gray basket-weave rind. Slightly briny, nutty flavor. Tiny holes	Table cheese. In salads. Can be grated
PROVOLONE	Whole cow's milk. Shaped like a pear, sausage, or round ball. Pale yellow with yellow to golden-brown rind. Sharp flavor. Elastic, oily. May be smoked	Table cheese, with olives, bread, raw vegetables, salami. In sandwiches. Great melting cheese
RICOTTA SALATA	Whole sheep's milk. Pure white cylinder. Salty, nutty flavor. Smooth but crumbly	In pasta, salads. Table cheese, with salami, fruit, and vegetables
GRUYÈRE	Whole raw cow's milk. Flat beige wheels with brown rind. Fruity, nutty flavor. Smooth; may have crystals	In fondue, gratins, soups, sandwiches. As cooking ingredient

---

Indian Grilled Lamb with Fresh Mango Chutney

Makes 10 servings

6 lb/2.72 kg boneless lamb leg, broken down into subprimal cuts (see page 384)

MARINADE

1 tsp/2 g ground green cardamom

1 tsp/2 g ground cumin

½ tsp/1 g ground nutmeg

4 oz/113 g minced onion

¾ oz/21 g minced garlic

¾ oz/21 g minced ginger

1 tsp/2 g ground black pepper

4 fl oz/120 mL plain yogurt

20 fl oz/600 mL Fresh Mango Chutney (recipe follows)

1. Trim the lamb and separate it into individual muscles. Remove all interior fat and gristle. Cut the meat into long strips, 1 by 4 by ½ in/3 by 10 cm by 3 mm.

2. To make the marinade, toast the cardamom and cumin lightly in a dry sauté pan. Add the nutmeg, onions, garlic, ginger, and pepper and toast until fragrant. Let cool. Add to the yogurt.

3. Pour the marinade over the lamb in a hotel pan and turn to coat evenly. Marinate the lamb, covered, in the refrigerator for 8 hours or overnight.

4. Preheat the grill. Thread the lamb onto metal skewers and allow the excess marinade to drain away.

5. Place the lamb presentation side down on the grill rods. Grill undisturbed for about 1 minute. (Optional: Give each skewer a quarter-turn to achieve grill marks.)

6. Turn the skewers over and complete cooking to the desired doneness, or a minimum internal temperature of 145°F/63°C.

7. Serve 3 or 4 skewers per person with 2 fl oz/60 mL of the chutney.

Fresh Mango Chutney

Makes 32 fl oz/960 mL

2 lb/907 g small-dice mangos

2 fl oz/60 mL lime juice

4 tsp/4 g roughly chopped cilantro

2 tsp/6 g minced ginger

1 tsp/3 g minced jalapeño (optional)

Salt, as needed

Ground black pepper, as needed

Combine all the ingredients, including the minced jalapeño, if using. Let the chutney rest in the refrigerator for up to 2 hours to allow the flavors to marry. Adjust seasoning before serving, if necessary, with additional lime juice, salt, or pepper.

The Professional Chef
The Culinary Institute of America

RESTAURANT

The Culinary Institute of America, Hyde Park, New York, USA, founded in 1946

BOOK DETAILS

First published 1974, CBI Publishing Co., 1212 pages; this edition published 2011, John Wiley & Sons, 1232 pages, photography by The Culinary Institute of America

"Almost every profession has an outstanding training ground. The military has West Point, music has Juilliard, and the culinary arts has The Institute."

CRAIG CLAIBORNE, THE *NEW YORK TIMES*

Founded in Connecticut in 1946, in order to offer vocational training to returning veterans from World War II, the Culinary Institute of America (CIA) has an impressive reputation, regarded internationally as one of the leading culinary institutions. No less a chef than the revered Paul Bocuse (see p.108, 182) has called it, "The best culinary school in the world." Students here are offered courses that are noted for the depth of information imparted, the knowledge of the teaching staff, and their commitment to hands-on learning. While classic Western cooking techniques remain central to the school's curriculum, it also teaches its students about world cuisine. An influential institution, its impressive roll call of alumni includes chefs Anthony Bourdain and Roy Choi.

This hefty tome takes the job of imparting information to would-be chefs with a conscientious seriousness. As one would expect from an esteemed educational establishment, this is a book designed to be used as a teaching aide. The introduction states: "It is our hope that this book will function both as a springboard to future growth and as a reference point to give ballast to the lessons still to be learned." The book begins with an introduction to the chef's profession. There is a clear and comprehensive outline of the classic French brigade system, for both the kitchen and the dining room, as introduced by twentieth-century chef Auguste Escoffier to streamline and simplify work in hotel kitchens. The encyclopaedic nature of the book ensures a thoroughness of approach. Food safety, nutrition, tools, and ingredients are covered at the start of the volume, ensuring a useful basis for actual cooking techniques and an international range of recipes, drawn from many different cuisines. Illustrations offer clear guidance to kitchen skills such as jointing a rabbit or knife cuts, such as *paysanne*, with measurements included. When it comes to cooking methods, the book offers the information in a variety of ways: a basic formula, the method at a glance, expert tips, and the method in detail. As befits its credentials, this is a comprehensive and informative book.

The highly respected and influential Culinary Institute of America has trained generations of chefs.

Dabbous: The Cookbook
Ollie Dabbous

RESTAURANT
Dabbous, London, UK, opened 2012

BOOK DETAILS
Published 2014, Bloomsbury Publishing, 304 pages, photography by
Joakim Blockstrom

"Dabbous is so hot you could fry an egg on its reputation, to be served on a hunk of their own black pudding, spun through with apple and caramelized onions, and smeared with a butch mango chutney."
JAY RAYNER, THE *GUARDIAN*

When chef Ollie Dabbous opened his eponymous restaurant in a sleepy London backstreet, he had taken a massive gamble: "I am perhaps proudest of all of the fund-raising: securing the capital we needed when this wasn't my natural territory, no one had heard of me, the site was a concrete shell and the country was in the middle of a recession," he writes. His chutzpah and self-belief paid off as rave review after rave review came in and he became London's "hottest" chef. Getting a booking at Dabbous became nigh impossible, with diners flocking to eat his creative cooking—imaginative dishes such as Braised Halibut with Coastal Herbs or Ripe Peach in its Own Juice—in the restaurant's industrial-chic surroundings, with its concrete floor and metalwork screens.

As one might expect from his clever cooking, Dabbous writes intelligently and well, outlining his principles and aesthetic with the confidence of his conviction. He vividly describes his struggle to get Dabbous off the ground. Lack of finances meant minimal resources; the restaurant opened with four teapots, frantically washed up between orders. "Economy forces you to be creative and, perversely, renders decision-making so much easier because it eliminates the luxury of choice," he reflects, looking back at this period.

It might seem an affectation for an urban chef to structure his cookbook seasonally, but there is a thoughtful respect for what the seasons mean, even for city-dwellers, reflected in his menus. His spring starters offer a "sense of freshness and invigoration"; summer is "when food is served at its most naked"; fall is a time for "very British, almost medieval" food; and winter dishes possess "an inherent rusticity." The recipes are visually arresting, innovative, and imaginative, from his famous Coddled Egg, Smoked Butter and Mushrooms to Mixed Alliums in a Chilled Pine Infusion; each one expressive of Dabbous and his restaurant's ethos. "The thought process behind the food I create is shaped by my defining principles: individuality, simplicity, and value."

Talented young British chef Ollie Dabbous, acclaimed for his bold, creative cooking.

Braised Halibut with Pink Purslane

Warm Apple Cake; Chilled Rice Milk with Camomile

Coconut

Coddled Egg, Smoked Butter & Mushrooms

Ris de veau doré, blettes en gratin, râpée de « tuber magnatum pico »

PAR JEAN-FRANÇOIS PIÈGE

Raviolis de mascarpone avec épinards, chanterelles et parmesan

PAR ALESSANDRO STRATTA

L'Atelier de Alain Ducasse: Les maîtres de la gastronomie
Alain Ducasse and Jean-François Revel

RESTAURANT

Le Louis XV, Monte Carlo, Monaco, opened 1987

BOOK DETAILS

Published 1998, Hachette Livre, 248 pages, photography by Hervé Amiard; published in English as *L'Atelier of Alain Ducasse: The Artistry of a Master Chef and His Protégés*, 2000, Wiley

"I am greedy and I am curious—two faults I intend to keep."
ALAIN DUCASSE

With a glittering string of restaurants around the world, French chef Alain Ducasse is a phenomenon in the world of fine dining, a formidable entrepreneur and businessman as well as a great culinary talent. His skill at creating top-notch establishments is such that he was the first person ever to receive three Michelin stars for restaurants in three different cities from the influential dining guide. In his own cuisine, Ducasse draws on France's great culinary heritage, which he respects and cherishes, but he also looks to other cuisines for inspiration: "My roots carry me, but do not tie me down. I travel a great deal, always on the lookout for new discoveries." Understanding, respecting, and using quality ingredients is at the very heart of his cooking.

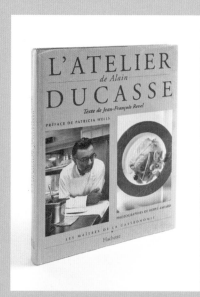

Given the scale of Ducasse's international operations, it is clear that he cannot actually be cooking in all of these restaurants, a fact he has always been open about. The analogy in the book's title evokes the world of the Renaissance painters and their students, and the cookbook itself offers an insight into the way Ducasse works, teaching his chefs his philosophy so that they reflect his approach in their cooking in his restaurants. "When asked, all Alain Ducasse students quote the mantra by which the master defines good cuisine: 60% ingredient, 40% technique."

The book begins with a description of key ingredients, such as Taggiasca olives from Italy or Menton lemons from France, and the sourcing and attention to provenance undertaken by Ducasse to ensure quality. "Products are the foundation on which I build my recipes," he says. "I never do it the other way round."

Next, Ducasse and five of his chefs (Frank Cerutti, Jean-Louis Nomicos, Jean-François Piège, Sylvain Portay, and Alessandro Stratta) each give recipes based on the ingredients. Ducasse's wheat recipe, for example, is for Semi-dried Pasta with Cream Sauce, Truffles, and Ragoût of Cockscombs and Chicken Kidney, whereas Cerutti makes a spelt soup. It is a fascinating exercise, allowing the reader to see how each chef responds to the product. What comes across is a sense of Ducasse as the leader of a team.

An acclaimed master of French haute cuisine, the legendary chef Alain Ducasse.

Le Guide culinaire
Auguste Escoffier

RESTAURANT

The Savoy Hotel, London, UK, 1890–1898 (Escoffier was head chef)

BOOK DETAILS

Published 1903, Flammarion, 943 pages, illustrations by Victor Morin; published in English as *A Guide to Modern Cookery*, 1907, William Heinemann

"I am the emperor of Germany, but you are the emperor of chefs."

EMPEROR WILLIAM II TO ESCOFFIER

Chef, restaurateur, and hotelier, Auguste Escoffier is a towering figure in the world of French cuisine. His career saw him cook for the top echelons of society at establishments including the Grand Hotel, Monte Carlo, and the Savoy and Carlton hotels in London. He famously created the dessert La Pêche Melba in honor of the celebrated singer Nellie Melba when she stayed at the Savoy in 1893. Despite his immense culinary talents, however, Escoffier's lasting legacy is in terms of restaurant management. In order to simplify service and make it smooth-running, he established the brigade system, still widely used today around the world, where each person in the kitchen or at front of house has a specific job and clearly defined role, allocating roles from the *plongeur* (dishwasher) to the *chef de partie*.

Among his publications, *Le Guide culinaire* or *The Complete Guide to the Art of Modern Cookery* is the most famous and influential; it is respected as an authoritative source on French cuisine. An impressive tome, it contains 5,000 recipes, with Escoffier explaining that the book "is a collection of the traditions of French cookery rather than a personal work."

Aimed at chefs and kitchen staff, it was conceived of as an educational aid, a book to teach from, written with a glorious confidence and exuding calm authority. In it, Escoffier set out the foundations for good French food. In Part 1, explaining the "Fundamental Elements of Cooking," he writes of stock: "Indeed, stock is everything in cooking, at least in French cooking. Without it, nothing can be done. If one's stock is good, what remains of the work is easy. If on the other hand, it is bad or merely mediocre, it is quite hopeless to expect anything approaching a satisfactory result." Having outlined "the general," he then moves on to "the particular," outlining recipes, how to prepare them, and giving their numerous variations. Recipes such as Poularde Talleyrand and Pudding à la Richelieu and Karoly Eclairs, "stuffed with a purée made from the entrails of woodcock with champagne" evoke the grandeur of classic French cuisine. However, Escoffier notably championed the move toward a less elaborate way of cooking. "Above all, keep it simple" remains his most famous and widely quoted maxim.

The redoubtable Auguste Escoffier, whose influence in structuring restaurants continues to this day.

légèrement liée à la mayonnaise collée. Croûtonnage en gelée blanche.

Lina-Munte. — Œufs mollets affranchis des deux sous, enrobés de sauce chaud-froid blanche additionnée d'un tiers de purée de champignons. Dressés sur anneaux de gelée dentelée autour d'un dôme de gelée hachée. Entourés d'une chaîne de tout petits champignons renversés chaud-froités avec bille de truffe glacée dans chaque. Perle de truffe sur chaque œuf.

Maupassant. — Œufs pochés enrobés de sauce matelote rouge en chaud-froid. Croûtonnage à la gelée rose de poisson.

Mosaïque. — Moules demi-ovoïdes chemisées de gelée blanche, foncés en mosaïque avec petits losanges de langue écarlate, blanc d'œufs pochés, truffes, haricots verts. Un œuf dans chaque moule et remplir de gelée blanche. Dresser autour d'une salade russe liée, moulée en moule à dôme également foncé en mosaïque.

Moscovite. — Œufs durs affranchis légèrement des deux bouts, et cerclés en bas et en haut de 2 lanières de filets d'anchois. Point de truffes au milieu pour simuler la bonde du tonneau. Les œufs vidés à la colonne, garnis de caviar monté en cône, dressés en fonds d'artichauts bien blancs garnis de caviar.

Nantua. — Œufs durs, vidés à la colonne, apprêtés en tonneaux comme ci-dessus, et remplis d'un salpicon d'écrevisses lié à la mayonnaise, laquelle additionnée de la purée des carcasses passée à l'étamine. — Garnir en dôme et décorer avec 4 demi-queues d'écrevisses et 4 losanges de truffes. Napper à la gelée et dresser sur fonds d'artichauts garnis de la même mayonnaise.

Niçoise. — Croustades à tartelettes garnies en médaillon de haricots verts, pommes de terre cuites à l'eau et tomates crues, coupé en petits dés réguliers. Un œuf moulé, froid, masqué de mayonnaise additionnée d'un cinquième de purée de tomate crue sur chaque tartelette.

Polignac. — Œuf moulé à la Polignac, et mis en belle vue en moule plus grand, avec gelée bien blanche. Dresser avec croûtonnage de gelée légèrement colorée.

Reine. — Brioches à tête cuite en moules cannelés et parées au ras des cannelures. Évider en croustade, tapisser l'intérieur d'un fin hachis de blanc de volaille lié à la mayonnaise, légère-

ment relevé au cayenne; placer dans chaque un œuf mollet. Napper de mayonnaise. Petite perle de truffe sur l'œuf, et lustrer à la gelée.

Rosita. — Œufs pochés enrobés d'une sauce chaud-froid à la gelée et de corail de homard. Dresser en croissant de truffes de grandeurs graduées; dresser tampon de gelée blanche et entourer d'une bordure de tomates marinées (grosseur d'une noix) farcis au thon.

Ravigote. — Chemiser des moules ovoïdes et les décorer avec détails de cornichons, câpres et feuilles d'estragon. Verser dans chaque un œuf de rissolé encore liquide, et placer l'œuf dedans de suite, si de façon à ce que le ravigote en remontant. Dresser sur croûtons ovales cannelés en gelée blanche.

Rubens. — Assaisonner de sel et poivre du moulin des jets de houblon frais cuits au consommé; ajouter persil et cerfeuil hachés, et coulis de tomates additionnée de gelée, juste ce qu'il en faut pour assurer la liaison. Mouler en moules à tartelettes huilés. Napper les œufs de sauce chaud-froid blonde, décorer avec détails de feuilles d'estragon et lustrer à la gelée. Dresser sur les tartelettes avec crête de gelée coupée sur chaque œuf, et gelée hachée au milieu.

Viveurs. — Œufs mollets affranchis du dessous, enrobés de sauce de homard à l'américaine liée à la gelée. Dresser autour d'une salade de pommes de terre à la parisienne, et placer une escalope de queue de langouste sur la mayonnaise. Turban de petites rondelles de pommes de terre et betteraves marinées autour des œufs.

Coulibiac (d') B. — Les mêmes éléments de garniture que pour le coulibiac A. — Avec 500 grammes de rognures de feuilletage bien reposées, faire une abaisse ronde de 25 centimètres de diamètre, ou tenant les bords un peu plus mince que le centre. Garnir comme ci-dessus, fermer l'abaisse en chausson, en plaçant les bords légèrement mouillés en bourrelets. Ménager un ouvreau, dorer, rayer et cuire au four moyen. Temps de cuisson 30 à 35 minutes. — Introduire du beurre fondu comme dans le coulibiac en pâte à brioche.

Coulibiacs (d') Petits. — Détailler, en abaisses rondes cannelées de 12 centimètres de diamètre, 500 grammes de pâte à brioche.

sans sucre. Garnir des éléments indiqués ci-dessus, en mettant 2 petites escalopes d'anguille dans chaque coulibiac. Fermer en pâte russe, c'est-à-dire la soudure en haut et au centre. Laisser lever la pâte, et traiter comme le coulibiac A.

Pour les petits coulibiacs en rognures de feuilletage : abaisses de mêmes dimensions (12 centimètres de diamètre), mêmes garnitures et fermeture (soudure en haut). Temps de cuisson pour l'un et l'autre : 18 minutes à four moyen.

Durand (à la). — Anguille en tronçons de 7 centimètres, désossés, farcis (farce de brochet ou de merlan), remis en forme, enveloppés en mousselines et ficelés. Les pocher dans une mirepoix de même nom, c'est-à-dire la soudure au court-bouillon au vin de Pouilly et un tiers d'eau. — Déballer et glacer les tronçons au four avec 25 grammes de beurre et 2 cuillerées de cuisson réduite.

— Accomp. : La cuisson réduite aux deux tiers (bordelaise complétée), montée avec 150 grammes de beurre, légèrement relevée au cayenne.

Florimond (à la). — Grosse pièce ciselée, marinée au citron à l'heure à l'avance, enveloppée de papier huilé, roulée en cerceau et rôtie au four. Accomp. et garnir : 150 grammes de beurre maître d'hôtel, additionné de 50 grammes d'échalotes tombées au vin blanc et passées à l'étamine. Grosses rondelles de terre cuites en beurre à cru.

Frites. — Toutes petites anguilles ciselées, enibrochées en 8 et enilées comme poissons frits ordinaires. Dresser avec persil frit. — Accomp. facultatif : purée d'oseille braisée.

Frite à l'anglaise. — Anguille désossée. Les filets en aiguillettes marinées pendant 1 heure avec assaisonnement, aromates, huile et citron. Paner à l'anglaise et frire. — Accomp. : sauce bâtarde au beurre d'anchois.

Gourmets (des). — Anguille divisée en tronçons de 8 centimètres, pochés au court-bouillon au chablis; dresser après cuisson et mis dans un demi-litre de sauce béchamel, avec les queues de 20 belles écrevisses cuites comme pour bisque. Mise à point avec beurre d'écrevisses tiré des carcasses (50 grammes de beurre).

Matelote (en). — Traitement selon le genre. (Voir Matelotes.)

Melunoise. — Grosse pièce ciselée, marinée 1 heure à l'avance, roulée et ficelée en spirale, et rôtie au four. — Accomp. à part : sauce Robert maigre. Plat bordé de cornichons.

Ménagère. — Anguilles moyennes tronçonnées en parties de 7 à 8 centimètres. Ciseler, assaisonner et griller à cru. Accomp. : beurre maître d'hôtel additionné d'une cuillerée de moutarde par 100 grammes. Plat bordé de cornichons.

Meunière. — Anguilles petites, tronçonnées, assaisonnées, farinées et cuites au beurre. — Accomp. : beurre noisette acidulé au citron; persil haché.

Orly. — Petites anguilles détaillées en aiguillettes, légèrement aplaties, assaisonnées, panées à l'anglaise ou trempées à la pâte à frire et frites. — Accomp. : sauce tomate.

l'intérieur du plat). Légère semis de truffes hachées sur les filets, sauces crevettes, et le corail haché sur roux sauces généreusement. Au milieu garniture en bouquet de 150 grammes queues de crevettes liées à la liaison.

Manon (à la). — Filets farcis, roulés en paupiettes pochées à la cuisson de champignons. Dressés en couronne, un plat bordé en pomme duchesse, pochés à la douille cannelée au gros cordon tremble coloré au four. Garniture de pointes d'asperges, julienne de truffes et champignons au milieu. Les paupiettes légèrement nappées de sauce fines herbes, sans toucher les truffes.

Marcelle (à la). — Filets pliés, légèrement masqués de farce à la crème, décorés d'une rosace, ou simplement d'une lame de truffe cannelée, pochés au beurre et sur papier. Les obtenir très blancs. — Dresser sur barquettes garnies de purée de laitances truffée, mise à l'état de coulis par addition de quelques cuillerées de sauce vin blanc.

Marguery (à la). — Filets pochés en longueur au fumet de poisson, dressés avec garniture de moules et crevettes. Saucés au vin blanc et glacés.

Marinière. — Pochés en longueur au fumet de poisson. Garnis de petites moules pochées et ébarbées; nappés de sauce à la marinière (voir Sauces), et glacés.

Marquise (à la). — Pliés et pochés au vin blanc, fumet et beurre. Dressés en turban sur plat bordé d'une guirnade de pomme duchesse, additionnée de purée de saumon, sans coloration au four. Pochés à la douille cannelée, garniture au milieu : mousseline de saumon à la cuillère à café, queues de crevettes et truffes en olives. Sauce crevettes pâle.

Mexicaine (à la). — Filets farcis et roulés en paupiettes pochées au fumet. Dressées sur champignons grillés garnis d'une demi-cuillerée de tomates concassées fondues au beurre. Les paupiettes masquées d'une béchamel tomatée aux poivrons, dans les proportions de 2 décilitres de purée de tomate, et 50 grammes de poivrons en dés par litre de sauce.

Mirabeau (à la). — Filets pochés au fumet et en longueur. Saucés au vin blanc et genevoise alternés avec 1 lanière de filet

d'anchois entre les filets. Lame de truffe sur les filets marinés à l'huile et feuilles d'estragon blanchies sur ceux à beurre.

Miramar (à la). — Filets escalopés en trois, assaisonnés et sautés au beurre. — 40 petites rondelles d'aubergines assaisonnées, farinées et sautées au beurre également. Réunir escalopes de filets et aubergines, et dresser en timbale, fondée autour de riz pilaw. Arroser avec 50 grammes de beurre noisette en servant.

Mogador (à la). — Filets de soles parés en rectangles réguliers, légèrement masqués de farce mousseline, et décorés sur un côté d'une belle lame de truffe cannelée. Pocher au beurre et jus de citron, à couvert. — Dresser en couronne sur bordure basse de farce mortes à la crème, truffée, et en faisant apparaître le côté truffé. Verser au milieu une garniture Nantua, sans toucher les filets qui doivent rester intacts. Autour de la bordure : 12 coffres d'écrevisses emplis d'un salpicon de queues de crevettes lié avec un peu de farce. — Pour services rapides : coucher la bordure sur plat beurré, à la poche et douille cannelée, en superposant 2 cordons de farce l'un sur l'autre. Pocher à l'entrée du

Mousselines de solet Alexandra.

Montreuil (à la). — Filets pochés en longueur et en fumet, entourage de pommes de terre en boules, cuites à l'anglaise. Napper les filets de sauce vin blanc, et masquer la garniture d'un cordon de sauce crevettes.

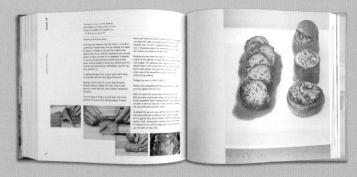

The Fundamental Techniques of Classic Cuisine
The French Culinary Institute with Judith Choate

INSTITUTION

The French Culinary Institute, New York City, New York, USA, founded in 1984 (now the International Culinary Center)

BOOK DETAILS

Published 2007, Stewart, Tabori & Chang, 496 pages, photography by Matthew Septimus

"I often reflect that our school is a bit like Florence during the Renaissance, with many masters working in their studios where aspiring artists can watch and work alongside."

DOROTHY CANN HAMILTON

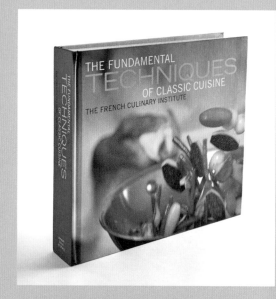

Founded in New York in 1984 by the redoubtable Dorothy Cann Hamilton, the French Culinary Institute was set up to offer a classic French culinary training to aspiring chefs. It soon became noted both for the depth and breadth of its training and the impressive speed at which it was accomplished. As Hamilton writes in the book: "Acknowledged as one of the top cooking schools in the world, the French Culinary Institute has been extremely successful at turning out some of the best chefs in the country. And the most startling fact is that the course is completed in a brief six to nine months!" Among the institution's famous alumni are chefs Bobby Flay, Wylie Dufresne, and David Chang (see p.192), with deans including Alice Waters (see p.46, 294, 335) and Jacques Pépin (see p.268).

An imposing, hefty work, complete with endorsing quotes from culinary legends Thomas Keller (see p.18, 86, 138, 230), Charlie Trotter, and Danny Meyer (see p.335), the book offers a chance to learn the first thirty-five percent of the French Culinary Institute's professional culinary program. "You will learn the 250 basic techniques that are fundamental to classic French cooking," writes Hamilton. "If you follow the book as directed, read it (and read it again and again), study it and practice the techniques that it lays out, you, too, can start to feel the confidence of the trained chef."

As one would expect given its impeccable credentials, the book is impressively comprehensive, beginning with how to set up one's workstation and the principles of sanitation, then progressing to working with food, from making stocks and sauces ("a crucial component of French cuisine") to meat, poultry, vegetables, fish, and seafood. The tone throughout is authoritative and encyclopaedic; this is a professional book aimed at people who are serious about learning how to cook. Useful practical information includes insightful "notes" from chef teachers. The illustrations, like the text, are about imparting information or demonstrating a technique. A respectful reverence for French cuisine—"the foundation upon which most of our Western cuisine is built"—is at the heart of the book.

Dorothy Cann Hamilton, who founded the influential French Culinary Institute in 1984.

Sex & Drugs & Sausage Rolls
Graham Garrett and Cat Black

RESTAURANT

The West House, Biddenden, UK, opened 2002

BOOK DETAILS

Published 2015, Face Publications, 288 pages, photography by Adrian Franklin

"Everything I make I try and make better than the time before. We're constantly evolving the food, the menus, always looking at suppliers. I get excited by suppliers, produce and finding things."

GRAHAM GARRETT

Born in London, Graham Garrett enjoyed a successful career as a rock star, a drummer touring the world in bands including Dumb Blondes, Panache, and Ya Ya. A long-held interest in cooking, meant, however, that at the age of thirty-one, he decided to follow his other dream, that of becoming a chef. He then worked in the kitchens of notable chefs Nico Ladenis (see p.238) and Richard Corrigan (see p.52). In 2002, with his wife Jackie, Garrett opened his restaurant The West House in the picturesque Kent village of Biddenden. While the setting is traditional and the menu has long championed local food, Garrett's intelligent cooking is contemporary and sophisticated. In addition to gaining a loyal following, his restaurant was soon recognized with critical plaudits, including a Michelin star.

As the humorous title succinctly suggests, this is no conventional cookbook. Rather than offering a classic collection of recipes, with an introduction outlining the chef's career, this graphically presented, entertaining read of a book takes you on a journey through Garrett's life: from boyhood to the creation of his beloved West House, interspersing recipes, text, and images en route. Garrett's voice—laconic, irreverent, and down-to-earth—comes across loud and clear in a series of vivid memories, from the Robert Carrier cookbook he bought as a boy for his mother, then kept under his bed and read, to a memorable anecdote of how "Indiana Jones liked my pork belly." The autobiographical format allows the reader to understand the importance of food in Garrett's life, with his travels as a rock star to countries including Japan, the United States, and Russia feeding his open-minded curiosity and informing his cooking. His candid accounts convey the sheer hard graft of working in a professional kitchen and the stresses and strains of opening one's own restaurant. What also comes across—through both the writing and the recipes, such as his sausage rolls (cheekily filled with foie gras) or his accomplished Milk and Honey dessert— is the sheer love of food and cooking that this rock star-turned-chef has.

Following a career as a rock star, Graham Garrett now displays his talents as a Michelin-starred chef.

ESCABECHE-OF-SEA-BASS

IBERICO-PORK-PRESA, RAZOR-CLAMS, WILD-GARLIC-BUTTER

STEAMED-HARE-BUN, CHOCOLATE-SAUCE

SIKA-DEER, MASHED-SWEDE, CHANTERELLES, TWIGLETS

ROAST-DUCK-BREAST, MUSHROOM-TORTELLINI, LAPSANG-SOUCHONG

HEDGEROW

TREACLE-TART

SERVES 8

salad of pink, red and golden beetroot with fig, goat's curd cylinder and truffle honey

Quay: Food Inspired by Nature
Peter Gilmore

RESTAURANT

Quay, Sydney, Australia, opened 1988 (Gilmore joined in 2001)

BOOK DETAILS

Published 2010, Murdoch Books, 288 pages, photography by Anson Smart

"What I aim to achieve with my food is a balance that takes into consideration a number of things: the texture of ingredients, mouthfeel, harmony of flavors, and the overall elegance of the visual presentation and proportions."

PETER GILMORE

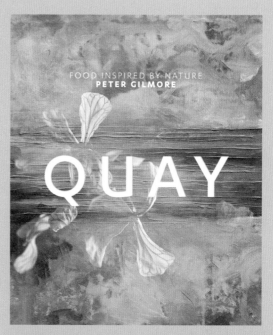

Peter Gilmore is regarded as one of the great Australian chefs and it is fitting that his acclaimed restaurant Quay should be located in the iconic surroundings of Sydney Harbour. Gilmore's desire to become a chef saw him begin working in restaurants at the age of fifteen, with a period spent traveling as a young man in Europe providing a formative experience. His talent was such that restaurateur Leon Fink took a chance on the young chef, installing him at Quay in 2001. The rest is Australian culinary history, with the restaurant under Gilmore rapturously received. Gilmore's imaginative ability at creating dishes, combined with precise, masterful techniques and meticulously sourced ingredients, has gained him a loyal following.

This lavish cookbook, complete with stunning photographs of Sydney Harbour as seen from the Quay restaurant, celebrates Gilmore's cooking in style. A thoughtful introduction by Gilmore explains how important nature is in his work, and he cites Michel Bras (see p.10, 36, 54, 188), Andoni Luis Aduriz (see p.10, 16, 158), and René Redzepi (see p.278) as inspirations. When it comes to him creating dishes, he reveals, texture is "as important as flavor" and he acknowledges Japanese cuisine, with its respect for the seasons, as an influence. As an Australian chef, he understands and relishes the freedom of cooking in a country that is "not bound by tradition,"

feeling that, when done well, this open-minded approach offers exciting opportunities. Gilmore's own creativity is amply demonstrated by this collection of sophisticated recipes, grouped together by themes: "The Garden," "The Sea," "The Land," "Heaven." Here are signature Quay dishes, notably his Sea Pearls, an original and complex set of jellies shaped into edible pearls. His notes on the textures and flavors he brings together offer an illuminating insight into how Gilmore develops dishes. The dishes themselves, such as Raspberries with Vanilla, Almond, and Violet, look enchantingly natural, belying the huge amount of work and skill taken to create them.

Acclaimed Australian chef Peter Gilmore draws his culinary inspiration from nature.

North: *The New Nordic Cuisine of Iceland*
Gunnar Karl Gíslason and Jody Eddy

RESTAURANT

Dill Restaurant, Reykjavík, Iceland, opened 2009

BOOK DETAILS

Published 2014, Ten Speed Press, 354 pages, photography by Evan Sung

"Chefs like Gunni and his restaurant Dill are immensely important: they rediscover lost traditions, breathe life into old techniques, and support the good people out there producing food with quality and deliciousness as their only guiding principles."

RENÉ REDZEPI

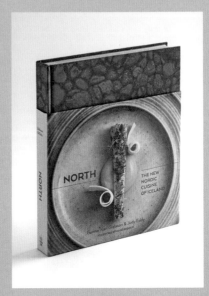

A culinary pioneer, championing new Nordic cuisine with integrity and verve, chef Gunnar Karl Gíslason is a charismatic figure in Iceland's gastronomic scene. His restaurant Dill—a place he envisioned celebrating the foods and cooking techniques of the North—faced disaster just before it opened as Iceland's banks collapsed, plunging the economy into a tailspin. Gíslason's investors withdrew their support, leaving him with a mountain of debt, a situation he faced with courage and tenacity. His suppliers promised to send him ingredients either free or at low cost until he could afford to pay them back. Their faith in the chef was rewarded; Gíslason's restaurant achieved an international reputation, becoming one of the must-visit restaurants for visitors to Reykjavík.

Gíslason's cooking, as befits his philosophy, is very much about a sense of place, with his dishes featuring traditional Icelandic ingredients such as *hardfiskur* (ocean-dried wolffish), *rugbraud* (sweet rye bread), and *skyr* (a yogurt-like cheese). Appropriately, therefore, especially given the role they played in saving his restaurant during Iceland's economic crisis, food producers share the pages of his cookbook. Portraits, visual and verbal, of producers such as Elvar Reykvalín ("the bacalao producer") or Bergrún Arna Thorsteindottir ("the birch and mushroom forager") give a rooted quality to the book; an appreciation of the environment, climate, and culture that have shaped Icelandic cuisine. Conversations with the producers on their relationship with Gíslason give an insight into the collaborative nature of this partnership between hard-working people who are committed to good food. The recipes themselves, themed by ingredients, are for imaginative dishes, inspired by traditional foods yet distinctly creative: Crispy Oats Cooked in Beer with Malt Cream; Pine-Sautéed Redfish, Salsify, Pine Tree Sauce, and Burned Butter Vinegar; and Bird Meringue, Buttermilk Pudding, and Birch Granita. This book offers a beguiling glimpse of Iceland's cuisine and one chef's celebration of it.

Charismatic Gunnar Karl Gíslason champions the traditional foods of his native Iceland to great effect.

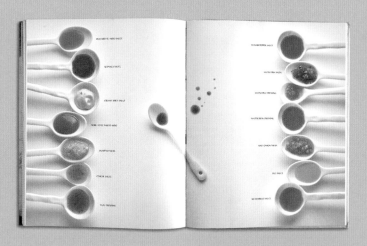

winter

Sunday Suppers at Lucques: Seasonal Recipes from Market to Table
Suzanne Goin with Teri Gelber

RESTAURANT

Lucques, Los Angeles, California, USA, opened 1998

BOOK DETAILS

Published 2005, Alfred A. Knopf, 398 pages, photography by Shimon and Tammar

"When Suzanne started working at Chez Panisse, we all knew right away that one day she would have a restaurant of her own and that other cooks would be coming to her for kitchen wisdom and a warm welcome."

ALICE WATERS

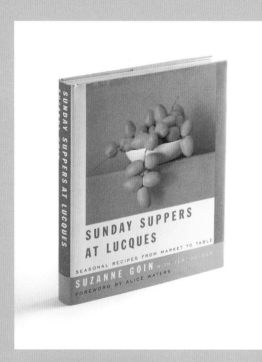

A love of food shaped Suzanne Goin's life from an early age: "Food was an absurdly large part of my childhood," she observes. Her parents planned holidays in France around the restaurants they wanted to visit and this fascination with food transmitted to Goin who, after completing a degree, decided to follow "the route of a self-taught chef." Formative experiences working at Al Forno and Chez Panisse in California followed, and in 1998, Goin opened Lucques in Los Angeles, garnering both diners and critical acclaim. From the start, Goin's vision of what she wanted her restaurant to be was clear, with the emphasis on conviviality and hospitality: food as a way of bringing people together. Good ingredients, sourced from farmers' markets, are at the heart of her cuisine, changing with the seasons.

There is a seasonal structure to Goin's cookbook, with each season followed by a selection of menus. The Sunday Menus, based on produce sourced at farmers' markets, are a Lucques tradition, inspired by her time in France. Goin's understanding of ingredients and her ability to combine them creatively comes across in the recipes: Sauté of White Asparagus, Morels and Ramps Over Polenta; Warm Squid Salad with Spinach, Chorizo, and Black Olives; Olive Oil Cake with Crème Fraîche and Candied Tangerines. As Alice Waters observes in her foreword: "The ingredients they use at Lucques are supremely well chosen and appropriate but never utterly obvious." Adding a personal dimension, too, are Goin's recollections on what has shaped her approach to food. She reveals her thoughts on what makes a good cook— highlighting the need to take pleasure from cooking. The recipes, from French and Italian traditions, have a rusticity about them, but their simplicity is deceptive as they are rooted in a deep understanding of how to cook, which Goin shares. "The most important thing to learn from this recipe is the technique," she writes, and that thoughtful, intelligent approach to understanding food and cooking shines through.

California chef Suzanne Goin is known for her expressive cooking, which is inspired by seasonal ingredients.

bills Sydney Food
Bill Granger

RESTAURANT

bills, Sydney, Australia, opened 1993

BOOK DETAILS

Published 2000, Murdoch Books, 192 pages, photography by Elsa Hutton, Tony Lyons, and Con Poulos

"I was struck by the freshness of the ingredients in California and how eating Japanese food leaves one feeling so clean."

BILL GRANGER

Australian café culture, from its obsession with excellent coffee to its informal offer of accessible but well-made food, has been influential around the world. And one man—Bill Granger—has come to typify that. A former art student turned chef and restaurateur, when Granger opened his first small, eponymous café in Darling Point in Sydney, he struck a chord that resonated with Sydney diners. The appeal of what he created with that first eating place has now extended far beyond Australia, with the rise of bills outlets in countries including Japan, Korea, and the United Kingdom. An affable and appealing figure, Granger is an excellent ambassador for his own light, easy-to-enjoy food.

The appeal of the Australian café goes way beyond simply the food on offer, although that must be good. In today's hectic, harassed world, the idea of a welcoming neighborhood café, a mellow place in which one can drop by, be greeted with friendly hospitality, and hang out with friends in a convivial atmosphere is an alluring one. "When I opened bills in 1993 it had council restrictions that allowed us to seat only thirty-five people at a time. I put in the big communal table to fill the space in an inviting way. It turned out to be what Sydneysiders wanted." Granger's cookbook is filled with bright, cheerful images of food and lifestyle shots of people enjoying sunny Sydney. His recipes, for dishes such as Sweetcorn Fritters with Roast Tomato and Bacon or Avocado Toast with Lime, Pepper and Coriander, are fresh and simple. They draw on the multicultural culinary influences—Asian, Italian, Greek— that are very much part of contemporary Australian food. Dishes such as spring rolls and papaya salad sit alongside mushrooms with Taleggio or crab spaghettini. The book, aimed at home cooks, celebrates the opportunities brought by urban living. A chapter on shopping for ingredients in the city highlights fresh Australian fish such as blue swimmer crab; the fresh herbs and vegetables found in Thai, Chinese, and Vietnamese green grocers; and the riches offered at Italian shops. Just as his cafés are hospitable places, so too is this cookbook relaxed and accessible.

Australian chef Bill Granger, whose famous eponymous café is a Sydney institution.

BREAKFAST

Tide dsk, Bondi Icebergs Pool, Bondi Beach

SCRAMBLED EGGS

SPRING ONION PANCAKE WITH GRAVLAX

SPICY PRAWN CAKES

CORIANDER DIPPING SAUCE

VIETNAMESE LEMONADE

DINNER

Twilight, Sydney Opera House Forecourt, Bennelong Point.

CHOCOLATE AND RASPBERRY TARTS

Linguine al Granchio
Linguini with Crab

Serves 10

2 large live male crabs, about 2–3 kg (4.1/2–6.1/2 lb) total weight

3 fresh red chillies, seeded and finely chopped

3 handfuls flat-leaf parsley, finely chopped

Juice of 4 lemons

3 garlic cloves, peeled and ground to a paste with a little salt

250 ml (8 fl oz) olive oil

500 g (18 oz) linguine

sea salt and freshly ground black pepper

extra virgin olive oil

Get the fishmonger to kill the crabs for you. In a saucepan large enough to hold both, bring enough water to the boil to cover the crabs. Boil gently for 20 minutes, then remove from the water and leave to cool.

Remove the claws and legs. Break the bodies open carefully. Remove the brown meat from inside the shell and transfer along with any juices to a bowl. Remove the white meat from the claws and legs and add to the brown meat in the bowl. Mix together.

Add the chilli and most of the chopped parsley, the lemon juice and crushed garlic to the crab mixture. Stir in the olive oil. This sauce should be quite liquid.

Cook the linguine in a generous amount of boiling salted water then drain thoroughly. Stir into the crab sauce, but do not reheat. Serve sprinkled with the remaining chopped parsley and a generous amount of extra virgin olive oil.

Fish and Shellfish
5

Branzino Arrosto
Roasted Marinated Sea Bass

The grilling of the skin before baking gives the bass a distinctive and interesting flavour

Serves 4–6

1 x 2.25 kg (5 lb) sea bass, scaled and cleaned but not filleted (see page 192)

2 tablespoons fennel seeds

sea salt and coarsely ground black pepper

2 red onions, peeled and sliced thinly

2 lemons, sliced

a few parsley stalks

2 fresh fennel bulbs, trimmed and sliced

juice of 1 lemon

5 tablespoons olive oil

75 ml (2.1/2 fl oz) white wine

Preheat the oven to 190°C/375°F/Gas 5. Preheat the grill.

Put half the fennel seeds and some salt and pepper inside the cavity of the fish, brush the skin with a little olive oil and grill for about 5–6 minutes on each side until the skin is lightly charred.

Place half the onion and lemon slices, parsley stalks, fennel slices and the remaining fennel seeds in a large ovenproof dish, lay the fish on top and cover with the remaining onion, lemon, parsley and fennel. Pour over the lemon juice, olive oil and white wine, and bake in the oven for about 30 minutes, or until the flesh is firm to the touch.

Serve either hot or cold with Salsa Verde (see page 220).

The River Cafe Cookbook
Rose Gray and Ruth Rogers

RESTAURANT
The River Cafe, London, UK, opened 1987

BOOK DETAILS
Published 1995, Ebury Press, 318 pages, photography by Jean Pigozzi and Martyn Thompson

"The River Cafe was conceived deliberately along domestic lines, with a small open kitchen, a menu that would change for every meal, and the unconventional idea that the waiters and kitchen porters would be involved in the preparation of the food."

ROSE GRAY AND RUTH ROGERS

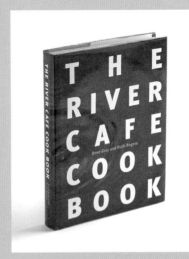

When in 1987 two good friends, American chefs Rose Gray and Ruth Rogers, opened a restaurant in the west London architectural practice of Ruth's husband, Richard Rogers, they had a clear vision for it. They would offer the authentic Italian food they both knew and loved, presenting it in a clear, straightforward fashion. The kitchen was open-plan, a calm place run with respect for the staff, and the seasonal, ingredients-led menu changed with every meal. This approach, rooted in their personal convictions, struck a phenomenal chord, with The River Cafe gathering first a cult following, then international renown. Its championing of Italian food changed perceptions of that cuisine in the United Kingdom and generations of talented chefs have been influenced by working there.

At the heart of Italian cuisine is the understanding of good ingredients. Simple dishes such as a typical Tuscan panzanella salad, thriftily made from stale bread, rely on tomatoes that are sweet, juicy, and flavorful to make it work. Gray and Rogers understand the importance of ingredients, and this respectful knowledge is at the heart of their cooking. The recipes in this, their first cookbook, are classically Italian, from Linguini with Crab to Pork Cooked in Milk. Reading through them gives you a rich sense of both Italy's regionality and the seasonality that underlies the cuisine. The tone in which the book is written, from the informative essays to the actual recipes, is refreshingly straightforward and clear. There is a generous sharing of information, as Gray and Rogers seek to convey their love of Italian cuisine and what makes it great. The ample glossary, with its detailed entries on key ingredients, from anchovies to olive oil, offers practical guidance as to how to find them and use them. With its striking, graphic appearance—the simple, text-led jacket, the use of clean-cut font, and the bold colors on the pages—the look of this cookbook, as well as the style of cooking it portrays, has proved hugely influential.

Friends Ruth Rogers and Rose Gray shared a vision of how they wanted The River Cafe to be.

Cuisine Minceur
Michel Guérard

RESTAURANT

Les Prés d'Eugénie, Eugénie-les-Bains, France, opened 1974

BOOK DETAILS

Originally published as *La Grande Cuisine Minceur*, 1976, Éditions Robert Laffont, 412 pages, photography by Didier Blanchat, illustrations by Michel Guérard; published in English as *Cuisine Minceur*, 1977, Macmillan London Ltd

"I play with the joy of flavors the way Mozart used to play with notes—impertinently, inquisitively, and poetically."

MICHEL GUÉRARD

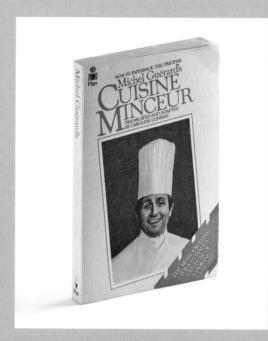

Supremely talented and creative, chef Michel Guérard, hailed as the father of *nouvelle cuisine*, is a hugely influential figure in French cooking. In 1974 as a two-star Michelin chef, he moved with his wife Christine to Eugénie-les-Bains to work at her spa and its restaurant, gaining in rapid succession first one, then two, then, in 1977, three Michelin stars, which he has retained ever since. It was during this period at Eugénie-les-Bains, that, prompted by the fact that he, himself, had gained a lot of weight, Guérard invented his *cuisine minceur*, offering a healthier, leaner version of classical French cooking. His cooking moved away from the classic dependence upon butter, cream, oil, and egg yolks to add luxury, offering instead dishes which, while elegant and flavorful, were also far lighter in terms of calories.

Despite *Cuisine Minceur* being, in effect, a manifesto for a new type of French cooking, there is a charm to the book in Guérard's own voice, from his humorous introduction to his poetic descriptions of ingredients: "I have been a dreamer for forty-two years," begins the book, in a Dante-esque, midlife crisis fashion. "My poor body, heavy with the residue of so many rich and delectable sauces, was so well-covered that it weighed me to the ground, where dreams cannot take flight." His effort to lose weight saw him beginning a "long trudge through acres of grated carrot." Despairing at the monotony and dullness of healthy food, Guérard instead decided to draw on his knowledge of classic French cooking to create a refined, sophisticated cuisine that would be healthier. The cookbook, which Guérard conceived of as "a complete festival of light meals for slimming," outlines the primary ingredients for *Cuisine Minceur*—such as mushroom purée or his chicken stock and fish fumet—then shares his techniques, such as the use of vegetable purées for thickening sauces or making light foams rather than creamy sauces. His recipes—such as Saffron-Steamed Turbot Studded with Anchovies or Veal Kidneys in a Green Waistcoat—demonstrate amply that this is gourmet territory, a world away from the grated carrot. *Cuisine Minceur* is a cookbook that is at once radical and classic.

French chef Michel Guérard, an eloquent and witty advocate of a healthier way of cooking.

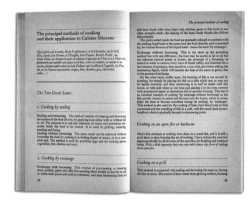

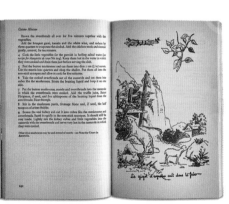

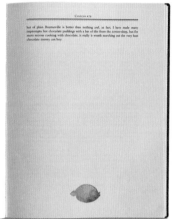

Roast Chicken and Other Stories
Simon Hopkinson and Lindsey Bareham

RESTAURANT

Bibendum, London, UK, opened 1987 (cofounder Hopkinson was chef until 1995)

BOOK DETAILS

Published 1994, Ebury Press, 230 pages, illustrations by Flo Bayley

"Good cooking, in the final analysis, depends on two things: common sense and good taste. It is also something that you naturally have to want to do well in the first place, as with any craft."

SIMON HOPKINSON

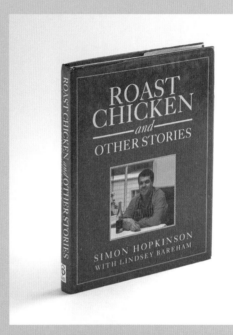

Chef, author, and broadcaster Simon Hopkinson has played an important part in helping shape Britain's culinary landscape, both through his cooking while a chef, but also with his approach to food and cooking expressed in his books and television series. Born in Bury in Lancashire, he worked as a young chef under Yves Champeau at his restaurant, the Normandie, in Birtle in the north of England, an experience of French cooking that profoundly influenced him. Having moved to London to work, he struck up a partnership with the dynamic restaurateur Terence Conran, an admirer of Hopkinson's cooking, with the two cofounding Bibendum, atmospherically housed in the old Michelin building in Chelsea. Here, Hopkinson's always eminently delicious cooking won him and the restaurant many plaudits.

This beguiling cookbook, the first he ever wrote, offers a wonderful insight into the food that Hopkinson loves to cook and loves to eat. Part of this book's enduring appeal is its capacity to make its readers hungry, as Hopkinson works his way affectionately through an eclectic assortment of his favorite ingredients, offering a few excellent recipes for each. Simple foods such as cream, onions, and liver are made inviting through his writing and suggestions for how to cook them in dishes such as Crème Brûlée, Onion Tart, and Calves' Liver Venetian Style. Part of Hopkinson's allure while at Bibendum was the fact that he was not afraid to champion dishes that were not currently in fashion; although naturally a shy and modest man, he has the courage of his convictions when it comes to food. What is notable about this book is the quality of the recipes themselves. His recipe for Crème Chantilly, for example, is not simply flavored with vanilla and sugar, but also incorporates ice at a key stage during the whipping: "The addition of a little water (melted ice) adds to the insubstantiality, which is the secret of a good Crème Chantilly," he observes. Hopkinson not only knows how to cook, he also knows how to write recipes that work. Unpretentious and conveying a great love of food, this is an invaluable book for home cooks.

British chef Simon Hopkinson, noted for both his cooking and his expressive food writing.

Eleven Madison Park: The Cookbook
Daniel Humm and Will Guidara

RESTAURANT

Eleven Madison Park, New York City, New York, USA, opened 1998 (Humm and Guidara joined in 2006)

BOOK DETAILS

Published 2011, Little, Brown, 384 pages, photography by Francesco Tonelli

"Restaurants are an art form, both theatrical and visual. When approached the right way, they enable you to enrich people's lives, either by creating one of their most lasting memories or in giving them a break from their reality."
WILL GUIDARA

It was restaurateur Danny Meyer who put together the culinary dream team of Swiss chef Daniel Humm and general manager Will Guidara to breathe new life into his New York restaurant Eleven Madison Park, housed in the iconic art deco Metropolitan Life North Building. It was something that they achieved with panache. Daniel Humm's considerable talents had marked him as a young chef to watch, with Meyer having to coax him over from San Francisco to New York. The joint vision for the revitalized restaurant involved reinventing the classic high-end dining experience for a contemporary audience, taking the starched formality out of eating out, while retaining impeccable standards. As such, Eleven Madison Park, with its mix of stylish food and hospitable warmth, has influenced chefs around the world.

There is an energy and an enthusiasm about this substantial tome. It is a reflection of the drive of the talented trio involved in creating this celebrated New York restaurant—Danny Meyer, Daniel Humm, and Will Guidara. The book charts the restaurant's history in detail, offering insights into how Humm and Guidara think about food through a sequence of essays. One learns of Humm's and Guidara's dreams and aspirations; the lows and highs of their careers. A photograph of the jazz musician Miles Davis seems puzzling at first, until one reads that Miles, who was technically perfect but broke the rules, was a source of inspiration for them. The recipes are grouped by season, focused on ingredients appropriate to that time of year. While the ingenious, playful dishes look artfully lovely, the recipes are technically complex and intricate—much work goes into creations such as Asparagus Textures with Shrimp and Anise Hyssop or Foie Gras Terrine with Plums and Bitter Almond. Reading this book, however, reinforces the truism that great restaurants are about so much more than food; the service, the setting, and the ambience all play their part in delighting diners. This is a book that is as much about restaurants as recipes.

The partnership behind New York's successful Eleven Madison Park: Will Guidara and Daniel Humm.

LAMB
HERB-ROASTED
WITH LETTUCE, MORELS AND
MUSTARD SEEDS

MILK
AND HONEY

CORN
GRILLED SOUP
WITH LOBSTER

TOMATO

CHERRY
CRUMBLE
WITH PISTACHIO

CHOCOLATE
ON MILK WITH
BANANA, YUZU
AND SESAME

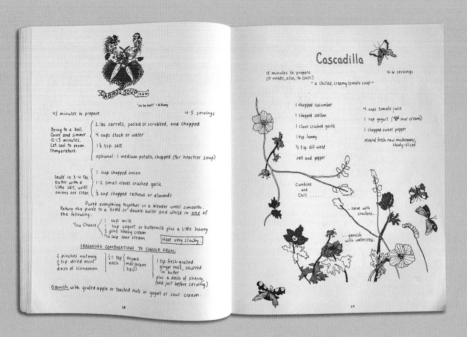

CARROT SOUP ★★★

"it's the best!" — B. Bunny

45 minutes to prepare.   4-5 servings

Bring to a boil.
Cover and simmer
12-15 minutes.
Let cool to room
temperature.

- 2 lbs. carrots, peeled or scrubbed, and chopped
- 4 cups stock or water
- 1½ tsp. salt
- optional: 1 medium potato, chopped (for heartier soup)

Sauté in 3-4 Tbs.
butter with a
little salt, until
onions are clear.

- 1 cup chopped onion
- 1-2 small cloves crushed garlic
- ⅓ cup chopped cashews or almonds

Purée everything together in a blender until smooth.
Return the purée to a kettle or double-boiler and whisk in one of
the following:

You Choose
- 1 cup milk
- 1 cup yogurt or buttermilk plus a little honey
- ½ pint heavy cream
- ¾ cup sour cream

Heat very slowly.

SEASONING COMBINATIONS TO CHOOSE FROM:

2 pinches nutmeg ½ tsp. dried mint dash of cinnamon	1-1 tsp. each thyme marjoram basil	1 tsp. fresh-grated ginger root, sautéed in butter plus a dash of sherry. (add just before serving)

Garnish with grated apple or toasted nuts or yogurt or sour cream.

28

Cascadilla

15 minutes to prepare   4-6 servings
(it needs, also, to chill.)
~ a chilled, creamy tomato soup ~

- 1 chopped cucumber
- 1 chopped scallion
- 1 clove crushed garlic
- 1 tsp. honey
- ½ tsp. dill weed
- salt and pepper
- 4 cups tomato juice
- 1 cup yogurt (½ sour cream)
- 1 chopped sweet pepper
- several fresh raw mushrooms, thinly-sliced

Combine and chill...

...serve with croutons...

...garnish with watercress.

29

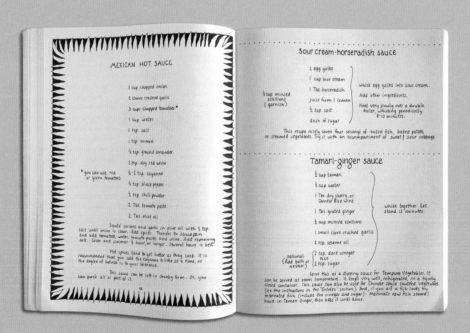

MEXICAN HOT SAUCE

- 1 cup chopped onion
- 2 cloves crushed garlic
- 3 cups chopped tomatoes *
- 1 cup water
- 1 tsp. salt
- 1 tsp. cumin
- ¼ tsp. ground coriander
- 2 Tbs. dry red wine
- ¼-⅓ tsp. cayenne
- ¼ tsp. black pepper
- ¼ tsp. chili powder
- 2 Tbs. tomato paste
- 2 Tbs. olive oil

* you can use red or green tomatoes

Sauté onions and garlic in olive oil with ¼ tsp.
salt until onion is clear. Add spices. Transfer to saucepan
and add tomatoes, water, tomato paste and wine. Add remaining
salt. Cover and simmer ½ hour, or longer. Several hours is best.

Hot spices tend to get hotter as they cook. It is
recommended that you add the cayenne a little at a time, so
the degree of hotness is to your tolerance.

This sauce can be left in chunky form. Or, you
can purée all or part of it.

78

Sour cream-horseradish sauce

¼ cup minced scallions (garnish)
- 2 egg yolks
- 1 cup sour cream
- 1 Tbs. horseradish
- juice from 1 lemon
- ½ tsp. salt
- dash of sugar

Whisk egg yolks into sour cream.
Add other ingredients.
Heat very slowly over a double
boiler, whisking periodically.
8-10 minutes.

This recipe nicely covers four servings of baked fish, baked potato,
or steamed vegetables. Try it with an accompaniment of sweet & sour cabbage.

Tamari-ginger sauce

- ¼ cup tamari
- ¼ cup water
- 1 Tbs. dry sherry, or Chinese Rice Wine
- 1 Tbs. grated ginger
- ¼ cup minced scallions
- 1 small clove crushed garlic
- 1 tsp. sesame oil

Whisk together. Let stand 15 minutes.

optional:
(Add both or neither.)
- 2 tsp. dark vinegar
plus
- 2 tsp. sugar

Serve this as a dipping sauce for Tempura Vegetables. It
can be served at room temperature. It keeps very well, refrigerated, in a tightly
closed container. This sauce can also be used for Chinese-style sautéed vegetables
(see the instructions in the "Entrées" section). And, if you are a fish-lover, try
marinated fish (include the vinegar and sugar). Marinate raw fish several
hours in Tamari-Ginger, then bake it until done.

Moosewood Cookbook
Mollie Katzen

RESTAURANT

Moosewood Restaurant, Ithaca, New York, USA, opened 1973

BOOK DETAILS

Published 1977, Ten Speed Press, 228 pages, illustrations by Mollie Katzen

"Mollie appeals to people who like to eat well but don't want to make a big deal out of it. She helped make vegetarian cooking accessible to everyone. She's unpretentious and homespun."

ALICE WATERS

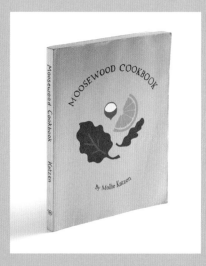

"Moosewood (named after a local maple tree) was begun in September 1973 by a group of friends who enjoyed getting together to cook and eat, and who wanted to engage in a community project," explains Mollie Katzen, one of the cofounders. The collective found an old school building in Ithaca and set about converting the gymnasium. The resulting natural foods restaurant—offering predominantly vegetarian dishes—has become famous around the world, largely through the bestselling cookbook. The restaurant offered daily changing menus, posted on blackboards, with Sunday night being "ethnic night" when the menu focused on one cuisine. Offering tasty, freshly cooked food, part of its appeal was its lack of strict dogma, which meant that many of its customers were not strict vegetarians themselves.

Moosewood Cookbook was "compiled, edited, illustrated, and hand-lettered" by Mollie Katzen, and initially self-published in 1974. Its hand-written appearance gave it a distinctive and striking feel. The recipes in it were drawn from the notebooks in which she recorded the changing recipes used at the restaurant, adapted by Katzen for home use. Look through the book and, at once, the cheerfully eclectic, globe-trotting nature of the recipes leaps out from the pages: Brazilian Black Bean Soup, Miso Soup, Russian Cabbage Borscht, Polenta Pizza, Samosas, Szechuan Eggplant and Tofu, Finnish Whipped Fruit Puddings, Apple-Cheddar Strudel. . . . This rich, cosmopolitan variety came from the democratic sharing of each member of the team's culinary heritage, with many recipes in the book based on family dishes. "Moosewood's cooks," points out Katzen, "also frequent the library, to read about the foods of other cultures."

The restaurant was created by a group of friends coming together to act collaboratively through principles of sharing and accessibility to good, natural food. The cookbook conveys this sense of sharing and passing on recipes and information in a helpful way. Katzen's tone is friendly and conversational, with her simple, hand-drawn illustrations adding a charming, personal touch.

Mollie Katzen, whose cookbook expressed the spirit of the vegetarian movement in America.

The French Laundry Cookbook
Thomas Keller

RESTAURANT

The French Laundry, Yountville, California, USA, opened 1978
(Keller became the chef-owner in 1994)

BOOK DETAILS

Published 1999, Artisan Books, 326 pages, photography by Deborah Jones

"When you acknowledge, as you must, that there is no such thing as perfect food, only the idea of it, then the real purpose of striving toward perfection becomes clear: to make people happy. That's what cooking is all about."
THOMAS KELLER

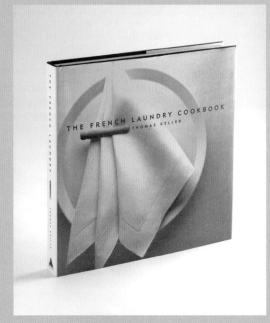

Within the world of international gastronomy, American chef and restaurateur Thomas Keller has a very special place, admired, respected, and held in great affection among his peers. Having begun cooking from a young age in the kitchen of the Palm Beach restaurant managed by his mother, he traveled to France and worked in restaurants including Guy Savoy and Taillevent. He then made his name with his own celebrated and much-lauded restaurant The French Laundry in Napa Valley. Renowned as a perfectionist in the kitchen, Keller's signature Franco-American food, rooted in classic French techniques, gained an appreciative following. Today Keller's restaurant group includes Ad Hoc and Bouchon, also in Yountville, and Per Se and another Bouchon in New York. Famed as a great teacher and mentor, many of today's new generation of talented young chefs have worked for Keller, with names such as Grant Achatz (see p.154), Corey Lee (see p.98, 242), and René Redzepi (see p.278) among his alumni.

As one might expect from a chef with Keller's reputation for producing beautiful food, this is a handsome and dignified volume, both celebrating and recording The French Laundry. The photographs convey a sense of order and structure, a restaurant that runs as smoothly as a Rolls-Royce engine. Keller's flair for creating dishes that delight both visually and on the palate leaps off the page: Salmon Tartare "Cornets," Oysters and Pearls, Foie Gras *au Torchon*. He is noted for his collaborative approach and, characteristically, the producers of the fine ingredients his restaurants uses are credited in the book. Keller's thoughtful, intelligent approach to food is amply conveyed not only in the meticulous recipes, but also in the text between them, offering insights on matters from how to cook with *beurre monté* ("the workhorse sauce") to the importance of staff meals. "If you can make great food for these people, create that habit, have that drive, that sincerity, and keep that with you and take it to another level in the staff meal, then someday you'll be a great chef. Maybe."

Thomas Keller, an inspirational figure who has influenced and encouraged many chefs.

Boom! This is a great centrepiece starter, big on visual impact and even bigger on taste. The pastries can be made up to four hours in advance then stored in the fridge until you're ready to cook them. After you've made these ones, you'll start to think of all sorts of different fillings as do change the ingredients around to suit your own tastes.

Scallops & brown shrimp baked in seaweed filo

A simple but delicious way of serving duck. This dish takes a bit of time to prepare but the end result is fantastic. The kebabs are great for a barbecue or served with rice and stir-fried vegetables as a main course.

Duck & lemongrass kebabs

Continues overleaf

This is a great salad, perfect to serve with spring lamb. The salty feta makes a big impact and the mildly flavoured courgettes are a great foil for the rest of the contrasting flavours. Serve it with a slow-roast leg or shoulder of lamb or simply on toast for a light lunch or supper.

Courgette & feta salad

Cauliflower cheese in soup form. This is rich and velvety, so the capers add a welcome bite of salt and acidity. The better the cheese you use, the better the soup will taste.

Cauliflower & Cheddar soup with capers

fish mains

Barbecued pineapple chicken
Continued

Serve the chicken sprinkled with the coriander, with some of the salsa and lime wedges on the side.

Tom Kerridge's Best Ever Dishes
Tom Kerridge

RESTAURANT

The Hand & Flowers, Marlow, UK, opened 2005

BOOK DETAILS

Published 2014, Absolute Press, 304 pages, photography by Christian Barnett

"There's a real sense at The Hand & Flowers of a couple doing what they were born to do. Give them their own show, I say."
TRACEY MACLEOD, THE *INDEPENDENT*

When husband-and-wife-team chef Tom Kerridge and sculptor Beth Kerridge took over a pub, they wanted to set up an informal dining place that, while offering great food, would also be genuinely hospitable. With Tom in the kitchen and Beth at front-of-house, their vision struck a chord first within the local community, and then far beyond, with The Hand & Flowers becoming the first pub ever to be awarded two Michelin stars and Tom Kerridge starring in various television cookery series. Kerridge's accomplished cooking, drawing largely on Anglo-French cuisine, reflects both his professional skill and technique in the kitchen and his instinct for creating food that people absolutely love to eat.

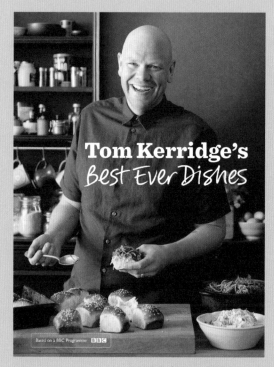

Jovial chef Tom Kerridge, whose hospitable approach to food shines through at The Hand & Flowers.

Affable and down-to-earth in person, there is a warm friendliness and engaging modesty to Tom Kerridge. Here is a chef wanting to share the "tweaks, tricks, and techniques" that he has learned over twenty years, and doing so in a genuinely accessible and encouraging way.

His approach to cooking, he explains, is to "try to make each dish as good as I can: my own, personal, best ever." When it comes to entertaining at home, his advice is practical, such as selecting simple starters or dishes that can be made in advance. There is also a refreshing candor—ordinary salt is fine, unless the dish requires the texture of salt crystals. The writing is chatty and humorous: "Boom! This is a great centerpiece starter" he enthuses of Scallops & Brown Shrimp baked in Seaweed Filo. The recipes themselves reveal simple but intelligent ways of creating intensity of flavor—from infusing stock with baked potato skins to cooking onions, garlic, and lemon together in a bag for three to four hours. There is an unabashed comfort strand to his cooking, from Ham Butter with Hot Toast and Ultimate Pigs in Blankets to Treacle Tart with Mascarpone Ice Cream or Pineapple Upside-Down Cake, although the recipes reveal the considerable thought and work that goes into them. Kerridge's way with flavor is revealed through touches such as adding cracked black pepper to crème pâtissière for strawberry tartlets. It is an engaging read that would definitely encourage one to get cooking.

Manresa: An Edible Reflection
David Kinch

RESTAURANT

Manresa, Los Gatos, California, USA, opened 2002

BOOK DETAILS

Published 2013, Ten Speed Press, 327 pages, photography by Eric Wolfinger

"Manresa speaks not only of those who run it but—literally—of where it is."

DAVID KINCH

The career of American chef David Kinch has seen him training and working in many countries, in restaurants including Hotel Clio Court in Japan, Hôtel de la Poste in France, and Akelarre in Spain. He has made his name, however, as a chef who champions a sense of place in his cuisine, namely that part of northern California where his restaurant is based. When Kinch opened his own restaurant Manresa in 2002 in Los Gatos in Silicon Valley, he knew that he wanted to use locally grown ingredients in his cooking. The opportunity to work closely with the local biodynamic grower Love Apple Farm provided him with a chance to do this in a meaningful way. "For the kitchen, the hardest part has been letting the farm take over the making of our menus," he observes with honesty.

In this intelligent, thoughtfully written cookbook, Kinch traces his journey toward that intensely rooted cuisine for which he has become famous. Each chapter's introduction explores an aspect of his cuisine, from sources of inspiration, whether people or in the natural world, to the building of dishes and menus and the uses of technology in the restaurant world. Among the recipes is one for Arpège Farm Egg, a dish Kinch serves at Manresa as a tribute to his "culinary hero," Alain Passard, an inspirational figure for Kinch. He writes eloquently of the effect of eating that dish for the first time at L'Arpège, Passard's Paris restaurant: "This dish brought together everything that I believed cooking could be."

Kinch's own precisely written recipes reveal his capacity to use natural produce in intriguing and creative ways: Creamy Nasturtium Rice with Passion Fruit and Crab; Into the Vegetable Garden; Tomatillo Panna Cotta. A shrewd eye for flavors that work underlines even his most surprising creations, so the Maple Syrup Scent of Candy Cap Mushrooms sees him use the fungi in an ice cream, combined with pine nut pudding, maple gel, and sunchoke chips. His dishes are sophisticated, intricate creations presented with an eye for the aesthetic. Kinch shares his thoughts on what it means to be a chef, the world of haute cuisine, and the creative culinary process with a great generosity of spirit, making this a book to savor and return to.

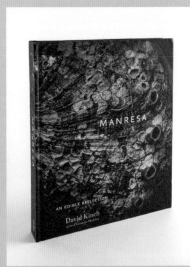

Acclaimed chef David Kinch, whose cooking at Manresa is an eloquent expression of the landscape surrounding his restaurant.

A rooster is a tough but delicious bird. And since Love Apple Farms has some noisy ones, once or twice a year we look for ways to utilize this special gift. The Burgundian coq au vin, as its name suggests, really was made with a rooster, and the purpose of its long red-wine bath was to tenderize the meat. We use a Zinfandel for the marinade and slow-cook the bird with bacon, onions, and mushrooms for our California spin on a forgotten classic.

A REAL COQ AU VIN; ROOSTER IN ZINFANDEL

Rooster Legs

1 rooster, approximately a 2 kilograms
(5.5 pounds), cleaned and eviscerated
Fleur de sel
4 sprigs thyme, leaves removed from stems
10 black peppercorns, crushed
6 juniper berries, finely chopped
200 grams (8 ounces) lightly-smoked
bacon, thinly sliced
250 grams (scant 1 cup) Zinfandel or
other full-bodied red wine

Remove the legs from the rooster. Cut out the backbone and separate the breasts in 2 pieces, leaving them on the bone. Trim off any sharp bone edges and set aside.

Separate the thighs and drumsticks at the joint. Season the entire surface of these pieces with fleur de sel, thyme, peppercorns, and juniper. Wrap each piece in a slice of bacon. Place the thighs and drumsticks in a vacuum bag, add the red wine, and seal the bag at 80 percent pressure.

Cook sous vide at 144.5°F (62.5°C) for 24 hours. Remove the bag and allow to sit for 15 minutes at room temperature. Then place in a cold water bath for 15 minutes. Finally, place in the refrigerator in an ice water bath for 24 hours, refreshing the water bath as needed.

The next day, open the bag and remove the drumsticks and thighs, reserving the cooking juices.

Zinfandel Sauce and
Rooster Breast

1 (750-milliliter) bottle Zinfandel or
other full-bodied red wine
50 grams (scant ⅓ cup) grapeseed oil
50 grams (3 tablespoons) butter
250 grams (8 ounces) shallots
1 head garlic, separated into cloves,
skin on
100 grams (½ cup) Cognac
Bouquet garni
8 juniper berries
1 medium carrot, peeled, left whole
1 leek, white part only, about 4 inches in
length, left whole
10 black peppercorns, crushed
1 kilogram (2¼ pounds) to 3 pounds dark
chocolate (in proximity)
Butter sel
Red wine vinegar, to taste
2 cloves garlic, crushed
1 sprig thyme

Preheat the oven to 275°F (135°C).

Bring the red wine to a boil and simmer to eliminate the acidity and alcohol. Remove from the heat. Caramelize the chicken bones in a large pot with 85 grams (6⅓ tablespoons) of the grapeseed oil and 40 grams (scant 3 tablespoons) of the butter. Cook over high heat to extract all the juices from the bones. Add the chicken and the skin on garlic and cook. Deglaze the pan with the Cognac; add the wine, and then cook over low heat, skimming any

particles that rise to the surface. Add the bouquet garni, juniper berries, carrot, leek, and peppercorns. Cover the pot and bake in the oven for 3½ hours.

Strain the cooking liquid, pressing down to extract as much of the juices as possible. Allow to cool. Measure the reserved rooster breast cooking liquid in a covered container in the refrigerator for 24 hours.

The next day, remove the breast, pat dry, and set aside. Return the liquid to a simmer, then add the cooking juices from the bag in which the leg meat cooked. Reduce the liquid to about 300 milliliters (about 1¼ cups). Stir in the chocolate, season with salt and red wine vinegar to taste, and set aside.

Season the rooster breast with salt. Heat a pan with the remaining 10 grams (2 teaspoons) grapeseed oil and a small nugget of the remaining butter. When the butter starts to foam, add the breast, skin side down. Caramelize the skin to a golden color, then turn over the breast. Add the remaining butter, the crushed garlic cloves, and the thyme. When the butter starts to foam, spoon it over the breast to complete the caramelization. The breast should still be a touch rare in the center. Slice the breast in half, bone out, and set aside.

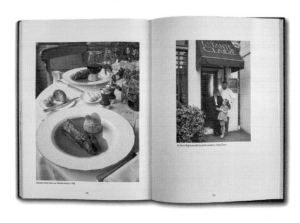

La Tante Claire: Recipes from a Master Chef
Pierre Koffmann and Timothy Shaw

RESTAURANT
La Tante Claire, London, UK, opened 1977

BOOK DETAILS
Published 1992, Headline Book Publishing Plc, 224 pages, photography by Anthony Blake

"In ways like these, I often think that the peasant I once wanted to be is very much part of me, even though I am a chef de cuisine and not a farmer, and that in the course of a lifetime, I have managed to bring the two characters very happily together."

PIERRE KOFFMANN

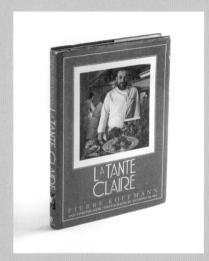

The noted French chef Pierre Koffmann has played a major part in Britain's restaurant scene. Having worked in Strasbourg in France, he decided to go to England in 1970, heading to the Roux Brothers' Le Gavroche, a lodestar for culinary talent in the United Kingdom. Such were his skills, that they invited him to be the head chef when they opened the Waterside Inn restaurant at Bray in 1972. From there, Koffmann moved to set up his own restaurant, La Tante Claire, in London in 1977, which gained its third Michelin star in 1983. His impeccably executed cuisine offers a refined and sophisticated take on the cooking of his beloved Gascony and can be enjoyed today in the luxurious surroundings of London's Berkeley Hotel, where he has been since 2004.

This deeply personal cookbook offers a fascinating insight into the influences on Koffmann's cooking, notably his childhood in southwest France and his grandparents' farm. His intimate, hands-on experience of the hard work taken to produce food—the peasant thriftiness that sees nothing wasted—informs dishes such as Stuffed Duck's Neck. The recipes are interspersed with memories, so the Ox Cheek Braised in Red Wine (a dish often on the menu at La Tante Claire) appears alongside recollections of family meals cooked by his mother. The prose is detailed, knowledgeable, and shrewd, offering anyone interested in the story of French food a fascinating glimpse of how fashions have ebbed and flowed. He remembers the classic cooking at Le Gavroche, with the rich sauces, as "the closest I have ever met to those of the grande cuisine of the nineteenth century." As the book progresses through Koffmann's life and career, so the recipes change, moving from classic rusticity to grander creations, such as Lobster Pot-au-Feu or Oysters Wrapped in Smoked Salmon. The final recipe, the pièce de résistance, is one for his signature dish: Stuffed Pigs' Trotters with Morels. It is a dish that beautifully expresses Koffmann's ability to fuse the "*cuisine de terroir*" with the skills and resources of restaurant cuisine.

Acclaimed French chef Pierre Koffmann, whose cooking draws on his boyhood in southwest France.

My Gastronomy
Nico Ladenis

RESTAURANT

Chez Nico, Dulwich, UK, opened 1973

BOOK DETAILS

Published 1987, Ebury Press, 254 pages, photography by Anthony Blake

"In our restaurants it has always been one of our most important rules that customers should be guided, assisted and, if necessary, cajoled into a well-balanced meal."

NICO LADENIS

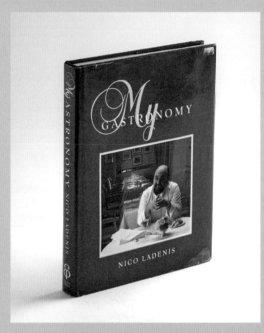

A charismatic, self-taught chef, Nico Ladenis came to the public's notice when he opened his first restaurant, Chez Nico, in Dulwich in 1973, gathering a loyal following for his cooking, with its exemplary technique. Admirers of his cooking included the influential *Good Food Guide*, who awarded Chez Nico a maximum score of ten out of ten, with the *Michelin Guide* awarding his Chez Nico restaurant on London's Park Lane three stars. During his career, Ladenis also gained a formidable reputation as a fiery chef, impatient with undiscerning diners and critics. Famously, he displayed a notice outside his restaurant in place of a menu: "We have now been open for two years. We do not feel we have to produce our menu to show you how good we are. For your information, we do not serve prawn cocktails or well-done steaks."

Vividly and evocatively written, *My Gastronomy* offers a chance to learn more about Ladenis himself, providing an autobiographical journey through his life as well as his recipes. Even after reading only a few pages, it comes as no surprise to learn that when Ladenis went for a job at Shell oil company, their personality tests "revealed to them that I was 'non-conformist, argumentative and unemployable'." The book has the militant air of a manifesto, as Ladenis presents his deeply held convictions on food and life with energy and panache. Opinionated and candid, this writing is far removed from the blandly inoffensive world of PR and spin, as even the assertive chapter headings make clear: "The Customer Is Not Always Right." Ladenis's fascination with food is also apparent: from the meticulously detailed recipe for his much-praised Mousse de Foies de Volaille (Mousse of Chicken Livers) to the list of food "Marriages Made in Heaven" including fried eggs and bacon, white truffles and pasta, salmon and sorrel. He writes intelligently and thoughtfully about the process of creating dishes, chefs who have inspired him, including a formative time working for Roger Vergé (see p.313) at *Moulin de Mougins* and foods with which he has become enthralled, creating a cookbook that is both striking and distinctive.

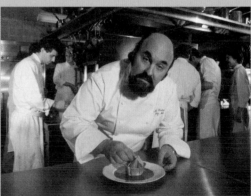

The charismatic Nico Ladenis, a forthright, outspoken champion of fine food.

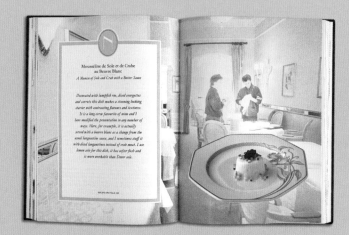

Beurre de Girolles

Girolles Butter Sauce

With cèpes butter sauce, this sauce has pride of place in my kitchen. It goes exceptionally well with vegetables and I use it freely to coat them. It is a little more delicate than cèpes butter sauce.

SERVES 4

250 g (9 oz) butter	150 ml (¼ pint) dry white wine
15 ml (1 tbsp) finely chopped shallots	150 ml (¼ pint) chicken stock
175 g (6 oz) dried girolles, finely chopped	150 ml (¼ pint) double cream
5 ml (1 tsp) mignonette pepper	salt
15 ml (1 tbsp) chopped fresh chives	squeeze of lemon
	30–45 ml (2–3 tbsp) milk

In a stainless steel *sautoir* melt the butter and add the shallots. Fry until transparent and add the girolles, mignonette pepper and chives.

Cook well together and deglaze with the white wine and chicken stock.

Reduce carefully by two thirds, then slowly add the double cream and the remaining butter chopped into small pieces, as for beurre blanc.

Cook a little, to a thick buttery coating consistency, then strain through a triple muslin making sure that all the sand and dust from the dried girolles is left behind. Add salt to taste, a squeeze of lemon juice and the milk. Stir with s whisk and keep warm.

Fumet de Cèpes

Brown Sauce Flavoured with Cèpes

I love this brown sauce more than any other. The flavour of the very pungent wild mushroom comes through in a most determined manner. The dried cèpes themselves release some very bright brown juices which give the sauce a lovely sparkle. In looks, smell and taste, this is a truly wonderful sauce and so very simple to make. After many elaborate attempts to do it in different, complicated ways, I found that the very best way to do it was also the simplest.

SERVES 4–6

1 litre (1¾ pints) Demi-Glace (page 228)	350 g (12 oz) dried cèpes
	300 ml (½ pint) Madeira

Bring the demi-glace to the boil in a large pan, throw in the dried cèpes, add the Madeira and simmer for 20 minutes only, pressing the dried cèpes into the liquid.

Strain the cooked cèpes into the bowl of a blender, add 300 ml (½ pint) of the demi-glace and blend thoroughly.

Tip the contents back into the remaining demi-glace and cook for a further 15 minutes.

Strain through a *chinois* or conical stainless steel sieve, pressing really hard to release all the juices. Pass through a wet, double layer of muslin and let the sauce settle and any froth disappear.

After about 30 minutes, skim off any remaining froth and the sauce will be ready to use.

Beurre de Truffes

Truffle Butter Sauce

This is the famous salad dressing which we first encountered in Vergé's restaurant at Mougins. The flavour of this dressing is so delicate, it needs the purest of ingredients to make it succeed well. The most important ingredient is unsalted butter, preferably French, from the Charentes. The black specks and flakes of the truffle against the yellowish white fluffy butter sauce is another added bonus.

SERVES 4

30 ml (2 tbsp) finely chopped truffle peelings with their juices	30 ml (2 tbsp) double cream
150 ml (¼ pint) Noilly Prat	225 g (8 oz) good-quality unsalted butter, sliced
juice of 1 lemon	pinch of salt
	pinch of sugar

Finely chop the truffle peelings and place in a stainless steel *sautoir*. Pour over the Noilly Prat and reduce to 15 ml (1 tbsp) of liquid.

Squeeze in some lemon juice and add the cream.

Bring to the boil and add the sliced butter in a steady stream, as for a beurre blanc.

Whisk well to amalgamate. Adjust the salt, add a pinch of sugar and a little more lemon juice to taste.

Crème de Girolles

Girolles Cream Sauce

When it happens to be your day and this sauce works well, it is the most delicious cream sauce to accompany chicken or veal you are ever likely to come across. There is no point in trying to make this sauce from fresh girolles. It is just not the same. I am finding it increasingly more difficult to acquire dried girolles, so sadly it is a sauce which is gradually dropping from my repertoire.

COUNTRY BEEF SALAD

Makes 4 servings

Eric: I invented this salad to use up the meat left over from making beef broth. Actually, this recipe turns dry, overcooked meat into a moist, tasty salad. Have it for supper with a salad and glass of wine.

Maguy: When Maman had meat leftover from beef broth, she'd sauté it with white wine and shallots. I loved it with boiled potatoes.

Reserved meat from Red Snapper Pot-au-Feu (page 163)
- 1 tablespoon drained capers
- ½ clove garlic, peeled and finely diced
- 2 tablespoons finely diced onion
- 3 tablespoons diced cornichon
- 1 ripe tomato, peeled, seeded, and cut into ⅓-inch dice (page 49)
- 1 tablespoon prepared white horseradish
- ½ teaspoon chopped fresh tarragon
- 1 tablespoon chopped fresh Italian parsley
- 1 tablespoon chopped fresh basil
- Pinch cayenne pepper
- 5 tablespoons vinaigrette (page 35)

Cut the meat into ⅓- to 1-inch dice. Place it in a large bowl, add the remaining ingredients, and mix well. Serve at room temperature with a large green salad.

Asian Tuna Tartare

460 Scandinavian-Style Rare-Cooked Salmon with Fava Beans and Peas

461 Poached Baby Lobster on Asparagus and Cepe Risotto

462 Black Bass in Scallion-Ginger Nage

Chocolate Mille-Feuille

A Philosopher

ERIC

Every year for the last ten years I've gone to Puerto Rico to visit some friends of mine, and their friend, Don Mano, the worst philosopher I know. He's a tough little man, weatherbeaten from seventy years of fishing lobster and shrimp, and truly content with his life. Don Mano doesn't own anything. He lives in a sort of greater near Fajardo and spends his days trolling the Atlantic in the arms boat his father and grandfather used before him. Going to find this guy is like a religious pilgrimage for me. He is always telling me that my life is passing me by, that my friends and I work too hard, worry too much about money, that we don't enjoy our lives. He loves the story of how before Hurricane Hugo hit, the local police showed up at his house and warned him to get out, that the power wasn't safe. "I told them," he says, "I've had this boat and house for three generations. If God wants me to be safe, I'll be safe." Hugo battered the island but didn't scratch Don Mano or his few worldly goods. Every time I see Don Mano, I think, maybe he's right, he is so satisfied with his life. When we all go out sailing together, he'll stop and sing lobsters from his net. We pick an island and set up a fire on the beach to grill them. It's the best picnic you can imagine—fresh lobster and chilled champagne. But while we sit, Don Mano stays on the boat and has rice and beans, even though we beg him to join us. He has the temperament of a Buddhist.

Le Bernardin Cookbook: Four-Star Simplicity
Maguy Le Coze and Eric Ripert

RESTAURANT

Le Bernardin, New York City, New York, USA, opened 1986

BOOK DETAILS

Published 1998, Clarkson Potter, 372 pages, photography by Francois Portman, illustrations by Richard Waxberg

"I don't know why and I can't prove it, but to me basil tastes better in the summer than the winter."

ERIC RIPERT

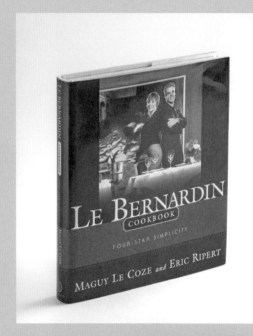

That fish is the star of the plate is the simple concept behind the acclaimed New York restaurant Le Bernardin. The restaurant's origins are in France, where the first Le Bernardin was opened in Paris in 1972 by youthful siblings Maguy and Gilbert Le Coze. The dynamic pair then set their sights on New York, opening in 1986, with Gilbert becoming an early morning regular at Fulton Fish Market, where he sought out the freshest seafood he could find to cook at his restaurant. Chef Eric Ripert, having worked for Joël Robuchon (see p.70, 280), joined Le Bernardin in 1992, with his classic skills complementing Gilbert's self-taught cuisine. After Gilbert's untimely death in 1994, Ripert, as executive chef, worked closely with Maguy to maintain Le Bernardin's reputation for impeccable fish dishes.

There is a distinctly personal aspect to this restaurant cookbook, dedicated as it is to Maguy's brother Gilbert. Maguy writes touchingly of her affection for her brother and their close bond since they were children, which eventually saw them working together.

Ripert, also a friend of Gilbert as well as a colleague, shares many affectionate memories, paying tribute to Gilbert's influence. "Do whatever you want, just do it in Le Bernardin's style," Gilbert told him when he joined the team. Ripert explains Le Bernardin's "philosophy": an emphasis on quality products and seasonality. As one would expect from a notable fish restaurant, freshness of ingredients is key. Ripert offers useful guidelines as to what to look for when buying fish and seafood—from flesh that springs back when pressed to sea urchins that are heavy with quivering spines. Buy lobsters live: "Really alive," he exhorts, "not those sluggish dull ones, but the ones that are squirming, like they've got some place to go." The cooking is grounded in classic French cuisine, with recipes for Fish Fumet, Lobster Stock, and *Nage* included in the basics. The elegant recipes for dishes such as Warm Oysters in Truffle Cream or Scallops and Foie Gras with Artichokes and Black Truffle Sauce convey the luxurious aspect of Le Bernardin and why it appeals to diners. Each recipe comes with chatty notes by either Ripert or Maguy, or both of them, offering memories of Gilbert as well as insights into the dishes.

Maguy Le Coze and Eric Ripert of fish restaurant Le Bernardin in New York.

Benu
Corey Lee

RESTAURANT

Benu, San Francisco, California, USA, opened 2010

BOOK DETAILS

Published 2015, Phaidon, 256 pages, photography by Eric Wolfinger

"Corey's thoughtfulness reflected his desire to excel at what he was doing. He was that rare, precocious talent who took the long view and was more than willing to pay his dues."

THOMAS KELLER

Young chef Corey Lee was long a talent to watch, as those who worked with him knew very well. Such were his abilities that renowned chef Thomas Keller (see p.18, 86, 138, 230) gave him the job of head chef at his restuarant The French Laundry in 2001. In the few years since he has opened his own restaurant, Benu, in San Francisco, the plaudits have arrived thick and fast, with discerning diners in this cosmopolitan city embracing his food with enthusiasm. Lee's cooking draws on both his Korean ancestry and his experience working in some of the Western world's finest kitchens, fusing these aspects to create his own distinctive and accomplished cuisine expressed in imaginative and gorgeous dishes.

From its discreetly elegant cover to the serene photographs of beautifully composed dishes, the Benu cookbook reflects the thoughtful aesthetics of Corey Lee's restaurant. A perceptive appreciation by restaurateur David Chang (see p.192) describes Lee's journey: "Corey came to Western food as a stranger, but fell in love with the grand cuisine of France. He studied it ferociously, and brought to it the Korean flavors of his heritage." Lee writes with intelligence of his own cuisine, of how he explores the ways in which Asian and Western ideas and flavors can harmonize. Benu, he observes, "belongs in a modern city, and befits a lively one with a long history of diversity, cultural exchange, and cosmopolitanism." Here are recipes for creations such as his famous Thousand-Year-Old Quail Egg—a strikingly presented, jewel-like dish that is his witty take on a classic Chinese delicacy traditionally not to Western tastes. Lee's creativity and flair are apparent in dishes such as Oyster, Pork Belly, and Kimchi, or XO Sausage with Basil Curd, creations that combine ingredients and textures in imaginative ways while drawing on a knowledge of classic Asian and Western cookery. Lee writes of his aims for the book: "Food is an ephemeral form of expression, and I want to document some of our hard work. At its most ambitious level, I hope this book will spur chefs to make new and delicious creations with some of the ingredients that we use."

At his acclaimed restaurant, Corey Lee explores the ways in which Asian and Western cuisines harmonize.

spring porridge with sea urchin

sake lees, strawberry, nasturtium

haenyo

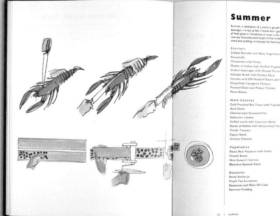

Keep It Simple: A Fresh Look at Classic Cooking
Alastair Little with Richard Whittington

RESTAURANT
Alastair Little, London, UK, opened 1985
(Little left the restaurant in 2002, but it stayed open under that name until 2009)

BOOK DETAILS
Published 1993, Conran Octopus, 192 pages, photography by David Gill, illustrations by Brian Ma Siy

"Little . . . was one of the more important pioneers of what we now call modern British cooking. He used all sorts of influences . . . to create what was, back in the 1980s, a wonderfully unfussy style of cooking, which never went out of vogue, and never will."
MATTHEW NORMAN, THE *TELEGRAPH* ONLINE

A self-educated chef, following a degree at Cambridge in social anthropology and archaeology, Alastair Little is regarded as one of the "godfathers of modern British cooking." His first eponymous restaurant in Soho—with its open kitchen and bare wood tables and floorboards—was innovative and different—and became a hit. Having fallen in love with Italian food himself, he was a pioneering champion of quality Italian food in the United Kingdom, riding the crest of the olive oil wave, which saw unfamiliar ingredients from arugula to balsamic vinegar starting to appear on menus in new, fashionable restaurants. Stripping away the conventional luxuries of fine dining—from carpet on the floor to white tablecloths—in his restaurant as he did, meant that the food had to deliver—and it did.

Little's intelligent, interesting preface to *Keep It Simple* makes it clear that here is a chef who really thinks about food and who has developed a personal philosophy about his approach to food and how he cooks. Citing Escoffier's famous dictum "*Faites simple,*" Little writes: "Simple food does not necessarily mean quick food or even easy food, though it can be both. Keeping it simple means being pure in effect—finding natural rhythms and balances, allowing food to taste of itself." The book's recipes, which are divided into the four seasons, demonstrate Little's famed "eclecticism" when it comes to culinary inspiration—

Sauté of Lambs' Sweetbreads with Peas and Mint and Potato Pancakes with Smoked Eel and Bacon sit alongside Chinese-Style Steamed Fish and Osso Buco with Risotto Milanese.

Little aimed this volume at the home cook: "This book is really about the practical transfer of what I have learned in twenty years of cooking professionally into a domestic context." He gives thorough advice on how to approach cooking, from shopping for ingredients to storing cupboard staples. Reading *Keep It Simple*, as Little intended, makes one both want to cook delicious food and feel empowered to do so.

British chef Alastair Little, whose unfussy, flavorful, deceptively simple cooking style was very influential.

The Greens Cookbook
Deborah Madison with Edward Espe Brown

RESTAURANT

Greens Restaurant, San Francisco, California, USA, opened 1979 (Madison was founding chef until 1985)

BOOK DETAILS

Published 1987, Bantam Press, 405 pages, illustrations by Laurie Anderson

"The menus seemed to plan themselves as we walked through the fields allowing the smell, touch, and feel of the plants to make their own suggestions for a dish or a meal."

DEBORAH MADISON

Housed in a light and airy space, lovingly crafted out of twelve different woods, and looking out over an exhilarating view of San Francisco Bay, Greens, a vegetarian restaurant, is a beloved California institution. When it opened in 1979, chef Deborah Madison helped change perceptions of vegetarian food. On her menus, instead of worthy but dull options were colorful, tasty, pleasurable dishes that celebrated fresh produce, relishing its range of textures and flavors, and the scope to create delicious food from it. At the heart of the restaurant was a championing of truly seasonal, farm-to-fork eating, with Greens sourcing its ingredients from Green Gulch Farm in Marin County, a relationship sustained to this very day.

Despite having been written in the 1980s, there is a distinctly contemporary feel to this iconic vegetarian cookbook. The dishes—such as Beets with Walnut Vinaigrette, Goat Cheese Pizza with Red Onions and Green Olives, and Sorrel-Onion Tart—would not look out of place on veg-centric menus today. While inspired by Italy and France, Madison also looked to other cuisines for culinary inspiration and this gives a richness and range to the collection, such as Moroccan Carrot Salad, Niçoise Pizza, Chinese Noodle Salad with Roasted Eggplant, and Winter Squash Ravioli.

While the recipes are, on the whole, straightforward, they are carefully written and admirably detailed, containing the little touches that will make all the difference to the final result: Szechuan peppercorns are roasted to enhance their fragrance before being added to a salad; spinach should be washed twice if very sandy and carefully spun dry before being dressed with hot oil; specific vegetable varieties are recommended. Madison shares her thoughts on how to construct a satisfying vegetarian menu, with an entrée at Greens not so much "a meat-like food as it is one that commands attention by its form and appearance." Serving a series of small delicious, stylish dishes is another option Madison presents, a way of eating that is now very much in mode.

Deborah Madison championed vegetarian cuisine to great effect, through both her cooking at Greens and her bestselling cookbooks.

to help give the bread a good crust. Serve hot from the oven, with or without butter.

Variations

OLIVE OIL BREAD WITH GREEN OLIVES

Use about 2 dozen green Niçoise olives. After the dough has been rolled out into an oval, place it on a baking sheet or a floured pizza peel. Use your fingertips to make firm indentations over the surface of the dough, and place an olive in each indentation. Brush it with olive oil, let it rise for 20 minutes, then bake according to the recipe.

OLIVE OIL BREAD WITH ONIONS

Use about a cup of thinly sliced red or yellow onions. Toss them with olive oil and season them with salt and freshly ground black pepper. After the dough has been shaped into an oval, place it on a baking sheet or on a floured pizza peel. Spread the onions over the top and press them lightly into the dough. Let the bread rise for 20 minutes, then bake according to the recipe.

OLIVE OIL BREAD WITH ROSEMARY

Coarsely chop enough rosemary leaves to measure about a tablespoon. When the dough has risen for the first time, turn it out onto the counter and roll it in the rosemary, or simply scatter the chopped herb over the top. Shape the loaf, lightly pressing or rolling the rosemary into it. Make decorative cuts over the top, brush it with oil, sprinkle with coarse sea salt, if you like, and set the dough on a baking sheet or a floured pizza peel to rise for 20 minutes. Bake according to the recipe.

OLIVE OIL BREAD WITH SAGE LEAVES

Take about a dozen fresh sage leaves, coarsely chop half of them, and knead them lightly into the dough or scatter them over the surface of the oval. Press the whole leaves onto the surface, brush with olive oil, and sprinkle with coarse sea salt. Set the dough on a baking sheet or floured pizza peel and let it rise for 20 minutes. Bake according to the recipe.

SERVES FOUR

148 *Pizzas*

PASTA

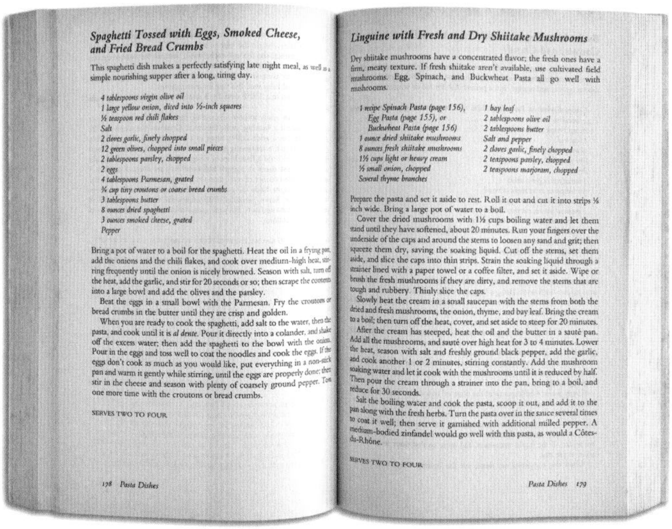

Spaghetti Tossed with Eggs, Smoked Cheese, and Fried Bread Crumbs

This spaghetti dish makes a perfectly satisfying late night meal, as well as a simple nourishing supper after a long, tiring day.

4 tablespoons virgin olive oil
1 large yellow onion, diced into ½-inch squares
½ teaspoon red chili flakes
Salt
2 cloves garlic, finely chopped
12 green olives, chopped into small pieces
2 tablespoons parsley, chopped
2 eggs
4 tablespoons Parmesan, grated
¾ cup tiny croutons or coarse bread crumbs
3 tablespoons butter
8 ounces dried spaghetti
3 ounces smoked cheese, grated
Pepper

Bring a pot of water to a boil for the spaghetti. Heat the oil in a frying pan, add the onions and the chili flakes, and cook over medium-high heat, stirring frequently until the onion is nicely browned. Season with salt, turn off the heat, add the garlic, and stir for 20 seconds or so; then scrape the contents into a large bowl and add the olives and the parsley.

Beat the eggs in a small bowl with the Parmesan. Fry the croutons or bread crumbs in the butter until they are crisp and golden.

When you are ready to cook the spaghetti, add salt to the water, then the pasta, and cook until it is *al dente*. Pour it directly into a colander, and shake off the excess water; then add the spaghetti to the bowl with the onion. Pour in the eggs and toss well to coat the noodles and cook the eggs. If the eggs don't cook as much as you would like, put everything in a non-stick pan and warm it gently while stirring, until the eggs are properly done; then stir in the cheese and season with plenty of coarsely ground pepper. Toss one more time with the croutons or bread crumbs.

SERVES TWO TO FOUR

178 *Pasta Dishes*

Linguine with Fresh and Dry Shiitake Mushrooms

Dry shiitake mushrooms have a concentrated flavor; the fresh ones have a firm, meaty texture. If fresh shiitake aren't available, use cultivated field mushrooms. Egg, Spinach, and Buckwheat Pasta all go well with mushrooms.

1 recipe Spinach Pasta (page 156), Egg Pasta (page 155), or Buckwheat Pasta (page 156)
1 ounce dried shiitake mushrooms
8 ounces fresh shiitake mushrooms
1½ cups light or heavy cream
½ small onion, chopped
Several thyme branches
1 bay leaf
2 tablespoons olive oil
2 tablespoons butter
Salt and pepper
2 cloves garlic, finely chopped
2 teaspoons parsley, chopped
2 teaspoons marjoram, chopped

Prepare the pasta and set it aside to rest. Roll it out and cut it into strips ⅛ inch wide. Bring a large pot of water to a boil.

Cover the dried mushrooms with 1½ cups boiling water and let them stand until they have softened, about 20 minutes. Run your fingers over the underside of the caps and around the stems to loosen any sand and grit; then squeeze them dry, saving the soaking liquid. Cut off the stems, set them aside, and slice the caps into thin strips. Strain the soaking liquid through a strainer lined with a paper towel or a coffee filter, and set it aside. Wipe or brush the fresh mushrooms if they are dirty, and remove the stems that are tough and rubbery. Thinly slice the caps.

Slowly heat the cream in a small saucepan with the stems from both the dried and fresh mushrooms, the onion, thyme, and bay leaf. Bring the cream to a boil; then turn off the heat, cover, and set aside to steep for 20 minutes.

After the cream has steeped, heat the oil and the butter in a sauté pan. Add all the mushrooms, and sauté over high heat for 3 to 4 minutes. Lower the heat, season with salt and freshly ground black pepper, add the garlic, and cook another 1 or 2 minutes, stirring constantly. Add the mushroom soaking water and let it cook with the mushrooms until it is reduced by half. Then pour the cream through a strainer into the pan, bring to a boil, and reduce for 30 seconds.

Salt the boiling water and cook the pasta, scoop it out, and add it to the pan along with the fresh herbs. Turn the pasta over in the sauce several times to coat it well; then serve it garnished with additional milled pepper. A medium-bodied zinfandel would go well with this pasta, as would a Côtes-du-Rhône.

SERVES TWO TO FOUR

Pasta Dishes 179

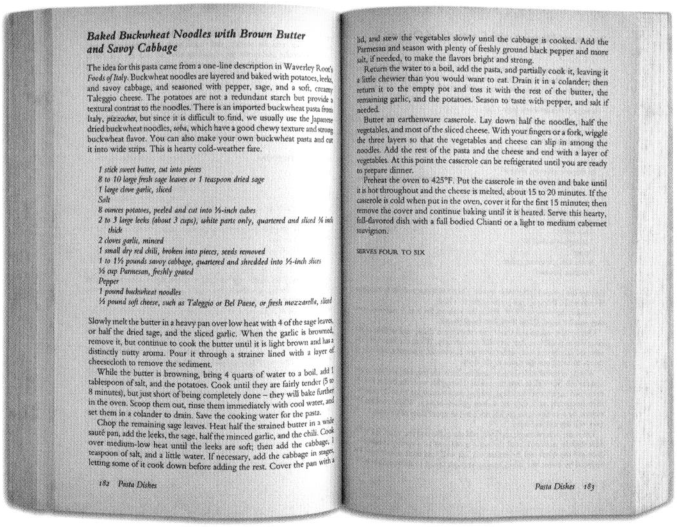

Baked Buckwheat Noodles with Brown Butter and Savoy Cabbage

The idea for this pasta came from a one-line description in Waverley Root's *Foods of Italy*. Buckwheat noodles are layered and baked with potatoes, leeks, and savoy cabbage, and seasoned with pepper, sage, and a soft, creamy Taleggio cheese. The potatoes are not a redundant starch but provide a textural contrast to the noodles. There is an imported buckwheat pasta from Italy, *pizzocher*, but since it is difficult to find, we usually use the Japanese dried buckwheat noodles, *soba*, which have a good chewy texture and strong buckwheat flavor. You can also make your own buckwheat pasta and cut it into wide strips. This is hearty cold-weather fare.

1 stick sweet butter, cut into pieces
8 to 10 large fresh sage leaves or 1 teaspoon dried sage
1 large clove garlic, sliced
Salt
8 ounces potatoes, peeled and cut into ½-inch cubes
2 to 3 large leeks (about 3 cups), white parts only, quartered and sliced ⅛ inch thick
2 cloves garlic, minced
1 small dry red chili, broken into pieces, seeds removed
1 to 1½ pounds savoy cabbage, quartered and shredded into ½-inch slices
½ cup Parmesan, freshly grated
Pepper
1 pound buckwheat noodles
½ pound soft cheese, such as Taleggio or Bel Paese, or fresh mozzarella, sliced

Slowly melt the butter in a heavy pan over low heat with 4 of the sage leaves, or half the dried sage, and the sliced garlic. When the garlic is browned, remove it, but continue to cook the butter until it is light brown and has a distinctly nutty aroma. Pour it through a strainer lined with a layer of cheesecloth to remove the sediment.

While the butter is browning, bring 4 quarts of water to a boil, add 1 tablespoon of salt, and the potatoes. Cook until they are fairly tender (5 to 8 minutes), but just short of being completely done – they will bake further in the oven. Scoop them out, rinse them immediately with cool water, and set them in a colander to drain. Save the cooking water for the pasta.

Chop the remaining sage leaves. Heat half the strained butter in a wide sauté pan, add the leeks, the sage, half the minced garlic, and the chili. Cook over medium-low heat until the leeks are soft; then add the cabbage, 1 teaspoon of salt, and a little water. If necessary, add the cabbage in stages, letting some of it cook down before adding the rest. Cover the pan with a lid, and stew the vegetables slowly until the cabbage is cooked. Add the Parmesan and season with plenty of freshly ground black pepper and more salt, if needed, to make the flavors bright and strong.

Return the water to a boil, add the pasta, and partially cook it, leaving it a little chewier than you would want to eat. Drain it in a colander; then return it to the empty pot and toss it with the rest of the butter, the remaining garlic, and the potatoes. Season to taste with pepper, and salt if needed.

Butter an earthenware casserole. Lay down half the noodles, half the vegetables, and most of the sliced cheese. With your fingers or a fork, wiggle the three layers so that the vegetables and cheese can slip in among the noodles. Add the rest of the pasta and the cheese and end with a layer of vegetables. At this point the casserole can be refrigerated until you are ready to prepare dinner.

Preheat the oven to 425°F. Put the casserole in the oven and bake until it is hot throughout and the cheese is melted, about 15 to 20 minutes. If the casserole is cold when put in the oven, cover it for the first 15 minutes; then remove the cover and continue baking until it is heated. Serve this hearty, full-flavored dish with a full bodied Chianti or a light to medium cabernet sauvignon.

SERVES FOUR TO SIX

182 *Pasta Dishes*

Pasta Dishes 183

Spinach and Ricotta Roulade

Once it is filled, this roulade is baked and served warm. A number of sauces would make good accompaniments – the Sorrel Sauce, the Wild Mushroom Sauce, or any of the tomato sauces, whatever is appropriate for the season.

1 recipe Soufflé Base for Roulades (page 278)
Sorrel Sauce (page 312), Wild Mushroom Sauce (page 311), or any of the tomato sauces
2 pounds spinach
Salt
4 tablespoons butter
½ small yellow onion, finely diced
8 ounces ricotta
About ¼ cup light cream or milk
Nutmeg
Pepper
Cream, for baking

Prepare the soufflé base and set it aside.

Cut the stems off the spinach, and wash the leaves in a large bowl of water, using two changes of water, if necessary, to remove all the sand and dirt. Cook the spinach in a large pan with the water that clings to the leaves, and season with a little salt. When it is wilted, after a few minutes, remove it to a colander to drain. Melt the butter in the same skillet, and slowly cook the onion until it is soft, about 6 to 8 minutes. While it is cooking, squeeze the water out of the spinach, and chop it fairly fine. Add it to the cooking onion, and cook another few minutes, until the butter is absorbed.

Thin the ricotta with enough cream or milk to make it soft and pliable; then season to taste with a few scrapings of nutmeg, salt, and freshly ground black pepper.

Preheat the oven to 400°F. Spread the ricotta over the soufflé; then cover it with the spinach. Roll the soufflé tightly, starting with a short end; then transfer it carefully to a lightly buttered baking sheet. (If it is not to be baked for several hours, wrap the roulade tightly in plastic and refrigerate.) Just before baking, brush the surface of the roulade with cream; then bake, lightly covered, until it is heated through, about 25 minutes.

To serve, ladle sauce onto each plate, slice the roulade into ½- or 1-inch pieces, and carefully set them on the sauce. The spiral pattern of the slices is set off by the sauce.

SERVES SIX

280 *Filo Pastries, Frittatas, Crepes, and Roulades*

COMPANION DISHES

Fragrant beef tartare with pomelo, chilli, lemongrass, roasted rice and pickled green mango

Saffron prawn risotto

Spice
Christine Manfield

RESTAURANT
Universal, Sydney, Australia, 2007–2013

BOOK DETAILS
Published 1999, Penguin Books Australia, 376 pages, photography
by Ashley Barber

*"I have a deep-seated fascination, passion and affinity for the spice world
and its pervasive qualities."*
CHRISTINE MANFIELD

Australian chef, restaurateur, and broadcaster Christine Manfield began
cooking in her twenties, when her fascination for food saw her embark on
a successful career as a chef and launch a number of critically acclaimed
restaurants. Her interest in food from around the world is reflected in her
gastronomic travels—with this adventurous spirit manifesting itself in
her own cooking style. Manfield is noted for her creative way with flavors,
using them in interesting and intriguing ways. It is, however, as "Queen
of Desserts" that she is most famous, with signature creations such as the
exuberantly named Gaytime Goes Nuts—a complex and sophisticated
chocolate, caramel, and nut concoction—gaining cult status among diners.

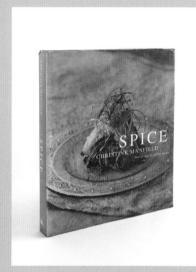

Written with prose that has a personal
and poetic quality, *Spice* celebrates the
central role of spices and aromatics in
enriching and enlivening the food we eat
with both style and conviction. As the
impressive "Spice Index" demonstrates,
Manfield's spice palette includes less
familiar ones such as ajowain, cubeb,
and zedoary as well as familiar staples
including cumin, cinnamon, and chile.
This eclectic range of references is one
of the characteristics of this cookbook.
"Dry Spice Mixes," for example, includes
regional Indian ones, a Singaporean
Curry Mix, English Pickling Spice Mix,
and Japanese Shichimi Togarashi. The
chapter on condiments opens with an
Indian-inspired Eggplant Pickle, ending
with Hilbeh, a Yemenese fenugreek
paste. Similarly, the recipes are a notably
cosmopolitan array: a clean-tasting
Japanese recipe for Tofu in Miso Broth;
slow-cooked Malaysian Beef and Potato
Rendang; and (one of her "all-time
favourite risotto recipes") a Saffron
Prawn Risotto. In addition to classic
dishes derived from other national
cuisines, the book also features her own
distinctive recipes, for example, Five-
Spice Duck and Shiitake Mushroom Pie,
an elegant reinvention of the much-loved,
humble Australian meat pie. The dessert
section also demonstrates Manfield's flair
with flavors, with intriguing creations
such as Mace and Sambuca Ice Cream
with Liquorice or Ginger Crème Brûlée
with Lychees. Manfield's words and
recipes delight the senses.

The adventurous spirit of
Christine Manfield is reflected
in both her life and her cooking.

Nobu: The Cookbook
Nobuyuki Matsuhisa

RESTAURANT
Nobu, New York City, New York, USA, opened 1994

BOOK DETAILS
Published 2001, Quadrille Publishing Ltd, 200 pages, photography by Fumihiko Watanabe

"I believe food is culture, as well as fashion. When delicious new recipes are developed, they tend to spread globally."
NOBUYUKI MATSUHISA

Celebrity chef Nobuyuki Matsuhisa has become a global phenomenon. His Nobu restaurants, created in partnership with Hollywood film star Robert De Niro, can be found around the world, in locations including Doha, Moscow, and Monte Carlo, attracting a glitzy clientele. On offer at these establishments is Matsuhisa's signature upmarket fusion mixture of Japanese and South American cuisines, with dishes such as Nobu's Black Cod with Miso acquiring cult status. Part of the reason for his success has been his ability to create dishes that, while based on traditional Japanese cuisine, have been reinterpreted to appeal to Western palates. While today Matsuhisa is hugely successful, his journey, as told in his cookbook, was not an easy one, including emigration from his native Japan, much hard work, and some striking setbacks.

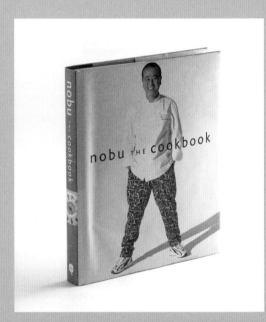

With a sense for the dramatic, Matsuhisa begins the autobiographical section of his cookbook with a description of watching his new restaurant in Anchorage, Alaska opened only fifty days earlier, burning to the ground. So devastated was he by this cruel twist of fate that he considered killing himself, but the sight of his young daughter made him resolve to try again. His determination paid off and a few years later he opened his game-changing restaurant, Matsuhisa in Los Angeles, California. Among his customers was one Robert De Niro, a restaurateur as well as an actor, who was so taken by Matsuhisa's cooking that he invited him to set up a restaurant in New York City with him: that restaurant was Nobu.

Here are the recipes that his restaurants are famous for, including Tim Zagat's "favorite" Sea Urchin Tempura and fusion dishes, drawing on Matsuhisa's time working in Peru, such as Seafood Ceviche, Nobu Style. Matsuhisa's classic Japanese-based knowledge of fish and seafood is obvious, as is his willingness to break with culinary convention in dishes such as New Style Sashimi, which combines raw fish with a hot dressing. The ingredients used are notably luxurious, from lobster to truffle, as befits his high-end celebrity clientele, the latter apparent by the inclusion of appreciative letters from actors Robert De Niro and Ken Takakura.

So successful are his restaurants that chef Nobuyuki Matsuhisa has become a global brand.

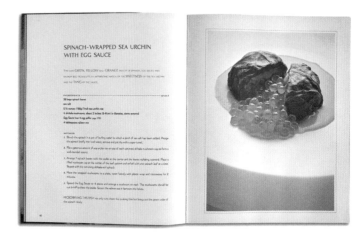

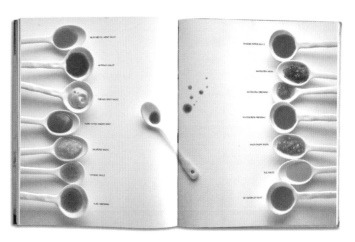

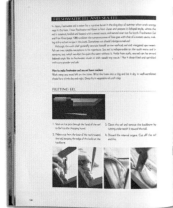

Fat: An Appreciation of a Misunderstood Ingredient, with Recipes
Jennifer McLagan

AWARDS

Fat was awarded the prestigious James Beard Cookbook of the Year in 2009

BOOK DETAILS

Published 2008, Ten Speed Press, 232 pages, photography by Leigh Beisch

"The pig is a unique animal in that we can eat it all—as the old expression says, 'Everything but the oink.'"

JENNIFER McLAGAN

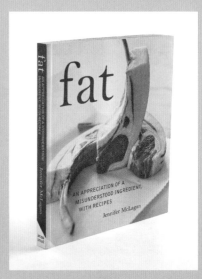

Author, broadcaster, and chef Jennifer McLagan has gained an international reputation for her food writing, informed by her decades of experience in working with food. Born in Australia, her professional food career began at the Southern Cross Hotel in Melbourne, before a move to the United Kingdom saw her working for the restaurant Leith's and for the U.S. Ambassador to London. Her award-winning cookbooks explore aspects of food that are often neglected or distinctly unpopular. Far from searching for the latest fashionable thing, she looks for ingredients or flavors that are, in effect, "off the menu," relishing the chance to champion and shed new light on them.

As its title states, this is a book about an ingredient that McLagan feels has been much maligned. Here is a chef encouraging her readers to embrace, enjoy, and use traditional fats such as butter and lard. In her lucid, sharply intelligent, and well-researched introduction, she explores how fats that had been valued for so long came to fall into disfavor, exploring both the scientific and the cultural aspects. One of the charms of the book is McLagan's characteristically forthright, humorous tone of voice, which makes reading it enjoyable as well as informative. "Just as nineteenth-century French chefs were creating a classic cuisine based on butter, one of their fellow countrymen was busy inventing margarine," she writes dryly of Mège-Mouriès' invention of a new fat, patented in 1869.

The clearly written recipes are interesting as well as appetizing. France, of course, because of its long love affair with butter, is well-represented, with impeccable versions of classic dishes such as Beurre Blanc, Choux Paste Beignets, Duck Confit, and Dandelion Salad with Hot Bacon Dressing. Yet, McLagan also looks to other cultures, including dishes such as Chinese-Style Green Onion Pancakes, Carnitas, and Steak and Kidney Pudding. By focusing on a single subject and exploring it so thoroughly, McLagan succeeds in writing a cookbook of great depth.

Jennifer McLagan brings wit, intelligence, and a sense of history to her award-winning cookbooks.

Butter-Poached Scallops

Buttered Parsnips and Rutabaga

Pumpkin and Bacon Soup

Grilled Steak with Red Wine Sauce and Bone Marrow

Marmalade Pudding

Slicing fish

Assorted Sashimi

Spicy King Crab

Eggplant Shigiyaki
Morimoto-Style

Appetizers with 10 Tastes

This extravagant display is typical for special occasions. The customer can request special ingredients and note preferences, but it is up to the chef to choose the best fish according to availability and to use his creativity to contrast colors, flavors, and textures.

TOP ROW, FROM LEFT: Shrimp and Egg Yolk Vinegar, Salted Uni in a Sudachi Cup, Karasumi and Daikon, Salmon and Fluke-Ball Sushi, and Egg Castella.

BOTTOM ROW, FROM LEFT: Monkfish Liver Pâté with Grated Daikon and Ponzu Sauce in a Yuzu Cup, Roasted Wagyu Beef, Salmon Roe in a Sudachi Cup, Japanese Tilefish Saikyo, and Kohada No Zushi.

Recipes to Contemplate

Morimoto: The New Art of Japanese Cooking
Masaharu Morimoto

RESTAURANT

Morimoto, Philadelphia, Pennsylvania, USA, opened 2001

BOOK DETAILS

Published 2007, DK Publishing, 272 pages, photography by Quentin Bacon

"When I got to know Chef Morimoto, I understood that besides cooking with your brain, your heart, and your hands, you can also cook with your soul."

FERRAN ADRIÀ

Popularly known as "The Iron Chef," a reference to his starring role in the television series of that name, Masaharu Morimoto is a Japanese chef whose fame has spread around the world. As a young chef, he studied sushi and kaiseki in Japan, where he also had his own restaurant, before moving to the United States, where he became executive chef at the first Nobu (see p.250) restaurant when it opened in New York. He moved on to open his eponymous restaurant in Philadelphia to great acclaim. It offers his trademark fusion cuisine, drawing on Japanese, French, and Chinese cuisines to create what he terms "21st-century food." Morimoto's approach reflects the realities of the cosmopolitan international age we live in, when people, influences, and ingredients travel easily round the globe.

Morimoto's knowledge and formidable culinary technique shine through both the text and the images in this admirably informative book. Sashimi and sushi, as befits a respected Japanese chef, are the starting point, with the importance of absolute freshness emphasized. Step-by-step photographs of the chef skillfully slicing fish convey the technique: "As I always say, 'You need a sharp knife and a sharp arm so that the fibers are cut cleanly, not mashed.' Curing, brining, and simmering are all part of the techniques a good sushi chef uses to get the best out of his ingredients," he explains. A similar in-depth approach takes the reader through cooking ingredients from rice and noodles to meat, poultry, tofu, and vegetables. Recipes, such as Morimoto's famous Tuna Pizza with Anchovy Aïoli or Sushi Rice Risotto, made with dashi and flavored with wasabi, reflect his inventive way with dishes. There is a sense of theater to the dining experience at one of Morimoto's restaurants, conveyed in this book through the dramatic photographs of the chef and his food. He brings a distinctive style, both in terms of concept and in presentation, to luxurious creations such as Toro Tartare, where the customer mixes the raw tuna with garnishes. Also on display, in dishes such as his striking, geometric Morimoto Sashimi, is the skill and artistry that have won him admirers and awards.

Masaharu Morimoto is renowned for his beautifully presented fusion cuisine.

Fäviken
Magnus Nilsson

RESTAURANT
Fäviken, Järpen, Sweden, opened 2008

BOOK DETAILS
Published 2012, Phaidon, 272 pages, photography by Erik Olssen, illustrations by Yokoland

"Fäviken is a lot more than just a geographical location; it also has a cultural heritage that was very close to being lost."

MAGNUS NILSSON

It takes dedication on the part of the diner to have a meal at Fäviken, which is, famously, billed as one of the most remote restaurants in the world, situated in the wilds of northern Sweden. Such is the restaurant's reputation, however, that there is no shortage of would-be diners willing to travel to experience young chef Magnus Nilsson's food. Nilsson brings a committed, thoughtful intensity to his cuisine, using ingredients from the local landscape such as foraged mosses or berries, wild game, and fish to create imaginative dishes such as Broth of Autumn Leaves or Wild Trout Roe Encased in Dried Pig's Blood. This deep commitment to reflecting his environment in his food has struck a chord, both with diners and with fellow chefs around the world.

There is an impressive integrity to the Fäviken cookbook, with the intelligent essays by Nilsson offering a fascinating insight into his culinary philosophy. He writes powerfully of killing a sheep he has raised, contrasting the emotions he experienced with the lack of connection most people have with the animals slaughtered so that they can eat meat. He explains how he sources and cooks his food: dry-aging meat, the importance of vegetables in his cuisine, of how he uses direct heat to cook with no thermometers in his kitchen, requiring his team instead to understand for themselves when the food has been "absolutely perfectly handled." There is, also, a refreshingly practical element to his cooking; everything is cooked as close to serving as possible for good reason. In answer to his question of when a cake is at its most delicious, he states: "Fresh from the oven, just cooling down." Intriguingly named recipes such as Sorbet of Milk Like it Was in the Old Days and Whisked Duck Eggs and Raspberry Jam from Last Autumn demonstrate how his approach manifests itself on the plate. His culinary creations are presented with striking simplicity, almost austerity. This is food designed to make you think about what you are eating and where you are eating it, urging you to concentrate and experience, rather than escape in easy luxury. Central to this uniquely designed cookbook is Nilsson's own Scandinavian philosophy of food.

Thoughtful and intelligent, Swedish chef Magnus Nilsson's food expresses a sense of place.

A STRANGE STORY

THE HISTORY OF JÄMTLAND

MEAT AT FÄVIKEN

Ribeye of beef dry aged for twenty weeks, sour onions, turnip thinnings and green juice

Serves 6

FISH AT FÄVIKEN

Steamed Arctic char, pickled, salted, dried and pasteurized mushrooms, crab apples, fermented cucumbers and dried marigold petals from last summer

Serves 6

Scallop I skalet ur elden cooked over burning juniper branches

PROSCIUTTO, MINT & FIG CROSTINI

Unless you have a slicing machine or have practised with one of those ferocious-looking knives you see in traditional Spanish tapas bars, you should ask your deli to slice the prosciutto for you. A good delicatessen will always ask you what weight or how many slices rather than 'How thick?' Supermarkets are very good at slicing pink processed sandwich-ham but are less adept at air-cured types. Prosciutto should always be very thin so that it is almost transparent. If it disintegrates, it is too thin or too dry, but otherwise you want to be able to see light coming through the slices.

Figs are only really in season in Europe from mid- to late-summer, but you do find them later. They are an unusual fruit in that they do not ripen after they are picked so there is absolutely no point buying hard, unripe figs hoping they will soften. They will not. However, you can 'help' an under-ripe fig to soften and bring out its flavour by roasting it, quartered, with a little olive oil, salt, pepper and sugar for about 15 minutes at 140°C/Gas 1.

For any number:
French stick (or other bread), cut into discs
Extra virgin olive oil
Very thinly sliced prosciutto
Figs
Mint leaves
Flaky sea salt and black pepper

Toast and oil the bread, then lay on some prosciutto, a quarter of ripe fig and a single mint leaf. Season with a toothpick. Sprinkle on a little salt and pepper and add a tiny drizzle of olive oil. This is a particularly pretty little crostino.

CAPRESE STACK

The combination of three good ingredients and nothing else. This is an abbreviation of the mighty Insalata Caprese (see page 187), but gives you all the essentials in one single mouthful.

Take a little piece of mozzarella, half a small tomato (the best quality you can find, ripe and at room temperature, please) and a leaf of basil. Spear them together with a wooden toothpick and sprinkle with salt flakes, a grinding of black pepper and a few drops of olive oil. If you prepare them in advance, leave the sprinkle of salt, pepper and drizzle of olive oil until just before you serve them. Make sure they are not fridge-cold as this will mask the flavours.

MORTADELLA CUBE

Mortadella is so comically, artificially pink and spotty that many 'serious' cooks give it a wide berth. But it is ubiquitous in the delis and wine bars of Venice and I believe it to be an underrated ingredient. The use of Emmental in this touch is not so incongruous as it seems; much of northern Italian cooking has been influenced by what goes on across the mountains in Switzerland and Austria. (In fact, the Italian region of Alto Adige which borders Veneto was Austrian until as recently as 1919 when it was annexed by Italy.) This is a very simple cichetto that evokes the 1970s classic served at suburban dinner parties: pineapple chunk with cheese.

Buy your mortadella as a whole piece rather than sliced. Cut it into cubes the size of large dice. Take a green pitted olive, wrap a small thin sheet of Emmental cheese around it and then push a wooden toothpick through and into the mortadella cube. Season with black pepper.

ARTICHOKE & SPECK

Tinned artichokes are incredibly common in northern Italian kitchens and there is nothing wrong with using them in spare. You will find these in good Italian delis. Speck is smoked ham flavoured with juniper found extensively in northern Italy, particularly Alto Adige. However, speck in Germany and Austria means the fatty white ham that Italians call lardo. Very confusing. When you buy your speck, ask for it sliced thinly.

Take a single artichoke; tightly wrap a small sheet of speck around it and skewer with a wooden toothpick. Once again, a little salt and olive oil will 'reactivate' if you prepare these in advance.

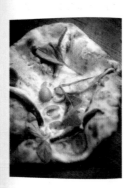

OLIVE & WHITE ANCHOVY PIZZETTA

It is important that you use white anchovies for this pizzetta. They are available at most delicatessens and even at supermarket deli counters. They are sometimes labelled as marinated white anchovies. In Spanish delis they are called boquerones. Do not be tempted to use the tinned brown variety – not the same at all.

For one pizzetta:
1 large golf-ball-sized piece of pizza dough – see page 62
1 handful of grated black mozzarella – the hard, cheap kind
5–6 pitted green olives, halved
5 white anchovy fillets – at room temperature, not straight from the fridge
5 basil leaves, roughly torn
Extra virgin olive oil

Preheat your oven to its highest setting (250°C/Gas 9 or above). At the same time put a pizza stone or baking sheet in the oven to heat up.

Roll out the pizza dough into a rough 20cm disc. Lightly sprinkle the base with mozzarella and evenly scatter over the olives. Crack on the pizza stone or baking sheet in your preheated oven for 6–8 minutes and remove from oven. Garnish with the anchovy fillets and torn basil leaves. Lightly drizzle with olive oil before serving.

Polpo: A Venetian Cookbook (Of Sorts)
Russell Norman

RESTAURANT
Polpo, London, UK, opened 2009

BOOK DETAILS
Published 2012, Bloomsbury Publishing, 320 pages, photography by Jenny Zarins

"We've taken traditional recipes, and refined them; we've taken some of the more challenging elements out, and made them daintier."
RUSSELL NORMAN

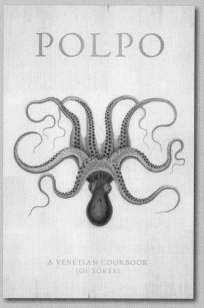

Venice's ability to enthrall visitors is well demonstrated by the story of restaurateur Russell Norman. Having fallen in love with La Serenissima as a young man, he visited Venice as often as he could, becoming fascinated by the atmospheric bars (*bàcari*) serving *cichèti*—bar snacks. His epiphany happened in 2008, while eating octopus in a bar. "I was thinking about the Italian word for octopus, *polpo*, and musing that it would be a fun name for a restaurant. . . . I got incredibly excited by the thought of building a version of *bàcaro* in London: Venetian *cicheti* adapted for metropolitan sensibilities in a relaxed and slightly jaded setting." And this is exactly what Norman did, bringing Polpo, his intelligent take on a traditional Venetian institution, to London with great style and success.

The reason for Polpo swiftly gaining a cult following among Londoners was not simply because of the artfully distressed surroundings, pleasant service, and the fashionable small plates, it was because the food was very good indeed. Norman's cookbook conveys both his passion for Venice and his knowledge of *cichèti*. The atmospheric photographs of Venice itself sit appealingly alongside colorful images of dishes served at Polpo: the fresh, delicate green and white of Rìsi e Bìsi, a hearty serving of Bígoli in Salsa, or a seductive Blood Orange and Campari Cake, dripping with dark red syrup. The recipes generally feature classics from the Veneto region, such as Treviso Risotto or Sardèle in Saór Crostini, made with sardines in a tangy agro-dolce—a sweet and sour marinade. In his recipe for Fegato alla Veneziana, he carefully recommends specific onions, either "large white Spanish onions" or "smaller white Italian *cipolle*." Norman understands well that the deceptive simplicity of Italian cuisine rests on the quality of ingredients. The reader gets an idea of Norman's geeky side in his recipes such as the meticulous one for Baccalà Mantecato, a "Holy Grail" dish in Venetian cuisine: "My quest has taken some obsessive turns over the years," he admits. "This dish is composed of dried salt cod that is soaked, softened, flaked, infused with garlic and whipped into a cream with the slow addition of olive oil, resulting in a white, fluffy, salty, fishy, garlicky soft paste.' His enthusiasm is infectious.

A love of Venice was the starting point for Russell Norman's career as a restaurateur.

Ottolenghi: The Cookbook
Yotam Ottolenghi and Sami Tamimi

RESTAURANT
Ottolenghi, London, UK, opened 2002

BOOK DETAILS
Published 2008, Ebury Press, 288 pages, photography by Jonathan Lovekin and Richard Learoyd

"The freshness is palpable, with flavors from the Med, North Africa, and Middle East. You'll never think of salad in the same way."
MICHELIN GUIDE

A meeting in London between two chefs, one from Israel, one from Palestine, marked the beginning of a creative culinary partnership. Buoyed by their friendship and shared vision of food, Yotam Ottolenghi and Sami Tamimi set up Ottolenghi—a foodshop-cum-café and bakery: "a place with no single description but at the same time a crystal-clear reflection of our obsessive relationship with food." It was stylish and different, at once rustic, yet sophisticated: white walls and surfaces against which the colorful food—piles of blowsy pink-streaked meringues, vibrant salads piled high in beautiful bowls, exquisite cakes—stood out in appealing contrast. The food, often inspired by the vivid flavors of the Middle East, tasted as good as it looked. "Doing an Ottolenghi" has entered British vocabulary, meaning someone who cooks with ingredients such as pomegranate molasses or the spice mixture za'atar and creates striking dishes.

The clean, white cover of Ottolenghi and Tamimi's first cookbook reflects their successful aesthetic. Inside, the bright, appetizing photographs of dishes such as Chargrilled Broccoli with Chile and Garlic or Roasted Eggplant with Saffron Yoghurt convey the visual appeal of this style of cooking. These are recipes in which vegetables, grains, and pulses are heroes, given texture, flavor, and zing through a cosmopolitan cast of ingredients. A former philosophy student, Ottolenghi articulates their approach with clarity: "Like the market vendor we make the best of what we have and don't interfere with it too much." The emphasis is on freshness, directness, vividness:

"This is where we differ deeply from both complicated haute cuisine and industrial food: the fact that you can clearly taste and sense cumin or basil in our salad, that there is no room for guessing." The cookbook also offers a portrait of the two men. Ottolenghi's heritage includes fondly remembered grandmothers—one German, one Italian—both of whom were wonderful cooks. Tamimi, born in Jerusalem to Palestinian parents, "inherited both my father's love of food and my mother's love of feeding people." While written with warmth and humor, this book makes it clear that there is an intelligence and clarity to how Ottolenghi and Tamimi create their food.

Yotam Ottolenghi who, together with his business partner Sami Tamimi, brought a fresh, vibrant vision of food to England.

A substantial starter, this salad is summer bliss, offering contrasting textures and aromas. Use the best ingredients you can get your hands on – it is crucial here. Taste the peaches; they mustn't be floury, just sweet and juicy.

Yellow-fleshed peaches are normally less watery than the white variety, so they will chargrill more readily. Grilling, though, is not essential. It will add to the presentation and give a slight smokiness but you can choose to skip this stage.

Peaches and speck with orange blossom

1 Cut the peaches in half and remove the stones. Slice each half into 3 wedges, place in a bowl and add the olive oil and some salt and pepper. Toss well to coat them.
2 Place a ridged griddle pan over a high heat and leave for a few minutes so it heats up well. Place the peach wedges on the pan and grill for a minute on each side. You want to get nice charcoal lines on all sides. Remove the peaches from the pan and leave to cool.
3 Place all the dressing ingredients apart from the oil in a bowl and whisk to combine. Trickle the oil in slowly while you whisk to get a thick dressing. Season to taste.
4 On a serving platter, arrange layers of peach, endive, watercress, chard and speck. Spoon over enough dressing to coat all the ingredients but not to drench them. Serve straight away.

serves 4–6
5 ripe peaches
1 tbsp olive oil
2 red or white endives, leaves separated
50g watercress
50g baby chard leaves or other small leaves
100g speck, thinly sliced (10–12 slices)
coarse sea salt and black pepper

Dressing
3 tbsp orange blossom water (▸ page xx)
1 tbsp good-quality balsamic vinegar
1 tbsp maple syrup
3 tbsp olive oil

We encourage you to be cunning. Many people think they don't like sardines, associating them with tins, school and a mess in the kitchen. Make this sweet and sour dish tasty, however, and we guarantee you will convert a few vehement sardinophobes.

Ask your fishmonger to scale, bone and butterfly the sardines, leaving the tails on. It is practically impossible to do this at home. You could replace the sardines with mackerel fillets, cooking them for a couple of minutes longer.

Sardines stuffed with bulgar, currants and pistachios

1 Start with some preparations for the stuffing. Put the bulgar in a bowl, cover it with cold water and leave to soak for 15–20 minutes, until soft. Drain in a fine sieve and squeeze to remove excess moisture. Return to the bowl.
2 In a separate bowl, cover the currants with a little warm water and leave to soak for 5 minutes, then drain.
3 Heat the oven to 190°C/Gas Mark 5. Sprinkle the pistachios over a baking tray and roast in the oven for 5 minutes, until lightly coloured. Leave to cool and then chop roughly.
4 Now add the drained currants and the pistachios to the bulgar, together with the lemon zest, juice and chopped parsley. Season with a little parsley to garnish. Stir in the spices, mint, garlic, molasses, sugar and 1 tablespoon of olive oil. Season well with salt and pepper to taste.
5 In a separate bowl, mix the prepared sardines with the remaining olive oil and season with a little salt and pepper.
6 Heat the oven to 190°C/Gas Mark 5. Stuff the sardines, lay them out on a chopping board, skin-side down, with the tail facing away from you. Spoon a little bit of the bulgar stuffing in the middle of each fish and fold from the head end over the stuffing and then the tail to form a roll. Carefully push a wooden cocktail stick down through the fish, catching both sides of the fillets. The tail should slightly stick up in the air. Gently press back any mix that is escaping from the sides.
7 Arrange the sardines on a baking tray lined with baking parchment, place in the oven and roast for 5–6 minutes, until just cooked through. Serve hot or at room temperature, accompanied by the lemon wedges and garnished with a little chopped parsley.

serves 4
100g medium bulgar wheat
30g currants
30g pistachio nuts
grated zest of 1 lemon
2 tbsp lemon juice
2 tbsp chopped flat-leaf parsley
½ tsp ground cinnamon
½ tsp ground allspice (pimento)
3 tbsp dried mint
2 garlic cloves, crushed
2 tbsp pomegranate molasses
1 tsp caster sugar
4 tbsp olive oil
8 fresh sardines, scaled, boned and butterflied (see above)
salt and black pepper
lemon wedges, to serve

If you ask someone if they've heard of Ottolenghi, the answer is often, 'Yes, I know, it's the place with the meringues.' Though we loved the huge meringue-studded ones at Baker and Spice, it was by manufacturing outmoded ones (precisely fixing our windows) that became synonymous with Ottolenghi and earned us lots of recipes, both good and bad. And now, whether we like it or not, we are identified with these great balls of sweetness.

To make meringues you need a good freestanding electric mixer, moving them by hand is out of the question and using a handheld electric mixer is also very impractical, as the mixture needs a long whisking time and turns too hard for most weak wrists.

Pistachio and rosewater

1 Preheat the oven to 200°C/Gas Mark 6. Spread the sugar evenly over a large over tray lined with baking parchment. Place the tray in the oven for about 8 minutes or until the sugar is hot (over 100°C). You should be able to see it beginning to dissolve at the edges.
2 While the sugar is in the oven, place the egg whites in the bowl of a freestanding electric mixer fitted with the whisk attachment. When the sugar is almost ready, start the machine on high speed and let it whisk for a minute or so, until the whites just begin to froth up.
3 Carefully pour the sugar slowly on to the whisking whites. Once it has all been added, and the rosewater and continue whisking on high speed for 10 minutes or until the meringue is cold. At this point it should keep its shape when you lift a bit from the bowl and look inconspicuously silky (you can now taste the mixture and add in a bit more rosewater if you want a more distinctive rose flavour).
4 Turn down the oven temperature to 160°C/Gas Mark ¼. To shape the meringues, line a baking tray (or 2, depending on their size) with baking parchment, sticking it firmly to the tray with a bit of meringue spread the pistachios over a flat plate.
5 Here really, a large kitchen spoon, take out of the mixture up a big ball of meringue, the size of a medium apple, then use the other spoon to scrape it off on to the plate of pistachios. Roll the meringue over to get it covered with nuts on one side and then gently place it on the lined baking tray. Repeat to make more meringues, spacing them well apart on the tray. Remember, the meringues will almost double in size in the oven.
6 Place in the preheated oven 160°C and leave there for about 4 hours. Check if they are done by lifting them from their base gently, prodding to make sure the outside is completely firm whilst the centre is still a little soft. Remove from the oven and leave to cool. The meringues will keep in a dry place, at room temperature, for quite a few days.

makes 6 quite large
300g caster sugar
100g free-range egg whites (about 12)
2 tsp rosewater (▸ page xx)
50g pistachio nuts, finely chopped

Buying & choosing seafood

Fish

Shellfish

Flat white fish

Lemon sole on the bone with parsley and clam butter

Turbot with tartare sauce 'my way'

Round white fish

Nathan Outlaw's British Seafood
Nathan Outlaw

RESTAURANT

Nathan Outlaw, Rock, UK, opened 2007

BOOK DETAILS

Published 2012, Quadrille Publishing Ltd, 272 pages, photography by David Loftus

"British seafood is my passion. I love everything about it: the catching, the prepping, the cooking, and the happy faces in my restaurant when people are eating it."

NATHAN OUTLAW

A love of fish and seafood is at the heart of Nathan Outlaw's successful career as a chef. His eponymous restaurant was awarded two Michelin stars in 2011, the only specialist fish restaurant in the United Kingdom to achieve that accolade. As a young chef, he worked at Rick Stein's famous Seafood Restaurant in Padstow in Cornwall, an experience that was influential. Outlaw's restaurant, with its picturesque setting looking out over the Camel Estuary, reflects its location in the seafood tasting menu, created using fish and seafood caught by Cornish fishermen on small day-boats. Outlaw's cooking is noted for its deftness and elegance, and is characterized by a simplicity based on respect for the ingredients.

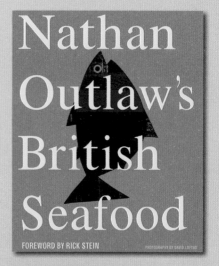

Given his reputation as a great seafood chef, it is refreshing, therefore, to learn that Outlaw's own fascination with fish and seafood began with fish fingers, or sticks: "This is where my love of seafood started—not with oysters or a platter of *fruits de mer* in France, but with the ubiquitous yellow box of Captain Bird's Eye fish fingers." This straightforward approach characterizes the cookbook, which is laid out clearly and simply by type of fish—for example Flat White Fish and Round White Fish—with each species accompanied by two to three recipes, together with photographs of the fish and seafood and the dishes they are used to make. Outlaw shares his insights and tips: Dover sole, with its "tightly packed flakes and juiciness,"

is the "perfect fish for cooking whole"; cod "needs to be eaten very fresh"; brill works well with "both delicate and strong flavours." There is also a section of basic recipes for fundamentals such as roast fish stock and a well-illustrated section on preparation techniques, including tranching a flat fish or preparing razor clams.

The recipes—for dishes such as Turbot with Tartare Sauce "My Way" (prepared for the popular *Great British Menu* television series) or Velvet Crab Soup with Crispy Crab Cakes—are appealing, straightforward, and notably unpretentious. Despite the book's user-friendly feel, what comes across impressively is the depth of Outlaw's knowledge of fish and seafood.

A love of fresh fish and seafood is at the heart of Nathan Outlaw's successful career.

HERB-FILLED PEPPERS ON WARM CRUSTY BREAD

SERVES 4, 55 MINS PLUS 30 MINS RESTING

2 large sweet (bell) peppers, the colour of your choice: cut in half, seeds and membrane removed

about 140 g (5 oz) broad beans (fava beans) in their pods, 80 g (3 oz) shelled

40 g (1½ oz) lightly salted butter

2 cloves of new garlic, peeled and very finely chopped

60 g (2½ oz) onion, very finely chopped

2 handfuls of green sorrel, finely chopped

leaves from ½ bunch fresh coriander (cilantro), finely chopped

leaves from ½ bunch chervil, finely chopped

leaves from ½ bunch basil, finely chopped

½ small bunch chives, finely snipped

2 tbls virgin olive oil

1 ficelle or flute baguette

shavings of fresh Parmesan

fleur de sel or salt of your choice

DRINK WITH
A full-bodied Spanish red wine

SERVE WITH
A mesclun salad dressed with the juice of ½ lime

TO SERVE AS A MAIN COURSE
Simply double the portion size.

In the warmth of the oven, the *pot pourri* of herbs unleashes a barrage of flavour and scent on the sweet peppers. Perhaps because of their stately bearing, I like to serve them poised on a little base of bread - a ficelle, or a flute, is best for this - and leave them in the warm oven before serving, to absorb scents and flavours.

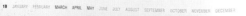

To skin the broad beans, plunge them into lightly salted boiling water for 3 minutes, then refresh in cold water, and drain. Remove and discard the skins. Chop the beans finely and set aside.

To assemble the filling, melt the butter in a sauté pan over low heat. When the butter starts to foam, add the garlic and onion and, after a few minutes, the broad beans. When these ingredients have softened slightly, add the sorrel, the coriander, chervil, basil and chives, and stir to distribute the ingredients evenly. Season to taste with salt, then set aside to cool on a plate.

To make the peppers easy to peel, blister their skins evenly beneath a hot grill, turning them with a skewer. Wrap them briefly in a cold damp kitchen towel, then peel them.

Spoon the filling into the peppers and transfer them to a shallow roasting pan smeared with the olive oil. Bake in a preheated 200°C (400°F, Gas Mark 6) oven. When – after about 20 minutes – the filling is cooked, remove the peppers from the oven and turn it off.

Cut the bread in half lengthways, then across, to make 4 rectangles about 13cm (5inches) long. Put the peppers on top and return them, in the roasting pan, to the warm oven for 30 minutes, leaving the door of the oven wide open.

Just before serving, adjust the seasoning and scatter with shavings of Parmesan. Offer the peppers with a mesclun salad.

AUBERGINE (EGGPLANT) *with* GREEN CURRY

SERVES 4, 30 MINS

GLOBE ARTICHOKES *with* BAY LEAVES AND LIME

SERVES 4, 1 HR 30 MINS PLUS 1 HR COOLING

Collages & Recettes
Alain Passard

RESTAURANT

L'Arpège, Paris, France, opened 1986

BOOK DETAILS

First published 2010, Éditions Alternatives, 112 pages, illustrations by Alain Passard; published in English as *The Art of Cooking with Vegetables*, 2012, Francis Lincoln

"Passard, who recognized the importance of a cook's relationship to the land and those who work it long before it became fashionable, is now rightly considered a visionary by the best chefs in the world."

DAVID KINCH

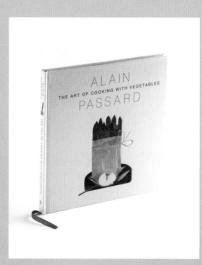

There is a visionary quality to French chef Alain Passard, the sense of a man who, compelled by his belief, is not afraid to challenge preconceptions and gastronomic orthodoxy. Having achieved three Michelin stars for his restaurant L'Arpège, which he opened in 1986, he announced in 2002 that he was introducing a vegetable-focused menu without red meat. It was a radical step in the world of French haute cuisine at the time, and one that has since resonated with and inspired chefs around the world. In order to have access to vegetables of the quality he wanted, Passard established three farms in different areas of France, each with different soils, expressing a distinctive terroir. His menus feature seasonal vegetables and fruits in unexpected combinations, thus creating a very different dining experience.

Passard's willingness to break with convention is amply demonstrated in this slender book, created to celebrate L'Arpège's twenty-fifth anniversary. At first glance, it looks like a children's picture book, with each recipe joined by a picture of collage, rather than a photograph, to illustrate it. Passard, it turns out, is an artist as well as a chef. "The collages in this book," he writes, "express marvelously well the influence of color in my cooking: for me, it is a true source of inspiration, one which urges me to search for partnerships between ingredients in a quest for gastronomic and visual harmony." The atmospheric collages, in a palette ranging from subdued to vivacious, remind one of inlaid Florentine marble and, with his poetic text, offer an expressive insight into Passard's personality and creativity.

The imaginative recipes are intriguing, ranging from Ratatouille Brittany-Style in Butter—which transposes the olive oil–drenched Provençal cuisine to the north of France—to Avocado Soufflés with Dark Chocolate. While the recipes are short and far from complex, this is deceptive. Passard's knowledge of vegetables and flair at combining flavors—he writes of confronting subtly bitter turnips with a "mighty blast of flavor" from basil and lemon confits—underlies the book.

Visionary chef Alain Passard, whose culinary creativity delights diners and inspires other chefs.

Coi: Stories and Recipes
Daniel Patterson

RESTAURANT

Coi, San Francisco, California, USA, opened 2006

BOOK DETAILS

Published 2013, Phaidon, 304 pages, photography by Maren Caruso

"Daniel is constantly looking beyond what he already knows to find fresh facets of deliciousness and meaning. So his dishes reward attentive savoring. They also simply reward!"

HAROLD McGEE

Thoughtful and intelligent, Daniel Patterson opened his restaurant Coi in San Francisco seeking to express himself and California through his food in a deeply personal way. What he offered was far from being in mode— an ambitious, technically complex tasting menu in surroundings that were natural in style. The integrity of his vision, however, and the quality of his imaginative food struck a chord and Coi has been much acclaimed around the world. Exquisite dishes, constructed with meticulous care at every step of the way—including the concept behind them, the quality of ingredients, and the cooking method—have gained Patterson a reputation as a hugely creative chef. In 2015, Patterson stepped away from his role as Executive Chef at Coi, and turned his attention to LocoL, working with Roy Choi.

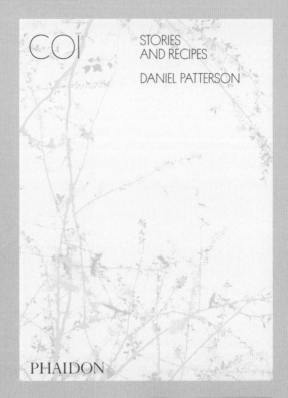

Characteristically, this book is far from a quickly assembled collection of recipes. Instead, through its pages, Patterson offers a meaningful insight into how he thinks about food and how he cooks. A key turning point in his career as a chef came about when his wife Alexandra lost her mother and he cooked to comfort her: "I remembered, after so many years of producing fancy restaurant food, what it meant to cook for someone. It was then that I began to think about the restaurant that would become Coi." His vision for the restaurant was to express California through his food, using ingredients such as carrots, pork, Douglas fir (pine needles), wild sage, wheatgrass, and avocado. He outlines elements that are key to how he cooks at Coi: ingredients at their peak, seasonality, seasoning, balance, texture, and process. Each of the recipes—for beautifully put together, intriguing dishes such as Earth and Sea New Harvest Potatoes, Cucumber, Coastal Plants; Pan-Grilled Matsutake, Potato Pine Needle Purée; or Wood Sorrel—display the level of skill and culinary craftsmanship. Most interesting, however, are the essays accompanying each dish, in which Patterson writes of what inspired the dish—an ingredient, emotion, or experience that was the starting point—giving an enthralling glimpse into the creative processes of a truly remarkable chef.

American chef Daniel Patterson has gained acclaim for his skillful cooking, which is deeply expressive of a sense of place.

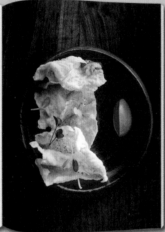

10. Fleurs en Truffes *(Black Truffle Flowers)*

MOUSSE DE FOIES DE VOLAILLE
(Poultry Liver Mousse)

Color plate 4. Décoration du saumon

Color plate 5. Daube de boeuf en gelée, poulet en saucisse

Color plate 6. Terrine de ris de veau, pâté de faisan en croûte, pâté maison

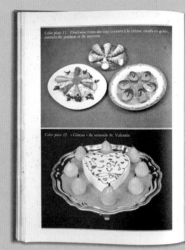

Color plate 7. Bûche de Noël, tarte Tatin

Color plate 8. Gâteau moka, gâteau kirsch

Color plate 9. Clockwise from the right: vacherin melba, petit vacherin melba, meringue chocolatée, meringue torsadée

Color plate 10. Crème anglaise, charlotte royale, charlotte au chocolat

Color plate 11. Clockwise from the top: cornets à la crème, oeufs en gelée, cornets de jambon et de saumon

Color plate 12. Gâteau de semoule St. Valentin

Color plate 13. Top: vol-au-vent à l'ancienne et à la moderne. Center: fleurons, bouchées, allumettes aux anchois, palmiers. Bottom: diablotins, allumettes aux anchois (forme poisson), paillettes au fromage

Color plate 14. Clockwise from the top: bande d'abricots, tarte aux pommes, tarte à l'orange

80. Pommes Pailles, Allumettes et Pont-Neuf *(Potato Sticks)*

ANGLAISE

La Technique
Jacques Pépin

CAREER

Television personality since 1975. Dean of special programs at the International Culinary Center

BOOK DETAILS

Published 1976, Times Books, 470 pages, photography by Léon Perer

"I have often noticed when speaking with people, or teaching a cooking class, that the greatest drawback to a good performance in the kitchen is an inadequate knowledge of basic techniques."

JACQUES PÉPIN

French chef Jacques Pépin has an international reputation, and is particularly well known in the United States, where he has lived and worked since 1959. His career as a chef in France saw him working at La Plaza Athénée in Paris and as a personal chef to General de Gaulle. In the United States, he has starred in television series including *The Complete Pépin*, based on his bestselling book *La Technique*, and *Julia and Jacques Cooking at Home* with the legendary Julia Child, which made him a household name. Throughout his career, he has championed classic French cooking and is respected for his in-depth knowledge of haute cuisine and French gastronomy, about which he has written numerous books.

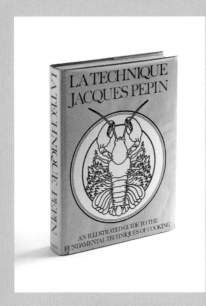

La Technique was conceived to offer a thorough grounding in "the fundamental techniques of cooking." It is illustrated throughout with detailed photographs, and progresses from simple techniques to more complex ones. It soon becomes clear that following this book will entail hard work, a fact that Pépin makes clear both in his introduction and his pointed dedication for the book: "To the chefs who sweat to create friendliness and cordiality among men." It gives insight into the considerable skills required in the professional chef's kitchen, such as the deft knife work involved in techniques such as trimming a rack of lamb, filleting a fish, or cleaning a squab. Here, too, is an intriguing insight into a now largely vanished world of elaborately presented dishes, with a huge section of instructions on how to create decorations, from carved watermelons to hold fruit salad to potato roses and olive rabbits. The cuisine depicted is a formal one, filled with rules as to the right way to present everything, from the dishes to the intricately folded napkins. Pépin's knowledge of ingredients is impressive; he often laments the difficulty of finding foods such as brains or sea urchins in the United States. With dry humor, he cites "practice" as one of the ingredients needed to make the perfect omelette. Authoritative and extensive, this encyclopaedic work is serious in tone, with Pépin, who worked hard to acquire his own knowledge, expecting the same from the reader.

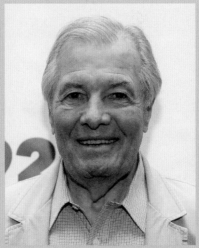

French celebrity chef and broadcaster Jacques Pépin, whose writings emphasize the importance of acquiring culinary technique.

Balance & Harmony: Asian Food
Neil Perry

RESTAURANT
Rockpool, Sydney, Australia, opened 1989

BOOK DETAILS
Published 2008, Murdoch Books, 400 pages, photography by Earl Carter

"Our food style takes advantage of our diverse produce ... We take advantage of going to the market for English spinach and being able to pick up the bok choi displayed in the stall nearby."
NEIL PERRY

An influential figure in Australia's fine-dining scene, chef and restaurateur Neil Perry has played a key part in the movement to create a modern Australian cuisine. His career began in Sydney with Sails Restaurant at McMahons Point, where he worked initially in restaurant management but was drawn toward the kitchen. In 1986, he opened the Blue Water Grill at Bondi Beach to instant acclaim, and Rockpool, which he opened in 1989, is regarded as one of Sydney's iconic fine-dining restaurants. His cooking showcases Australia's high-quality ingredients, such as stunning fish and seafood, and is notably influenced by Asian cuisine, both in terms of ingredients and culinary techniques and aesthetic presentation. His catchphrase regarding his cuisine is "balance and harmony."

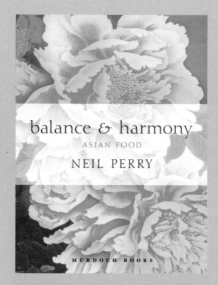

In this cookbook, Perry shares his long-held love of Asian cooking, an affection that he traces back to when he was six and his father took him shopping for ingredients in Chinatown. He was introduced to Thai cooking through chef David Thompson; part of the appeal for Perry is that Asian food is often designed for sharing, but he is also attracted to its intense flavors. While many of the recipes in *Balance & Harmony* are inspired by Chinese cooking, he also draws on Southeast Asian food: "I am absolutely convinced that my love of Asian cooking has made me a much better cook of Western food. It has taught me so much about the texture of food and, just as crucially, about aroma."

Written in an affable, down-to-earth style, the book provides an insight into Asian food, beginning with a grounding in fundamental Asian cooking techniques such as stir-frying, steaming, deep-frying, and braising. It moves on to the section "Advanced Recipes and Banquet Dishes," containing "lots of great recipes that I have cooked in my restaurants and at home": Lobster with XO Sauce; Double-Boiled Pigeons with Shiitake Mushrooms; Crispy Pressed Duck with Mandarin Sauce. He also offers succinct insights to the reader—among them "look to balance each dish"—and his affection for and fascination with Asian cooking permeates every page of the book.

Neil Perry has played an important part in creating modern Australian cuisine.

STOCKS AND SOUPS

Good stock is the basis of many great Chinese soups and main dishes. A welcome addition to any steamed dish, you can just pour good stock into a bowl with the meat, poultry or fish and seasoning to make a dish worth savouring.

Chinese-style stock is very simple to master. It requires none of the roasting of bones or vegetables and deglazing that a French-style stock does. The reason being that we are looking for a clear, light broth that has the body and essence of the chicken, but is not clouded with the taste of vegetables. The best way to handle stock at home is to make a big batch and freeze it in small containers. We always have lots of this in the freezer at home so it can be pulled out for a soup or a stir-fry. It also makes a great base for risottos and, as luck, my wife uses it for tofu-based fermented with vegetables and pushed it gives baby food more taste and body; our children love it. I now find that at work and at home this is the only chicken stock I use.

...

WARM SALAD OF SPICY MINCED CHICKEN

This is a style of large or salad, from the north of Thailand, although it's really a stir-fry served on lettuce. The heat from the chillies and the flavour of fresh lime make it irresistible with a bowl of rice. It's truly a great meal. Thank it to a Isan Dua Sang Chin Sia.

...

SPICY PRAWN SALAD

This is one of the simplest seafood salads you will ever make — the combination of lime and chilli is so fresh it will soon be a favourite. It's easy to substitute any seafood you like for the prawns.

500 g (1 lb 2 oz) cooked king prawns (shrimp), peeled and deveined with tails left intact
juice of 1 lime
1 tablespoon fish sauce
1 teaspoon caster (superfine) sugar
6 small wild green chillies, finely sliced
1 lemongrass stalk, tough outer leaves removed, finely sliced
2 red shallots, finely sliced
1 large handful of mint leaves
1 large handful of coriander (cilantro) leaves
2 kaffir lime leaves, very finely shredded

METHOD

Whisk together the lime juice, fish sauce and sugar. Toss the prawns, chillies, lemongrass, shallots, mint, coriander and lime leaves with the dressing, taste and adjust the seasoning if necessary. Serve immediately.

SPICY BEEF BRISKET BRAISE

A very simple braise. This relies on slow cooking and the wonderful flavour and kick of chilli bean paste.

...

BRAISED DUCK LEGS IN SOY SAUCE

Another complete dish. This can be served as a cold cut or hot with its broth and some fresh ginger and spring onion julienne. Chicken legs could also be used.

4 duck legs
6 cloves garlic, finely chopped
1 small knob of galangal, roughly chopped
1 teaspoon sea salt
1 teaspoon five-spice powder
1 teaspoon sugar
2 tablespoons dark soy sauce
fresh chilli sauce (page 46), to serve

METHOD

...

QUICHE

YIELD
{ one 10-inch quiche: 6 to 8 servings }

THERE ARE TWO SMALL BUT IMPORTANT DIFFERENCES between this quiche filling and most others. The first is that part of the liquid is crème fraîche, which makes the filling smoother and slightly tart. The other is the presence of a small amount of flour. This idea comes from Boulangerie Artisanal des Maures, a bakery that Chad and I apprenticed at in the Var region of France. This recipe is just one of many that we learned there, each of which has some small, unique, and usually simple little trick to it.

Fully baked and cooled 10-inch Flaky Tart Dough shell baked in a deep 10-inch tart pan or a 10-inch pie pan (page 194)	1	
Large eggs	5	
All-purpose flour	3 tbsp	45 ml
Crème fraîche	1 cup	8 oz/250 ml
Whole milk	1 cup	8 oz/250 ml
Salt	1 tsp	5 ml
Black pepper, freshly ground	½ tsp	2 ml
Fresh thyme, finely chopped	1 tbsp	15 ml

KITCHEN NOTES: You also can add 1 cup uncooked coarsely chopped leafy greens, such as chard or spinach to the egg mixture. If you have difficulty pouring all of the batter into the pastry shell and then transferring the dish to the oven without spills, here's what we do for a nice high quiche with no filling loss. Fill the pastry shell as high as you can without worry of mishap, bake the quiche until the top is ever so slightly set, and then, with the tip of a paring knife, make a hole in the center, pour in the rest of the filling, and continue baking until the quiche is done.

Have the pie shell ready for filling. Preheat the oven to 375°F.

Place 1 egg and the flour in the bowl of a stand mixer or in a large mixing bowl and mix at high speed or by hand with a whisk until smooth. Mix or whisk in the remaining 4 eggs until blended. In a medium bowl, whisk the crème fraîche until it is perfectly smooth and then whisk in the milk. Pour the egg mixture through a fine-mesh sieve held over the milk mixture. Whisk in the salt, pepper, and thyme. (You can prepare the custard up to 4 days in advance before baking; cover and refrigerate. The flour, thyme, and pepper will settle to the bottom of the storage container and can stick to it, so whisk well before using.)

Pour the egg mixture into the pastry shell. Place in the oven and bake for 10 minutes. Reduce the oven temperature to 325°F and bake until the filling is just set, about 30 minutes longer. The center of the quiche should feel slightly firm, rather than liquidy, when touched. Let cool on a wire rack for at least 20 minutes to allow the custard to set up, so that it will slice neatly. It can be served warm or at room temperature. To serve a fully cooled quiche warm, cover it with aluminum foil and reheat it in a 325°F for about 15 minutes.

TRIFLE OF SUMMER FRUIT

YIELD
{ 8 to 10 servings }

I DON'T KNOW WHY THIS DESSERT isn't more popular on restaurant dessert card in homes. Every time we make it at the bakery it sells out instantly. When made in a clear glass trifle bowl, it is a beautiful dessert showpiece of layers of sliced fruit, whipped cream, pastry cream, and cake intertwined with a genoise red fruit purée. Traditionally, trifle is no more than leftover cake and jam with whipped cream and custard. Here, you can use whatever summer fruit you like, from berries to peaches to nectarines. Choose a spirit for the purée that complements the fruit you are using. This dessert is sumptuous and refreshing.

Fruit Purée		
Berries or sliced fruit	1½ cups	12 oz/340 g
Sugar	⅓ cup	2 oz/60 g
Clearebrad, Grand Marnier, sweet sherry, white wine, or kirsch (optional)		
Heavy cream, very cold	1½ cups	12 oz/375 ml
Sugar	2 tbsp	30 ml
Génoise (page 196) or any type of chiffon cake (pages 200–201)	1	
Berries or sliced fruit	3 cups	20 oz/565 g
Pastry Cream (page 210, cold)	2 cups	16 oz/500 ml

KITCHEN NOTES: Use fruits that are so ripe that they couldn't wait another day before they are eaten. If you don't have a trifle bowl a straight-sided nested bowl, usually on a piecherd), substitutes any clear glass bowl. Or, it you are not concerned about presentation, use any type of bowl.

To make the fruit purée, combine the fruit and sugar in a blender and on on high speed until very smooth. It is not necessary to strain the purée unless you have used berries with seeds and prefer a purée without seeds. Transfer to a bowl, stir in the spirit to taste (⅓ using), and set aside. You should have about 3 cups (24 fluid ounces/750 ml).

Using a mixer fitted with the whisk attachment or a whisk, whip the cream until thickened. Add the sugar and whip until the cream holds soft peaks. Set aside.

Split the cake horizontally into 3 layers each ½ inch to ½ inch thick. Cut a cake layer to fit into the bottom of a trifle bowl about 8 inches in diameter and 8 inches deep (or to within ¾ inch of the fruit purée. Pour ½ cup (4 fluid ounces/90 ml) of the fruit purée over the cake. This will appear to fruit to be an excessive amount, but it will soak into the cake. Top the purée with one-third of the fruit. If using more than one type of fruit, you can mix them or use them all at once or use a different fruit for each layer. If you are using sliced fruit, place some of the slices with their cut sides facing outward against the sides of the bowl, so that the slices are visible in cross section. Spoon half of the pastry cream over the fruit. Spoon half of the whipped cream on top, filling in any gaps in the pastry cream. Top with a second cake layer, repeat trimming as needed. Pour on 1 cup (8 fluid ounces/250 ml) of the fruit purée, top with half of the remaining fruit, all of the remaining pastry cream, and all of the remaining whipped cream. Place your last cake layer on top and gently press down on it. Brush with the rest of the fruit purée and top with the last of the fruit.

Chill the trifle well before serving. It will keep in the refrigerator for up to 1 day.

COOKIES

SHORTBREAD 250 · CHOCOLATE-OATMEAL WALNUT COOKIES 254
ORANGE-OATMEAL-CURRANT COOKIES 256 · WALNUT CINNAMON SLICES 258
ALMOND ROCHERS 260 · SOFT GLAZED GINGERBREAD 262 · HAZELNUT BISCOTTI 266
DELUXE DOUBLE-CHOCOLATE COOKIES 268

Tartine
Elisabeth M. Prueitt and Chad Robertson

RESTAURANT

Tartine Bakery and Café, San Francisco, California, USA, opened 2002

BOOK DETAILS

Published 2006, Chronicle Books, 224 pages, photography by France Ruffenach

"The stone hearth–baked loaves have spawned a café menu of artfully prepared sandwiches, but bread bought unadorned is still the best way to experience Robertson's way with flour, salt, water, and wild yeast."
SAVEUR MAGAZINE

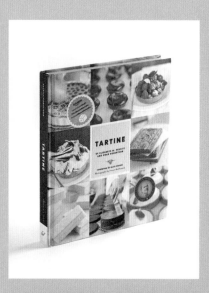

Following their training at the Culinary Institute of America, a shared passion for baking saw pastry chef Elisabeth M. Prueitt and her husband, baker Chad Robertson, travel to Europe, where they lived and worked in France to learn about French baking traditions. Upon their return to California, they opened a small bakery in Point Reyes, baking bread in a wood-fired brick oven and making elegant pâtisserie, inspired by their time in France. With the Berkeley Farmers' Market as a showcase for their talents, and attracting the attention of food doyenne Alice Waters (see p.46, 294, 335) no less, word spread. In 2002, they opened Tartine, their famous and influential bakery and café in the heart of San Francisco. Waters writes in her introduction to their first book: "Tartine is about as authentic—and as indispensable—as a bakery and café can get. No wonder people are still lining up."

Baking is an area of cooking that requires precision when it comes to measuring ingredients and following recipes, as well as depth of knowledge when it comes to handling dough and pastry. Recognizing this, Prueitt and Robertson include introductory notes and kitchen notes, offering practical guidance and useful tips, in addition to their recipes. The tone is clear and accessible and the recipes—for baked goods ranging from time-consuming croissants, carefully and patiently made in the traditional way, to mouthwatering pies, cakes, and cookies—are admirably detailed and informative.

The cookbook also reveals how Tartine is run; there are no night shifts, the reader learns. Work begins in the morning and continues through the day: "baking in real time." What comes across is the strength of Prueitt and Robertson's shared vision: "We're both purists when it comes to ingredients and presentation: we believe in keeping it simple. We want our cakes to look as natural as the flowers we use to decorate them, our pies and tarts and fruit desserts to change with the seasons, and our cookies to look like they're made with loving hands. But most of all, we want everything we make to taste of what was used to make it."

Elisabeth M. Prueitt, who, with her husband Chad Robertson, founded the influential Tartine Bakery and Café.

Relæ: A Book of Ideas
Christian F. Puglisi

RESTAURANT

Relæ, Copenhagen, Denmark, opened 2010

BOOK DETAILS

Published 2014, Ten Speed Press, 447 pages, photography by Per-Anders Jorgensen

"Christian Puglisi is meticulous in his technique, rigorous in his thinking, and—even more impressive—humble in his delivery."

DAN BARBER

Talented young Sicilian-Norwegian chef Christian Puglisi lived in Denmark from the age of seven and began working in restaurants as a teenager. His career saw him working for Ferran Adrià at elBulli in Spain (see p.156) and then for René Redzepi at Noma in Denmark (see p.278), two great chefs from whom he learned much. Puglisi left Noma, however, to set up his own restaurant, inspired by his vision of producing great food in the simplest surroundings and in an informal atmosphere. With his business partner, Kim Rosen, another ex-Noma employee, he set up Relæ, his small organic restaurant in Copenhagen in 2010, offering extraordinary food in a relaxed, bistro-style atmosphere. Such is the quality of Puglisi's cooking that the restaurant has gained numerous plaudits and an international reputation.

Just as Puglisi's restaurant surprises and intrigues, so too does this, his debut cookbook, break with convention. As suggested by the subtitle—"A Book of Ideas"—there is a philosophical aspect to the work, which contains a series of thoughtful essays by Puglisi as well as carefully written, detailed recipes that link to the essays. "I wanted to show you the creative process behind our work and the ideas that inform the fundamentals of our kitchen," he explains. Puglisi expresses his views—from the importance of restaurant staff in great gastronomy to the role that *sous vide* (under vacuum) cooking plays in his cuisine—with clarity and conviction. There is also a refreshingly grounded quality to the text, which illuminates the practicalities of cooking in a restaurant kitchen. On his use of smoked nut milks, for example, Puglisi explains that they allow Relæ to keep its vegetarian cooking "complex and flavorful while still freeing us from heavy sauces." A determination to use foods in their entirety, with the understanding that the skins of vegetables are packed with flavor, sees the Relæ cooks scrubbing carrots "for hours at a time." Having learned from Noma chef René Redzepi the importance of acidity in unlocking flavor, Puglisi explains the importance of the "acidic arsenal"—from lemon juice to sea buckthorn berries—in his kitchen. This is an illuminating, interesting, and engaging cookbook.

Great food in simple surroundings is Christian Puglisi's vision for Relæ.

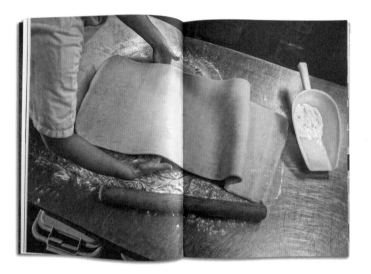

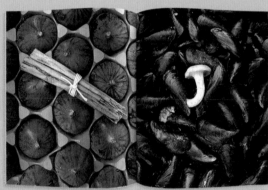

A Chef for All Seasons
Gordon Ramsay with Roz Denny

RESTAURANT

Restaurant Gordon Ramsay, London, UK, opened 1998

BOOK DETAILS

Published 2000, Quadrille Publishing Ltd, 224 pages, photography by Georgia Glynn Smith

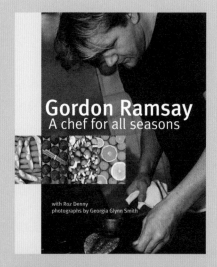

"The success of our menus depends on a balance of popular choices and experimenting with new flavors and ideas to push the boundaries out still further. Perfection of skills and technique reassures our customers, but constant creativity keeps them coming back for more."

GORDON RAMSAY

Successful television series such as *Kitchen Nightmares*, *Hell's Kitchen*, and *MasterChef* have ensured that British chef and restaurateur Gordon Ramsay is a household name around the world. A formidable reputation as a perfectionist is part of the Ramsay brand. Ramsay's career is marked by determination and ambition, with time put in at the kitchens of notable chefs including Marco Pierre White (see p.20, 116, 296) and French chefs Guy Savoy and Joël Robuchon (see p.70, 280, 314). He made his name as chef at Aubergine in London before moving on to open Restaurant Gordon Ramsay in Chelsea, to great critical acclaim. Today, Ramsay has numerous restaurants around the world, ranging in style from the relaxed and informal to upmarket establishments offering elegant haute cuisine.

This accessible, colorfully illustrated cookbook focuses on Ramsay's interest in seasonality and features a collection of recipes chosen by him to reflect each season. "This book is a collection of recipes using foods not only at their best in the seasons, but also recipes that suit the seasons," he explains. Each section begins with a series of his reflections on the foods that best represent that time of year, ingredients such as morels or Jersey Royal new potatoes in summer and cèpes and mussels in fall. The tone of these essays is enthusiastic and chatty, with snippets of autobiography from his days as a young chef dotted within text on how to use the ingredients. So, broad beans (fava beans) bring with them reminiscences of preparing beans "for hours" at Joël Robuchon's famous restaurant Jamin: "for the light, fantastic, 'cappuccino' of fèves with baby lobster, one of the favorite spring starters on his menu." Opinions on how to handle and cook ingredients are firmly expressed, giving an insight into his reputation as a perfectionist in the kitchen. The recipes in this collection reflect Ramsay's love for French food, drawing on classic techniques to create elegant dishes such as a chilled Light Tomato Broth with a Paysanne of Vegetables; Roasted Cod with Garlic Pomme Purée; Orange and Lemon Tart; and Praline Soufflés.

British chef Gordon Ramsay, whose television shows have made him a household name.

Noma: Time and Place in Nordic Cuisine
René Redzepi

RESTAURANT

Noma, Copenhagen, Denmark, opened 2004

BOOK DETAILS

Published 2010, Phaidon, 368 pages, photography by Ditte Isager

"He is already influencing chefs around the world not just with his cooking but with his philosophy. That is why I am convinced that his influence will endure."

FERRAN ADRIÀ

René Redzepi is a truly signicant figure in today's world of gastronomy. Credited with reinventing and reinvigorating Nordic cuisine, his influence extends far beyond his native Denmark, and he inspires chefs around the world. At fifteen, he got "the bug for cooking" and his early career saw him work at both elBulli (see p.156) and The French Laundry (see p.18, 86, 138, 230). Then, at twenty-four, he became head chef and cofounder of Noma, a restaurant in an eighteenth-century warehouse in Copenhagen that is now internationally renowned. It was here that Redzepi relinquished the conventional tropes of international fine dining, seeking instead to bring something truly expressive of Denmark, the country and the natural environment, to the table. Famously, the menu at Noma draws on wild, foraged foods that are truly seasonal—edible fungi, roots, seashore plants, lichens, weeds—and that Redzepi transforms into distinctive, poetic food.

This is an atmospheric and informative book, generously intended as a way of giving readers a genuine insight into Redzepi's intellectual journey and his astonishing food. Looking back to the founding of Noma, which is located in a North Atlantic cultural center, he sensed that it offered "the chance to create our own way of expressing ourselves, our own signature." The idea of exploring the landscape, using it as a larder for "new" ingredients, came to him, and the book includes his diary of a research trip to the North Atlantic in 2003, shortly before Noma opened. It is filled with excitement and enthusiasm for his ambitious project. He writes about the challenges presented by the long, dark winters and with great respect for his producers, offering affectionate portrayals of suppliers of briefly available ingredients such as birch sap, sea urchins, and rowanberries. The aesthetically presented, truly beautiful dishes have a particular sensibility to them, one that is rooted in his intimate understanding of the natural world: Sea Urchin and Elderberries, Rose Hips and Vinegar, Pork Neck and Bulrushes, Violets and Malt, Milk Ice and Barley, Poached Egg and Liquorice—even their simple titles have a freshness to them.

With his pioneering vision of a new Nordic cuisine, René Redzepi has influenced chefs around the world to explore a sense of place in cooking.

BROAD BEANS AND BABY ONIONS
WITH SMOKED BACON

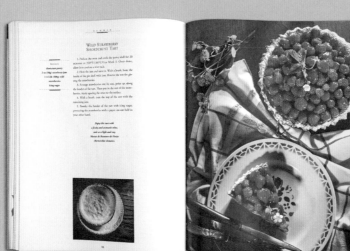

WILD STRAWBERRY
SHORTCRUST TART

FRIED FRESH COD
WITH CABBAGE

Les Dimanches de Joël Robuchon
Joël Robuchon

RESTAURANT
Jamin, Paris, France, opened 1981 (Robuchon retired in 1996)

BOOK DETAILS
First published 1993, Editions du Chêne, 184 pages, photography by Hervé Amiard; published in English as *La Cuisine de Joël Robuchon: A Seasonal Cookbook*, 2001, Cassell & Co

"The simpler the food, the harder it is to prepare it well. You want to truly taste what it is you're eating."

JOËL ROBUCHON

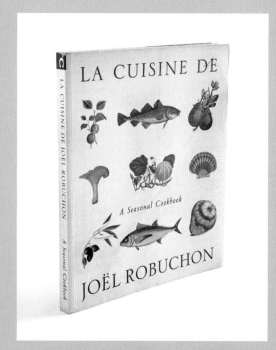

A highlight of a distinguished career saw French chef Joël Robuchon attain first one Michelin star for his newly opened restaurant Jamin, then two, and then three in successive years; he is the first chef to achieve this feat. Noted for his relentless quest for perfection, he also played an important part in moving French cuisine away from excess, toward a simpler, more natural style focusing on ingredients. Robuchon now has several successful, critically lauded restaurants—the L'Atelier de Joël Robuchon group—around the world, as well as a career in broadcasting. The L'Atelier concept, inspired by the sushi bars of Japan and the tapas bars of Spain, is for a more relaxed dining experience, with diners facing the kitchen.

This attractive cookbook is devised as a culinary chronicle and is structured as a seasonal journey through a calendar year. For each season, Robuchon presents a selection of appropriate ingredients, offering not only recipes but also essays, in which he writes at length about what the ingredient means to him and how to cook with it. His text is both poetic and practical, informed by his in-depth knowledge of food. "Incomparable and always seductive, the delicate asparagus makes its appearance in March," begins his essay on that much-loved vegetable. He moves on to offer detailed advice as to how to select and cook it; he is aware of appearance as well as texture and flavor. "There are some restaurants who cook asparagus in advance and reheat it as the orders come in, but this is a method I find repugnant." The foods chosen embrace both the luxurious and the everyday—lobster, foie gras, and caviar sit alongside salt, cabbage, and potatoes. He expresses his culinary convictions with verve and charm: "Here are the seven commandments for preparing french beans," he declares. The recipes are elegant, both in concept and method. Reading this book, one appreciates the understanding of ingredients that is central to Robuchon's cuisine. Often his preference is for straightforward ways of cooking. He uses methods that allow the subtle flavors of the ingredients to come through—for example, pheasant, he feels, is best simply roasted in the oven or on a spit.

Legendary French chef Joël Robuchon, noted for his perfectionism in the kitchen.

The Zuni Cafe Cookbook
Judy Rodgers

RESTAURANT

Zuni Cafe, San Francisco, California, USA, opened 1979 (Rodgers became head chef in 1987; she died in 2013)

BOOK DETAILS

Published 2002, W. W. Norton & Company, 548 pages, photography by Gentl & Hyers

> *"The best meals are more than a succession of great dishes resulting from a number of great recipes. They are fashioned with wisdom and experience and are shaded, always, with spontaneity."*
>
> JUDY RODGERS

As a young exchange student, chef Judy Rodgers spent a formative year at Les Frères Troisgros, the three Michelin–starred restaurant in Roanne, France, watching the brothers at work and making notes. That experience was to stay with her as she traveled and worked in places including Italy, Catalonia, and Greece, learning about the food of these places. A time at Alice Waters's iconic Chez Panisse (see p.46, 294, 335), with its commitment to seasonality, was a key experience in forming her approach to food. Zuni Café, the relaxed restaurant of which she was chef-owner, saw her serve her own cuisine, informed by her travels and her sense of what makes good food. Rodgers installed a brick oven in the middle of Zuni's dining room, where her famously delicious, characteristically hospitable roast chicken for two with bread salad became a signature dish.

There is a generosity of spirit to *The Zuni Cafe Cookbook*, just as there was to Rodgers herself and her beloved restaurant. A substantial book, the recipes are long and detailed, filled with useful information and helpful touches, including numerous variations. Her in-depth knowledge of ingredients, from fresh artichokes to skirt steak, is amply shared. Her interest in what makes good food is infectious: "Cookbooks will give you ideas, but the market will give you dinner," she writes. There is a grounded, practical aspect to the book: "Even the most expensive egg," she observes justly, "makes a very economical meal." The recipes, for dishes such as Carpaccio with Fried Potatoes and Truffle; Pasta with Giblet-Mushroom Sauce; or Peach Crostata, draw on the cuisines of France and Italy. What is also apparent, however, is that Rodgers had developed her own cuisine, using techniques she felt worked well when handling meat or poultry and creating her own characteristic flavor combinations. A sense of Rodgers's personality is on every page. In sentences such as "Carefully layered like a dish of baked lasagne, it is uncharacteristically orderly for Zuni" or "The beginning of a meal is a good place to be adventurous when menu planning, and when learning to cook," one hears her voice, and it is a warm, kind, and wise one.

American chef Judy Rodgers, whose love of food informed her characterful cooking style.

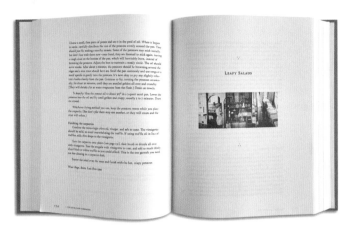

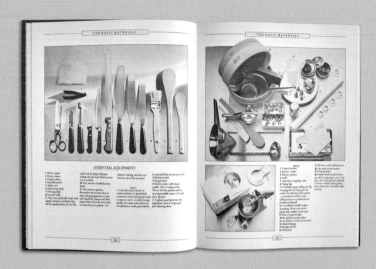

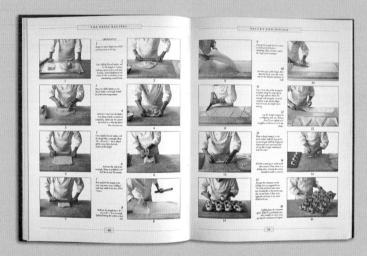

La Pâtisserie des frères Roux
Michel and Albert Roux

RESTAURANT

The Waterside Inn, Bray, UK, opened 1972

BOOK DETAILS

Published 1986, Éditions Solar, 256 pages, photography by Anthony Blake; published in English as *The Roux Brothers on Patisserie*, 1986, Macdonald & Co

"I cook for myself. I cook what I like to eat—and so far everyone else has wanted to eat it too."
MICHEL ROUX

The influence of "the Roux Brothers," as French chefs and restaurateurs Albert and Michel Roux are affectionately known, on Britain's gastronomic scene has been remarkable. Their luxurious restaurants, Le Gavroche, which opened in 1967, and The Waterside Inn, opened in 1972, set high standards of what the fine-dining experience should be, offering immaculately executed, classic French food and impeccable service. Beacons attracting talent, the Roux brothers have employed many young chefs who have gone on to make their own marks, including Marco Pierre White (see p.20, 116, 296), Gordon Ramsay (see p.276), and Pierre Koffmann (see p.90, 94, 236). Their knowledge of French cuisine—and the care and attention required to produce food of such quality—has ensured their names are hugely respected within the restaurant world.

The extent of that expertise is manifest in their cookbooks, among them this classic text on French pâtisserie. Michel is a master pastry chef, a fact formally recognized with his award of the title Meiller Ouvrier de France, a huge honor in the world of French pâtisserie, entitling the holder to teach at the highest technical level. "In this book you will find many recipes, hints and tricks of the trade, gleaned from years of experience, right back to our earliest years in the profession," writes Michel in his introduction, and there is a real sense of wisdom shared. The cookbook offers an extensive overview of what working as a pastry chef at this standard involves, covering basic recipes, cold and hot desserts and sweets, ice creams and sorbets, canapés and petit fours, decoration and presentation. The recipes, accompanied by notes offering extra information or suggesting variations, are concise but, importantly, include the salient points, grounded in the practical realities of making dishes that work well. Simple but practical pointers—such as applying two coats of eggwash for "a really shiny finish" or staggering rows of pastries on trays in order to ensure even cooking, provide an interesting insight into the meticulous care and attention needed to produce cooking of the caliber of the Roux Brothers.

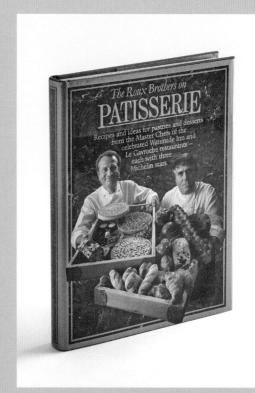

The gastronomic talents of Albert and Michel Roux were influential in shaping Britain's restaurant scene.

Le Pigeon: Cooking at the Dirty Bird
Gabriel Rucker and Meredith Erickson with Lauren and Andrew Fortgang

RESTAURANT

Le Pigeon, Portland, Oregon, USA, opened 2006

BOOK DETAILS

Published 2013, Ten Speed Press, 352 pages, photography by David L. Reamer

"His cuisine is all about balance, with a dash of American nostalgia. He gets it."
DANIEL BOULUD

The journey toward becoming a chef can often be one with twists and turns along the way. Having dropped out of culinary school at the age of eighteen, Gabriel Rucker worked at restaurants including Portland's Gotham Building Tavern and Paley's Place. At the age of twenty-five, he opened his own restaurant, the intimate Le Pigeon in Portland, offering his personal creative take on French food. Wonderfully indulgent, exuberant creations such as Foie Gras Profiteroles and Bacon Butter gained him a cult following among the city's youthful diners, along with critical acclaim. Today, his umami-rich, deliciously decadent comfort food is also on offer at his second Portland restaurant, an informal bistro named Little Bird.

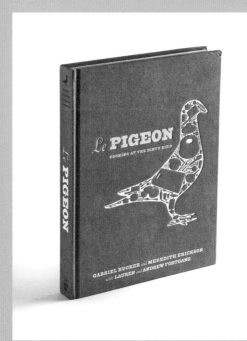

The irreverence and humor that characterizes Rucker's approach to cooking comes across from the minute one opens the book: with its cartoon-like endpapers of pigeons dining out in a restaurant and a graphic photograph of an entire roast pigeon, complete with head and claws, resting in a dish. That beak-to-tail approach to food is very much part of Le Pigeon's ethos—as recipes for dishes such as BBQ Beef Tongue, Fried Rice, Pigeon Liver Crostini, or Elk Tongue Stroganoff demonstrate. Rucker's noted affection for foie gras is apparent in the array of dishes featuring it, from Foie Gras Bacon, Brioche ("our take on bacon and eggs") to Foie Gras Ice Cream. The dishes have been conceived with a trademark wittiness; one can sense the fun that Rucker has creating his menus. What also comes across is his ability to create imaginative dishes that people want to eat—cleverly executed creations so rich and tasty that they linger on in the mind. The introduction tells Rucker's story, including that of his partnership with Andy Fortgang, his general manager, whose shrewd business sense helped keep Le Pigeon running. Rucker tells the story with verve: from the precarious economics of their early days, when they were known as "an offal den," to the creation of hit dishes and seeing off those who had predicted they would fail. Down-to-earth and creative, this cookbook captures the sense of a truly individual chef and his restaurant.

An affection for French cuisine is at the heart of Gabriel Rucker's exuberant cooking.

In this recipe, hearts of romaine are grilled to a nice char on one side, giving you a hot-and-cold effect on the plate. We use a couple of different techniques with lemon here: roasting, for a bright vinaigrette to drizzle on the plate, and preserving, to brighten a creamy dressing. This salad is all about depth of flavor and contrast: Hot versus cold. Preserved versus roasted. Acidic versus creamy. [SERVES 4]

GRILLED ROMAINE, PRESERVED LEMONS

Preserved Lemon Dressing
1 egg yolks
2 cloves garlic, minced
2 white anchovies (boquerones)
½ cup (20 g) grated Parmesan
2 tablespoons minced Preserved
  Lemons (page 326)
2 tablespoons freshly squeezed
  lemon juice
½ teaspoon freshly ground white
  pepper
½ teaspoon kosher salt
¾ cup (180 ml) extra-virgin olive oil

Honey Lemon Vinny
6 lemons, halved
4 sprigs thyme
3 cloves garlic
2 shallots, sliced ¼ inch (6 mm) thick
2 tablespoons water
1 tablespoon freshly ground black
  pepper
1 teaspoon kosher salt
½ teaspoon red pepper flakes
⅓ cup (80 ml) honey
½ cup (125 ml) olive oil

2 hearts of romaine, trimmed
3 tablespoons olive oil, plus more for
  brushing
Kosher salt and freshly ground black
  pepper
Juice of ½ lemon
2 teaspoons Seasoned Bread Crumbs
  (page 327)
½ cup (30 g) Parmesan shavings

1. To make the dressing, add the egg yolks, garlic, anchovies, Parmesan, preserved lemon, lemon juice, white pepper, and salt to a food processor. Set to puree and, with the motor running, add the oil in a thin, steady stream to create an emulsion. It should be the consistency of a loose aioli, very creamy. When the dressing is smooth, turn off the machine and set the dressing aside. Store leftovers in the refrigerator for up to 1 week.

2. Preheat the oven to 175°F (190°C).

3. To make the honey lemon vinny, in a Dutch oven, toss together the lemons, thyme, garlic, shallots, water, black pepper, salt, and red pepper flakes. Roast in the oven, uncovered, until the lemons are browned, about 45 minutes. Remove from the oven and, using a ladle, push the mixture through a chinois, trying to extract as much liquid as you can. Let the liquid cool to room temperature.

4. Add the cooled liquid and honey to a blender or food processor. Set to puree and, with the motor running, add the oil in a thin, steady stream to create an emulsion. You want a deep lemon flavor, slightly sweet. Turn off the machine and set aside.

5. Preheat a gas grill or prepare a charcoal grill for cooking over very high heat. Remove a few outer leaves from the romaine hearts and slice them thinly crosswise, into a chiffonade. You should have about 1 cup (40 g). Cut the romaine hearts in half, brush them with oil, and season with salt and pepper. Grill the romaine, cut side down, until the lettuce has grill marks and the edges look nice and charred, about 3 minutes.

6. Toss the sliced romaine with the lemon juice and 3 tablespoons of olive oil. Season with salt.

7. In the center of a plate, spoon a nice circle of the preserved lemon dressing. Top with the sliced romaine. Toss the grilled romaine hearts in a bowl with the remaining preserved lemon dressing and place, grilled side up, on top of the sliced romaine. Drizzle the salad with the honey lemon vinny and sprinkle with bread crumbs. Top with shaved Parmesan and serve.

Lobster Roe Pappardelle, Crab, Lemon, Crème Fraîche, *continued*

5. Bring a large pot of heavily salted water to a boil. Meanwhile, in a large sauté pan over medium heat, combine the crème fraîche with the preserved lemon and crabmeat and sauté to reduce the sauce and thicken slightly. Drop the pasta in the boiling water and cook until al dente, 3 to 4 minutes. Drain the noodles and add them to the sauté pan with the sauce. Cook for 10 seconds, just long enough to marry the flavors. Stir in the chives, parsley, chervil, and tarragon and taste for seasoning. The mixture should be saucy but not runny.

6. Divide the pasta among four bowls, making sure you get all of that crab and sauce out of the pan, and serve.

carrots, carrot juices, chestnut

duck, smoked beet juice, dried berries, cocoa mass

happy fruit organic almonds

Origin: The Food of Ben Shewry
Ben Shewry

RESTAURANT
Attica, Melbourne, Australia, opened 2005 (Shewry took ownership in 2015)

BOOK DETAILS
Published 2012, Murdoch Books, 304 pages, photography by Colin Page

"I like to create dishes that are a pure expression of their ingredients—dishes that make you sit up and pay attention. For me, that's the ultimate respect I can pay the farmer and the core ingredient."

BEN SHEWRY

Ben Shewry has traveled a long way from his rural childhood in New Zealand to the success of his internationally acclaimed restaurant Attica in Melbourne. His desire to follow that course existed from an early age: "I decided that I was going to be a chef when I was five years old. When I was ten I wrote to four restaurants asking for work experience: only one, The Mill in New Plymouth, responded." Deeply fascinated by ingredients, his creative and distinctive cuisine is characterized as "Modern Australian," and draws on the natural bounty of high-quality Antipodean foodstuffs, from wallaby, paired with bunya pine and begonia, and seafood to beechwood honeydew, used to create Honeydew Honey, an extraordinary dessert made to resemble honeycomb.

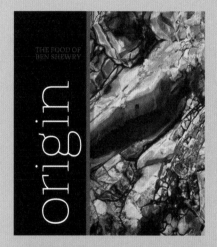

There is a monumental quality to this huge book, with its striking photographs. It is also a very personal book, written with a thoughtful intensity: "This book is a reflection of my life and my personality. It's an open and honest document and I haven't held much back," it begins. There is good reason for this autobiographical dimension to the cookbook, as Shewry—in his own characterful cuisine, often described as "narrative food"—draws on his own personal experiences to create dishes. Narrative text, in which he writes vividly of formative childhood memories such as watching his cattle farmer father kill a bullock and so understanding the need to respect meat, is interspersed with recipes inspired by his life, such as his famous A Simple Dish of Potato Cooked in the Earth it Was Grown, or Sea Tastes, which was triggered by his memories of nearly drowning as a boy of ten while picking mussels. The poetically titled recipes—for example Lettuce in a Natural State—are creative and technically accomplished, with the large photographs conveying the sheer beauty of his creations. The accompanying, intelligent text not only illuminates Shewry's own life and approach to food and cooking, but vividly conveys the long, tough slog it takes to become a chef and the formidable pressures faced by head chefs in particular.

Ben Shewry, whose expressive cooking at his Melbourne restaurant has gained him international renown.

Simple Good Food: Fusion Flavors to Cook at Home From a Four-Star Chef
Jean-Georges Vongerichten and Mark Bittman

RESTAURANT

Jean-Georges, New York City, New York, USA, opened 1997

BOOK DETAILS

Published 1998, Broadway Books, 240 pages, photography by Quentin Bacon; this edition published in 1999, Kyle Cathie Ltd

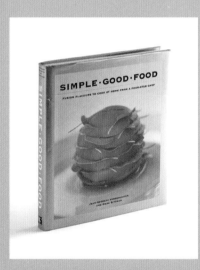

"Jean-Georges . . . is the essence of sophistication and gastronomic marksmanship. The cuisine is uniquely his, melding French Alsatian and Asian influences."
MICHAEL WHITEMAN

In the competitive world of New York's dining scene, chef and restaurateur Jean-Georges Vongerichten has a legendary status, with his eponymous restaurant lauded by critics and loved by customers. Born in Alsace, France, he began his career with training at the prestigious L'Auberge de L'Ill. His work as a chef took him to Thailand and Singapore, an experience that was to have a profound influence on his personal cuisine, introducing him to regional ingredients such as lemongrass and coconut milk. Moving on to open his own restaurants, he created his own characteristically light yet flavorful, elegant fusion cuisine, incorporating techniques and foodstuffs from both East and West in accomplished style and to great effect.

In this engaging book, Mark Bittman, the journalist co-author working with Jean-Georges, writes candidly of his own surprise at learning for himself just how accessible Jean-Georges's recipes were: "When we got through the first two recipes, I realized that Jean-Georges wasn't kidding: many of his recipes contain only a few ingredients, and more than a few take less than a half hour to prepare." Here are dishes beloved by diners at Jean-Georges, such as Steamed Chanterelles with Shallots and Sprouts and Seared Tuna with Szechuan Peppercorns, and what is also noticeable is how straightforward they are.

His flavor combinations are often original, sometimes startling—for example, Salmon and Grapefruit in Cucumber Milk or Scallops and Cauliflower with Caper-Raisin Sauce. As is traditional in both French and Asian cuisine, sauces are used to deliver hits of flavor, with recipes for Tamarind Ketchup or Vong Peanut Sauce sitting alongside Rich Chicken Stock and Fish Fumet. Unusually for a chef's cookbook, there is no introduction by Jean-Georges, who, as described by Bittman comes across as a modest, humorous, and creative person. It is a cookbook devoid of chef's ego, yet filled with his personality.

Talented chef Jean-Georges Vongerichten, master of creative French-Asian fusion food.

COUNTER-CLOCKWISE:

BEETROOT AND GINGER SALAD,

BEETROOT RAVIOLI WITH BEETROOT

SAUCE, CARAMELISED BEETROOTS

AND TURNIPS, BEETROOT TARTARE

COUNTER-CLOCKWISE:

FENNEL AND APPLE SALAD WITH

JUNIPER, WATERMELON-GOAT'S

CHEESE SALAD, SIMPLY THE BEST

CRAB SALAD WITH CUMIN CRISPS

CHICKEN WITH LEMONGRASS

BEEF WITH GINGER

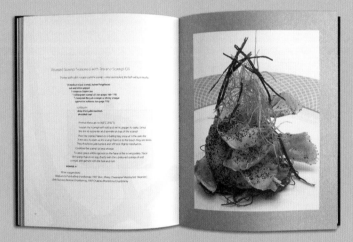

Tetsuya: Recipes from Australia's Most Acclaimed Chef
Tetsuya Wakuda

RESTAURANT
Tetsuya's, Sydney, Australia, opened 1989

BOOK DETAILS
Published 2000, HarperCollins Publishers Australia, 192 pages, photography by Takashi Morieda, Louise Lister, and David Lange

"His amazing technique, Asian heritage, sincere humility, worldwide travels, and insatiable curiosity combine to create incredible, soulful dishes that exude passion in every bite."

CHARLIE TROTTER

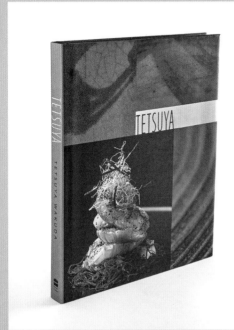

There is an appealing modesty to Tetsuya's account of his life and career in his introduction. Born in Japan, he was fascinated by all things foreign, setting off at twenty-two years of age to live and work in Australia. He arrived in Sydney with very limited English and no knowledge of Western cooking. Working at Kinselas gave him a grounding in classic French techniques, which continues to inform his cooking. In 1989 he opened a small restaurant in simple premises in a Sydney suburb. His exquisite, balanced cooking saw him achieving critical plaudits, and today, his famed eponymous restaurant is housed in style in a large, heritage-listed property. Tetsuya writes affectionately that, "The restaurant is my life and my home" and he considers the people who work and eat there as his family.

A love of ingredients, Tetsuya writes, is what comes first, especially seafood, with a morning visit to the fish market to see what is "fresh and wonderful for that day" as his starting point. Open-minded and interested, Tetsuya combines the best Australian produce with Japanese, Chinese, and French influences on the dishes. At the heart of his cooking, however, as he recognizes, is a profoundly Japanese approach: "Make simplicity seem like abundance—this is the lesson I take away from Japanese cuisine."

The recipes in the cookbook include many of the sophisticated signature dishes served at Tetsuya's, but made approachable or "domesticated" for

the home cook. Here, for example, is his signature dish of Confit of Petuna Ocean Trout with Fennel Salad. Initially, he explains, he used salmon for this, but, when the salmon season ended, his supplier offered him ocean trout and he came to prefer its "complex, rich taste." His in-depth knowledge of ingredients shines through strongly in the recipes, as he describes how the dishes should both look and feel. His aesthetic sensibility, which sees Tetsuya working with ceramic artist Mitsuo Shoji in a relationship of mutual respect and admiration, is expressed in the distinctly elegant dishes portrayed on these pages. The book lives up to its subtitle: "Recipes from Australia's Most Acclaimed Chef."

Tetsuya Wakuda's exquisite dishes have garnered a devoted following for his cooking.

The Chez Panisse Menu Cookbook
Alice Waters

RESTAURANT
Chez Panisse, Berkeley, California, USA, opened 1971
BOOK DETAILS
Published 1982, Random House Inc., 318 pages, illustrations by David Lance Goines

"My one unbreakable rule has always been to use only the freshest and finest ingredients available."
ALICE WATERS

The influence of chef, restaurateur, writer, and food activist Alice Waters has been widely felt around the world. A longtime champion of locavore (locally produced) food, the organic movement, and education, she has inspired many people in many countries, and continues to do so. She made her name with Chez Panisse, the much-loved restaurant she opened in Berkeley, California, in 1971. Having fallen in love with food while traveling in France, she bought a copy of Elizabeth David's *French Country Cooking*, and "wanted a restaurant that had the same feeling as the pictures on the covers of her books." Waters's quest for the best ingredients for the restaurant saw her working closely with growers and food producers. Her concerns about sustainability in the food chain—a dislike of "phony" food—have seen her undertake food campaigning initiatives such as the creation of the Edible Schoolyard in 1996 to connect children to food growing in a meaningful way.

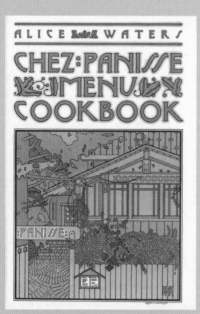

This cookbook, notably modest and understated in appearance, is a profound and wise work, which articulates clearly and eloquently Waters's own food philosophy. Food in her world is emotionally charged—something to be treasured, treated with respect, and enjoyed, from its cooking to its eating. A person who responds to cooking "with a genuine glow of delight is likely to be, or become, a very good cook indeed," she observes. The famous emphasis on ingredients, which saw Waters long ago hunting out local farmers, cooking seasonally, and embracing organic food, is absolutely central.

Her affection for ingredients is palpable in the role they play in the recipe titles: Garden Lettuces with Hyssop and Rocket [Arugula] Flowers; Shrimp Grilled on Rock Salt; and Whole Baked Garlic with White Cheese and Peasant Bread (part of a menu she created for the food writer James Beard). The influence of France and Italy is apparent in the dishes, with the recipes at once simple yet sophisticated, and with a refreshing capacity to surprise at how ingredients have been combined. Filled with excellent, unpretentious advice, this book offers an insight into a remarkable woman and her restaurant.

The remarkable Alice Waters, a hugely influential figure in shaping America's gastronomic culture.

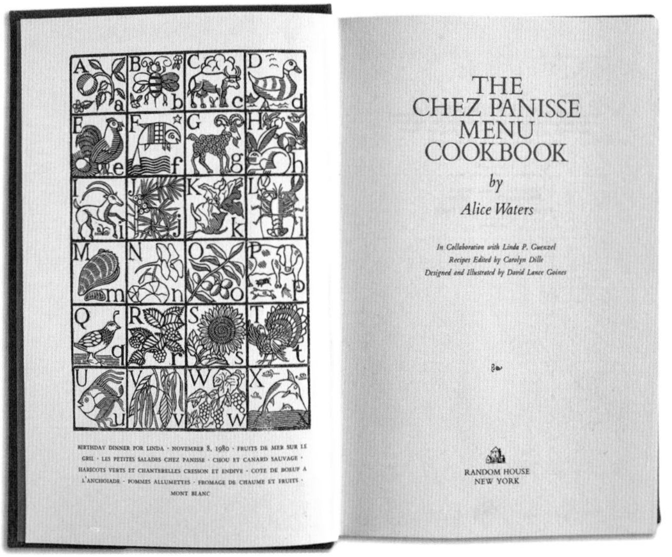
BIRTHDAY DINNER FOR LINDA · NOVEMBER 8, 1980 · FRUITS DE MER SUR LE GRIL · LES PETITES SALADES CHEZ PANISSE · CHOU ET CANARD SAUVAGE · HARICOTS VERTS ET CHANTERELLES CRESSON ET ENDIVE · COTE DE BOEUF A L'ANCHOIADE · POMMES ALLUMETTES · FROMAGE DE CHAUME ET FRUITS · MONT BLANC

THE CHEZ PANISSE MENU COOKBOOK

by

Alice Waters

In Collaboration with Linda P. Guenzel
Recipes Edited by Carolyn Dille
Designed and Illustrated by David Lance Goines

RANDOM HOUSE
NEW YORK

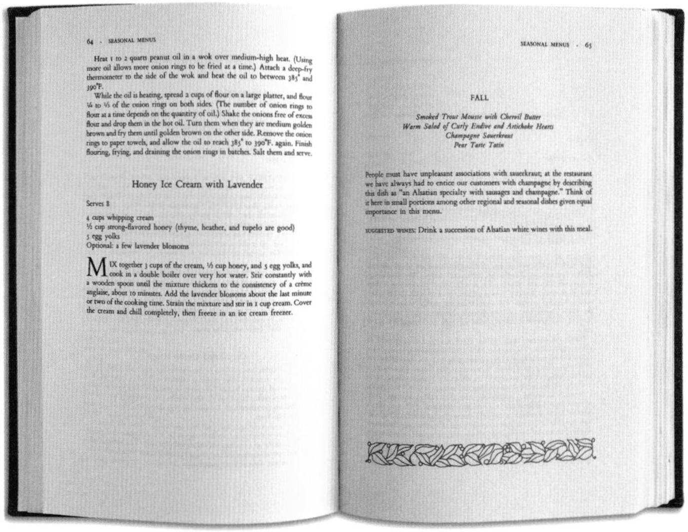
64 · SEASONAL MENUS

Heat 1 to 2 quarts peanut oil in a wok over medium-high heat. (Using more oil allows more onion rings to be fried at a time.) Attach a deep-fry thermometer to the side of the wok and heat the oil to between 385° and 390°F.

While the oil is heating, spread 2 cups of flour on a large platter, and flour ¼ to ⅓ of the onion rings on both sides. (The number of onion rings to flour at a time depends on the quantity of oil.) Shake the onions free of excess flour and drop them in the hot oil. Turn them when they are medium golden brown and fry them until golden brown on the other side. Remove the onion rings to paper towels, and allow the oil to reach 385° to 390°F. again. Finish flouring, frying, and draining the onion rings in batches. Salt them and serve.

Honey Ice Cream with Lavender

Serves 8

4 cups whipping cream
½ cup strong-flavored honey (thyme, heather, and tupelo are good)
5 egg yolks
Optional: a few lavender blossoms

MIX together 3 cups of the cream, ½ cup honey, and 5 egg yolks, and cook in a double boiler over very hot water. Stir constantly with a wooden spoon until the mixture thickens to the consistency of a crème anglaise, about 10 minutes. Add the lavender blossoms about the last minute or two of the cooking time. Strain the mixture and stir in 1 cup cream. Cover the cream and chill completely, then freeze in an ice cream freezer.

SEASONAL MENUS · 65

FALL

Smoked Trout Mousse with Chervil Butter
Warm Salad of Curly Endive and Artichoke Hearts
Champagne Sauerkraut
Pear Tarte Tatin

People must have unpleasant associations with sauerkraut; at the restaurant we have always had to entice our customers with champagne by describing this dish as "an Alsatian specialty with sausages and champagne." Think of it here in small portions among other regional and seasonal dishes given equal importance in this menu.

SUGGESTED WINES: Drink a succession of Alsatian white wines with this meal.

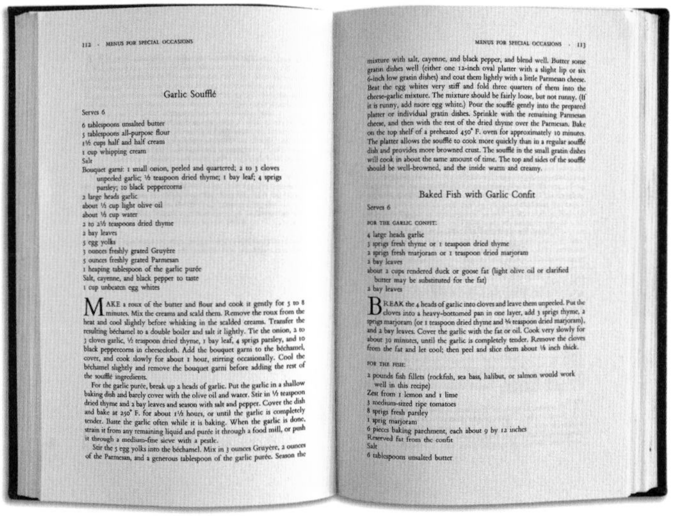
112 · MENUS FOR SPECIAL OCCASIONS

Garlic Soufflé

Serves 6

6 tablespoons unsalted butter
5 tablespoons all-purpose flour
1½ cups half and half cream
1 cup whipping cream
Salt
Bouquet garni: 1 small onion, peeled and quartered; 2 to 3 cloves unpeeled garlic; ½ teaspoon dried thyme; 1 bay leaf; 4 sprigs parsley; 10 black peppercorns
2 large heads garlic
about ½ cup light olive oil
about ½ cup water
2 to 2½ teaspoons dried thyme
2 bay leaves
5 egg yolks
3 ounces freshly grated Gruyère
5 ounces freshly grated Parmesan
1 heaping tablespoon of the garlic purée
Salt, cayenne, and black pepper to taste
1 cup unbeaten egg whites

MAKE a roux of the butter and flour and cook it gently for 5 to 8 minutes. Mix the creams and scald them. Remove the roux from the heat and cool slightly before whisking in the scalded creams. Transfer the resulting béchamel to a double boiler and salt it lightly. Tie the onion, 2 to 3 cloves garlic, ½ teaspoon dried thyme, 1 bay leaf, 4 sprigs parsley, and 10 black peppercorns in cheesecloth. Add the bouquet garni to the béchamel, cover, and cook slowly for about 1 hour, stirring occasionally. Cool the béchamel slightly and remove the bouquet garni before adding the rest of the soufflé ingredients.

For the garlic purée, break up 2 heads of garlic. Put the garlic in a shallow baking dish and barely cover with the olive oil and water. Stir in ½ teaspoon dried thyme and 2 bay leaves and season with salt and pepper. Cover the dish and bake at 250° F. for about 1½ hours, or until the garlic is completely tender. Baste the garlic often while it is baking. When the garlic is done, strain it from any remaining liquid and purée it through a food mill, or push it through a medium-fine sieve with a pestle.

Stir the 5 egg yolks into the béchamel. Mix in 3 ounces Gruyère, 2 ounces of the Parmesan, and a generous tablespoon of the garlic purée. Season the

MENUS FOR SPECIAL OCCASIONS · 113

mixture with salt, cayenne, and black pepper, and blend well. Butter some gratin dishes well (either one 12-inch oval platter with a slight lip or six 6-inch low gratin dishes) and coat them lightly with a little Parmesan cheese. Beat the egg whites very stiff and fold three quarters of them into the cheese-garlic mixture. The mixture should be fairly loose, but not runny. (If it is runny, add more egg white.) Pour the soufflé gently into the prepared platter or individual gratin dishes. Sprinkle with the remaining Parmesan cheese, and then with the rest of the dried thyme over the Parmesan. Bake on the top shelf of a preheated 450° F. oven for approximately 10 minutes. The platter allows the soufflé to cook more quickly than in a regular soufflé dish and provides more browned crust. The soufflé in the small gratin dishes will cook in about the same amount of time. The top and sides of the soufflé should be well-browned, and the inside warm and creamy.

Baked Fish with Garlic Confit

Serves 6

FOR THE GARLIC CONFIT:

4 large heads garlic
3 sprigs fresh thyme or 1 teaspoon dried thyme
2 sprigs fresh marjoram or 1 teaspoon dried marjoram
2 bay leaves
about 2 cups rendered duck or goose fat (light olive oil or clarified butter may be substituted for the fat)
2 bay leaves

BREAK the 4 heads of garlic into cloves and leave them unpeeled. Put the cloves into a heavy-bottomed pan in one layer, add 3 sprigs thyme, 2 sprigs marjoram (or 1 teaspoon dried thyme and ¾ teaspoon dried marjoram), and 2 bay leaves. Cover the garlic with the fat or oil. Cook very slowly for about 30 minutes, until the garlic is completely tender. Remove the cloves from the fat and let cool; then peel and slice them about ⅛ inch thick.

FOR THE FISH:

2 pounds fish fillets (rockfish, sea bass, halibut, or salmon would work well in this recipe)
Zest from 1 lemon and 1 lime
3 medium-sized ripe tomatoes
8 sprigs fresh parsley
1 sprig marjoram
6 pieces baking parchment, each about 9 by 12 inches
Reserved fat from the confit
Salt
6 tablespoons unsalted butter

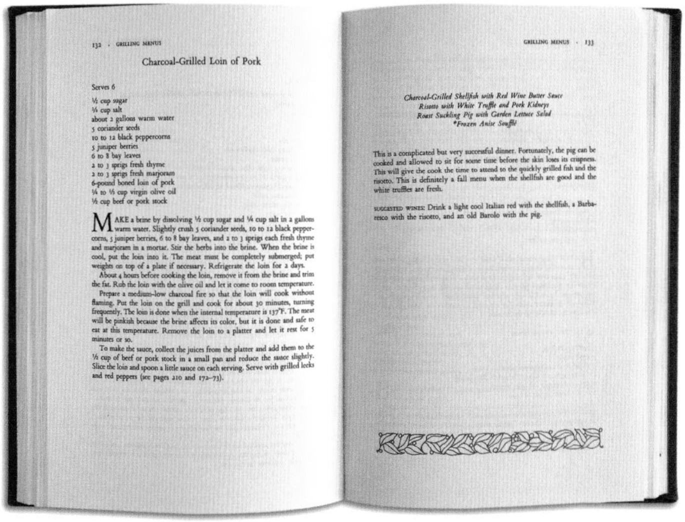
132 · GRILLING MENUS

Charcoal-Grilled Loin of Pork

Serves 6

½ cup sugar
¼ cup salt
about 2 gallons warm water
5 coriander seeds
10 to 12 black peppercorns
5 juniper berries
6 to 8 bay leaves
2 to 3 sprigs fresh thyme
2 to 3 sprigs fresh marjoram
6-pound boned loin of pork
¼ to ⅓ cup virgin olive oil
½ cup beef or pork stock

MAKE a brine by dissolving ½ cup sugar and ¼ cup salt in 2 gallons warm water. Slightly crush 5 coriander seeds, 10 to 12 black peppercorns, 5 juniper berries, 6 to 8 bay leaves, and 2 to 3 sprigs each fresh thyme and marjoram in a mortar. Stir the herbs into the brine. When the brine is cool, put the loin into it. The meat must be completely submerged; put weights on top of a plate if necessary. Refrigerate the loin for 2 days.

About 4 hours before cooking the loin, remove it from the brine and trim the fat. Rub the loin with the olive oil and let it come to room temperature.

Prepare a medium-low charcoal fire so that the loin will cook without flaming. Put the loin on the grill and cook for about 30 minutes, turning frequently. The loin is done when the internal temperature is 137°F. The meat will be pinkish because the brine affects its color, but it is done and safe to eat at this temperature. Remove the loin to a platter and let it rest for 5 minutes or so.

To make the sauce, collect the juices from the platter and add them to the ½ cup of beef or pork stock in a small pan and reduce the sauce slightly. Slice the loin and spoon a little sauce on each serving. Serve with grilled leeks and red peppers (see pages 210 and 172–73).

GRILLING MENUS · 133

Charcoal-Grilled Shellfish with Red Wine Butter Sauce
Risotto with White Truffle and Pork Kidneys
Roast Suckling Pig with Garden Lettuce Salad
**Frozen Anise Soufflé*

This is a complicated but very successful dinner. Fortunately, the pig can be cooked and allowed to sit for some time before the skin loses its crispness. This will give the cook the time to attend to the quickly grilled fish and the risotto. This is definitely a fall menu when the shellfish are good and the white truffles are fresh.

SUGGESTED WINES: Drink a light cool Italian red with the shellfish, a Barbaresco with the risotto, and an old Barolo with the pig.

"You can tell the scallops are fresh by checking they're closed. We only deal with hand-dived scallops, not dredged scallops – they get smashed, damaged. Dredged scallops should be banned."

"A lot of people say I look like a rock star or a designer punk. But I swear it's the job that has carved my face. It's the hours, the stress and the pressure. It's not me trying to look like this."

4 × 675g/1½lb live lobsters
1.75l/3pts court-bouillon (see page 117)

for the sauce:
250ml/9fl oz jus d'homard (see page 118)
200ml/¼pt classic vinaigrette (see page 118)
15g/½oz butter
salt and freshly ground white pepper

for the garnish:
48 very thin baby leeks, trimmed
225g/8oz tagliatelle (see page 119)
knob of butter

TO MAKE THE SAUCE:
1 Reduce the jus d'homard by one-third over a high heat, yielding about 175ml/6fl oz.
2 Whisk in the vinaigrette and finish with a little butter, incorporating it by making waves in the sauce. Taste and adjust the seasoning, if necessary. Keep warm.

TO MAKE THE GARNISH:
1 In a pan of boiling salted water, cook the leeks until just soft. Drain thoroughly.
2 Just before serving, re-heat them in an emulsion of butter and water, seasoned with salt and pepper.
3 Re-heat the tagliatelle in the

same way and then form into 4 balls as described on page 119.

TO COOK THE LOBSTERS:
1 Humanely kill the lobsters as described on page 36. Separate the tail and claws and reserve the heads for garnish, if wished.
2 In a large pan, bring to the boil the court-bouillon (enough to cover the lobsters – you can add some water to the court-bouillon if necessary). Poach the lobsters gently in it for 3½ minutes. Drain and then carefully remove the flesh from the shells in whole pieces (1 tail and 2 claw pieces per lobster).

TO SERVE:
1 Arrange 12 leeks in a bed on the lower part of each of 4 warmed plates, with the white bands radiating outwards.
2 Cut the lobster tails into 3 lengthways and fan these out over the beds of leek.
3 Place the 2 claws at 4 o'clock and 10 o'clock respectively on each plate, with the lobster head between them if using.
4 Place a ball of pasta at the base of the lobster tail fan or serve it on a separate side plate.
5 Spoon the sauce over the lobster flesh.

SERVES 4

LOBSTER WITH ITS OWN VINAIGRETTE

"When lobsters are in tanks they feed on their own flesh. You can have a majestic beast fished out for you, but it may be on its last legs, it may have almost eaten itself up, inside. You can tell that by feeling the weight of its tail. If it feels heavy and solid then you know it's a good lobster; if it's light, then it's been in the tank for a while. This dish is so simple that you need good lobsters. It's just lobster with lobster."

White Heat
Marco Pierre White

RESTAURANT
Harveys, London, UK, 1987–1993

BOOK DETAILS
Published 1990, Mitchell Beazley, 128 pages, photography by Michael Boys
and Bob Carlos Clarke, illustrations by Edward Bawden

*"Marco Pierre White was the original rock-star chef—
the guy who all of us wanted to be. . . . He made history."*
ANTHONY BOURDAIN

Driven, ambitious, and supremely talented, Marco Pierre White was, at the age of twenty-eight, the youngest chef to be awarded two Michelin stars; a few years later he went on to become the first British chef to be awarded three Michelin stars. He made his name with Harveys, the restaurant he opened in 1987 at the age of twenty-six. So stunning was the food—such as Tagliatelle of Oysters with Caviar—that despite its unfashionable location in Wandsworth in London, Harveys became the place to dine.

White Heat, published in 1990, was a groundbreaking cookbook, both in how it looked and read. White's forceful, confrontational personality leaps out from the pages. "You're buying *White Heat* because you want to cook well? Because you want to cook Michelin stars? Forget it. Save your money. Go and buy a saucepan," it starts uncompromisingly. Blood, sweat, and tears, declares White, are what's needed to cook at this level. "The boys in my team know that if they want to get to the top they've got to take the shit. Harveys is the hardest kitchen in Britain."

White's personal story is accompanied by striking black-and-white reportage photography by Bob Carlos Clarke. The images capture the hard work, camaraderie, and tension of a Michelin-starred restaurant, with the charismatic figure of the young White—lighting up a cigarette; knife in hand, deftly opening up a scallop; intently plating up—every inch the hero of the drama.

In striking contrast, the color food photography is elegant and orderly. The complex recipes for luxurious creations such as Roast Pigeon from Bresse with a Ravioli of Wild Mushrooms and a Fumet of Truffles, however, are cut through with terse comments from White. His voice—intelligent, sardonic, passionate—is loud and clear. Reading this cookbook brings home the force of Marco Pierre White's personality, and the extent of his talent, and offers an enduring record of his legendary career. The allure of a charismatic chef and the tough world of the professional restaurant are celebrated with style and verve here. Macho, intimate, and powerful, this was the cookbook that marked the dawn of the era of the celebrity chef.

The supremely talented British chef Marco Pierre White, a legend in his own lifetime.

Chapter Three
Cookbook Directory

Food is a multifaceted subject—and cookbooks reflect that in their range and variety. Here we feature the cookbook in all its diversity, bringing together a collection of classic works from around the world. One important strand is those cookbooks that offer an insight into national cuisines, with their authors setting out to share their knowledge of a specific culinary heritage. Many of these books by authors such as James Beard, Anna del Conte, or Claudia Roden, have played an important part in introducing these cuisines to a wider audience. Cookbooks, of course, help us to cook. The titles within "General Cookbooks" include much-loved books, whose authors—such as Stephanie Alexander, M. F. K. Fisher, and Nigel Slater—have inspired so many people to discover the pleasures of food and cooking. The "Specialty" section features cookbooks that have focused on a particular aspect of cooking, such as preserving or the science of food. Baking is prevalent, reflecting the fascination with this particular area and the number of interesting books about it. The "Historical" section contains titles that have played a role in shaping our food cultures: famous authoritative voices such as Mrs. Beeton and Fannie Farmer. Reading these books, it is clear that the issues which concerned the food writers of the past—how to make good food that tastes appetizing, healthy food that nourishes, while avoiding waste and extravagance—continue to resonate across the centuries.

THE
DEAN & DELUCA
COOKBOOK

David Rosengarten
with
Joel Dean and Giorgio DeLuca

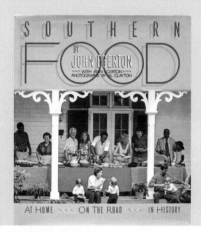

The Dean & DeLuca Cookbook
David Rosengarten with Joel Dean
and Giorgio DeLuca (Pub 1996,
Random House Inc, 563pp)

Southern Food
John Egerton
(Pub 1987, Alfred A. Knopf,
408pp)

The abundant variety within the cuisine of the United States reflects both its history as a nation founded through colonization and immigration as well as the great size of the American continent itself. Generations of settlers coming from diverse countries have arrived in the United States, bringing with them their own distinctive food traditions as well as their own ingredients, which have helped form and enrich the "melting pot" of US cuisine. The regional diversity of US food, which reflects the considerable geographic range within the country, is another notable characteristic. Cookbooks by writers including James Beard and Irma S. Rombauer with Marion Rombauer Becker have charted this rich, pluralistic food scene with affection and energy, helping to define a national cuisine.

In 1977, two men opened an upmarket food shop in the run-down New York district of SoHo. Their strikingly displayed stock was sophisticated and introduced the city's food lovers to what were then novel ingredients such as balsamic vinegar and sun-dried tomatoes. Today, Dean & DeLuca enjoys an international reputation and this book celebrates the part the gourmet food store has played in America's "gastronomic revolution." Delights include the store's bestselling sandwich recipes and insights on how to assemble salads. Both the ingredients used and the recipes themselves are cosmopolitan, reflecting the multiculturalism of New York's food scene.

This important work in the chronicling of Southern cuisine is written with both fondness and insight by John Egerton, who spent a great deal of time and energy researching it. It is, he writes, "a book about what the people of the South have eaten down through the years and how these foods have become a part of the region's character." It is a wide-ranging book: Egerton includes a history of Southern cuisine, a journey through "the most interesting restaurants," recipes for classic Southern dishes from Watermelon Rind Pickles to Burgoo, and a bibliography of cookbooks. His knowledgeable enthusiasm makes him an entertaining guide to this region's vibrant culinary heritage.

James Beard's American Cookery

American Cookery
James Beard

BOOK DETAILS

Published 1972, Little, Brown, 877 pages

Among the culinary legacies left by the acclaimed American chef and food writer James Beard is this impressive cookbook on American cuisine. "Food and eating habits have fascinated me throughout my life, and after sixty-five years I have come to the conclusion that perhaps American cooking is one of the most fascinating culinary subjects of all," he writes in the introduction, and his interest is infectious. The book offers a witty and engaging mixture of history and well-written recipes, with Beard's knowledge bringing depth to the content. The histories of iconic American dishes such as the hamburger or fried chicken are traced, then numerous recipe versions presented, giving an insight into the great range and vitality of American cooking.

Joy of Cooking
Irma S. Rombauer and Marion Rombauer Becker

BOOK DETAILS

Published 1931, Macmillan, 852 pages

First published in the 1930s, this bestselling cookbook retains a very special place in the hearts of Americans. The book was written by Irma S. Rombauer with the help of her daughter, Marion Rombauer Becker. The very first edition was self-published by Irma, who had recently been widowed and was in financial difficulties. Despite the onerous circumstances that Irma was facing (bearing in mind, too, that the book was being published against the background of the Great Depression), Irma's resilient spirit, humor, and common sense come through its pages. "When you are entertaining, try not to feel that something special is expected of you as hostess. It isn't. Just be yourself," she writes in the introduction to "Entertaining," and that calm, friendly, chatty voice was much appreciated by generations of the book's readers.

The size and scale of this book also reflect the Rombauers's energetic response to the question "What shall we eat?" Here are dishes for every social occasion, from canapés for drinks parties to homely brunch dishes, such as Beef and Ham Hash with Potatoes and Mushrooms. There is an impressive thoroughness to both the overall advice given and the breadth of recipes presented. On preparing pancakes, for example, three important factors in making them successfully are identified: "the consistency of your batter, the surface of your griddle or pan, and its even heat." Recipes including ones for Graham Griddle Cakes; Blintzes; and Crêpes Suzette follow. The tone is encouraging and practical throughout. Offering, as it does, a selection of classic American recipes, this book became the default "turn to" cookbook for thousands of home cooks.

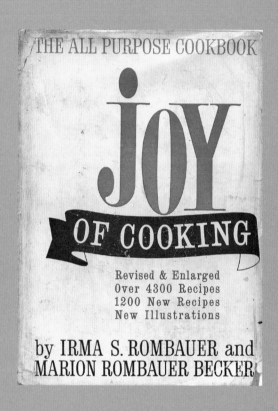

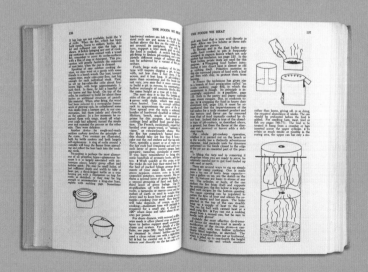

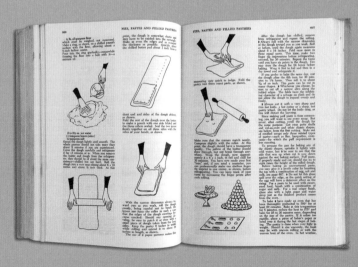

The Silver Palate Cookbook
Julee Rosso and Sheila Lukins
with Michael McLaughlin (Pub
1982, Workman Publishing, 362pp)

Jasper White's Cooking from New England
Jasper White (Pub 1989, HarperCollins, 367pp)

Chef Paul Prudhomme's Louisiana Kitchen, Paul Prudhomme
(Pub 1984, William Morrow and Company, 352pp)

The New York Times Cook Book
Edited by Craig Claiborne
(Pub 1961, Harper & Row, 723pp)

This much-loved cookbook is written by Julee Rosso and Sheila Lukins, the partnership behind a popular gourmet takeout shop in New York City. Reflecting the duo's catering background, the book is aimed at the home cook looking for dinner party inspiration. It opens with a chapter of "Fancy Finger Food" such as Gougère Puffs; Phyllo Triangles; and Avocado Dip. In addition to the well-written recipes, a key part of the book's appeal rests in its cheerful, lively tone of voice, with Rosso and Lukins offering tips on the practicalities of entertaining and cooking as well as chatty notes. With its encouraging air and useful information, it is clear why readers view it with such affection.

Jasper White's passion for the cuisine of New England, which he both knowledgeably charts and joyfully celebrates, permeates this book. Structured by ingredients, it opens, naturally, with a chapter on shellfish: "I can think of no better way to start a meal—or a book—than with oysters." Each chapter is enriched with much information on how to choose, prepare, and use the foods in question. While White shares the history and traditions of the region, he also roots the book firmly in the contemporary world. His recipes include classic regional dishes—Anadama Bread, New England Fish Chowder—as well as innovative ones—Salad of Scallops, Pear, and Celery; and Maple-Sugar Crème Caramel.

This cookbook, by the renowned chef, broadcaster, and cooking teacher Paul Prudhomme, celebrates Louisiana's traditional Cajun and Creole cuisines. Prudhomme was hailed by no less an authority than Craig Claiborne (see right), as "the greatest practitioner of Louisiana cookery." The chef's pride in and affection for his rich culinary heritage is palpable. From the illuminating introduction, which explains the similarities and differences between Cajun and Creole cooking and highlights key ingredients, to the recipes for classic dishes such as Shrimp Creole; Dirty Rice; and Seafood Filé Gumbo, Prudhomme is an informed guide to this fascinating regional American cuisine.

Edited by the eminent critic and writer Craig Claiborne, this cookbook contains around 1,500 recipes, selected from the thousands that have appeared in the *New York Times*. While it begins with advice on the correct way to serve caviar and foie gras, it also features more down-to-earth offerings: Egyptian Beans; Irma's Onion Sandwiches ("one of the finest and most popular appetizers served in New York"); Caraway and Cheese Spread. In fact, this volume is characterized by a varied content that offers a snapshot of US life. Reflecting the nation's rich immigrant heritage, its recipes are cosmopolitan: Budapest Beef Goulash; Chicken Curry Jaipur; Steak au Poivre; Rotisserie Chinese Duck.

Gran Cocina Latina: The Food of Latin America, Maricel E. Presilla (Pub 2012, W. W. Norton & Company, 902pp)

Brazilian Food
Thiago Castanho and Luciana Bianchi (Pub 2014, Mitchell Beazley, 256pp)

The influence of Central and South American food culture has been experienced around the globe with a number of key regional ingredients being exported to many countries—chiles, potatoes, tomatoes, chocolate—that originate from this part of the world. An abundant natural larder—with the potential of the Amazon still to be explored—and varied geography, together with a complex history, means that the cuisine of this part of the world is multifaceted. Through their acclaimed restaurants, chefs such as Peruvian Gaston Acurio, Argentine Francis Mallmann, and Mexican Enrique Olvera have done much to draw attention to the food of Latin America. Recent cookbooks by these chefs and others play an important part in chronicling and communicating the region's fascinating and multistranded culinary heritage.

The sheer scale of this book, both intellectually and physically, is impressive. Writing with authority and sensitivity, Cuban chef and restaurateur Maricel E. Presilla charts Latin American cuisine and the influence of Iberian colonialism: "In fact, no matter how far I travelled to find Latin dishes, I kept finding medieval Spain—sometimes in techniques that have died out in Spain itself." Presilla traveled extensively through the region to research this book, and her experiences inform the text and recipes, allowing her to reveal the historical context of dishes such as Mote Pelado (Andean hominy) or Arepas Caraqueñas (Arepas in the style of Caracas). A remarkable culinary chronicle.

The cuisine of Brazil reflects both the varied geography of this vast country—including the influence of the Amazon—and its diverse ethnic make-up. Young Brazilian chef Thiago Castanho, noted for his innovative food in his Belém restaurants, offers an accessibly presented taste of his country's varied, still-evolving cuisine, which he describes as "a mosaic of flavours and cooking methods." Distinctive Brazilian ingredients, such as *bacuri* (an Amazonian fruit) or *macaxeira* (a type of cassava) are clearly explained. Castanho includes recipes from other noted Brazilian chefs, including Roberta Sudbrack and Rodrigo Oliveira, to convey a sense of the cuisine's range and variety.

Mexico

Mexico from the Inside Out
Enrique Olvera

BOOK DETAILS
Published 2015, Phaidon, 280 pages

With this stylish, sophisticated cookbook, acclaimed Mexican chef Enrique Olvera of the restaurant Pujol, presents his vision of Mexican cuisine with charisma and flair. Inspiration for Pujol's dishes comes from a variety of sources: the powerful emphasis on flavor at the heart of Mexican food, the vibrant street food scene, the diverse range of key Mexican ingredients. The book describes the journey Olvera has taken in creating his own distinctive cuisine: "Since 2008, I've delved into the taco's form and taken it from the streets to Pujol." Dishes such as Baby Corn with Chicatana Ant, Coffee and Chile Costeña Mayonnaise; and Mother Mole reflect Olvera's capacity to play creatively with the venerable traditions of his native cuisine. "Tradition is one of our many starting points and we use it above all as a gustatory reference," he explains. While his cooking is contemporary and innovative, it is informed by a great sense of Mexican heritage.

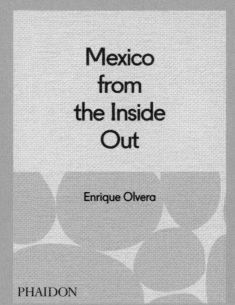

Mexico

Peru

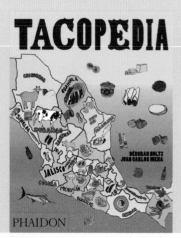

The Cuisines of Mexico
Diana Kennedy
(Pub 1972, HarperCollins,
378pp)

Tacopedia
Deborah Holtz and Juan
Carlos Mena
(Pub 2015, Phaidon, 320pp)

Peru: The Cookbook
Gastón Acurio
(Pub 2015, Phaidon, 432pp)

Ceviche: Peruvian Kitchen
Martin Morales
(Pub 2013, Weidenfeld &
Nicholson Ltd, 256pp)

Widely respected as a leading authority on Mexican food, this cookbook is an absorbing reflection of writer and cooking teacher Diana Kennedy's fascination with and respect for Mexican gastronomy. The deliberate use of the plural "cuisines" in the title refers to the extraordinary richness and diversity of food on offer here: "Indeed there are many cuisines that have grown up and flourished from pre-Columbian times to the present day," says Kennedy. Her deep interest manifests itself in the carefully written ingredients section, which notes the importance of "good pork lard," and in the lovingly written recipes for dishes such as tortillas and Salsa de Chile Pasilla.

From the jaunty jacket and illustrations to the title and lively tone of voice, there is an engaging quality to this volume, billed as the definitive taco manual. Written with tangible fondness as a chronicle of the taco, it traces the history of this quintessentially Mexican food, beginning with its origins "between 500 and 1000 BC as a kind of edible spoon." Information on aspects from the history of the tortilla to the story of pork carnitas sits alongside authentic recipes for dishes such as Maguey Worm Tacos or Fish Mixiote Tacos, with the "Tacography map" further conveying the diverse regional variety of Mexico's enormously vibrant taco heritage.

Written by acclaimed chef Gastón Acurio, this celebrates the cuisine of his beloved native Peru. In the introduction, he outlines the nature of Peruvian cuisine, including its different strands influenced by immigration, including Nikkei—Japanese-Peruvian—and Chifa—Chinese-Peruvian. The book begins with a chapter on ceviche—Peru's best-known dish—and ends with basic recipes, including the flavorful pastes and condiments that are so important in this cuisine. The range of dishes covered—from Huancaína Potatoes or *Quinoa Solterito* to Theologian's Soup or *Picarones* (Squash and Sweet Potato donuts)—is impressive and gives a sense of the cuisine's diversity.

Following a successful career in music, Peruvian-born Martin Morales decided to follow his dream and open a Peruvian restaurant in London, Ceviche. This cheerful cookbook, brightly illustrated with photographs of ingredients and dishes, provides a great introduction to Peruvian food, with Morales's affection for his native cuisine clearly apparent. It opens, naturally, with a chapter on ceviche, Peru's best-known dish internationally, including the restaurant's signature Don Ceviche. The recipes, which range from street food to desserts and drinks, are well written, with a chapter on the "Peruvian Larder" offering a useful guide to typical ingredients such as *chuño* (Andean dehydrated potatoes).

Argentina

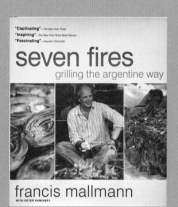

Seven Fires: Grilling the Argentinan Way
Francis Mallmann
with Peter Kaminsky

BOOK DETAILS
Published 2014, Artisan Books, 278 pages

Charismatic South American chef and TV star Francis Mallmann—noted for acclaimed restaurants such as Francis Mallmann 1884 in Argentina—went on a journey with his own career. As a young man, he worked with great French chefs including Paul Bocuse (see p.108, 182), before returning to cook in Argentina. An epiphany, however, led him to move away from fine dining and he chose instead to embrace the rustic roots of Argentinian cuisine. Written with eloquence and humor, the book explores cooking with fire and outlines the key "commandments" of this way of cooking—the first being "Don't Touch!"—together with seven different methods: the barbecue; cast-iron griddle; little hell; clay oven; embers and ashes; the iron cross; and the cauldron. The appetizing recipes—from the deceptively simple Skirt Steak and Fry Bread or celebratory Carbonada in a Pumpkin to Caramelized Endives with Vinegar or a signature creation, 7½-Hour Lamb Malbec with Rosemary and Lemon—convincingly convey the potential of cooking over flames and the range of dishes possible. Mallmann's happy fascination with this cooking method shines through the pages. As the book states: "Nothing wakes up the appetite quite like food cooking over an open fire."

EUROPE   Scandinavia   UK

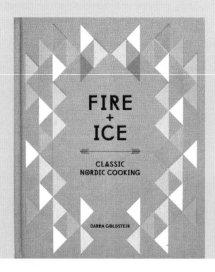

Fire + Ice: Classic Nordic Cooking
Darra Goldstein
(Pub 2015, Ten Speed Press, 296pp)

English Food
Jane Grigson
(Pub 1974, Macmillan London
Ltd, 322pp)

The continent of Europe with its long, complex cultural history, encompasses a widely diverse range of cuisines within it—from the olive-centric Mediterranean influence of Italian, Greek, and Spanish food in southern Europe to the clean flavors and authentic simplicity of Scandinavian cooking. It therefore offers a particularly rich culinary vein to tap for inspiration. French cuisine, of course, has long been hugely influential in the world of fine food and restaurants, and a deep fascination with French food is reflected in the time and attention paid to it by venerable food writers including Julia Child and Richard Olney. The regional pleasures of Italian food have also been eloquently championed by writers from Elizabeth David and Claudia Roden to Keith Floyd and Giorgio Locatelli.

A Professor of Russian who has long been interested in the cuisines of the Far North, Darra Goldstein offers an inviting introduction to Scandinavian food with this book. While traveling in the area to research it, she discovered "commonalities" such as cured salted fish, game, and pickled vegetables, but she also gained an insight into the striking, regional differences. The accessible recipes—for dishes such as Norwegian Buttermilk-Marinated Leg of Lamb with Parsley or Finnish Whipped Berry Pudding—are informatively set into context. With its appealing images of simple yet elegant food, the book provides an evocative insight into the region's cuisine.

"English cooking—both historically and in the mouth— is a great deal more varied and delectable than our masochistic temper in this matter allows," declares Jane Grigson (see p.74, 100, 102, 106) in this book. With characteristic intelligence and forthrightness, she makes her case for English food, offering dishes of quality as well as "surprises." Recipes include classics such as Cornish Pasty, Hot Cross Buns, and Lancashire Hotpot as well as less familiar dishes—Mackerel with Gooseberry Sauce or Singing Hinnies (griddle cakes). Her writing is both well-informed— filled with literary and historical references—and rooted in commonsense knowledge of ingredients and how to cook them.

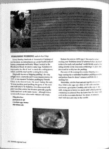

British Regional Food
Mark Hix

BOOK DETAILS
Published 2008, Hardie Grant Books, 240 pages

A long-time champion of British cooking and British food producers, chef Mark Hix (see p.76) was well-placed to write this book, and his affection for the subject comes across admirably. The book opens with a chapter on London, the great, cosmopolitan city treated—quite rightly—as its own region. While Hix writes of iconic dishes associated with the capital—such as fish and chips or eels, pie, and mash—he also identifies its open-mindedness to other cuisines from around the world as a special trait. The book then explores the rest of the United Kingdom and Ireland, with Hix proving a humorous and down-to-earth guide to regional variety: "The food of the North is generally considered working man's grub. Indeed, many Northern dishes are often based on economical ingredients and use all types of offal rarely seen in other parts of the country." The recipes—St. George's Mushrooms on Toast, Crab and Samphire Salad, Stargazy Pie (made with baked pilchards protruding through the piecrust)—are rooted in the ingredients and traditions of Britain, set in a context of history and place. Hix's knowledge of Britain's food producers, many of whom he has worked with over the years, is considerable; his warm tributes to those working hard to produce top ingredients are at the heart of the book. An engaging mixture of history, producer profiles, memories, and "traditional and original" recipes makes this a good read as well as a good cookbook.

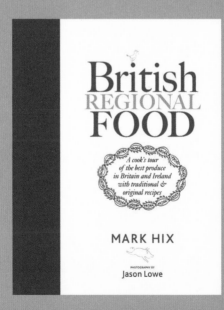

UK

Spain

Historic Heston
Heston Blumenthal
(Pub 2013, Bloomsbury
Publishing, 432pp)

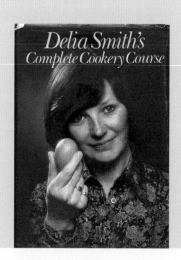

*Delia Smith's Complete
Cookery Course*
Delia Smith (Pub 1978,
BBC Books, 711pp)

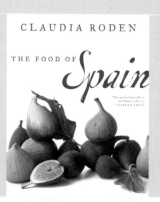

The Food of Spain
Claudia Roden
(Pub 2012, Michael Joseph, 512pp)

1080 Recipes
Simone and Inés Ortega
(Pub 1972, Phaidon, 976pp)

Acclaimed chef Heston Blumenthal (see p.180) is famed for his avant-garde culinary creations, yet he is also deeply fascinated and inspired by Britain's historical cuisine. "Tradition is the mainspring of innovation: we use the past as a springboard to leap towards the new," he writes in the introduction. This interestingly conceived, exuberantly written, intelligent cookbook takes the reader on an engaging journey through Britain's culinary history. It begins with Blumenthal's characteristically creative recipe inspired by *The Forme of Cury*, England's oldest cookbook, for Mock Turtle Soup. If anyone doubted that British food has an impressive heritage, this book convincingly shows otherwise.

Writer Delia Smith (see p.118) has a special place in British affections, trusted and respected for her "recipes that always work." Through her popular TV series and best-selling cookbooks, she has been a hugely influential figure in shaping the nation's tastes. Always writing for the home cook, her collection of recipes is admirably comprehensive, ranging from eggs to leftovers. Within its pages are an array of classic, much-loved British dishes, familiar to generations: Seville Orange Marmalade, Yorkshire Pudding, Cornish Pasty, Steak and Kidney Pie. Her famously detailed recipes are clear and easy to follow, while her tone of voice is reassuring and encouraging.

The distinguished food writer Claudia Roden (see p. 317, 319) digs deep into the heart of a cuisine—a quality that is amply demonstrated in this key book on Spanish food. Many years of research and travel underlie this fascinating cookbook. In its pages Roden traces the many different historic strands within Spanish food—including Moorish and Jewish—offering a vivid picture of the cuisine. The lovingly collected recipes—from Pan Con Tomate (Catalan Tomato Bread) to Tarta de Santiago (Almond Cake) are characteristically clear and elegantly written, each set in a context of region, history, and religion, with Roden's shrewd eye for the practical details of cooking also manifest.

A revered Spanish bestseller, written by highly regarded Spanish food expert Simone Ortega and her daughter Inés, this hefty tome offers a comprehensive insight into Spanish cuisine. Within its pages are recipes grouped together by food type or style of dish, including both classics such as Gazpacho or Catalan Cream and less familiar dishes such as Fried Hake Cheeks or Rabbit with Liver, Pine Nut, and Bell Pepper Sauce. The book's thoroughgoing nature is expressed, for example, in the section on paellas, with a number of recipes—including Simple Paella; My Paella; and Salt Cod Paella—demonstrating the considerable range and variety of this iconic rice dish.

France

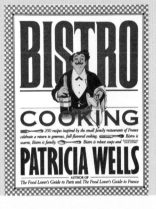

Tante Marie's French Kitchen
Trans. Charlotte Turgeon
(Pub 1949, Ulisse Editions,
323pp)

La Cuisine en dix minutes
(Cooking in Ten Minutes)
Édouard de Pomiane (Pub 1930,
Éditions Paul Martial, 152pp)

Mastering the Art of French Cooking
Julia Child, Louisette Bertholle,
Simone Beck (Vol 1, Pub 1961,
Alfred A. Knopf, 670pp)

Bistro Cooking
Patricia Wells
(Pub 1989, William Morrow
& Company, 291pp)

Based on the French cookbook *La Veritable Cuisine de Famille par Tante Marie*—"used by generations of French families" —this version translated and adapted by US chef and writer Charlotte Turgeon was aimed at offering the "American housewife" an introduction to French cuisine. It is a cuisine, asserts Turgeon, that "despite its reputation for quality and artistry, is basically simple." The original book was written for an audience obliged "to consider time and money" and there is a down-to-earth practicality to both the tone and content. The repertoire of recipes is classically Gallic, from the introductory chapter on "Sauces" to the one on "Liqueurs and Brandied Fruits."

Written with wit and flair by scientist and food writer Édouard de Pomiane, this characterful and charming cookbook combines affable asides together with thoroughly sensible advice on how to conjure up a meal quickly. The author's scientific turn of mind reveals itself in the clearly outlined principles of cooking and the precisely written recipes for Ultra-Rapid Soups and Some Delicate, If Hasty, Meat Dishes. However, he also has an appealing turn of phrase, poetic but without being flowery. There is a sensuousness to the way in which he writes about dishes such as Oysters and Sausages, which shows that here is a man who both loves his food and knows perfectly well how to cook it.

This seminal cookbook aimed— and admirably succeeded—at introducing French cuisine to a domestic US audience: "Anyone can cook in the French manner anywhere, with the right instruction," being its self-avowed mission statement. Written in a clear, calmly authoritative voice, it outlines the fundamental cooking techniques needed to cook French food, with recipes for classic dishes such as Boeuf à la Mode (Beef Braised in Red Wine) or Crêpes Suzette written in detail with great care. The cookbook's classic status saw it inspire Julie Powell's blogging project, in which she attempted to cook all the recipes in the book in one year, an endeavor that was turned into the movie *Julie & Julia* in 2009.

A fascination with French food has been a defining feature of US food writer Patricia Wells's career, and through her books she has done much to introduce it and champion it to her compatriots. In this accessible cookbook, she celebrates a much-loved aspect of French cuisine—the homely fare found in France's neighborhood restaurants. Here are classic, simple recipes, lovingly garnered from bistro owners from across France by Wells over several years: Salade Niçoise, Daube de Boeuf, Pommes Boulangere, Tarte aux Pommes. Wells is both a discriminating and affectionate guide, describing personalities and restaurants well and setting the appetizing dishes in an atmospheric Gallic landscape.

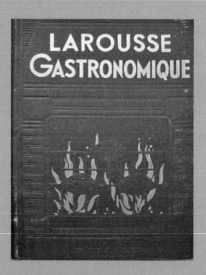

Larousse Gastronomique:
The Encyclopedia of
Food, Wine & Cookery
Prosper Montagné

BOOK DETAILS
Published 1938, Larousse, 1350 pages

Ambitiously conceived and thoroughly executed, this renowned, stately encyclopaedia of French gastronomy continues to be regarded as a key reference work. First written by chef Prosper Montagné, and featuring prefaces from chefs Auguste Escoffier (see p.206) and Phileas Gilbert, it offers an impressively thorough survey of French cuisine. While later editions, in a recognition that "gastronomy is not static" have increasingly widened the frame of reference, it is the Gallic content that is its forte. Beginning with *Abaisse* (a term for rolled-out pastry) and ending with *Zuppa Inglese*, the book offers a huge array of information. Among its riches are numerous recipes for classic

dishes, from Chestnut Soufflé to Snails à la Bourguignonne Reflecting its gourmet origins, ingredients such as foie gras and truffles are dealt with lovingly and at length, with detailed advice on how to source and prepare these luxuries. Here, too, are entries on culinary techniques, such as *chiffonade* (thin shreds) of lightly sautéed sorrel or lettuce, descriptions of cookware, and biographies of chefs and notable gastronomes—Brillat-Savarin (see p.345), Carême, and Escoffier. As with the best reference books, part of the pleasure of reading this is coming across pieces of intriguing information, whether learning what constitutes a *Freneuse* (a turnip and potato

soup), the origins of that Gallic institution, the brasserie, or reading about the "golden age" of French cooking under King Louis XV. Furthermore, the range of the volume's entries offers an insight into the culture and society of France, as well as the opportunity to set its cuisine within a national context. Within its pages, for example, one can read of subjects such as Confréries, Orders, and Brotherhoods—historic associations dedicated to promoting local wines—or Appellation d'Origine Contrôlée, the framework of laws protecting historic foods and drinks, which have undoubtedly helped preserve many traditional treasures of France's rich and vibrant culinary heritage.

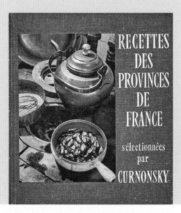

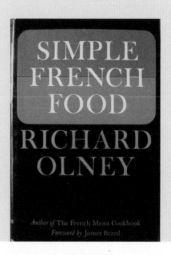

Les Fêtes de mon moulin (Entertaining in the French Style), Roger Vergé (Pub 1986, Flammarion, 320pp)

Recettes des Provinces de France (Traditional Recipes of the Provinces of France), Curnonsky (Pub 1961, Doubleday, 490pp)

Simple French Food Richard Olney (Pub 1974, Atheneum Books, 340pp)

The Cooking of South-West France Paula Wolfert (Pub 1983, Dial Press, 356pp)

The acclaimed French chef Roger Vergé, described by Gault Millaut as "the very incarnation of the French chef for foreigners," was an innovative, influential figure in French gastronomy. There is an infectious joie de vivre to this lavishly illustrated cookbook by Vergé, an exuberance to his writing: "A dinner with friends, that's fine. But a dinner with pals!" The book consists of a series of menus, each created for different occasions: Lunch in the Sun, On a Lovely Autumn Evening. In addition to recipes for luxurious, elegant dishes such as Stuffed Zucchini Flowers with Truffles, he also gives advice on table setting and accompanying wines. Warm and humorous, it is a book written with a hospitable spirit.

Known as the "Prince of Gastronomes," Curnonsky (aka Maurice-Edmond Sailland) was a French journalist, noted for his impeccable taste in many areas, including food. In this charming, humorous book, conceived of as a journey through France via its regional food, he advises his fellow gastronomist traveler: "Don't forget to stop!" Written with panache, in a lively, conversational style, Curnonsky begins with Paris ("the capital of our gastronomic world"), offering Parisian recipes such as Grives à la Parisienne. He continues with an atmospheric account of France's regions, from Brittany—"a paradise" for fish and seafood lovers—to Alsace, with its "original, lavish, and varied" cuisine.

Editor and writer Richard Olney's (see p.80) knowledge of French food ran deep. So fascinated was he by France that, as a young man, he moved from the United States to France, living there until his death. In this thoughtfully written cookbook, he celebrates the French food he loved, creating a classic cookbook imbued with his personality and intelligence. The recipes—for dishes such as Braised Stuffed Oxtail or Eggs in Aspic with Sorrel Mousse—are meticulously written, with Olney generously sharing useful information on ingredients and cooking methods. One can hardly open a page without coming across a striking phrase, making the book a pleasure to read as well as to cook from.

"The idea is that you, too, can possess the South-West not merely in words, but that most tangible and sensuous necessity of people's lives: the wonderful food they eat." So wrote Paula Wolfert (see p.58) in her eloquent introduction to a book in which she expresses her knowledge of and affection for the cuisine of southwestern France. In it she weaves together evocative writing of her experiences in the southwest: history, literature, and recipes. From its opening chapter celebrating key foods—foie gras, truffles, and *cèpes*—to the array of lovingly written recipes for classics such as Cassoulet de Toulouse or Pruneaux au Sauternes, this is an appetizing celebration of a region's cuisine.

> *"Robuchon taught me that the greatness of a cook can be measured by one's ability to work magic with the simplest of ingredients."*
>
> PATRICIA WELLS, *SIMPLY FRENCH*

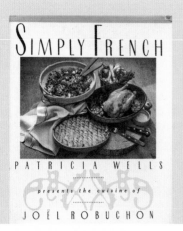

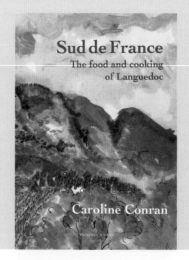

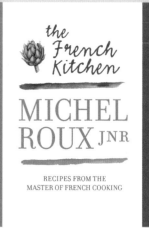

Simply French, Patricia Wells presents the cuisine of Joël Robuchon (Pub 1991, William Morrow and Company, 367pp)

Floyd on France
Keith Floyd
(Pub 1987, BBC Books, 272pp)

Sud de France: The Food and Cooking of Languedoc
Caroline Conran (Pub 2012, Prospect Books, 330pp)

The French Kitchen
Michel Roux, Jnr.
(Pub 2014, Weidenfeld & Nicholson Ltd, 352pp)

A collaboration between legendary French chef Joël Robuchon (see p.280) and respected American food writer Patricia Wells (see p.70)—with the latter presenting his cuisine—this book comes with impeccable credentials. The interview with Robuchon, in which he explains his thoughts on food and cooking, offers a fascinating insight into the man and his cuisine, compounded by the detailed, lucid recipes for elegant dishes including his signature Potato Purée or Blanquette de Veau. In her introduction, Wells explains that, as a home cook, having worked closely with the great chef on the book, she now divides her life "as a cook into two distinct periods: Before Robuchon and After Robuchon."

British chef and restaurateur Keith Floyd gained celebrity with his popular television cooking shows. A legendary *bon viveur*, Floyd's relaxed and candid presenting style, with a glass of wine in one hand, went down well. His genuine knowledge of and fondness for French food comes across in this accessible cookbook, which accompanied a television series of the same name. The straightforwardly written recipes for classic dishes come from throughout the various regions of France and contain a good deal of common sense and culinary advice. Giving the book character are Floyd's pieces of verbal scene painting, musings on French cuisine, and reminiscences.

Caroline Conran's respect and affection for the Languedoc shines through this heartfelt cookbook. The opening chapter offers an elegantly written account of the foods that have shaped the region, from truffles to *sel de mer* (sea salt), harvested on the shores of the Camargue. Conran's knowledge of food and cooking makes her a perceptive and informative guide, highlighting the cuisine's two aspects—mountain food and the food of the coast—influenced by the Greeks, Romans, Moors, and Catalonia. Her writing blends practical ingredients information, recipes, and history to elegant effect, creating a notably unsentimental sense of place rooted in shrewd observations.

As chef-owner of the acclaimed Le Gavroche in London, the restaurant founded by his father, the legendary Albert Roux, Michel Roux, Jr. (see p.284), has a formidable knowledge of classic French cuisine. In this accessible cookbook, he offers an affectionate portrait of regional French cooking. "Food in France has always been about more than mere sustenance," observes Roux, and his understanding of the importance of food in family and community life underlies the book. His recipes are for versions of classic dishes, such as Soupe à l'Oignon Lyonnaise or Boeuf Bourguignon, beloved for generations, and cooked by Roux both at home and in his restaurant Le Gavroche.

Italy

I Know How to Cook
Ginette Mathiot
(Pub 1932, Phaidon, 976pp)

Entertaining all'Italiana
Anna del Conte
(Pub 1991, Transworld, 398pp)

Il Talismano della Felicità
(The Talisman of Happiness)
Ada Boni (Pub 1929, Editore
Colombo, 416pp)

Passione: The Italian Cookbook
Gennaro Contaldo
(Pub 2003, Headline
Publishing Group, 256pp)

A cookbook with a special place in French affections, Ginette Mathiot's reassuringly authoritative and comprehensive book is aimed at the home cook. As Mathiot puts it with admirable self-confidence, her book will be genuinely useful to people wanting to cook as it will "avoid second-rate recipes or those that are too complicated for the way we live now." The fundamentals of French cooking, such as how to poach fish in a *court-bouillon* or which cuts of beef suit a particular cooking method, are laid out clearly, while her economically written recipes for such classics as Brochet au Beurre Blanc (Pike with Beurre Blanc) or Oeufs à la Neige (Eggs in Snow) are straightforward and lucid.

Anyone seeking inspiration when it comes to holding a dinner party should turn to this book, a charming classic by the Italian food writer Anna del Conte (see p.76). The book is structured as a series of menus, with themes including the four seasons but also "Harmonious," "Historical," "Special Occasion," and "My Favourite," the latter giving a clue as to the book's personal nature. The recipes are Italian, featuring both traditional classics and less familiar ones. Seeing how del Conte structures her meals, usually with a *primo* (first course), typically of pasta or rice, a *secondo*, and a *dolce*, offers a useful insight into Italian cuisine and the way dishes are balanced with each other to create a satisfying meal.

A much-loved, enduring chronicle of Italian cuisine, magazine editor Ada Boni's hugely popular cookbook has a long history of being given as a wedding present in Italy. Patriotic in tone, the author's pride in Italy's food culture is manifest: "We have a culinary tradition of the highest wealth," she declares stirringly. The importance of regionality in Italian cooking is made apparent; so, for example, a fish soup is given in numerous regional variations. The wide range of dishes covered in the book is impressive, with the emphasis on method rather than quantities. This comprehensive book is also expressive and eloquent, combining authority with charm.

Born in the Amalfi region of Italy, Gennaro Contaldo began working in local restaurants as a young boy. In England he made his name as a chef, working for restaurateur Antonio Carluccio at London's Neal Street Restaurant and, famously, inspiring young chef Jamie Oliver (see p.114, 331) with a love for Italian food. An affable figure, he has also enjoyed a successful career in broadcasting. This accessible and engaging cookbook, named after a restaurant that Contaldo opened in London in 1999, offers a mixture of classic Italian recipes and chatty reminiscences, from memories of going out fishing with friends as a boy and catching an enormous tuna fish to watching bullocks slaughtered.

Giorgio Locatelli

'My book of the year . . . puts everything else I have on my Italian shelf in the shade.'
Nigel Slater

Made In Italy Food & Stories

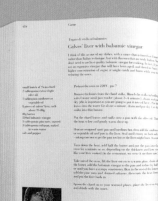

Made In Italy: Food & Stories
Giorgio Locatelli

BOOK DETAILS
Published 2006, Fourth Estate, 512 pages

This massive tome, handsomely illustrated with striking photographs of ingredients, dishes, and people, manages to deliver the "food and stories" of the book's subtitle. Italian chef Giorgio Locatelli weaves together engaging, often humorous, anecdotes from his journey as a boy growing up in Lombardy, Italy, to becoming chef-owner of acclaimed London restaurant Locanda Locatelli, together with recipes and detailed essays on food. Humble ingredients, such as *fagioli* (beans) are written about with the same respect and affection as *tartufi bianchi* (white truffles). Locatelli shares his insights on how to make classic dishes, such as risotto, *ragu alla Bolognese*, potato gnocchi, or fresh egg pasta. The recipes also chronicle the sophisticated Italian food he cooks at his restaurant: Razor Clam and Fregola Soup; Linguine with Lobster; Duck Breast with Broccoli; Mascarpone Ice Cream. A striking aspect of the book is the generosity of spirit with which it has been written; the range and depth of information about Italian food and cooking contained within its pages is impressive. Locatelli's deep-rooted love for Italian food and his desire to convey what makes this cuisine so special gives the book a vivacity and intensity that make it truly memorable.

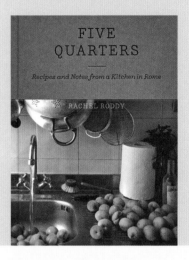

The Food of Italy
Claudia Roden
(Pub 1989, Chatto and Windus, 218pp)

Italian Food
Elizabeth David
(Pub 1954, Macdonald & Co., 368pp)

Il cucchiaio d'argento
Domus
(Pub 1950, Domus, 1263pp)

Five Quarters: Recipes and Notes from a Kitchen in Rome
Rachel Roddy (Pub 2015, Saltyard Books, 384pp)

The intensely regional nature of Italian cuisine is amply captured in this seminal work by Claudia Roden (see p.310, 319). Based on research undertaken for the British *Sunday Times Magazine*, it begins in the northeastern corner of Italy, in Piedmont and Val d'Aosta, then travels through the country, ending in the islands of Sicily and Sardinia, along the way offering a cornucopia of diverse and appetizing recipes. Well-informed introductions to each region give an evocative sense of what has shaped that particular cuisine, from the Arab legacy that enriched Sicilian cuisine to the simplicity that typifies the food of Tuscany, which is centered on locally produced ingredients such as good olive oil and wine.

Elizabeth David's (see p.84, 110, 332) ability to understand, appreciate, and communicate the key aspects of a national cuisine are well demonstrated in this classic and illuminating work. David wrote it in 1953, a time in Britain when postwar food rationing was still in place, Italian cuisine was little understood, and Italian ingredients were difficult to source. She conveys the knowledge of and respect for food lying at the heart of Italian cuisine with both conviction and elegance. While the book is grouped by ingredient or type of dish—*pasta asciutta* or sweets, for example—she shows the regional nature of Italian cooking while also setting dishes in a historical and cultural context in this fascinating book.

The extraordinary regional diversity of Italian cuisine is carefully chronicled in this massive tome. An Italian bestseller for decades, it is regarded as the authoritative volume on Italian cuisine. The scale of the book is reflected in the fact that it contains 2,000 recipes, collected from throughout Italy but arranged by meal type and ingredient, which allows the immense variety of Italian cooking to be appreciated. The section on veal, for example, contains classics such as Roman Saltimbocca and Milanese Osso Buco, but also less familiar dishes such as Spezzatino ai Sei Profumi (Six-Aroma Veal Stew) or Involtini ai Tartufi (Veal Bundles with Truffles).

An expression of the enduring regionality of Italian cuisine, this book celebrates the food of Rome. The title alludes to the Italian expression "*il quinto quarto*" (fifth quarter), which refers to the thrifty strand in Roman cuisine that uses offal. Living in Testaccio, the traditional slaughterhouse area of Rome, Roddy charts her experiences of both the city and its lively food scene. She conveys in appealing, characterful, candid prose her excitement at discovering Roman cooking. The recipes—for dishes such as Baccalà in Guazzetto (Salt Cod with Tomatoes, Raisins, and Pine Nuts) or Pasta e Lenticchie (Pasta and Lentil Soup)—add further insight into the food of the Eternal City.

MIDDLE EAST

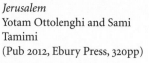

Jerusalem
Yotam Ottolenghi and Sami
Tamimi
(Pub 2012, Ebury Press, 320pp)

*Honey & Co.: Food From the Middle
East,* Sarit Packer and Itamar
Srulovich (Pub 2014, Saltyard
Books, 304pp)

The complex history of Middle Eastern cuisine, with its diverse, interwoven strands, was memorably charted by the food writer Claudia Roden in her groundbreaking, seminal work on the subject. Israeli food, which draws on the fascinating, multifaceted cuisine of the Jewish diaspora, is enjoying new popularity outside Israel itself thanks—in part—to the success of chefs such as Yotam Ottolenghi, Sarit Packer, and Itamar Srulovich, who have all championed vibrant salads, mezze dishes, and street food. Previously hard-to-source ingredients—such as pomegranate molasses, *za'atar* (spice blend), preserved lemons, and rose water—are becoming far more widely available as interest in Middle Eastern cuisine continues to grow, encouraged by an increasing number of cookbooks.

Israeli chefs Yotam Ottolenghi and Sami Tamimi (see p.260, 331) grew up in different parts of Jerusalem: Ottolenghi in the Jewish West and Tamimi in the Muslim East. This fascinating, jointly written cookbook offers an insight into the vibrant, diverse, complex food culture of their home. They chart, with intelligent affection, the way in which key ingredients such as aubergines or za'atar are used in cooking, with the recipes for flavorful dishes—Pureed Beetroot with Yoghurt & Za'atar or Mejadra—written with great care. Their cookbook is written with a sensitive appreciation of the divisive politics of the fractured region, offering food and hospitality as a possible meeting point.

Having worked for chefs such as Yotam Ottolenghi (see left, p.260, 331), the Israeli husband-and-wife team, Sarit Packer (see p.118) and Itamar Srulovich (see p.146) followed their dream and set up their own place, Honey & Co.—a restaurant in London's Fitzrovia—in 2012. The menu was inspired by their Israeli roots: a mixture of mezze, salads, mains, and cakes, flavored with ingredients such as preserved lemon, saffron, and tahini. Their colorful, home-style food, with its vivid and intriguing tastes, struck a chord and they acquired a cult following. This ebullient cookbook, interspersing carefully written recipes with chatty, humorous anecdotes, conveys the appeal of both the food and the place itself.

A Book of Middle Eastern Food
Claudia Roden

BOOK DETAILS

Published 1968, Nelson, 484 pages

This genuinely seminal work, published in 1968, first introduced Middle Eastern food to a Western audience. The origins of the book reflect the political complexities of the region. Born in Egypt, as a Sephardi Jew, Claudia Roden (see p.310, 317) along with family and friends, was exiled from her native land. She began collecting their recipes, trying, as she explains in the introduction, to recreate certain aspects of their previous life: "In particular the food, which meant so much in the Middle East and has come to mean even more in exile." Her first book on Middle Eastern food, based on this important act of chronicling, offers both an atmospheric and a detailed account of the region's cuisine, with its complex interwoven elements, among them the historical influence of the Persian and Ottoman empires, and the Bedouin. The range of the 500-plus recipes is extensive— from mezze such as Turkish Fried Mussels to Sephardic Orange and Almond Cake—with explanatory chapter introductions and notes setting the dishes in a historical or cultural context. This attention to context gives the book an academic character, although the clearly written recipes are, on the whole, simple and accessible. Roden's evocative, elegantly written anecdotes and memories bring an additional human interest, a sense of the importance of food to people as a source of pleasure, comfort, and identity.

ASIA

India

Lucky Peach Presents 101 Easy Asian Recipes, Peter Meehan and the Editors of *Lucky Peach*
(Pub 2015, Clarkson Potter, 272pp)

Madhur Jaffrey's Indian Cookery
Madhur Jaffrey
(Pub 1982, Vintage Books, 200pp)

Asian cuisine—an umbrella term that encompasses a vast geographical area of the world—includes the ancient and hugely influential cuisines of China and India, as well as those of Japan, Korea, and Southeast Asia. While the importance of rice as a staple food is a unifying factor, the diversity—both nationally and regionally—is notable: Indian cuisine, with its distinctive use of spices; Chinese cuisine, with an extraordinary omnivorous larder; the elegant precision of Japanese cuisine; Korea's strikingly tasty food; the tropical flavor palate of Southeast Asian cuisine. Through their books and teaching, great food writers, including Madhur Jaffrey, Ken Hom, Yan-kit So, Shizuo Tsuji, and Rosemary Brissenden, among others, have done much to introduce the glories of Asian food to a wider audience.

There is a jaunty quality to this cookbook, from the waving, golden lucky cat on the jacket to the chatty notes that accompany each recipe. Coming, as the book does, from the acclaimed *Lucky Peach* food and lifestyle journal, founded by David Chang of Momofuku fame (see p.192), it has excellent credentials in terms of the authenticity and the sheer lip-smacking tastiness of the recipes within it. Recipe groupings are both intelligent and playful: "Cold Dishes, Apps, and Pickly Bits" and "Super Sauces." The recipes include classics—Hot and Sour Soup, Five-Spice Chicken—as well as more innovative creations, such as Pesto Ramen or Miso Claypot Chicken (No Claypot).

A leading authority on Indian cooking, Indian actress Madhur Jaffrey, through her best-selling books and successful television cookery programs, has done a huge amount to promote knowledge and understanding of Indian cooking around the world. This paperback, written to accompany a popular BBC television series, neatly expresses her ability to convey the key aspects of a cuisine in an encouraging and clear way, from techniques to detailed recipes. Jaffrey herself began learning to cook Indian food as a homesick student in England, following recipes written in letters by her mother, so she understands how much information and guidance someone new to Indian cooking needs.

China

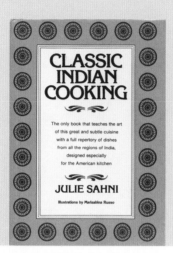

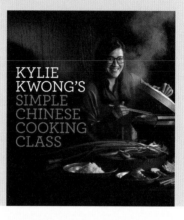

Classic Indian Cooking
Julie Sahni
(Pub 1980, Ecco Press, 542pp)

50 Great Curries of India
Camellia Panjabi
(Pub 1994, Kyle Cathie Books, 192pp)

A. Wong: The Cookbook
Andrew Wong
(Pub 2015, Octopus Books, 240pp)

Simple Chinese Cooking Class
Kylie Kwong
(Pub 2012, Penguin Books Australia, 314pp)

Julie Sahni is renowned as a cooking teacher and her authoritative cookbook offers a knowledgeable overview of Indian cuisine. It opens with an extensive section on spices, ingredients, equipment, techniques, and tips on how to serve an Indian meal, then moves on to recipes, grouped by food types, for example, "Meat," "Legumes," "Rice." The recipes—such as Chickpea Dumplings in Yogurt Sauce (*Kadhi*) or Minced Meat in Cashew Nut Sauce with Chickpeas (*Keema Matar*)—are drawn from across India; written in great detail and set within context, they give a sense of the intriguing regional differences within this rich cuisine. Sahni's own passion for Indian food pervades the book.

Indian restaurateur Camellia Panjabi is noted for promoting regional Indian food and for introducing it to new audiences through her work in restaurants around the world. In this richly illustrated cookbook, she uses the device of focusing on "curry"— that iconic Indian dish—to explore the diversity of Indian cuisine, with clearly written, explanatory recipes ranging from a Kashmiri dish of Lamb with Turnips to a Goan Fish Curry. Each dish is set in its own context with advice given on what the cook is looking to achieve. The introductory essays provide a useful insight into Indian cooking, including the nature of curries and the philosophy of Indian cuisine.

Chef Andrew Wong has acquired a cult following for the imaginative, contemporary Chinese food he serves at his small London restaurant, A. Wong. His exciting cooking draws on an understanding and respect for Chinese cuisine, but with dishes given a distinctive personal twist. Intricate recipes for stylishly presented creations such as 63-degree Tea Eggs or Macanese Prawns demonstrate the considerable work and skill that goes into his cuisine. Writing in a forthright, humorous voice, Wong makes clear that "patience and persistence" is required to cook this food. Just as the cooking at A. Wong is intelligent and creative, so, too, is this cookbook.

Australian chef, restaurateur, and broadcaster Kylie Kwong— the founder of noted restaurant Billy Kwong in Sydney—has championed Chinese food throughout her career, fostering a deeper knowledge and understanding of it through her cooking, TV work, and writing. This large, handsome cookbook aims to give readers a better understanding of how to cook Chinese food at home. Written in Kwong's encouraging tone of voice, it begins with the basics of making good Chinese stocks, then moves on through a succession of mouthwatering recipes, including Crystal Rock Sugar Pork Hock; and Scallop and Ginger Dumplings with Chili-Vinegar Dipping Sauce.

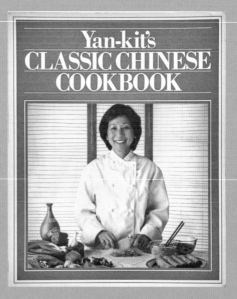

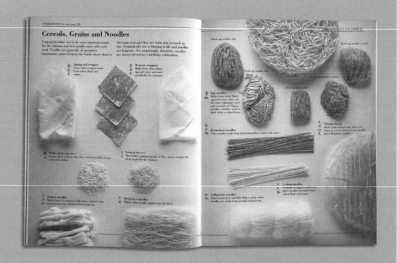

Yan-kit's Classic Chinese Cookbook
Yan-kit So

BOOK DETAILS
Published 1984, DK Publishing, 240 pages

Written out of a desire to make authentic Chinese food accessible to a wider, non-Chinese audience, this bestselling cookbook succeeded admirably in that aim. Yan-kit So discovered her ability to cook Chinese food as an impoverished post-graduate student in London. She realized that outside the Chinese community there was a widespread perception that Chinese cuisine was "generally incomprehensible" and set out with characteristic energy and flair to prove this wrong. She approached the task with great thoroughness, both in terms of content and design. Generous photographic illustrations show not only what the recipes should look like, but also demonstrate fundamental techniques, with step-by-step images, from how to cut ingredients with a cleaver to stir-frying and steaming. Yan-kit So's lucidly written recipes for classic dishes—such as Spiced Salt Prawns, Cantonese Roast Pork, Spring Rolls—are clear and straightforward, broken down into numbered steps for ease of following. However, at the same time, she gives an understanding of the regional nature of Chinese cooking and the richness of flavors and textures that this remarkable cuisine contains. One of the reasons why this cookbook quickly became a much-respected classic is that Yan-kit So wrote knowledgeably as well as clearly.

Japan

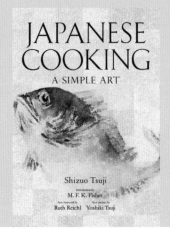

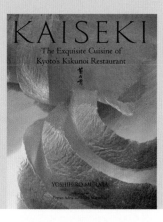

Sichuan Cookery
Fuchsia Dunlop
(Pub 2001, Michael Joseph,
276pp)

Complete Chinese Cookbook
Ken Hom
(Pub 2011, BBC Books, 352pp)

Japanese Cooking: A Simple Art
Shizuo Tsuji
(Pub 1980, Kodansha USA
Inc, 516pp)

*Kaiseki: The Exquisite Cuisine
of Kyoto's Kikunoi Restaurant*
Yoshihiro Murata (Pub 2006,
Kodansha USA Inc, 192pp)

Among the riches of China's great culinary heritage is its diverse, regional nature. Here, food writer Fuchsia Dunlop celebrates the cuisine of Sichuan in southwest China, which is noted within China for its flavor. Drawing on personal experience and research, Dunlop guides the reader through the key characteristics of Sichuanese cooking, including the use of trademark ingredients such as red chiles and Sichuan pepper, with its distinctive mouth-numbing effect. The detailed recipes for dishes such as Strange-Flavor Chicken (or Bang Bang Chicken) or Fish-Fragrant Eggplant illuminate the typical flavors and textures of Sichuan cuisine, as well as cooking methods, such as dry braising.

In this book, the Chinese chef, broadcaster, and author Ken Hom (see p.78) offers a characteristically accessible overview of Chinese cuisine, drawing on family recipes from his mother as well as from Chinese restaurants. Hom first outlines the regional differences within Chinese cuisine— southern, northern, eastern, and western—beginning with Cantonese, the best-known style in the West because of emigration from this southern region. The clear recipes, from appetizers to desserts, feature both the familiar—Hot and Sour Soup, Peanuts with Five Spice—and the less well-known—Garlic Chicken with Cucumber or Squirrel Fish. Hom is a helpful and encouraging guide to the cuisine.

This is an influential cookbook by Shizuo Tsuji, a man who has done a huge amount to introduce the principles of Japanese cuisine to Western audiences, partly through his work as a chef in France alongside leading lights of the *nouvelle cuisine* movement and through his influential Osaka-based academy for professional chefs. This authoritative, lucidly written cookbook provides an excellent understanding of Japanese cuisine and continues to be regarded as one of the key works on the subject. As Tsuji wrote in his introduction: "Here, for the very first time, the secrets of the simple yet complex art of Japanese cooking have been laid bare for all to see."

Kaiseki or Japanese haute cuisine—consisting of a series of courses and noted for its seasonal and aesthetic nature— holds a special place in Japanese culture. Renowned Japanese chef Yoshihiro Murata is well-placed to write this cookbook, being descended from generations of kaiseki chefs, with his Kyoto restaurant Kikunoi acclaimed for its kaiseki cuisine. According to his father, he explains: "The food we make should be refined and beautiful, but not too delicate." In this fascinating cookbook, Murata outlines the principles of kaiseki, with both his eloquently written text and its exquisite recipes conveying the sensibility and philosophy that underpins this elegant cuisine.

Southeast Asia

Everyday Harumi
Harumi Kurihara
(Pub 2009, Conran, 192pp)

Into the Vietnamese Kitchen: Treasured Foodways, Modern Flavors, Andrea Nguyen (Pub 2006, Ten Speed Press, 344pp)

Pok Pok
Andy Ricker with JJ Goode
(Pub 2013, Ten Speed Press, 295pp)

Burma: Rivers of Flavor
Naomi Duguid
(Pub 2012, Artisan Books, 372pp)

Written by Harumi Kurihara, a doyenne of Japanese cooking with a devoted following in her native Japan, this cookbook is intended as an introduction to Japanese cuisine, offering those unfamiliar with it the chance to understand it and begin to cook it. Kurihara begins with an informative glossary of essential Japanese ingredients, such as miso and mirin, describing their use within the cuisine. Her writing is clear and illuminating; sauces and dressings, for example, she explains, are an essential part of the "vocabulary" of Japanese cooking. The recipes within the book are straightforward, homely, and simple to cook, designed, as described, for everyday Japanese cooking.

Vietnamese cuisine—from tasty *banh mi* (baguette sandwich) to aromatic *bo kho* (beef stew)—is evoked in elegant and appealing style by Andrea Nguyen in her beautifully presented cookbook. As a child in 1975, Nguyen and her family fled from the soon-to-be-invaded South Vietnam to the United States, and an exile's interest in her culinary heritage characterizes this thoughtfully written book. Her cook's eye informs the recipes, with the useful inclusion of touches such as enriching the caramel sauce for a catfish dish with rendered pork fatback or the recommendation of knuckle and leg bones when it comes to making the beef broth for *pho*, Vietnam's best-known dish.

Having fallen in love with Thai cuisine, and after many years traveling there and researching it, American chef Andy Ricker opened his popular restaurant Pok Pok in Portland, Oregon, in 2005. This ebullient cookbook is written in an anecdotal and accessible style. In addition to recipes for dishes such as Som Tam Thai (Central Thai-Style Papaya Salad) or Kai Yang (Whole Roasted Young Chicken), he offers stories of people such as Mr. Lit—his "chicken mentor"—and recollections of memorable meals eaten. Beneath the conversational tone, however, Ricker's detailed knowledge of the complexities and regional nature of Thai cuisine is strongly apparent.

Years of political isolation and borders long closed to visitors have meant that Burmese cuisine is little known outside Burma. Naomi Duguid's appealing, colorful cookbook, illustrated with her own location photography, based on her many trips to Burma to research it, offers a chance to remedy this. Situated as the country is between China, India, and Thailand, Burmese cuisine reflects the influence of these great traditions in shared ingredients and cooking techniques, while being distinctive. Duguid is a clear, accessible guide to Burma's cuisine, offering recipes for dishes such as Classic Sour Soup or Crispy Shallot and Dried Shrimp Relish (*Balachaung*), mixed with atmospheric traveler's tales.

South East Asian Food
Rosemary Brissenden

BOOK DETAILS

Published 1969, Penguin Books, 448 pages

There is a labor-of-love quality to this remarkable work by academic Rosemary Brissenden. First published in 1969, it was a pioneering attempt to convey the richness of Southeast Asian food to a Western audience, written with palpable affection, respect, and an infectious interest. Taking the reader on a journey through the region, from Indonesia to Vietnam, Brissenden first sets the context for each cuisine, then explores it, offering a diverse selection of well-written, authentic recipes for traditional dishes. With characteristic intelligence, motivated by the desire to give a meaningful sense of each cuisine, Brissenden groups together dishes by typical cooking methods, for example, "Salads and Dressed Vegetables" or "Curries and Braised Dishes."

Recipes range from street food classics such as Malaysia's Roti Canai (a flat bread) or Vietnam's Hanoi Beef Noodle Soup (Pho Bo), each carefully set in context. Classic ingredients, such as lemongrass, galangal, and shrimp paste are explained, as too are cooking methods and utensils, providing a genuine foundation of knowledge. While she brings an admirable thoroughness to the massive task of chronicling the complexities of this region's cuisine, she also manages to be a lucid and straightforward guide. The discriminating food writer Elizabeth David declared this tome to be "A book that every serious cook should possess," and, undoubtedly, anyone genuinely interested in learning about Southeast Asian cuisines will find it rewarding reading.

AUSTRALIA

Maggie's Harvest
Maggie Beer
(Pub 2007, Penguin Books
Australia, 716pp)

The Cook's Companion
Stephanie Alexander
(Pub 1996, Pengiun Books
Australia, 816pp)

Australia is a continent in its own right and its history as a comparatively young nation-state is reflected in its cuisine. The historic relationship with the United Kingdom saw Australian cuisine reflecting its British roots for a long time, with roasts and pies very much part of the classic repertoire. Recent decades, however, have seen the rise of a distinctly Australian cuisine, one that celebrates the quality of Australian ingredients, such as the abundant, fresh seafood. This new Australian cuisine is also cosmopolitan, drawing inspiration from the culinary heritages of those who have settled there, weaving in, for example, Italian, Southeast Asian, Chinese, and Greek influences. Cookbooks by Australian chefs and writers including Stephanie Alexander and Maggie Beer have played an important part in helping to define and celebrate it.

Chef, broadcaster, food producer, and food writer Maggie Beer has been a major player in fostering Australia's food scene. In this book, she celebrates seasonal cooking, offering batches of her favorite recipes centered on ingredients from anchovies to vine leaves. The sheer scale of the book, as well as the generously described ingredient introductions and the ebulliently written recipes, conveys Beer's energy and interest in food. As befits someone who is a food producer herself—famously of verjuice—her text champions Australia's farmers, crediting those whose commitment to producing good ingredients has helped create Australia's current thriving food scene.

Stephanie Alexander wrote this classic Australian cookbook—impressive in its comprehensive nature—to encourage young people to cook at home. "Before you can cook with confidence, you need to understand the raw materials," she writes, and she therefore themes her book by ingredients, from anchovy to squash and zucchini. Each section gives advice on choosing and preparing, as well as a cosmopolitan selection of recipes for dishes such as Banana Cake or Yabby Bisque. There is a zestful energy to Alexander's writing, which makes her enthusiasm for food and cooking infectious. Memories and anecdotes add a personal dimension to the sound and frank culinary advice.

INTERNATIONAL

Time Life
Foods of the World

BOOK DETAILS
Published 1968, Time Life, 27 Volumes

An ambitious project to chart the world's cuisines in an illustrated reference format, this series of books spanning the globe achieved classic status. One of the reasons for the series's seminal status was the resources that were brought to the task of charting the world's cuisine in a meaningful way, and the thoroughness with which this was achieved. Each of the twenty-seven books sets out the context for a country or region's food—explaining the influence of history, geography, and climate in shaping the cuisine in question —and is accompanied by a separate spiral-bound collection of recipes. The photography included reportage images of food markets, harvesting, hunting, and fishing, as well as more formal images of the prepared dishes. Reflecting the publisher's origins, the United States is covered in the greatest depth, with eight titles exploring its cuisine through themes of regionality and immigration. Richard L. Williams, the editor of the series, assembled some notable food writing talent to participate, including renowned names such as M. F. K. Fisher (see p.328) on Provincial France, Waverley Root on Italian cuisine, and Craig Claiborne (see p.303), ensuring in the process a high level of knowledgeable content.

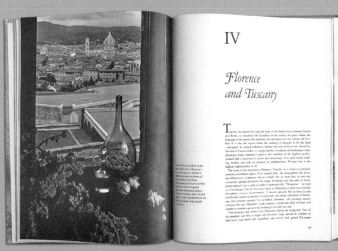

GENERAL COOKBOOKS

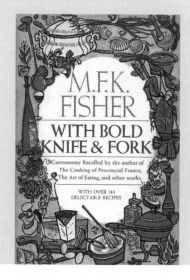

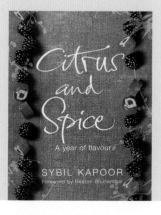

With Bold Knife & Fork
M. F. K. Fisher
(Pub 1969, G. P. Putnam's Sons,
318pp)

*Citrus and Spice: A Year
of Flavour*, Sybil Kapoor
(Pub 2008, Simon and
Schuster, 176pp)

The ways in which various cookbooks can introduce their readers to the joys of cooking is at the heart of this section. Great food writers such as Elizabeth David, M. F. K. Fisher, Jane Grigson, and Nigel Slater demonstrate an assured way with words as well as recipes. Here, too, are a number of cookbooks by chefs that are aimed at a domestic audience, among them titles by Yotam Ottolenghi, Alice Waters, Jamie Oliver, and Thomas Keller, all of whom share their considerable knowledge of and expertise in food and cooking. The section also includes Alan Davidson's *Oxford Companion to Food*, a learned but entertaining reference work rather than a cookbook, which reflects the author's own serious and deep-rooted commitment to food history and reminds anyone fascinated by food what a marvelous subject it is.

This collection of articles by the acclaimed American food writer M. F. K. Fisher is a book, she writes, "about how I like to cook, most of the time, for people in my world and it gives some of the reasons. These have made life enjoyable, so they may be of interest to other human beings." Written with charismatic flair and wit, the book contains her expressive, knowledgeable musings on subjects from "Teasers and Titbits" to how to make a good cup of tea. Embedded in her prose are recipes for a characterful array of dishes such as A Ceviche of Scallops and Vevey Market Mushrooms. A book that makes one think about food, as well as want to cook it.

In this interesting and imaginative cookbook, Sybil Kapoor explores the role of flavor in food, examining the way in which it evokes memories and triggers emotional associations. "Each type of flavour will produce different associations and responses to your food," she observes. Inspired by seasonally appropriate flavor sets—a bracing whiff of ozone for February, floral in June, or autumnal fungi in September—Kapoor offers a characteristically elegant collection of recipes: Spiced Swordfish Salad; Grilled Mackerel with Gooseberry Elderflower Relish; Parsnip Cake with Cinnamon Butter Icing. Kapoor's passion for food is obvious, as she showcases the role of flavors in cooking.

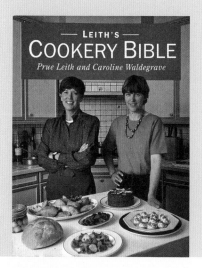

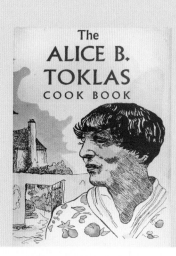

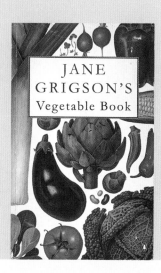

Leith's Cookery Bible
Prue Leith and Caroline
Waldegrave (Pub 1991,
Bloomsbury Publishing, 640pp)

The Kitchen Diaries
Nigel Slater
(Pub 2005, Fourth Estate,
406pp)

The Alice B. Toklas Cook Book
Alice B. Toklas
(Pub 1954, Random House Inc,
305pp)

Jane Grigson's Vegetable Book
Jane Grigson
(Pub 1978, Penguin Books,
518pp)

Famed for their highly regarded cooking school in London, Prue Leith and Caroline Waldegrave are respected authorities in the world of British cuisine. The book draws on the pair's considerable culinary experience gained through their school. As Leith writes in her foreword: "There are not many cookbooks whose recipes are tested over and over again by 100 students and 15 teachers." At the book's heart is the message that cooking well lifts food from a necessity to a pleasure. A comprehensive introduction, touching on healthy eating and cooking methods among other fundamentals, is followed by a classic collection of recipes, offering a thorough schooling in how to cook.

Acclaimed British food writer and broadcaster Nigel Slater has a way with words as well as with ingredients, which is amply demonstrated in this highly personal cookbook. Written in diary form, it takes the reader through a year in Nigel's life, offering an evocative mixture of text, recipes, and beautifully composed photographs. Naturally, this structural concept allows for the seasons to be mirrored, from the comfort of a Double Ginger Cake in January to a July dish of Zucchini Cakes with Dill and Feta. The reader also gains a pleasurable insight into how Slater thinks about food, from his accounts of shopping trips to the way in which he creates dishes to mirror his moods.

This is a characterful, idiosyncratic classic. Part of the appeal of this legendary cookbook rests in the social world it portrays. Alice B. Toklas was companion to the US writer Gertrude Stein for almost forty years, living with her in France, where she cooked food for Stein and her guests. Her recipes come replete with anecdotes, including such gems as Bass for Picasso, a colorfully decorated fish dish created for the artist, who on seeing it "exclaimed at its beauty" but said it should rather have been made for Matisse. Toklas's fascination with food is evident in her shrewd observations on French and US cooking, complemented by eclectic recipes from Sauce for Lampreys to Oeufs Francis Picabia.

There is a cheerfully practical aspect to this classic Jane Grigson cookbook, arranged alphabetically by name of vegetable: beginning with artichokes and ending with watercress. This simple way of structuring the content allows Grigson (see p.74, 100, 102, 106) to offer first an introductory history of each ingredient, followed by advice on how to use it, and a cluster of recipes. The wide-ranging, intelligent text conveys Grigson's genuine interest in the subject. The distinctive choice of recipes are drawn from various cuisines, notably French, Italian, and British. Drawing on her own hands-on experience, Grigson writes with knowledge and common sense of the pleasures of vegetables.

Plenty
Yotam Ottolenghi

BOOK DETAILS

Published 2010, Ebury Press, 288 pages

Based on Yotam Ottolenghi's (see p.260, 318) popular, weekly "New Vegetarian" column in U.K. newspaper the *Guardian*, this offers a wide-ranging collection of vegetarian recipes. Ottolenghi, as he explains, is not himself vegetarian, but was invited to write the column because of his acclaimed creative way with vegetables, which has been amply displayed at his stylish, eponymous restaurant-cum-deli. The book is divided, he observes, "in quite an unsystematic way," by favorite ingredients: "I tend to set off with this central element and then try to elaborate on it, enhance it, bring it out in a new way, while still keeping it in the centre, in the heart of the final dish." Ottolenghi is, famously, a cosmopolitan chef and he draws inspiration not only from his own Israeli heritage but from other cuisines around the world that attract his magpie-like curiosity. The "Mighty Aubergine" (eggplant) section, for example, offers not only a visually striking recipe for Aubergine with Buttermilk Sauce, but Soba Noodles with Aubergine and Mango; and Aubergine Croquettes—the latter inspired by fond memories of Dutch cheese balls. As the original newspaper column title suggests, the emphasis was on creating fresh ways of cooking with vegetarian ingredients and, as this book shows, Ottolenghi succeeded triumphantly. His way of mixing flavors and textures to create dishes that intrigue and satisfy has earned him a cult following.

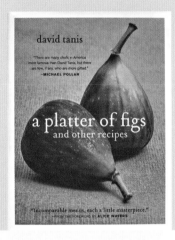

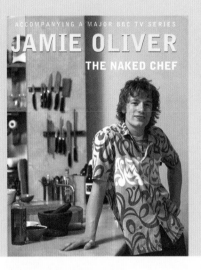

A Platter of Figs and Other Recipes
David Tanis
(Pub 2008, Artisan Books, 294pp)

Radically Simple: Brilliant Flavors with Breathtaking Ease
Rozanne Gold (Pub 2010, Rodale Inc., 340pp)

The Naked Chef
Jamie Oliver
(Pub 1999, Michael Joseph, 250pp)

The Gentle Art of Cookery
Mrs. C. F. Leyel and Miss Olga Hartley (Pub 1925, Chatto and Windus, 452pp)

There is an understated eloquence to this beguiling, personal cookbook by David Tanis, whose career notably included many years as chef with Alice Waters at Chez Panisse in California (see p.46, 294). Structured seasonally, the book offers batches of intriguingly named menus, from "Summer's Too Darned Hot, *Alors!*" to "Winter's North African Comfort Food." Tanis makes a persuasive and intelligent case for the pleasures of cooking simply but well, whether musing on what to do with a glut of zucchini or enthusing on the charms of chile heat. His recipes for savory mains such as Berber Pizza or a springtime dessert of Lavender Honey Ice Cream, reflect his love of good food.

Written with panache, this chic cookbook by US chef Rozanne Gold sets out to demonstrate that simply cooked dishes, made from just a few ingredients, can be sophisticated and full of flavor. The recipes are imaginative and inventive, offering intriguing combinations of flavors that draw on a notably cosmopolitan larder of herbs and spices. Dishes include Chicken Ras el Hanout with Tomato-Ginger Chutney and Seared Tuna with Fresh Corn and Wasabi "Cream." As befits a busy New Yorker, there is much emphasis on recipes that are quick to prepare and cook: Three-Minute Wasabi Salmon; Tomato-Anisette Soup with Tarragon; Salmon, and Mint in Crispy Grape Leaves.

A youthful British chef called Jamie Oliver (see p.114) made his name with the TV series that this cookbook accompanied. An Essex boy, Oliver began cooking in his parents' pub at the age of eight and was working in the kitchens at London's River Café when he was spotted by a TV producer. Oliver's refreshingly down-to-earth approach to cooking, coupled with an infectious enthusiasm for good food, gained him a large following. The book reflects not only his friendly, encouraging style, but also Oliver's genuine knowledge of food, with detailed recipes for cooking live lobster and making fresh pasta alongside simple dishes such as Potato Salad or My Perfect Roast Chicken.

This is a cookbook with charm and character, which begins with a cheerfully defiant listing of the seven ways "in which this cookbook differs from all others." Chapter headings range from the prosaic—"Eggs" and "Cold Supper Dishes"—to the eccentric—"Dishes from the Arabian Nights" and "Flower Recipes." The writing—as the opening to the vegetables section demonstrates—is acerbic, witty, and often insightful. This was a cookbook intended to promote a "modern" way of cooking in the United Kingdom, one which championed shopping in markets before planning a menu and eating more fresh vegetables and fruits. It is advice that does not seem at all old-fashioned.

> *"The best kind of cooking does not depend on exotic and expensive ingredients, only upon the best and freshest of whatever you decide to use. And upon the importance of taking time and trouble. Trouble that isn't really trouble, but love, care, thought; time that isn't so much time, as organization, method, planning, thinking ahead."*
>
> MARGARET COSTA, *FOUR SEASONS COOKERY BOOK*

Four Seasons Cookery Book
Margaret Costa
(Pub 1970, Thomas Nelson, 360pp)

Summer Cooking
Elizabeth David
(Pub 1955, Penguin Books, 234pp)

The Oxford Companion to Food
Alan Davidson
(Pub 1999, Oxford University Press, 892pp)

The Good Food Guide Dinner Party Book, Hilary Fawcett and Jeanne Strang (Pub 1971, Hodder & Stoughton Ltd, 184pp)

There is a lively and engaging quality to this much-loved cookbook by food writer and restaurateur Margaret Costa, with her distinctive voice emerging clearly from its pages. The recipes are grouped together by season and consist of a characterful selection of dishes she feels appropriate to the time of year, for example, "Omelettes and Pancakes" in spring and "Comforting Spices and Marmalade" in winter. Ingredients such as sorrel, game, or mushrooms are appetizingly evoked and explored in recipes and suggested dishes. She writes with an infectious enthusiasm of the pleasures of cooking, while also offering much sound culinary advice.

Anyone interested in the idea of seasonal food would find this a stimulating read. By summer cooking, "I do not necessarily mean cold food," writes Elizabeth David (see p. 84, 110, 317). Instead she explores "the suitability of certain foods to certain times of the year, and the pleasure of eating the vegetables, fruits, poultry, meat, or fish which is in season, therefore at its best, most plentiful, and cheapest." David's thoroughly grounded knowledge of ingredients manifests itself in the briskly written, well-observed recipes contained within the book's pages, from her tip on how to avoid "watery and clammy" fresh tomato salads to the pleasures of spring chickens, as opposed to "insipid" poussins.

An ambitious venture, this book was a twenty-year-long labor of love for the distinguished food historian Alan Davidson. His starting vision had been of a "good and detailed reference book on foodstuffs, of global scope" and in this he succeeded admirably. The book opens with an entry on the aardvark and ends with zucchini, crisscrossing the globe in a truly cosmopolitan fashion in between. The range of content is extensive and fascinating, offering rich pickings for anyone interested in food. While many people also contributed entries to the project, Davidson's elegant writing style and wit permeate the book, making it an engaging as well as informative read.

This idiosyncratic book showcases a collection of recipes coaxed out of restaurants, which featured in the 1971 edition of *The Good Food Guide*, an influential restaurant manual that played its part in changing postwar British gastronomy. "Its readers and users will, I hope, become demanding diners-out as well as cooks-in," wrote Christopher Driver, the editor of *The Good Food Guide*, in his introduction to the book. The dishes, each with the restaurant of origin credited, are grouped into seasonal dinner party menus, from a spring meal of Almond and Watercress Soup; Chicken de Vaux; and Sailor's Lament to a winter menu of Kipper Pâté; Kidneys in Madeira; and Lemon Syllabub.

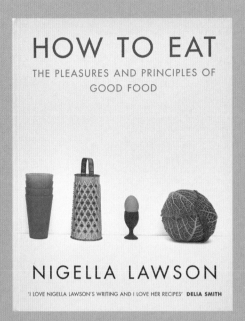

HOW TO EAT
THE PLEASURES AND PRINCIPLES OF GOOD FOOD

NIGELLA LAWSON

'I LOVE NIGELLA LAWSON'S WRITING AND I LOVE HER RECIPES' **DELIA SMITH**

How to Eat: The Pleasures and Principles of Good Food
Nigella Lawson

BOOK DETAILS
Published 1998, Chatto and Windus, 473 pages

There is an appealingly personal quality to British food writer and broadcaster Nigella Lawson's beautifully written first cookbook, a sense of her talking directly to her readers. In her conversational introductions to recipes, she muses on subjects such as the correct texture for a fish pie, the "nursery" pleasures of jam tarts, or how to use up leftover tabbouleh. As the subtitle suggests, the book offers both a sense of the enjoyment offered by good food and Lawson's thoughts on how to achieve it, with the target audience being the home cook. "I am not a chef. I am not even a trained or professional cook. My qualification is as an eater," she writes. The recipes here offer inspiration for solo diners as well as those seeking to entertain: Welcoming January Lunch For Six, Quick After-Work Supper For Four, Basic No-Effort Saturday Lunch. Lawson's sense of delight in feeding others shines through. Cooking, she writes, is "about developing an understanding of food, a sense of assurance in the kitchen, about the simple desire to make yourself something to eat." Her enthusiasm is infectious.

How to Cook
Everything
Simple Recipes for Great Food

Mark Bittman

How to Cook Everything:
Simple Recipes for Great Food
Mark Bittman

BOOK DETAILS
Published 2012, Houghton Mifflin Harcourt, 486 pages

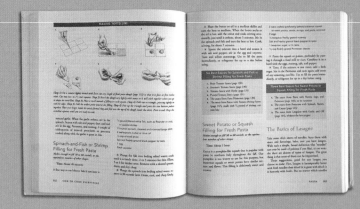

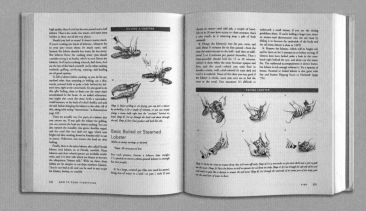

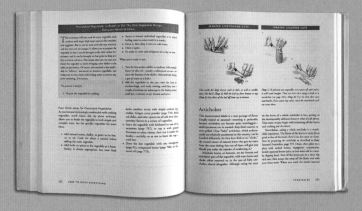

There is a tongue-in-cheek quality to the title, but this popular book by American journalist and food writer Mark Bittman has a serious message, namely that making good food is within the reach of everybody. "Anyone can cook, and most everyone should," he affirms. Rather than "convenience" food or "gourmet" food, Bittman makes a case for straightforward home cooking using easily available ingredients. His book is comprehensive by nature, beginning with advice on fundamentals—equipment and techniques—before moving on to clear, accessible recipes. Step-by-step illustrations are an illuminating element. Bittman's writing tone throughout is down-to-earth—aware of the time pressures of modern day living—

practical, demystifying, and friendly. There is an admirable thoroughness to his approach, demonstrated by the section on pizza, which includes a basic dough recipe (a food processor is recommended) and advice on shaping dough, choosing toppings, and cooking pizza. The range of recipes is cosmopolitan, reflecting Bittman's broad interest in food: Simple Roast Chicken, for example, comes with variations, one with Soy Sauce, the other flavored with Cumin, Honey, and Orange. Giving these possibilities for tweaking the dish in different flavor directions allows the reader to understand the principles involved, then riff accordingly. The satisfaction of making one's own food is communicated with clarity and relish.

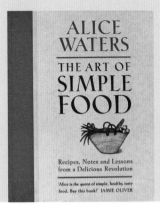

The Art of Simple Food
Alice Waters
(Pub 2007, Michael Joseph,
405pp)

A Return to Cooking
Eric Ripert and Michael
Ruhlman (Pub 2002, Artisan
Books, 330pp)

Ad Hoc at Home
Thomas Keller with
Dave Cruz (Pub 2009,
Workman Publishing, 360pp)

*The Union Square Café
Cookbook*, Danny Meyer
and Michael Romano
(Pub 1994, Ecco Press, 329pp)

"Gathering good ingredients" is the starting point to cooking well explains Alice Waters, whose acclaimed restaurant Chez Panisse in Berkeley, California (see p.48, 294), champions fresh, seasonal food, sourced from local farmers and producers. In this lucid, intelligent cookbook aimed at the home cook, she explains her principles of good cooking, drawing on years of experience to enlightening effect. The first part of the book is aimed at beginners and offers basic recipes such as Chicken Stock and Fresh Pasta. The second section gives elegantly written recipes for cooking every day, with Waters's love of Mediterranean cuisine manifest in dishes such as Braised Artichokes or Provençal-Style Fish Soup.

In this thoughtful, personal cookbook, chef Eric Ripert (see p.240) reconnects with his love of cooking and the fascination with food that saw him first embark on his quest to become a chef. He visits four meaningful places—Sag Harbor, Puerto Rico, Napa Valley, and Vermont—each in a different season, using these journeys to inspire a cluster of enticing recipes. The encountered ingredients and the sense of place result in diverse dishes ranging from Crab Salad with Chilled Gazpacho Sauce to Ash-Baked Potatoes with Smoked Salmon and Caviar. The elegant writing, together with the sophisticated recipes themselves, explores the fascinating nature of culinary creativity.

There is an intimate, personal quality to this cookbook by Thomas Keller (see p.18, 86, 138, 230). It opens with a menu—"Dinner for Dad," consisting of Barbecued Chicken with Mashed Potatoes and Collard Greens, followed by Strawberry Shortcake—and a moving memory of cooking this meal for his father shortly before he died. The recipes for dishes such as Braised Beef Short Ribs or Fresh Tuna Salad, as Keller promises, are approachable and aimed at home cooks: "No complicated garnishes, I promise." As usual with Chef Keller, there is a thoughtful intelligence displayed, with much useful advice, kitchen insights, and information offered alongside accessible recipes.

Just as the iconic, much-loved New York restaurant the Union Square Café is a hospitable, mellow place, so its cookbook is cheerfully exuberant and accessible. "Our suggestion is to use the book as if it were a marketplace, skimming through the different chapters to collect ideas, as you would peruse the stalls of your favorite farmer's markets." The straightforward recipes draw on the rustic traditions of Italy, France, and the United States to tasty effect: Black Bean Soup with Lemon and Sherry; Artichoke–Eggplant Hash; Herb-Roasted Chicken; "Reverse" Chocolate Chunk Cookies. The tone is friendly, with stories on how dishes were created and useful cooking tips.

SPECIALTY COOKBOOKS

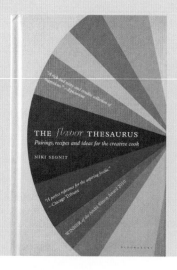

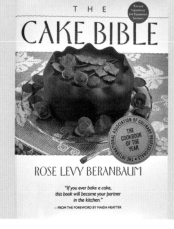

The Flavour Thesaurus
Niki Segnit
(Pub 2010, Bloomsbury
Publishing, 400pp)

The Cake Bible
Rose Levy Beranbaum
(Pub 1988, William
Morrow and Company, 636pp)

Cookbooks, by focusing on one aspect of cooking and looking at it more deeply, can offer genuine illumination on that topic. The intricacies of baking and pâtisserie, which demand precision in terms of measuring ingredients and following methods carefully and patiently, have been usefully explored by several bakers, chefs, and pâtissiers including Nancy Silverton, Dan Lepard, Chad Robertson, and Claire Clark, generously sharing their knowledge and insights through cookbooks. Barbecuing, the craft of charcuterie, the pleasures of baking, and, fascinatingly, an in-depth understanding of the science of food—with important works by Harold McGee, Nathan Myhrvold, and J. Kenji López-Alt—are among the other interesting subjects included in this eclectic section.

The beginnings of this best-selling food book lie in the determination of author Niki Segnit—a home cook, not a chef—to understand more about flavor combinations and therefore improve her cooking. The results of her thoughts on the elusive and subjective topic of flavors are presented in Segnit's distinctive personal voice. Having grouped together flavors—Roasted, Marine, Citrussy—Segnit shares her thoughts on a wide-ranging set of ingredient combinations—such as Potato and Caviar, Chile and Garlic, Banana and Coffee—referencing everything from chefs and food writer Harold McGee (see p337). to memorable meals abroad and Elvis Presley with wit and style.

Having instructed hundreds of students in the craft of cake making at her successful Cordon Rose Cooking School in New York City, Rose Levy Beranbaum was well qualified to write a definitive cookbook on the subject. Beranbaum's fascination with the subject, which saw her writing a dissertation on whether sifting affects the quality of a yellow cake, makes her an excellent guide, bringing an erudite knowledge to her clearly written recipes. Cakes—butter, fruit, custard, breakfast—and adornments from buttercream icing to fruit toppings are fully covered. While she offers genuine insights into techniques and an understanding of basics, her tone is friendly and accessible.

> *"Few pleasures are greater than turning out a perfect cake. And perfect cakes can be achieved by any cook who is careful and who is willing to follow recipe directions."*
>
> ROSE LEVY BERANBAUM, *THE CAKE BIBLE*

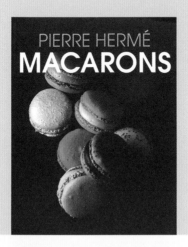

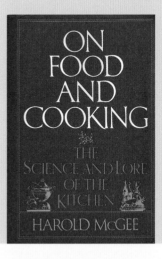

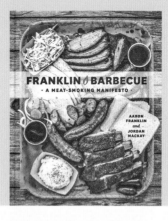

Macarons
Pierre Hermé
(Pub 2008, Agnès Viénot Éditions, 208pp)

Ready for Dessert: My Best Recipes
David Lebovitz (Pub 2011, Ten Speed Press, 278pp)

On Food and Cooking: The Science and Lore of the Kitchen
Harold McGee
(Pub 1984, Scribner, 684pp)

Franklin Barbecue: A Meat-Smoking Manifesto, Aaron Franklin and Jordan Mackay (Pub 2015, Ten Speed Press, 224pp)

Renowned pastry chef Pierre Hermé is known around the globe for his exquisite macarons—truly elegant creations in subtle, intriguing flavors. In this clearly laid out and visually striking cookbook, Hermé reveals the painstaking work that goes into his creations. The book opens with a well-illustrated step-by-step guide, demonstrating the journey from egg whites to cooked shells and instructions on how to make a chocolate ganache, laying the foundation for macaron-making. The recipes include classic macarons such as Rose, Salted Butter Caramel, and Lemon as well as his famous striking combinations, for example, Lime and Basil or Olive Oil and Vanilla.

This collection of David Lebovitz's "all-time favorite recipes" for desserts is an appetizing concoction from the former Chez Panisse pastry chef. Lebovitz's exuberant, conversational writing style makes him a companionable guide to the pleasures of baking, with sound common sense underlying his observations on subjects such as judging when something is ready, essential equipment, and the recommended amount of cacao solids in dark chocolate for baking. The recipes offer a tempting array of sweet treats, from his acclaimed Fresh Ginger Cake to Super-Lemony Soufflés. Underlying the buoyant presentation, Lebovitz's knowledge is impressive.

Harold McGee is a major figure in the modernist movement within cuisine, inspiring chefs such as Heston Blumenthal (see p.180, 310) and René Redzepi (see p.136, 278) with his approach. This seminal work introduced the idea of exploring the science of food and cooking to a wider audience. McGee himself began researching to find out the answers to self-posed questions such as: "why do eggs solidify when we cook them?" and "what makes bread bouncy?" This led to *On Food & Cooking*, which has become a key reference work. McGee's great achievement is not simply the scale of knowledge within this tome, but also the clear, readable style in which he conveys information.

Texan chef, restaurateur, and TV personality Aaron Franklin is known for his devotion to the craft of barbecue. As Franklin's thoughtful introduction explains, there are many variables involved in barbecue: wood, fire, cooker, meat, weather. Franklin sets out to share his knowledge with a generosity of spirit and admirable thoroughness and there is an emphasis on "DIY skills," based on Franklin's own experience. He writes about key elements: the smoker, the wood ("arguably the most important seasoning in the food"), fire and smoke, meat and cooking. Written in an encouraging tone, his enthusiasm for the subject come across well. Nothing beats experience, as far as he's concerned.

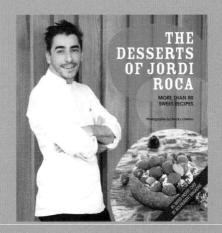

The Desserts of Jordi Roca
Jordi Roca

BOOK DETAILS

Published 2015, Peter Pauper Press, 247 pages

Celebrated pastry chef Jordi Roca (see p.128), head pastry chef of the acclaimed restaurant El Celler de Can Roca, here shares his love of desserts through this handsome book. "I feel an absolute need to express my life in sweets," he writes in "Breaking Molds", the title of the piece a reference to his famously creative, irreverent approach to his craft. The introductory section outlines the history of El Celler de Can Roca and the distinctive, "techno-emotional" cuisine offered at this world-famous restaurant, setting the context for Jordi Roca's creations. The recipes are grouped together by season, such as Grilled Watermelon with Almond and Vodka Granita for summer and Pear Compote with Chestnut Crudite for the fall. They are also usefully graded by difficulty, from "Easy" dishes, such as Tomato and Strawberry Gazpacho, to more challenging, intricate creations such as the "Very High" in difficulty Green Chromatism or Orange Blossom Cream. Full color illustrations of each dish offer both inspiration and a useful record of the beguiling presentation. As one would expect from a chef of Roca's caliber, these are complex creations, usually put together from a number of technically challenging elements. The laconically titled Dairy Dessert, for example, features guava fruit leather, dulce de leche, a dairy-based foam, ice cream, yogurt, and a "cloud" made from sugar and powdered milk. What is also apparent is the wide range of inspiration for Roca—the scent of perfume, a sense of place, a classic Spanish dish, vegetables, cocktails all offer starting points for his inventiveness. Reading the recipes one senses his delight in playing with flavor, texture, and preconceptions.

Short & Sweet: The Best of Home Baking
Dan Lepard
(Pub 2011, Fourth Estate, 562pp)

Baking: From My Home to Yours
Dorie Greenspan
(Pub 2006, Houghton Mifflin Harcourt, 514pp)

Breakfast, Lunch, Tea
Rose Carrarini
(Pub 2006, Phaidon, 188pp)

Desserts
Nancy Silverton
(Pub 1986, Absolute Press, 366pp)

Belying its title, this hefty cookbook by the acclaimed Australian baker, food writer, and broadcaster Dan Lepard is a substantial tome, densely packed with recipes for an array of baked goods, from bread to savory supper dishes. An experienced teacher and communicator, Lepard's tone is friendly and encouraging: "I truly believe that life is improved by cake," he writes cheerfully. At the same time, however, what is notable is the impressive depth of knowledge he brings to his subject, whether writing about flour and yeast or how to handle pastry or make meringues. The recipes—from Bourbon Pecan Brownies to British Gammon and Pork Pie—are clearly written and helpfully detailed.

Dorie Greenspan's career as a food writer saw her working closely on books with legendary chefs including Julia Child, Daniel Boulud (see p.186), and Pierre Hermé (see p.337). In this cookbook, she shares an impressive collection of recipes, garnered over many years, spanning breakfast sweets, cookies, cakes, pies, tarts, and desserts. These range from the homely—Granola Grabbers or Double Apple Bundt Cake—to the sophisticated—a classic French Tarte Noire or Rosy Poached Pear and Pistachio Tart. Famed for her ability to write user-friendly recipes, Greenspan's instructions are detailed, clear, and with notes offering advice on "playing around" with the recipes.

Having made their name on London's food scene with their delicatessen Villandry, husband-and-wife team Jean-Charles and Rose Carrarini moved to Paris and established the Rose Bakery, which showcased the eponymous Rose's considerable baking skills and their own distinctive style. This attractively designed cookbook, Rose's first, gives a taste of the bakery's cosmopolitan menu, which draws inspiration from an eclectic range of sources. Here are recipes for sweet and savory treats, including scones (much appreciated by the French, we learn), Pecan Pie, Eton Mess, Red Bean Sorbet, and the elegant, square Vegetable Tarts, which have gained Rose Bakery a cult following.

Among chef and baker Nancy Silverton's impressive career highlights is her opening of Spago in Beverly Hills, with this, her first cookbook, written while she worked there. "I've long believed that the two most important parts of a menu are the desserts and the appetizers," writes Wolfgang Puck in the foreword, crediting Silverton with making desserts "better." As befits a pastry chef, the recipes in her book are detailed and precisely written: "I've made every recipe in this book over and over, some of them hundreds of times," observes Silverton. Signature dishes include Individual Apple Calvados Tarts, with the careful instructions for each stage revealing the work behind them.

> *"Although I had apprenticed with some of the finest artisan bakers in the United States and France, none had taught me how to make the loaf I was envisioning. Instead, they gave me the tools to get there."*
>
> CHAD ROBERTSON, *TARTINE BREAD*

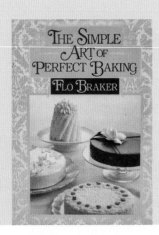

Charcuterie
Michael Ruhlman and Brian Polcyn (Pub 2005, W. W. Norton & Company, 320pp)

Biscuits, Spoonbread, and Sweet Potato Pie
Bill Neal (Pub 1990, Alfred A. Knopf, 334pp)

The Simple Art of Perfect Baking
Flo Braker (Pub 1985, Chronicle Books, 416pp)

Tartine Bread
Chad Robertson (Pub 2010, Chronicle Books, 304pp)

His first taste of a duck confit was an epiphany for Michael Ruhlman, one that inspired his fascination with charcuterie and this book, co-written with Brian Polcyn. Ruhlman's enthusiasm for the subject permeates the book, which offers an accessible introduction to the historic "techniques of preservation and economy." Ruhlman explains in clear, readable prose the science behind curing, from how salt works as a preservative by dehydrating microbes to the importance of acid in the dry-cure process. The recipes, grouped by curing process, range from Fresh Bacon to Ruhlman's beloved Confit, along with a chapter on sauces and condiments to accompany charcuterie.

As the appetizing title suggests, Bill Neal's cookbook is a celebration of "the glories of Southern baking." Neal presents a fine selection of recipes for sweet and savory baked dishes, grouping them by themed chapters, such as "The Pride of the South"—hot biscuits—or "The Gift of Corn"—breads, dumplings, pancakes, and fritters. The recipes—with wonderful names such as Hushpuppies, Big Mama's Everlasting Rolls, Zephyrinas, Divinity—are each set in a historical context. While the depth of knowledge is apparent throughout, Neal's engaging, conversational prose, often drawing on his own childhood memories, makes the book a beguiling read.

There is an admirable thoroughness to this classic American baking book, which explains its enduring popularity. Having learned from personal experience that attention to numerous details in the baking process was what brought about success, Braker sets out to share her knowledge and communicate the care required. She writes with a meticulous eye on subjects such as the importance of measuring precisely, for example, with her recipes including details such as the temperature of the ingredients. She is, also, however, a cooking writer who believes in empowering her readers: "Use your senses and don't be a slave to my baking times," she exhorts with good common sense.

Such is the reputation of the bread at San Francisco's famous Tartine bakery, that it sells out as quickly as it emerges freshly baked from the oven. In this handsome cookbook, baker Chad Robertson, who cofounded Tartine with his wife Elisabeth Prueitt, shares his considerable knowledge on how to bake great bread. Robertson conceived of the book as "a baker's guidebook," one that would work for the home baker. Writing thoughtfully and intelligently, he shares the long journey he himself took toward the goal of his "ideal loaf." There is a generosity of spirit in the way Robertson shares his knowledge, from how to make the leaven and mix the dough to the lovingly written recipes themselves.

There are just so many recipes I long to try out — my copy is littered with post-its.
NIGELLA LAWSON

Salt Sugar Smoke
Diana Henry

BOOK DETAILS
Published 2012, Mitchell Beazley, 272 pages

Recent years have seen a new interest in the subject of the craft of food among chefs and domestic cooks alike: the rise of home-baked sourdough bread and homemade butter and charcuterie on restaurant menus is a reflection of this fascination. Here, award-winning food writer Diana Henry turns her attention to the subject of preserving and, in characteristic style, manages to breathe new, imaginative culinary life into this traditional area of cooking. Henry's approach, as she explains, is that of a home cook: "I don't have masses of special equipment and I don't do things on a grand scale." Rather than offering intimidating geeky obsessiveness, Henry provides a helpful introduction to preserving,

emphasizing its pleasures and satisfactions. While she clearly explains the practicalities, the real joy of the book lies in her imaginative recipes, which are filled with intriguing flavor combinations: Blackberry and Pinot Noir Jam, Wok-Smoked Trout with Dill; Raspberry and Rose Cordial. The recipes draw inspiration from cuisines around the world—Persian, Italian, Polish, British, French, Thai— giving the book a cosmopolitan feel. Henry's love of food comes across vividly in her writing. The conversational introductions to the recipes—with their memories of ingredients encountered, meals shared, and interspersed essays—create an engaging, characterful framework for the book.

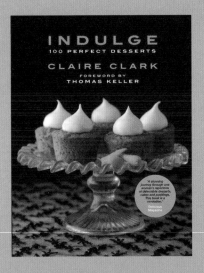

Indulge:100 *Perfect Desserts* Claire Clark

BOOK DETAILS

Published 2007, Absolute Press, 240 pages

Pastry chef Claire Clark—a recipient of Meilleur Ouvrier de Grande Bretagne—has had an impressive career in the world of restaurants and hotels. Drawn to baking ever since she was young, she worked as head pastry chef at Bluebird, followed by Claridges, and opened the Wolseley, the elegant London brasserie renowned for its breakfasts and afternoon teas. She later met legendary American chef Thomas Keller (see p.18, 86, 138, 230), and knew that she had to work with him. Keller, impressed by the quality and breadth of her execution, invited her to join the team at his acclaimed California restaurant The French Laundry. Of working for Keller, she writes: "I quickly learnt that he expects nothing less than excellence 24/7 in everything you do." This cookbook, written while Clark was working at The French Laundry, offers an insight into her considerable skills. The recipes, from biscuits to petits fours, are a mixture of the homely (her mother's recipe for shortbread) and the technically challenging, for example, Battenberg Cake or the Rich Chocolate Ganache Tart with Salted Caramel and Candied Peanuts she created for Keller. The recipes are clearly written, with Clark's professional eye for appearance manifest. In contrast to the precision and erfectionism required by the baking, her authorial voice is chatty and encouraging, mixing sound practical advice—"Don't cut corners or rush tasks—there are no compromises in baking"— with anecdotes from her career.

> *"Science is not an end in and of itself, but a path."*
>
> J. KENJI LÓPEZ-ALT, *THE FOOD LAB*

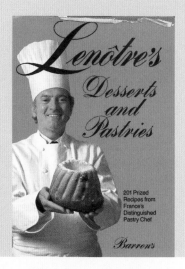

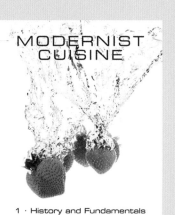

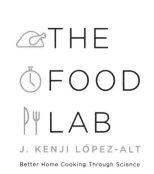

Lenôtre's Desserts and Pastries
Gaston Lenôtre
(Pub 1975, Flammarion, 312pp)

Modernist Cuisine
Nathan Myhrvold, Chris Young, and Maxime Bilet
(Pub 2011, Taschen, 2438pp)

The Food Lab: Better Home Cooking Through Science
J. Kenji López-Alt (Pub 2015, W. W. Norton & Company, 958pp)

Encyclopédie du chocolat (Cooking with Chocolate)
Frédéric Bau (Pub 2010, Flammarion, 416pp)

Acclaimed French pastry chef Gaston Lenôtre was noted not only for his high-quality pâtisserie but, through his school for pastry chefs at Plaisir-Grignon, France, for his willingness to share the "secrets" of his profession. In this cookbook, Lenôtre addresses amateur cooks and emphasizes the importance of using quality ingredients and of time, patience, and perseverance when it comes to creating pâtisserie. The recipes are from the classic French canon—with basics such as Génoise or Tarte aux Mirabelles (Mirabelle Plum Tart)—but also include elegant, signature Lenôtre creations, for example, Feuille d'Automne (Autumn Meringue Cake) and Rosace a l'Orange (Upside Down Orange Cake).

This fascinating, extraordinary work, spanning six volumes and well over 2,000 pages long, reflects Cooking Lab founder Nathan Myhrvold's obsession with food and the science of cooking. Each of the handsomely illustrated volumes deal with different aspects of food and cooking. The logically presented, clearly written, wide-ranging information is presented in numerous ways, including recipes, charts, tables, and instructions on matters such as "How to 'Cryosear' a Duck Breast" or "How to Extract Juice From Plants with Pectinase." As Ferran Adrià writes in his foreword, this work "will change the way we understand the modern kitchen and gastronomy."

Based on J. Kenji López-Alt's popular online Food Lab blog, this hefty tome taps into the current fascination with the science of food. "A Nerd in the Kitchen" is the enlightening title of the introduction, with López-Alt cheerfully admitting to a geeky obsessiveness when it comes to understanding cooking. Familiar, popular, homely American recipes—such as Corn Chowder, All-American Meat Loaf, or Caesar Salad—are explored and dissected in detail, with the science behind making them well clearly explained. López-Alt is an effective communicator, sharing his knowledge in a friendly tone of voice, although the level of his fascination is very clear.

Hugely respected French chocolatier and pâtissier Frédéric Bau founded the École du Grand Chocolat Valrhona, renowned for the quality of its teaching. Drawing on this educational experience, this cookbook sets out, as Bau writes: "to be a key reference work," offering an admirably comprehensive insight into how to work with chocolate. He outlines fundamental techniques, including tempering, and "building block" recipes with the meticulous instructions accompanied by step-by-step illustrations. Having constructed the foundation of basic knowledge, Bau then builds on it, offering over 100 recipes by notable pastry chefs for treats from Sachertorte to Truffled Ivory Macaroons.

HISTORICAL COOKBOOKS

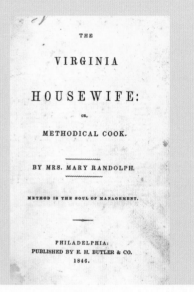

*The Virginia Housewife:
Or Methodical Cook*, Mrs.
Mary Randolph (Pub 1824,
E. H. Butler & Co., 180pp)

*Le Cuisinier François
(The French Cook)*
François Pierre de la Varenne
(Pub 1651, 294pp)

For much of human history, recipes and food knowledge were passed down and shared through word of mouth, by watching and learning, rather than recorded in written form. With the cooking of food an activity that continues to be important to this day, those cookbooks that have survived have the capacity to link us to the past in a very direct way. The cookbooks by writers such as Hannah Glasse or Alexis Soyer are concerned with the practicalities of household budgets, providing healthy, nutritious food, and entertaining hospitably, exactly as we still are today. Many chefs and food writers, among them Heston Blumenthal, Elizabeth David, and Jane Grigson, have drawn inspiration and knowledge from these historical works, and they constitute a fascinating resource to be treasured.

An important book in American culinary history, Mary Randolph's cookbook, published in the early years of the nineteenth century, is regarded as the first Southern cookbook and was hugely popular in its day. Randolph wrote the book to aid "the young, inexperienced housekeeper," declaring bracingly: "Management is an art that may be acquired by every woman of good sense and tolerable memory." Interspersed with recipes for dishes such as Gumbo, Chicken Pudding ("a favorite Virginia dish"), or Johnny Cake, is firmly expressed advice on matters such as the proper way to roast meats or, "for those who live in the country and butcher their own meats," on cleaning a calf's head and feet.

In the history of French cuisine, this bestseller by François Pierre de la Varenne (translated into English in 1653) is a seminal text. A professional chef, who worked for the aristocracy, la Varenne chronicled French cuisine at an important period. He wrote for fellow chefs, assuming knowledge of cookery but emphasizing salient points. His recipe for Eggs Poached in Water, for example, begins: "Take the newest you can get" and stresses careful handling. Many aspects of this cookbook— the importance and versatility of soups, the use of French culinary terms, the emphasis on choosing ingredients well—were hugely influential. Used by the great French chefs who came after him, it helped shape French cuisine.

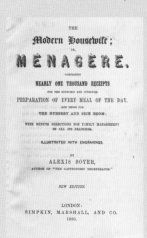

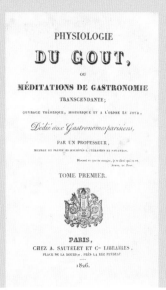

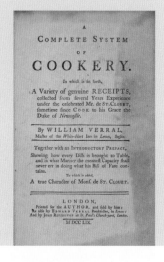

The Modern Housewife;
Or Menagere, Alexis Soyer
(Pub 1849, Simpkin, Marshall
and Co., 442pp)

The Boston Cooking School
Cook Book, Fannie Merritt
Farmer (Pub 1896, Little,
Brown, 567pp)

Physiologie du goût
(*The Physiology of Taste*)
Jean Anthelme Brillat-Savarin
(Pub 1825, 446pp)

A Complete System of Cookery
William Verral
(Pub 1759, Bibliolife, 240pp)

The dashing Victorian celebrity chef Alexis Soyer brought a characteristic verve and charm to this cookbook, a contemporary bestseller. Dedicated to "the fair daughters of Albion," the book is constructed as a series of letters between Mrs. B and her friend Mrs. L, the former offering advice to the latter on household management. Through this conceit, Soyer shares his views on how to cook well, with an awareness of both health and cost very much in mind. The conversational tone makes for an engaging as well as an informative read. On "Mephistophelian Sauce," a reassuring aside reads: "Do not be afraid of the title, for it has nothing diabolical about it."

"Food is anything which nourishes the body," opens Fannie Farmer's famous, best-selling American cookbook. This serious, educational tone, reflecting its cooking school origins, is maintained throughout her book, which begins with an explanation of food and cooking. Reading the book, with its advice on ingredients and cooking methods, offers an interesting glimpse into nineteenth-century domestic life. A practical thriftiness manifests itself in sections such as the one on "Warmed-Over Potatoes." The instructive nature extends to suggested menus, from hearty breakfasts to elaborate dinners, beginning with anchovy canapés and rounding off with desserts, cheese, and "café noir."

Playful, philosophical, and characterful, Jean Anthelme Brillat-Savarin's famous book enjoys the status of a cult classic, a fact that one feels would have deeply appealed to its author. His digressive "gastronomical meditations" cover subjects from "Taste" (which he links to smell) to "Digestion," explored with wit, energy, and a rambling curiosity. "Tell me what you eat, and I shall tell you what you are," remains his best-known aphorism. His style is entertaining and eloquent; the thought of "Truffled Turkeys" prompting the rhapsodic reflection: "They are like lucky stars, whose very appearance makes gourmands of every category twinkle, gleam and caper with pleasure."

William Verral was Master of the White Hart Inn in Lewes, Sussex, England. He is remembered now for his 1759 cookbook offering "A variety of genuine receipts, collected from several years experience under the celebrated Mr. de St. Clouet, sometime since cook to his Grace the Duke of Newcastle." Written in a jovial and anecdotal style, his aim was to show professional cooks "the whole and simple art of the most modern and best French cookery." He begins, in classic French style, with a recipe for how to make broth, using the cut of beef "which in London is called the mouse-buttock." Verral's pleasure in cooking and pride in his skillfully created dishes makes for an engaging read.

Beeton's Book of Household Management
Mrs. Isabella Beeton (Pub 1861, S. O. Beeton Publishing, 1112pp)

The Book of Ices
Agnes Bertha Marshall
(Pub 1885, Ward Lock, 67pp)

The Cook's Oracle and Housekeeper's Manual
William Kitchiner (Pub 1817, Samuel Bagster, 464pp)

The Art of Cookery Made Plain and Easy
Hannah Glasse
(Pub 1747, E. & J. Exshaw, 166pp)

A phenomenal bestseller in Victorian times, Isabella Beeton's well-known tome continues to impress with the scale of its ambition and depth of content: "I must frankly own, that if I had known, beforehand, that this book would have cost me the labour which it has, I should never have been courageous enough to commence it," she wrote. With the energetic confidence that characterized that era in Britain, she set out to make her work "something more than a Cookery Book," the book is therefore both wide-ranging and informative to an extraordinary degree, including, for example, natural history essays alongside recipes for dishes such as Beef à la Mode or Apple Charlotte.

Victorian businesswoman Agnes Bertha Marshall, usually known as Mrs. Marshall, is regarded as an eminent authority on ice-cream making, with admirers including the chef Heston Blumenthal. She and her husband set up a cooking school in London in 1883 and there is a practical, no-nonsense quality to this famous cookbook. The advice given is brisk and thoroughly sound: "Too much sugar will prevent the ice from freezing properly." Custards, used as the base for ice creams, are graded from the "Very Rich" to the "Common," the first containing eight egg yolks, the latter two. Less familiar recipes include Cucumber Cream Ice and Iced Spinach à la Crème.

A nineteenth-century bestseller, this engaging cookbook is "the result of actual experiments in the kitchen of a physician," declares its title page with characteristic verve. Its author, William Kitchiner, a member of the Royal Society, emphasizes the empirical base of his knowledge, offering "a bona fide register of practical facts, accumulated by a perseverance not to be subdued." Written in an endearingly digressive style, with eloquence and humor, the book contains both recipes and much advice, rooted in genuine knowledge. Cooking vegetables, he writes "requires the most vigilant attention. If vegetables are a minute or two too long over the fire—they lose all their beauty and flavor."

Written with the avowed aim of making every servant who read it "a tolerable good cook," Hannah Glasse's eighteenth-century bestseller still impresses with its forthright voice, pithy turn of phrase, and knowledge of cookery. She wrote, she explained, not "in the high, polite stile [sic]," but to address "the lower sort," and her instructions on such kitchen affairs as how to choose fresh meat, pickle ox palates, and cook French beans to retain their color are clear and succinct. The book champions good English cooking, with much grumbling on Glasse's part about the fashion of the age for extravagant French cooks and their unnecessarily expensive sauces.

Modern Cookery for Private Families
Eliza Acton

BOOK DETAILS
Published 1845, Longmans, 644 pages

Eliza Acton's influential nineteenth-century bestseller—written with intelligence and radiating a calm authority—deserves its classic status. Her intentions in writing the book are made clear by its subtitle: *Reduced to a System of Easy Practice, in a Series of Carefully Tested Receipts*. A concern to promote health through proper eating and to prevent food waste—two issues very much to the fore today—characterize her writing. She begins in a practical manner, with a chapter on soups, observing that "the art of preparing good, wholesome, palatable soups, without great expense, which is so well understood in France," be taken up in England. Her recipes were "carefully tested," written in detail with an eye for the salient points, rooted in genuine knowledge of cooking: "Every good cook understands perfectly the difference produced by the fast boiling or the gentle stewing of soups and gravies, and will adhere strictly to the latter method." Her awareness of seasonality is striking; she gives advice on which month's ingredients are at their best and seasonally appropriate dishes. Among Acton's admirers was Elizabeth David (see p.84, 110, 317, 331), who wrote: "Over and over again, reading *Modern Cookery*—for twenty years the book has been my beloved companion—I have marvelled at the illuminating and decisive qualities of Miss Acton's recipes."

Index

4 Saisons á la Table No. 5 82–3
50 Great Curries of India 321
1080 Recipes 310

Achatz, Grant 155
Acton, Eliza 347
Acurio, Gastón 306
Ad Hoc at Home 335
Adrià, Albert 156
Adrià, Ferran 17, 18, 156, 159, 255, 274, 278
Aduriz, Andoni Luis 6, 10–11, 17, 48, 159
Alastair Little, London 245
Alexander, Stephanie 326
Alford, Jeffrey 96
The Alice B. Toklas Cook Book 329
Alinea 154–5
Allen, Darina 12–13, 160
Allen, Myrtle 13
Alléno, Yannick 82
Allsop, Damian 129
American Cookery 301
Anaryllis, Scotland 73
André Garrett at Cliveden, Taplow, U.K. 57
Angela Hartnett at The Grill Room at the Connaught, London 73
Anthony, Michael 14–15, 163
AOC, Copenhagen 137
Aquavit, New York 29
Arabella Boxer's Book of English Food 34–5
Arcane, Hong Kong 117
The Art of Cookery Made Plain and Easy 7, 346
The Art of Simple Food 335
Artusi, Pellegrino 33
Arzak, Elena 16–17, 164
Arzak, Juan Mari 16–17, 164
Arzak, San Sebastián, Spain 17, 164
Arzak Secrets 164–5
Astrance 172–3
Astrance, Paris 44, 163, 172
Atala, Alex 167
Atelier Crenn: Metamorphosis of Taste 198–9
Atelier Crenn, San Franscisco 198
Atherton, Jason 7, 18, 168
Attica, Melbourne 289
Aubergine, London 277

Bains, Sat 20–1, 30, 171
Baking: From My Home to Yours 339
Balance and Harmony: Asian Food 270–1
The Ballymaloe Cookbook 12–13
Ballymoe Cookery School, Cork, Ireland 13, 121, 160
Barber, Dan 22–3, 274
Barbot, Pascal 172
Bareham, Lindsey 225
Barrafina, London 25
Barragán Mohacho, Nieves 24–5
Bau, Frédéric 343
Beard, James 301
Beck, Simone 311
Becker, Rainer 26–7
Beer, Maggie 326
Beeton, Mrs. Isabella 346
Beeton's Book of Household Management 346
Bengtsson, Emma 28–9
Bentley's Oyster Bar & Grill, London 52

Benu 7, 242–3
Benu, San Francisco 99, 242
Beranbaum, Rose Levy 336
Bertholle, Louisette 311
Bertolli, Paul 14, 175
Best, Mark 176
The Best of Jane Grigson 74–5
Betony, New York 141
Bianchi, Luciana 304
Bibendum, London 81, 225
The Big Fat Duck Cookbook 180–1
Bigar, Sylvie 187
Bilet, Maxime 343
bills, Sydney 62, 218
bills Sydney Food 218–19
Billy Kwong, Sydney 321
Biscuits, Spoonbread, and Sweet Potato Pie 340
Bistro Cooking 311
Bittman, Mark 290, 334
Black, Cat 52
Blake, Anthony 99, 122, 125
Blanc, Raymond 179, 180
Blue Hill at Stone Barns, New York 22, 163
Blue Water Grill, Sydney 122, 270
The Blueprint Café, London 100
Blumenthal, Heston 171, 180, 310
Bocuse, Paul 7, 109, 183, 187, 201, 307
With Bold Knife & Fork 328
Boni, Ada 315
The Book of Ices 346
A Book of Middle Eastern Food 7, 319
Bosi, Claude 30–1
The Boston Cooking School Cook Book 345
Bottura, Massimo 32–3, 184
Boudier, Alain 10
Boulud, Daniel 183, 187, 286
Bourdain, Anthony 191, 201, 297
Boxer, Arabella 34
Boxer, Jackson 34–5
Braker, Flo 340
Bras 188–9
Bras, Michel 10, 37, 55, 188
Bras, Sébastien 38–9
Brazilian Food 304
Breakfast, Lunch, Tea 339
Brillat-Savarin, Jean Anthelme 345, 346
Brioza, Stuart 40
Brissenden, Rosemary 325
British Regional Food 309
Brock, Sean 42–3, 191
Brown, Edward Espe 246
Brunswick House, London 34
Burma: Rivers of Flavor 324

The Cake Bible 336
Campton Place Restaurant, San Francisco 82
Carluccio, Antonio 315
Carrarini, Rose 339
Carrier, Robert 74
The Carved Angel, Dartmouth, U.K. 110
Castanho, Thiago 304
Castle Hotel, Taunton, Somerset 125
Ceviche: Peruvian Kitchen 306
Chang, David 192, 209, 242
Chapel, Alain 37
Charcuterie 340
Charcuterie and French Pork Cookery 100–3

Charmaine Solomon's Encyclopedia of Asian Food 62–3
Chef, La Grenouillère 44–5
A Chef For All Seasons 276–7
Chef Paul Prudhomme's Louisiana Kitchen 303
Chez Nico, Dulwich, U.K. 238
Chez Panisse, Berkeley, California 47, 58, 175, 217, 282, 294, 331, 335, 337
The Chez Panisse Menu Cookbook 46–7, 294–5
Chiang, André 44–5
Child, Julia 269, 311
Choate, Judith 209
Choi, Roy 201
The Cinnamon Club, London 142
Citrus and Spice: A Year of Flavour 328
City Rhodes, London 125
Claiborne, Craig 201, 303
Clark, Claire 342
Clark, Sam and Sam 195
Clarke, Sally 46–7
Clarke's, London 47
Classic Indian Cooking 321
The Classic Italian Cookbook 72–3, 134–5
Clorofilia 48
Cocinar Para Viver 16–17
Coi, San Francisco 266
Coi: Stories and Recipes 266–7
Colagraco, Mauro 48–9
Colicchio, Tom 50–1, 196
Collages & Recettes 264–5
Com Usar Bé de Beure e Menjar 6, 130
Complete Chinese Cookbook 323
A Complete System of Cookery 345
Conran, Caroline 314
Conran, Terence 81, 100, 225
Contaldo, Gennaro 315
Cooking by Hand 14–15, 174–5
The Cooking of South-West France 313
The Cook's Companion 326
Corrigan, Richard 52–3
Costa, Margaret 332
Craft, New York 51, 196
Craft London 121
Crenn, Dominique 198
Crewe, Quentin 7, 99, 122, 125
Cruz, Dave 335
Cuisine Actuelle 70–1
Cuisine Minceur 222–3
The Cuisines of Mexico 306
The Culinary Institute of America 201
Cumulus Inc., Melbourne, Australia 104
Curnonsky 7, 313

Dabbous, London 202
Dabbous, Ollie 202
Dabbous: The Cookbook 202–3
Daniel, New York 187
Daniel: My French Cuisine 186–7
David, Elizabeth 74, 85, 110, 294, 317, 332
Davidson, Alan 332
A day at elBulli 156–7
Dean, Joel 300
The Dean & DeLuca Cookbook 300
del Conte, Anna 77, 315
Delia Smith's Complete Cookery Course 310
Delia's Cakes 118–19
DeLuca, Giorgio 300

Denny, Roz 277
Desserts 339
The Desserts of Jordi Roca 338
Dill Restaurant, Reykjavík 214
Dock Kitchen, London 121
D.O.M. Rediscovering Brazilian Ingredients 166–7
Domus 317
Dorchester Hotel, London 66, 113
Ducasse, Alain 30, 89, 145, 205
Dufresne, Wylie 54–5, 209
Duguid, Naomi 96, 324
Dunlop, Fuchsia 323

Eddy, Jody 214
Egerton, John 300
Eiximenis, Francesc 6, 130
El Celler de Can Roca, Girona, Spain 126, 129, 130, 338
elBulli, Roses, Spain 18, 137, 156, 274, 278
Eleven Madison Park, New York 82, 226
Eleven Madison Park: The Cookbook 140–1, 226–7
Éloge de la cuisine Française 64–5
Encyclopédie du chocolat (Cooking with Chocolate) 343
English Food 308
Entertaining all'Italiana 315
Erickson, Meredith 286
Escoffier, Auguste 187, 201, 206
Essential Cuisine 54–5
Essentials of Classic Italian Cooking 148–9
Everitt-Matthias, David 102
Everyday Harumi 324

Farmer, Fannie Merritt 345
Fat 252–3
The Fat Duck, Bray, U.K. 180
Fäviken 6, 256–7
Fawcett, Hilary 332
Fearnley-Whittingstall, Hugh 40
Fera, London 132
Fifteen, London 114
Fire 60–1
Fire + Ice: Classic Nordic Cooking 308
Fisher, M. F. K. 328
Five Quarters: Recipes and Notes from a Kitchen in Rome 317
Flatbreads and Flavors 96–7
The Flavour Thesaurus 336
Flay, Bobby 209
Floyd, Keith 314
Floyd on France 314
Fombellida, Fernando 17
The Food Lab 343
The Food of Italy 317
The Food of Spain 310
Foods of the World 327
Fortgang, Andrew 286
Fortgang, Lauren 286
Four Seasons Cookery Book 332
Francis Mallmann 1884, Argentina 307
Franklin, Aaron 337
Franklin Barbecue: A Meat-Smoking Manifesto 337
French Country Cooking 294
The French Culinary Institute 208

The French House Dining Room, London 69
The French Kitchen 314
The French Laundry, California 18, 86, 99, 230, 242, 278, 342
The French Laundry Cookbook 7, 18–19, 138–9, 230–1
The French Menu Cookbook 80–1
French Provincial Cooking 84–5, 110–11
Fulham Road, London 52
Fullick, Roy 74
The Fundamental Techniques of Classic Cuisine 208–9

Galvin, Chris 57, 118
Galvin at Windows, London 57
Garrett, André 56–7
Garrett, Graham 52, 210
Gastronomy of Italy 76–7
Gauthier, Alexandre 44
Gelber, Teri 217
The Gentle Art of Cookery 331
Gidleigh Park, Dartmoor, Devon 74, 151
Gilmore, Peter 213
Girardet, Frédy 126
Gíslason, Gunnar Karl 214
Glasse, Hannah 7, 346
Goin, Suzanne 58–9, 217
Gold, Rozanne 331
Goldstein, Darra 308
Good Food 114–15
The Good Food Guide Dinner Party Book 332
Goode, J. J. 324
Gordon, Peter 60–1, 69
Gotham Building Tavern, Portland, Oregon 286
The Gramercy Tavern Cookbook 162–3
Gramercy Tavern, New York 14, 51, 163, 196
Gran Cocina Latina: The Food of Latin America 304
Grand Livre de Cuisine 88–9, 144–5
Granger, Bill 62–3, 218
Gray, Patience 93, 121
Gray, Rose 135, 221
Great Chefs of France 7, 98–9, 122–5
The Greenhouse, London 125
The Greens Cookbook 246–7
Greens Restaurant, San Francisco 246
Greenspan, Dorie 339
Grigson, Jane 74, 100, 102, 107, 308, 329
Guérard, Michel 64–5, 222
Guidara, Will 82, 141, 226
Guy Savoy, Paris 57, 90, 277
Gyngell, Skye 66, 146

Haeberlin, Jean-Pierre 26
Haeberlin, Paul 26
Hamilton, Dorothy Cann 209
The Hand & Flowers, Marlow, U.K. 89, 233
Hansen, Anna 68–9
Harris, Stephen 70–1
Hartley, Miss Olga 331
Hartnett, Angela 72–3
Harveys, London 297
Hazan, Marcella 73, 135, 148
Heath, Ambrose 114
Heller, Susie 18, 138
Henderson, Fergus 6, 25, 34, 69, 104
Henry, Diana 341

Herbs, Spices and Flavourings 132–3
Heritage 190–1
Hermé, Pierre 337
Hibiscus, Ludlow, U.K. 30
Hill, Shaun 74–5
Historic Heston 310
Hix, Mark 76–7, 309
HIX Oyster and Fish House, London 77
Hole in the Wall, Bath, U.K. 110
Holtz, Deborah 306
Hom, Ken 78–9, 323
Honey & Co., London 118, 146
Honey & Co.: Food From the Middle East 318
Honey From a Weed 92–3, 120–1
Hopkinson, Simon 57, 80–1, 225
How to Cook Everything: Simple Recipes for Great Food 334
How to Eat: The Pleasures and Principles of Good Food 333
Humm, Daniel 82–3, 141, 226
Husk, Charleston, South Carolina 43, 191

I Know How to Cook 315
Il cucchiaio d'argento 317
Il Talisman della Felicità (The Talisman of Happiness) 315
Indulge: 100 Perfect Desserts 342
Into the Vietnamese Kitchen: Treasured Foodways, Modern Flavors 324
Italian Food 317
The Ivy, London 77

Jaffrey, Madhur 320
Jamin, Paris 282
Jane Grigson's Fruit Book 106–7
Jane Grigson's Vegetable Book 329
Janse, Margot 84–5
Japanese Cooking: A Simple Art 323
Jasper White's Cooking from New England 303
Jean-Georges, New York 290
Jerusalem 318
Joe Beef, Montreal, Canada 109
Johnson, Hugh 179
Joy of Cooking 302

Kaiseki: The Exquisite Cuisine of Kyoto's Kikunoi Restaurant 323
Kalra, J. Inder Singh 142
Kaminsky, Peter 307
Kapoor, Sybil 328
Katzen, Mollie 229
Keep It Simple 244–5
Keller, Thomas 7, 18, 86–7, 99, 138, 168, 230, 242, 335, 342
Kennedy, Diana 306
Kerridge, Tom 89–90, 233
The Key to Chinese Cooking 78–9
Kikunoi, Osaka 323
Kinch, David 234, 265
Kinselas, Sydney 293
The Kitchen, Edinburgh 90
The Kitchen Diaries 329
Kitchin, Tom 90–1
Kitchiner, William 346
Knight, Florence 92–3
Koffmann, Pierre 6, 90, 94–5, 237
Koffmann's, Berkeley Hotel, London 94

Krasinski, Nicole 40, 96–7
Kuo, Irene 78
Kurihara, Harumi 324
Kwong, Kylie 321
La Cuisine c'est beaucoup plus que des recettes 36–7
La Cuisine du marché 7, 108–9, 182–3
La Cuisine en dix minutes (Cooking in Ten Minutes) 311
La Cuisine spontaneé 126–7
La Grenouillère, France 44
La Pâtisserie des frères Roux 284–5
La Place, Viana 51
La Plaza Athénée, Paris 269
La Pyramide, France 7, 37, 86, 183
La scienza in cucina e l'arte di mangiar bene 32–3
La Tante Claire, London 90, 94, 237
La Tante Claire: Recipes from a Master Chef 6, 236–7
La Technique 196, 268–9
la Varenne, François Pierre de 7, 344
Ladenis, Nico 57, 238
Larousse Gastronomique: The Encyclopedia of Food, Wine & Cookery 312
L'Arpège, Paris 30, 48, 58, 163, 172, 176, 234, 265
L'Atelier de Joël Robuchon 44, 281
L'Atelier of Alain Ducasse 204–5
L'Auberge de L'Ill, Alsace 26, 290
L'Auberge du Pont de Collonges, France 183
Lawson, Nigella 333
Le Bernardin Cookbook 240–1
Le Bernardin, New York 241
Le Caprice, London 77
Le Champignon Sauvage, Cheltenham, U.K. 102
Le Coze, Maguy 241
Le Cuisinier François (The French Cook) 344
Le Gavroche, London 237, 285, 314
Le Guide culinaire 187, 206–7
Le Louis XV, Monte Carlo 90, 145, 205
Le Manoir aux Quat' Saisons, Great Milton, U.K. 179, 180
Le Meurice, Paris 82
Le Mondrian, New York 196
Le Pigeon: Cooking at the Dirty Bird 286–7
Le Répertoire de la cuisine 94–5, 187
Le Taillevent, France 86
Lebovitz, David 337
Lee, Corey 6–7, 99, 242
Lee, Jeremy 100–1
Leith, Prue 329
Leith's Cookery Bible 329
L'Enclume, Cartmel, U.K. 132
Lenôtre, Gaston 343
Lenôtre's Desserts and Pastries 343
Lepard, Dan 339
Les Dimanches de Joël Robuchon 280–1
Les Fêtes de mon moulin (Entertaining in the French Style) 313
Les Frères Troisgros, Roanne, France 282
Les Prés d'Eugénie, France 65, 222
Les Recettes de Auberge de L'Ill 26–7
Les Secrets de la casserole 38–9
Leyel, Mrs. C. F. 331
Lindsay House, Soho, London 52
Little, Alastair 245

Little Bird, Portland, Oregon 286
Livre de Michel Bras 10–11
Locanda Locatelli, London 316
Locatelli, Giorgio 316
Loiseau, Bernard 48
López-Alt, J. Kenji 343
Loubet, Bruno 57
Lucky Peach Presents 101 Easy Asian Recipes 320
Lucques, Los Angeles 58, 217
LU.K.ins, Sheila 303

Ma Gastronomie 7, 86–7
Macaron 337
Mackay, Jordan 337
MacLeod, Tracey 233
Made In Italy: Food & Stories 316
Madhur Jaffrey's Indian Cookery 320
Madison, Deborah 246
Maggie's Harvest 326
Mallmann, Francis 307
Manfield, Christine 61, 249
Manresa, California 234
Manresa: An Edible Reflection 234–5
Marque 176–7
Marque, Sydney 176
Mastering the Art of French Cooking 311
Masui, Chihiro 172
Masui, KazU.K.o 82
Mathiot, Ginette 315
Matsuhisa, NobuyU.K.i 250
Maze, London 18
McConnell, Andrew 104
McGee, Harold 38, 180, 266, 337
McLagan, Jennifer 106–7, 252
McLaughlin, Michael 303
McMillan, David 7, 108–9
Mee, Rio de Janeiro, Brazil 78
Meehan, Peter 192, 320
Memories of Gascony 90–1
Mena, Juan Carlos 306
Merchant House, Ludlow, U.K. 74
Mexico from the Inside Out 305
Meyer, Danny 82, 163, 196, 226, 335
Michael Wignall at the Latymer, Surry 151
Millau, Christian 10
Mirazur, Menton, France 48
Modern Cookery for Private Families 347
The Modern Housewife; Or Menagere 345
The Modern Pantry, London 69
Modernist Cuisine 343
Molyneux, Joyce 110
MomofU.K.u 192–3
MomofU.K.u, New York 192
Mondrian, New York 51
Montagné, Prosper 312
The Moosewood Cookbook 228–9
Moosewood Restaurant, New York 229
Morales, Martin 306
Morimoto 254–5
Morimoto, Masaharu 255
Morin, Frédéric 7, 108–9
Moro, London 121, 195
Moro: The Cookbook 194–5
Mosimann, Anton 113
Moulin de Mougins, France 238
Much Depends on Dinner 6, 22–3
Mugaritz, San Sebastián, Spain 10, 48, 159

Mugaritz: A Natural Science of Cooking 6, 158–9
Murano, London 73
Murata, Yoshihiro 323
My Favourite Ingredients 146–7
My Gastronomy 238–9
Myhrvold, Nathan 343
The Naked Chef 331
Nathan Outlaw, Rock, U.K. 263
Nathan Outlaw's British Seafood 262–3
Neal, Bill 340
Neal Street Restaurant, London 315
Never Trust a Italian Skinny Chef 184–5
The New York Times Cook Book 303
Nguyen, Andrea 324
Nignon, Édouard 65
Nilsson, Magnus 6, 29, 256–7
Nobu, New York 250, 255
Nobu: The Cookbook 250–1
Noma, Copenhagen 274, 278
Noma: Time and Place in Nordic Cuisine 136–7, 278–9
Nopi, London 118
The Nordic Cookbook 6, 28–9
Norman, Matthew 245
Norman, Russell 93, 259
North: The New Nordic Cuisine of Iceland 214–15
Nose to Tail Eating: A Kind of British Cooking 24–5, 104–5
Nostrana, Portland, Oregon 148

Oblix, London 26
Oliver, Jamie 114–15, 315, 331
Oliveto, Oakland, California 175
Olney, Richard 81, 313
Olvera, Enrique 305
On Food and Cooking: The Science and Lore of the Kitchen 337
Opera dell'arte del Cucinare 112–13
Origin: The Food of Ben Shewry 6, 150–1, 288–9
The Orrery, London 57, 118̄
Ortega, Simone and Inés 310
Osborn, Shane 117
Osteria Francescana, Modena, Italy 33, 184
Ottolenghi, London 118, 260
Ottolenghi, Yotam 260, 318, 330
Ottolenghi: The Cookbook 260–1
Outlaw, Nathan 263
The Oxford Companion to Food 332

Packer, Sarit 118–19, 146, 318
Paley's Place, Portland, Oregon 286
Panjabi, Camellia 321
Parle, Stevie 120–1
Passard, Alain 30, 48, 176, 234, 265
Passione: The Italian Cookbook 315
Patanen, Pasi 176
Patterson, Daniel 266
Paula Wolfert's World of Food 58–9
Pépin, Jacques 196, 209, 269
Perfume 128–9
Perry, Neil 122–3, 270
Perry-Smith, George 110
Peru: The Cookbook 306
Petersham Nurseries, Richmond, London 66, 121, 146

Physiologie du goût (The Physiology of Taste) 345
Pied à Terre, London 117
Piège, Jean-François 90
Pierre Gagnaire, Paris 44
A Platter of Figs and Other Recipes 331
Plenty 330
Point, Fernand 7, 37, 86, 109
Pok Pok 324
Polcyn, Brian 340
Pollen Street Social, London 18, 168
Polpetto, London 93
Polpo, London 259
Polpo: A Venetian Cookbook (Of Sorts) 258–9
Pomiane, Édouard de 311
Prasha̅ d 142–3
Presilla, Maricel E. 304
Private Dining Club: Mosimann's, London 113
The Professional Chef 200–1
The Providores, London 61, 69
Prudhomme, Paul 303
Prueitt, Elisabeth M. 273
Puglisi, Christian F. 274
Pujol, Mexico 305

Quay, Sydney 213
Quay: Food Inspired by Nature 212–13
Quo Vadis, London 100

Radically Simple: Brilliant Flavors with Breathtaking Ease 331
Ramsay, Gordon 18, 73, 277
Randolph, Mrs. Mary 344
Rayner, Jay 202
Ready for Dessert 337
Recettes des Provinces de France (Traditional Recipes of the Provinces of France) 313
Recipes from Le Manoir aux Quat' Saisons 178–9
Redzepi, René 137, 176, 214, 274, 278
Relæ, Copenhagen 274
Relæ: A Book of Ideas 274–5
Restaurant André, Singapore 44
Restaurant Bras, Laguiole, France 37, 38, 55, 188
Restaurant Gordon Ramsey, London 145, 277
Restaurant Larue, Paris 65
Restaurant Sat Bains, Nottingham, U.K. 21, 30, 171
A Return to Cooking 335
Revel, Jean-François 205
Rhodes, Gary 124–5
Rhodes Twenty10, Dubai 125
Ricker, Andy 324
Ripert, Eric 241, 335
The River Cafe Cookbook 220–1
The River Cafe, London 121, 135, 221, 331
The River Cottage Meat Book 40–1
Roast Chicken and Other Stories 56–7, 81, 224–5
Robertson, Chad 273, 340
Robuchon, Joël 70, 277, 281, 314
Roca, Joan 126–7
Roca, Jordi 128–9, 338
Roca, Josep 130–1
Rockpool, Sydney 122, 270
Roddy, Rachel 317
Roden, Claudia 6, 7, 310, 317, 319

Rodgers, Judy 66, 282
Rogan, Simon 132–3
Rogers, Ruth 135, 221
Rohat, Christophe 172
Romano, Michael 335
Rombauer, Irma S. 302
Rombauer Becker, Marion 302
Rose Bakery, Paris 339
Rosen, Kim 274
Rosengarten, David 300
Rosso, Julee 303
Roux, Albert 285, 314
Roux, Michel 285
Roux Jnr., Michel 314
Rucker, Gabriel 286
Ruhlman, Michael 18, 138, 335, 340

Sahni, Julie 321
Sails Restaurant, Sydney 270
Salt Sugar Smoke 341
Saulnier, Louis 94, 187
The Savoy Hotel, London 206
Scappi, Bartolomeo 113
Seafood Restaurant, Padstow, U.K. 263
Searle, Adrian 156
Segnit, Niki 336
Selin, Søren 136–7
Seven Fires: Grilling the Argentinan Way 307
Sex & Drugs & Sausage Rolls 52–3, 210–11
Shaw, Timothy 90, 237
Shepherd, Chris 138–9
Shewry, Ben 6, 151, 289
Short & Sweet: The Best of Home Baking 339
Shuman, Bryce 140–1
Sichuan Cookery 323
The Silver Palate Cookbook 303
Silverton, Nancy 339
The Simple Art of Perfect Baking 340
Simple Chinese Cooking Class 321
Simple French Food 313
Simple Good Food 290–1
Simply French 314
Singh, Vivek 142
Slater, Nigel 195, 329
Smith, Delia 118, 310
Smyth, Clare 144–5
So, Yan-kit 322
Social Suppers 168–9
Soler, Juli 156
Solomon, Charmaine 62
South East Asian Food 325
Southern Food 300
Soyer, Alexis 345
Spago, Beverly Hills 339
Spice 248–9
The Sportsman, Seasalter, U.K. 70
Spring, London 66
Srulovich, Itamar 118, 146–7, 318
St. John restaurant, London 25, 34, 104
State Bird Provisions, San Francisco 40, 96
Stein, Rick 263
Stobart, Tom 332
Strang, Jeanne 332
Sud de France: The Food and Cooking of Languedoc 314
The Sugar Club, Wellington, New Zealand 61

Summer Cooking 332
Sunday Suppers at Lucque 216–17
Süskind, Patrick 129
Tacopedia 306
Tamimi, Sami 260
Tanis, David 331
Tante Marie's French Kitchen 311
Tartine 272–3
Tartine Bakery and Café, San Francisco 273, 340
Tartine Bread 340
The Tasting Room at Le Quartier Français, South Africa 85
Tetsuya 292–3
Thai Food 68–9
Think Like a Chef 196–7
Thirty Years at Ballymaloe 160–1
This, Hervé 38
Thompson, David 69, 270
Time Life 327
Toklas, Alice B. 329
Tom Kerridge's Best Ever Dishes 232–3
Too Many Chiefs, Only One Indian 30–1, 170–1
Trotter, Charlie 293
Tsuji, Shizuo 323
Turgeon, Charlotte 311

Underbelly, Houston, Texas 138
The Union Square Café Cookbook 335
Universal, Sydney 249
Unplugged Kitchen 50–1
The Unrivalled Cook-Book and Housekeeper's Guide 42–3

Vergé, Roger 238, 313
Verral, William 345
Verre, Dubai 73
The Virginia Housewife: Or Methodical Cook 344
Visser, Margaret 6, 22
Vongerichten, Jean-Georges 55, 290–1

Wakuda, Tetsuya 292–3
Waldegrave, Caroline 329
The Walnut Tree, Abergavenny, Wales 74
Washington, Mrs. 43
Waters, Alice 47, 160, 209, 217, 229, 294, 331, 335
Waterside Inn, Bray, U.K. 94, 237, 285
wd~50, New York 55
Wells, Patricia 70, 311, 314
The West House, Biddenden, U.K. 210
Whims, Cathy 148
White, Jasper 303
White, Marco Pierre 21, 116–17, 277, 296–7
White Heat 20–1, 116–17, 296–7
Whiteman, Michael 290
Whittingdon, Richard 245
Wignall, Michael 150–1
Wolfert, Paula 58, 313
Wong, Andrew 321
A. Wong: The Cookbook 321

Yan-kit's Classic Chinese Cookbook 322
Young, Chris 343

Zuma London 26
The Zuni Cafe Cookbook 6, 66–7, 282–3

Picture and Publisher Credits

Key: r, right; l, left; t, top; b, bottom; c, center; cr, center right; cl, center left

7, 8 Peter Dawson/Shutterstock 10, 11 l Éditions du Rouergue 11 r RAFA RIVAS/AFP/Getty Images 12 l, 13 Gill & Macmillan 12 r Kristin Perers 14, 15 l Random House Inc. 15 r Eshama John/Bloomberg via Getty Images 16 l, 17 Ediciones Destino 16 r Picture by Coconut 18 John Carey 19 Artisan Books 20 l Courtesy of Lotus PR 20 r, 21 Mitchell Beazley 22, 23 l McClelland and Stewart Ltd 23 r Susie Cushner 24 l, 25 © Fergus Henderson, 2004, Nose to Tail Eating, Bloomsbury Publishing Plc. 24 r John Carey 26, 27 l Flammarion 27 r David Griffen 28 l Courtesy of First Press Public Relations 28 r, 29 Reproduced from *The Nordic Cookbook* published by Phaidon Press Limited © 2015 Phaidon Press Limited. 30, 31 l Face Publications 31 r © REDA &CO srl/Alamy 32 l Paolo Terzi 32 r, 33 Marsilio Publishers 34, 35 l Hodder & Stoughton 35 r Tom Moggach for New Covent Garden Market 36 Éditions Robert Laffont 37 Bras/C. Bousquet 38, 39 l *Les Secrets de la casserole*, Hervé This, © Éditions Belin 2008 39 r Bras/C. Bousque 40 Ed Andereson 41 Hodder & Stoughton 42 l Andrea Behrends 42 r, 43 Harper & Brother 44, 45 l © 2014. Used by permission of Harry N. Abrams, Inc., New York. All rights reserved. Éditions de La Martiniére 45 r Edmond Ho 46 l Courtesy of Clarke's Restaurant 46 r, 47 Random House Inc. 48, 49 l Mugaritz 49 r Eduardo Torres 50 l Evan Sklar/Alamy 50 r, 51 William Morrow and Company 52, 53 t, 53 l Face Publications 53 r Courtesy of Cuff Communications 54 l Jaimie Trueblood/Bravo/NBCU Photo Bank via Getty Images 54 r, 55 Éditions du Rouergue 56 l Courtesy of Network London PR 56 r, 57 Ebury Press 58, 59 l Harper & Row 59 r Zuma Press Inc/Alamy 60 l, 61 Penguin Books Australia 60 r Courtesy of Peter Gordon 62, 63 t, 63 l William Heinemann Australia 63 r Mikkel Vang 64 l Corentin Mossière 64 r, 65 L'Édition d'art H. Piazza et Cie 66 Amber Rowlands 67 W. W. Norton & Company 68 l Courtesy of The Modern Pantry 68 r, 69 Ten Speed Press 70, 71 l William Morrow and Company 71 r Philip Harris 72 l Courtesy of Gerber Communications 72 r, 73 First edition published by Alfred A. Knopf; edition shown published by Macmillan 74, 75 r Michael Joseph/Grub Street 75 l Courtesy of Shaun Hill 76 l Courtesy of Eighty Four PR 76 r, 77 Bantam Press 78, 79 l Alfred A. Knopf 79 Allen Markey 80 l, 81 Simon & Schuster 80 r Rex/Shutterstock 82, 83 l Éditions Glenat 83 r Francesco Tonelli 84 l Hoberman Collection/Getty Images 84 r, 85 Michael Joseph 86, 87 l Flammarion 87 r Evan Hurd/Alamy 88 l Andrew Hayes Watkins 88 r, 89 Ducasse Books 90, 91 l Mitchell Beazley 91 r Marc Millar 92 l, 93 Harper & Row 92 r Courtesy of Fraser Communications 94, 95 l Flammarion 95 r Courtesy of the Maybourne Hotel Group 96, 97 l William Morrow and Company 97 r Ed Anderson 98 l © 1978. Used by permission of Harry N. Abrams, Inc., New York. All rights reserved. 99 Eric Wolfinger 100, 101 l Michael Joseph/Grub Street 101 r Jason Lowe 102 Lisa Barber 103 Michael Joseph 104 Earl Carter 105 © Fergus Henderson, 2004, Nose to Tail Eating, Bloomsbury Publishing Plc. 106 l Rob Fiocca 106 r, 107 © Jane Grigson, 2000 108 l David Cooper/Toronto Star via Getty Images 108 r, 109 Flammarion 110 Phil Scoble 111 © Elizabeth David, 1965, 1998 112 Arnaldo Forni Editore 113 Courtesy of Anton Mosimann 114, 115 l Faber & Faber Limited 115 r Dave Benett/Getty Images 116 Mitchell Beazley 117 Courtesy of Arcane 118, 119 t, 119 l Hodder & Stoughton 119 r Jeff Gilbert/Alamy 120 l, 121 Harper & Row 120 r Courtesy of HHB Agency 122, 123 l © 1978. Used by permission of Harry N. Abrams, Inc., New York. All rights reserved. 123 r Fairfax Media via Getty Images 124 l Courtesy of Jennie Rhodes 124 r, 125 © 1978. Used by permission of Harry N. Abrams, Inc., New York. All rights reserved 126, 127 l Éditions Robert Laffont 127 r Courtesy of El Celler de Can Roca 128 l Courtesy of El Celler de Can Roca 128 r, 129 Diogenes Verlag 130, 131 r Courtesy of El Celler de Can Roca 131 l Classics Curial 132, 133 l The International Wine and Food Publishing Company 133 r Courtesy of Network London PR 134 Alfred A. Knopf 135 David Loftus 136 l, 137 Reproduced from *Noma* published by Phaidon Press Limited © 2010 Phaidon Press Limited 136 r Signe Birck 138, 139 l Artisan Books 139 r Julie Soefer Photography 140 l Signe Birck 140 r, 141 Little, Brown 142 Nick Grega 143 Allied Publishers 144 l, 145 Ducasse Books 144 r Gordon Ramsey Group 146, 147 l Quadrille Publishing 147 r Jeff Gilbert/Alamy 148 Courtesy of Cathy Whims 149 Alfred A. Knopf 150 l, 151 Murdoch Books 150 r David Griffin 152 Peter Dawson/Shutterstock 154, 155 t Ten Speed Press 155 b Jim Newberry/Alamy 156 t, 157 Reproduced from *A Day at elBulli* published by Phaidon Press Limited © 2010 Phaidon Press Limited. 156 b Jerome Favre/Bloomberg via Getty Images 158, 159 t Reproduced from *Mugaritz* published by Phaidon Press Limited © 2012 Phaidon Press Limited. 159 b Rafa Rivas/AFP/Getty Images 160 t, 161 Kyle Books 160 b Eleanor Bentall/Getty Images 162, 163 t Clarkson Potter 163 b Eshama John/Bloomberg via Getty Images 164 t, 165 Grub Street Publishing Ltd 164 b Rafa Rivas/AFP/Getty Images 166, 167 t Reproduced from *D.O.M. Rediscovering Brazilian Ingredients* published by Phaidon Press Limited © 2013 Phaidon Press Limited. 167 b Nelson Almeida/AFP/Getty Images 168, 169 © Jason Atherton, 2014, Social Suppers, Bloomsbury Publishing Plc. 170, 171 t Face Publications 171 b Courtesy of Lotus PR 172 t, 173 Éditions du Chêne 172 b Jose Ignacio Unanue/Cordon Press/Getty Images 174, 175 t Random House Inc. 175 b Brant Ward/San Francisco Chronicle/Getty Images 176 t, 177 Hardie Grant Books 176 b Fairfax Media/Fairfax Media via Getty Images 178, 179 t Macdonald Orbis 179 b Andrew Fox/Alamy 180 t, 181 Bloomsbury Publishing 180 b EDB Image Archive/Alamy 182, 183 t Flammarion 183 b © Abilio Lope/Getty Images 184 t, 185 Reproduced from *Never Trust a Skinny Italian Chef* published by Phaidon Press Limited © 2014 Phaidon Press Limited. 184 b DavidCC/Alamy 186, 187 t Sphere 187 Cindy Ord/Getty Images for NYCWFF 188 t, 189 Éditions du Rouergue 188 b Photo by Pool Baudet/Le Corre/Gamma-Rapho via Getty Images 190, 191 t Artisan Books 191 b Johnny Nunez/WireImage/Getty Images 192 t, 193 Clarkson Potter 192 b Rene Johnston/Toronto Star via Getty Images 194, 195 t Ebury Press 195 b Eleanor Bentall/Getty Images 196 t, 197 Clarkson Potter 196 b Anna Carnochan/Retna Ltd./Getty Images 198 t, 199 Houghton Mifflin Harcourt 198 b Zuma Press Inc/Alamy 200, 201 t *The Professional Chef*, The Culinary Institute of America, © 2011. Reproduced with permission of John Wiley & Sons, Inc. 201 b Mira/Alamy 202 t, 203 © Ollie Dabbous, 2014, *Dabbous*, Bloomsbury Publishing Plc. 202 b Joakim Blockstrom 204, 205 t Hachette Livre 205 b ITAR-TASS Photo Agency/Alamy 206 t, 207 Flammarion 206 b © Hulton-Deutsch Collection/Getty Images 208, 209 t © 2007. Used by permission of Harry N. Abrams, Inc., New York. All rights reserved. Stewart, Tabori & Chang 209 b judithchoate.com 210 t, 211 Face Publications 210 b Face Publications 212, 213 t Murdoch Books 213 b Jack Atley/Bloomberg via Getty Images 214 t, 215 Ten Speed Press 214 b Giuseppe Cacace/AFP/Getty Images 216 Alfred A. Knopf, photography copyright Shimon and Tammar Photography Inc. 217 t Alfred A. Knopf 217 b Bernstein Associates/Getty Images 218 t, 219 Murdoch Books 218 b Mikkel Vang 220, 221 t Ebury Press 221 b dannyelwes.com 222 t, 223 Éditions Robert Laffont 222 b Icolas Tucat/AFP/Getty Images 224, 225 t Ebury Press 225 b Mike Abrahams/Alamy 226 t, 227 Little, Brown 226 b Richard Vines/Bloomberg via Getty Images 228, 229 t Ten Speed Press 229 b Ben Gabbe/Getty Images 230 t, 231 Artisan Books 230 b Nik Wheeler/Alamy 232, 233 © Tom Kerridge, 2014, *Tom Kerridge's Best Ever Dishes*, Bloomsbury Publishing Plc. 234 t, 235 Ten Speed Press 234 b Mark Holthusen 236, 237 t *La Tante Claire*, Pierre Koffmann and Timothy Shaw, Anthony Blake, Headline Book Publishing Plc 237 b Bloomberg 238 t, 239 Ebury Press 238 b Ian Bradshaw/Rex/Shutterstock 240, 241 t Clarkson Potter 241 b Maurice Rougemont/Gamma-Rapho via Getty Images 242 t, 243 Reproduced from *Benu* published by Phaidon Press Limited © 2015 Phaidon Press Limited 242 b jetsettimes.com 244, 245 t Conran Octopus 245 b Photoshot/Getty Images 246 t, 247 Bantam Press 246 b Aya Brackett 248, 249 t Penguin Books Australia 249 b realfoodfestivals.com 250 t, 251 Quadrille Publishing Ltd 250 b John Angerson/Alamy 252 t, 253 Ten Speed Press 252 b Rob Fiocca 254, 255 t DK Publishing 255 b Zuma Press Inc/Alamy 256 t, 257 Reproduced from *Fäviken* published by Phaidon Press Limited © 2012 Phaidon Press Limited. 256 b Vittorio Zunino Celotto/WireImage for Electrolux 258, 259 t © Russell Norman, 2012, *Polpo*, Bloomsbury Publishing Plc. 259 b Wenn Ltd/Alamy 260 t, 261 Ebury Press 260 b Jeff Gilbert/Alamy 262, 263 t Quadrille Publishing Ltd 263 b Stephen Perez 264, 265 t First edition published by Éditions Alternatives; copy shown published by Francis Lincoln 265 b © Owen Franken/Getty Images 266 t, 267 Reproduced from *Coi* published by Phaidon Press Limited © 2013 Phaidon Press Limited. 266 b Adam Pantozzi/Bernstein Associates, Inc./Getty Images 268, 269 t Times Books 269 b Mireya Acierto/FilmMagic 270 t, 271 Murdoch Books 270 b Sergio Dionisio/Getty Images 272, 273 t From Tartine © 2006 by Elisabeth M. Prueitt and Chad Robertson. Used with permission of Chronicle Books LLC, San Francisco. Visit ChronicleBooks.com. 273 b postcardPR/Tartine 274 t, 275 Ten Speed Press 274 b theinsatiablepalate.wordpress.com 276, 277 t Quadrille Publishing Ltd 277 b Oliver Knight/Alamy 278 t, 279 Reproduced from *Noma* published by Phaidon Press Limited © 2010 Phaidon Press Limited. 278 b Giovanni Tagini/Alamy 280, 281 t First edition published by Editions du Chêne; copy shown published by Cassell & Co 281 b © Francois Roboth/Sygma/Getty Images 282 t, 283 W. W. Norton & Company 282 b Kim Kulish/Getty Images 284, 285 Éditions Solar 286 t, 287 Ten Speed Press 286 b David Reamer 288, 289 t Murdoch Books 289 b Fairfax Media/Fairfax Media via Getty Images 290 t, 291 First edition published by Broadway Books; copy shown published by Kyle Cathie Ltd 290 b Michael Brennan/Getty Images 292, 293 t HarperCollins Publishers Australia 293 b Fairfax Media via Getty Images 294 t, 295 Random House Inc. 294 b Zuma Press, Inc./Alamy 296, 297 t Mitchell Beazley 297 b Virginia Sherwood/NBC/NBCU Photo Bank via Getty Images 298 Peter Dawson/Shutterstock 300 l Random House Inc. 300 r Alfred A. Knopf 301 Little, Brown 302 Macmillan 303 l Workman Publishing 303 cl HarperCollins 303 cr William Morrow and Company 303 r Harper & Row 304 l W. W. Norton & Company 304 r Mitchell Beazley 305 Reproduced from *Mexico From the Inside Out* published by Phaidon Press Limited © 2015 Phaidon Press Limited. 306 l HarperCollins 306 cl Reproduced from *The Tacopedia* published by Phaidon Press Limited © 2015 Phaidon Press Limited. 306 cr Reproduced from *Peru: the Cookbook* published by Phaidon Press Limited © 2015 Phaidon Press Limited. 306 r Weidenfeld & Nicholson Ltd 307 Artisan Books 308 l Ten Speed Press 308 r Macmillan London Ltd 309 Hardie Grant Books 310 l Bloomsbury Publishing 310 cl BBC Books 310 cr Michael Joseph 310 r Reproduced from *1080 Recipes* published by Phaidon Press Limited © 2007 Phaidon Press Limited. 311 l Ulisse Editions 311 cl Éditions Paul Martial 311 cr Alfred A. Knopf 311 r William Morrow and Company 312 Larousse 313 l Flammarion 313 cl Doubleday 313 cr Atheneum Books 313 r Dial Press 314 l William Morrow and Company 314 cl BBC Books 314 cr Prospect Books 314 r Weidenfeld & Nicholson Ltd 315 l Reproduced from *I Know How to Cook* published by Phaidon Press Limited © 2009 Phaidon Press Limited. 315 cl Transworld 315 cr Editore Colombo 315 r Headline Publishing Group 316 Fourth Estate 317 l Chatto and Windus 317 cl Macdonald & Co 317 cr Photo *Il Cucchiaio d'Argento* – Editoriale Domus spa, Cucchiaio d'Argento srl – All rights reserved. 317 r Saltyard Books 318 l Ebury Press 318 r Saltyard Books 319 © Claudia Roden, 1973 320 l Clarkson Potter 320 r Vintage Books 321 l Ecco Press 321 cl Kyle Cathie Books 321 cr Octopus Books 321 r Cover from *Kylie Kwong's Simple Chinese Cooking Class* by Kylie Kwong, photography by Earl Carter, published by Lantern on 2 July 2012, RRP $59.99 322 DK Publishing 323 l © Fuchsia Dunlop, 2003 323 cl BBC Books 323 cr Kodansha USA Inc. 323 r Reproduced by permission of Kodansha USA Inc. Excerpted from *Kasiseki: The Exquisite Cuisine of Kyoto's Kikunoi Restaurant* by Yoshihiro Murata 324 l Conran Octopus 324 cl Ten Speed Press 324 cr Ten Speed Press 324 r Artisan Books 325 © Rosemary Brissenden, 1974 326 l Cover from *Maggie Beer's Summer Harvest Recipes* by Maggie Beer, photography by Mark Chew, published by Lantern on 18 November 2015, RRP AU$29.99 326 r Penguin Books Australia 327 Time Life 328 l G. P. Putnam's Sons 328 r Simon and Schuster. Photography copyright Patrice de Villiers. Text copyright Sybil Kapoor. 329 l Bloomsbury Publishing 329 cl Fourth Estate 329 cr Random House Inc. 329 r © Jane Grigson, 1980 330 Ebury Press 331 l Artisan Books 331 cl Rodale Inc. 331 cr © Jamie Oliver, 1999 331 r Chatto and Windus 332 l Thomas Nelson 332 cl © Elizabeth David, 1998 332 cr Oxford University Press 332 r Hodder & Stoughton Ltd 333 Chatto and Windus 334 Houghton Mifflin Harcourt 335 l © Alice Waters, 2008 335 cl Artisan Books 335 cr Workman Publishing 335 r Ecco Press 336 l Bloomsbury Publishing 336 r William Morrow and Company 337 l Agnés Viénot Éditions 337 cl Ten Speed Press 337 cr Scribner 337 r Ten Speed Press 338 Peter Pauper Press 339 l Fourth Estate 339 cl Houghton Mifflin Harcourt 339 cr Reproduced from *Breakfast, Lunch and Tea* published by Phaidon Press Limited © 2006 Phaidon Press Limited. 339 r Absolute Press 340 l W. W. Norton & Company 340 cl Alfred A. Knopf 340 cr Chronicle Books 340 r From Tartine Bread © 2010 by Chad Robertson. Used with permission of Chronicle Books LLC, San Francisco. Visit ChronicleBooks.com. 341 Mitchell Beazley 342 © Claire Clark, 2010, *Indulge*, Bloomsbury Publishing Plc. 343 l Flammarion 343 cl Taschen 343 cr W. W. Norton & Company 343 r Flammarion 344 l E. H. Butler & Co, 344 r Maxtor France 345 l Simpkin, Marshall and Co. 345 cl Little, Brown 345 cr Charpentier editions, 1838 345 r Bibliolife 346 l S. O. Beeton Publishing 346 cl Ward Lock 346 cr Samuel Bagster 346 r E. & J. Exshaw 347 Longmans

Acknowledgments

First of all, many thanks to Ruth Patrick and Philip Cooper of Quintessence for commissioning me to write this book, which has been fascinating to research. My project editor Sophie Blackman has done much sterling work sorting out permissions and been a supportive, helpful, and encouraging presence throughout the process. Grazie mille to Angela Cuasse-Laurie, Nat Foreman of Phaidon Books, Zoe Hewetson, Anne McGlacken, and Hilary McNevin for their help—much appreciated. Grateful thanks, too, to the wonderful British Library, an amazing resource, which it was a pleasure to use.

The publishers would like to thank Namkwan Cho and Peter Dawson at Grade Design for their hard work and diligence throughout this project, and Leily Kleinbard at Abrams for her work on this book.